DATE DUE

JOHN GOWER

THE COURT OF CHANCERY

from an illumination in a 15th-century manuscript

...je ne suy pas clers,
Vestu de sanguin ne de pers,
Ainz ai vestu la raye mance.

Mirour de l'omme, lines 21772-74

John Gower

MORAL PHILOSOPHER AND

FRIEND OF CHAUCER

———◆———

By John H. Fisher

NEW YORK UNIVERSITY PRESS 1964

Publication of this work was aided by a
partial subvention from THE FORD FOUNDATION,
to whom the publishers make grateful acknowledgment.

Preface

T. S. Eliot has admonished us that "to bring the poet back to life is the great and perennial task of criticism." No English poet is more badly in need of such resuscitation than John Gower. Honored along with Chaucer for three centuries after his death as one of the "primier poetes of the nacion," his reputation so declined that there has never been a general study of his life and works. The best discussions have been in the introductions and notes to the excellent edition of his works by G. C. Macaulay in four volumes (1899–1901). However, the historical context and critical estimates these volumes provide were never intended as an organized study, and they are now more than sixty years old.

This book takes its departure from Macaulay's edition, attempting to organize, interpret, and amplify the mass of material there presented. It stresses historical context, structure, and literary relationships rather than esthetic criticism because these seem to me the most significant aspects of the writings. Gower did not have a profound philosophic mind nor was he a great literary artist. Yet five years of intensive reading and rereading of his poetry has made me appreciate what I feel Chaucer must also have valued in him: his absolute integrity, his coherent grasp of the values and ideals of his day, and his fearless expression of the moral judgments growing out of these ideals. These are no small virtues in a friend or in a poet.

The study grew out of a revision of the section on Gower for the new edition of J. E. Wells, *A Manual of Writings in Middle Eng-*

lish, when a survey of the scholarship revealed both the need and the potential wealth of material. In particular two articles by George R. Coffman, "John Gower in His Most Significant Role" (1945) and "John Gower, Mentor for Royalty" (1954), and the monograph by Maria Wickert, *Studien zu John Gower* (1953), provided the chart and compass by which to navigate the trilingual threat of Gower's 80,000 lines.

The impediment of languages is doubtless one factor which has discouraged readers from placing the *Confessio Amantis* in the context of the *Mirour de l'omme* and *Vox Clamantis* and recognizing it as part of an organized discussion "of those things by which King Alexander was trained, as much in his governing as in other things . . . into which the stories and the writings of poets are inserted for the sake of example," as Gower himself described it in his colophon. The linguistic impediment has now been largely removed by the publication of Eric W. Stockton's good translation of *The Major Latin Works of John Gower* (1962). Although I had wrestled long with Gower's Latin before I had access to Stockton's translation, I welcomed it with relief, have adopted most of its readings, and know that my discussion would be the poorer but for its assistance. The translator cannot, of course, be held accountable for any of the interpretations placed upon the texts.

Although Gower was a reasonably effective Latin stylist and much is lost in translation, the gain in intelligibility is so great that I have felt no qualms about Englishing the Latin throughout and omitting the original. On the other hand, I could not bring myself so to deal with the French. Particularly in the last chapter, where Gower's lines are compared with Chaucer's, loss of the original expression would have vitiated the whole argument. Hence, I have preserved the French text alongside the translation.

It is a pleasure to acknowledge the institutions and individuals to whom I am most deeply indebted for assistance in this project. Grants from the American Council of Learned Societies and the Duke University Research Council made it possible for me to examine the Gower manuscripts and search for biographical material in

Great Britain. The Duke University Library ordered original microfilms of forty of the manuscripts and prints of others that had
already been filmed, with the result that its fifty-one microfilms of
Gower manuscripts form the best collection of material now available for the study of Gower's text. The owners of the Gower manuscripts and librarians both in Great Britain and the United States
have been unfailingly generous in allowing me to examine the
manuscripts and have them photographed. Professors Paull F.
Baum, Morton W. Bloomfield, Rowland L. Collins, Alfred David,
Ruth Dean, Arthur Hogue, and William R. Parker read and criticized various parts of the typescript in various stages, and Professor
B. Q. Morgan read all the galleys. To them, more than to anyone
else, I apologize for the remaining errors and idiosyncrasies. Elizabeth Armstrong, Robert Cox, Howell Chickering, E. D. Dinkens,
Leon Leeds, and Jerome Wenker pursued and checked data, con-
scientiously and evidently with enjoyment. My wife, Jane Law
Fisher, has put up with John Gower for nearly a decade, typed the
manuscript, read proof, and offered the intellectual and spiritual
support without which the task could never have been completed.

Chorley Wood, Hertfordshire
August 1963

Contents

Preface   v

Abbreviations and Chronology   x

1. CRITICAL REPUTATION   1

2. LIFE RECORDS   37

3. LITERARY CAREER   70

4. MAJOR THEMES   135

5. GOWER AND CHAUCER   204

Appendix A. The Gower Manuscripts   303

Appendix B. The Colophons   311

Appendix C. Septvauns Inquisitions *de etate probando*   313

Note Abbreviations   320

Notes   321

Index   373

Abbreviations and a Chronology of the Writings of Gower and Chaucer

GOWER		CHAUCER	

Before 1374

| CB | *Cinkante Balades* | BD | *Book of the Duchess* |

ca. 1374–1385

MO	*Mirour de l'omme*	HF	*House of Fame*
VC	*Vox Clamantis*	PF	*Parliament of Fowls*
		KT	Knight's Tale
		TC	*Troilus and Criseyde*

After ca. 1385

CA	*Confessio Amantis*	LGW	*Legend of Good Women*
T	*Traitié pour essampler les amants marietz*	CT	*Canterbury Tales*
Cron	*Cronica Tripertita*		
PP	*In Praise of Peace*		

JOHN GOWER

1. Critical Reputation

It has been the fate of John Gower to appear to succeeding ages almost constantly in the company of Geoffrey Chaucer. All biographical comment until that of Sir Harris Nicolas (1828), and most of it since that time, can be characterized by the sentence with which John Leland concluded the first biographical notice (ca. 1540): "Sed de Govero plura in Chaucero dicemus." And to the present day the most favorable critical comment echoes the judgment of Thomas Warton (1774): "If Chaucer had not existed, the compositions of John Gower, the next poet in succession, would alone have been sufficient to rescue the reigns of Edward III and Richard II from the imputation of barbarism."[1] Since Gower biography and criticism are so inextricably intertwined with Chaucer, it behooves us to understand all we can about their relationship, both external and—to the extent that it can be reconstructed—internal. Such an understanding should lead to a more perceptive appreciation of the literary achievements of both authors.

By proceeding in this manner, we perpetuate the traditional and, to Gower, harmful contrast between Chaucer and Gower as poets. For this we make no apology. They were acquainted, they acknowledged one another in their writings, they reacted against the same social and spiritual shortcomings, and they wrote lyric, didactic, and narrative works with similar themes and forms. Comparison is inevitable. In the 19th century the comparison tended to be unreasonably hostile to Gower. For example, Taine (1877): "Comme les écrivains de la décadence latine, ces gens ne songent qu'à transcrire, à compiler, à abréger, à mettre en manuels, en mémentos rimés, l'encyclopédie de leur temps. Voulez-vous écouter le plus illustre, le grave Gower, 'Moral Gower,' comme on l'appelle? Sans doute, de loin en loin, il y a en lui quelque reste de brillant, quelque grâce. . . . Son grand poëme, *Confessio Amantis*, est un dialogue entre un amant et son confesseur. . . . C'est une charretée de décombres scholastiques. . . . Et quel style! si long, si plat, si interminablement traîné dans les redites. . . . Le régime scholastique a érigé en reine la lettre morte et peuplé la monde d'esprits morts." [2]

This obloquy was given by James Russell Lowell (1887) his own clever fillip: "In order to feel fully how much Chaucer achieved, let any one subject himself to a penitential course of reading in his contemporary, Gower. . . . Gower has positively raised tediousness to the precision of science, he has made dullness an heirloom for the students of our literary history. . . . He is the undertaker of the fair mediaeval legend, and his style has the hateful gloss, the seemingly unnatural length, of a coffin." [3] The same comparative estimate reappears in the remarks of J. J. Jusserand (1895): "A little above the copse around Chaucer another head rises; that of Chaucer's great friend, John Gower," who hated and despised the common people, and wrote immoderately and soporiferously, until "in the midst of the droning of his sermon, Gower suddenly screams, roars, flies into a passion—'Vox Clamantis!' His hearers open an eye, wonder where they are, recognize Gower, and go off to sleep again." [4]

These comprise some of the harshest and most influential judgments that have been passed upon Gower's writings. It will be the purpose of this chapter on Gower's critical reputation to show that they arise at least partly from a misinterpretation of his political career and supposed quarrel with Chaucer. The subsequent chapters will reveal the impressive unity of his moral philosophy and the coherent structure of his three major poems. Their dullness cannot be palliated, but it must be recognized for what it is—not failure, but success in its intended genre. Reaction to Gower's poetry has since the 18th century been colored by a shift in taste away from the generalized, moralistic mode of medieval complaint to the sharper, more specific mode of satire. The taste for satire virtually died out from the time of St. Jerome until it was revived in the Renaissance.[5] In the interim social criticism was overwhelmingly ecclesiastical and for reasons of Christian charity, if for no other, it deliberately eschewed the personal attitude, pungent tone, and specific reference of satire. Whereas Chaucer's achievement of satire has made him the most readable of early English authors, Gower's continued cultivation of complaint has made him one of the least read.

I

Until the 18th century, however, readers were less conscious of the stylistic differences between the writings of Gower and Chaucer than of their similarities in theme and technique. Most of the early allusions that mention both refer to their achievements in creating polished poetry in the vernacular.[6] It was in this vein that Lydgate praised "Gower Chaucers erthely goddes two" (ca. 1403),[7] and the author of the *Kingis Quair* dedicated his poem to the memory of "Gowere and chaucere, that oñ the steppis satt/ Of rethorike" (1423).[8] When George Ashby called these two and Lydgate "Primier poetes of this nacion" (ca. 1470),[9] he intended less a value judgment than a statement of chronological fact. To men of the Renaissance, English poetry as a cultivated art began with the introduction of continental technique and decorum at the end of the 14th century.

The convention of comparing the achievements of Chaucer and Gower to those of their classical and continental predecessors began in their lifetime. Chaucer himself had directed his *Troilus*: "Go, litel bok, . . ./ And kis the steppes, where as thow seest pace/ Virgile, Ovide, Omer, Lucan, and Stace" (TC, v.1768). Hoccleve compared Chaucer to Cicero in rhetoric and Aristotle in philosophy;[10] Lydgate compared him to Virgil, Dante, and Petrarch;[11] and the anonymous philosopher who complimented Gower upon finishing his trilogy compared his achievement to Virgil's *Aeneid*, *Bucolics*, and *Georgics*:

Eneidos Bucolis que Georgica metra perhennis
Virgilio laudis serta dedere scolis;
Hiis tribus ille libris prefertur honore poetis,
Romaque precipuis laudibus instat eis. (Macaulay 4.361)

(You take the metres of the *Aeneid*, the *Bucolics* [*Eclogues*],
and *Georgics* seeking to achieve the wreaths of praise surrendered by Virgil; for these three books the honor of poetry is
awarded you, and Rome presses special praises upon them.)

Erasmus showed his awareness of the renascence of national litera-
tures by remarking: "Habet gens Britannica, qui hoc praestiterunt
apud suos, quod Dantes ac Petrarcha apud Italos." That Erasmus'
preeminent ones were Chaucer and Gower is confirmed by *The
Defence of Poesie* (1595), in which Sidney observed: "So among the
Romans were *Livius Andronicus* and *Ennius,* so in the Italian language . . . were the poets *Dante, Boccace,* and *Petrarch,* so in our
English, were *Gower* and *Chaucer*; after whom, encouraged and
delighted with their excellent foregoing, others have followed." [12]

Gower is as much entitled as Chaucer to whatever credit attaches
to being "first," and Lydgate was their most assiduous follower. The
concept of these three as creators of English poetry and conscious
refiners of the language accounts for the trilogy established by Osbern Bokenham (ca. 1443), "For I dwellyd neuere/ wyth the fresh
rethoryens// Gower/ Chauncers/ ner wyth lytgate." [13] Like Ashby's
"primier," Bokenham's "fresh" is rather a temporal statement than
a qualitative judgment, a factual observation, that is, that the poetry
these three introduced was different from folk song and alliterative
narrative. The new craftsmanship that links them is recognized
again in *Praise of the Mass* (ca. 1500):

Yif eny crafte be in baled makyng
I reserve hyt to the poetys olde
Chaucers Gower and lydgatys wrytyng.[14]

Gavin Douglas certainly recognized Chaucer's intrinsic superiority
in *The Palis of Honoure* (1501):

Sa greit ane prees of pepell drew vs neir,
The hundreth part thair names ar not heir,

3it saw I thair of Brutus Albyon,
Geffray Chaucier, as *a per se* sans peir
In his vulgare, and morall Johne Goweir.
Lydgait the monk raid musing him allone.[15]

Stephen Hawes likewise praised (1506):

Moral Gower, whose sentencyous dewe
Adowne reflayreth, with fayre golden beames
And after Chaucers, all abroade dothe shewe.[16]

But Hawes used this praise of Chaucer and Gower merely to introduce Lydgate as his own "chefe original." The two are linked again
by William Dunbar, and at least six more commentators between
1520 and 1550, three of whom like Bokenham put Gower first,
then Chaucer and Lydgate; two Chaucer, then Gower and Lydgate;
and one, William Turner, who put *Piers Plowman* first, then Gower
and Chaucer.[17] The allusions which place Gower before Chaucer
are no more to be taken as indications that he was considered Chaucer's superior than the mere linkage that he was thought to be his
equal. But they are evidence of the early belief that Gower was the
senior, and perhaps, as we shall see, that he was Chaucer's mentor.[18]

It is interesting to observe the trilogy persisting into the History
of the English Language in Johnson's *Dictionary*. Denying that
Chaucer was the first refiner of English poetry, Johnson observed
that "he who reads the works of *Gower* will find smooth numbers
and easy rhymes, of which *Chaucer* is supposed to have been the
inventor, and *French* words, whether good or bad, of which *Chaucer*
is charged as the importer. Some innovations he might probably
make, like others, in the infancy of our poetry, which the paucity
of books does not allow us to discover with particular exactness; but
the works of *Gower* and *Lydgate* sufficiently evince, that his diction
was in general like that of his contemporaries." [19] The praise of
Gower as one of the innovators of the new poetry and polishers of
the English language continues to the present. It is nowhere better
expressed than by G. C. Macaulay in the introduction to his edition
of the *Confessio Amantis* (1900). Upon Macaulay is based the eval-
uation in the anonymous Memorial Essay in *The London Times*

Literary Supplement commemorating the 600th anniversary of Gower's birth (1932): [20] "Gower's little light has been dimmed by the brilliance of Chaucer. He cannot rival Chaucer's lively comedy and vivid realism, his variety and amplitude, nor has he the passionate sincerity of Langland; but he deserves to be remembered not only for his share in establishing the new tradition in English poetry and his faith in the future of the English tongue but for his actual achievement. He has a quite characteristic, and at times, charming, vein of poetry; his best stories are told so easily and clearly that we are hardly conscious of the poet's art, the story appears to tell itself, there is nothing to come between it and the reader. But to create this impression of absolute ease was, at the end of the fourteenth century, a real distinction. We remember, too, the quiet, pleasant melody of his verse like his river 'rennende upon the smale stones,' and the charm of his old romantic tales, suffused with tender feeling, awakening echoes of sorrows 'far off and very long ago.' " Macaulay and the *Times Literary Supplement* form the basis for the excellent appreciation of Gower's technical achievement in the fifth chapter of C. S. Lewis's *The Allegory of Love* (1936). There is no reason for us to trace this vein of criticism further through the intervening years.

When we go beyond comments on their linguistic and prosodic achievements, however, we can see that Chaucer from the first aroused an enthusiasm of which Gower has never had a part. Chaucer himself was content to dedicate the *Troilus*:

> O moral Gower, this book I directe
> To the, and to the, philosophical Strode,
> To vouchen sauf, ther nede is, to correcte,
> Of youre benignites and zeles goode. (TC, v.1856)

But Gower had Venus speak much more warmly at the conclusion of the *Confessio Amantis*:

> Adieu, for I mot fro the wende.
> And gret wel Chaucer whan ye mete,
> As mi disciple and mi poete:
> For in the floures of his youthe

In sondri wise, as he wel couthe,
Of Ditees and of songes glade,
The whiche he for mi sake made,
The lond fulfild is overal:
Wherof to him in special
Above alle othre I am most holde.
For thi now in hise daies olde
Thow schalt him telle this message,
That he upon his latere age,
To sette an ende of alle his werk,
As he which is myn owne clerk
Do make his testament of love,
As thou hast do thi schrifte above,
So that mi Court it mai recorde. (CA, viii.2940*)

It is important to emphasize here that the antecedent of "mi disciple and mi poete" is Venus. Misreading the "my's" as referring to Gower himself reinforced the 16th and 17th century belief that Gower was Chaucer's mentor. But Gower made no such claim. There are no allusions to him which match the "enthuasiastic reverential praise" of Miss Spurgeon's first period of Chaucer criticism,[21] no Hoccleves or Lydgates who acknowledge him as their "maister deere" and speak of his "gentilnes," his "fructuous entendëment," his "pleasuance" and "syffysance." These are terms that imply a delight in the poetry as such, and no matter how diligently the early Puritans sought to justify their enjoyment of Chaucer's naughty tales by imputing moral value to them (in the second edition of his *Ecclesiastical History* [1570], John Foxe remarked that he knew of "parties, that . . . by readyng of Chausers workes, they were brought to the true knowledge of Religion"),[22] this sheer delight has crept out whenever anyone has written more than two lines about him. Curiously, one of the few early comments on Gower's works in which they are not linked with Chaucer's implies that even his stories may contain too much "covert delight" (Foxe). In 1516 Alexander Barclay, author of *The Ship of Fools*, declined the request of his patron, Sir Giles Alington, that he make an abridgement of the *Confessio Amantis*:

Right honrable Master, ye me required late,
A Louers confession abridging to amende,
And from corrupte English in better to translate.
To your request would I right gladly condiscende,
Were not that some readers my worke would reprehend,
As to my age and order muche inconuenient,
To write of thing wanton, not sad but insolent.

And though many passages therin be commendable,
Some processes appeare replete with wantonnes,
And also the labour great, longe and importable,
Unto my weake wittes, my mindes might oppresse.
For age it is folly and ieopardie doubtlesse,
And able for to rayse bad name contagious,
To write, reade or commen of thing venerious.[23]

But only an elderly monk could be counted on to find much wan-
tonness in the works of Gower. For the most part, when his matter
was praised, it was as by Caxton in *The Book of Curtesye* (1477):

Redith Gower in his writyng moralle,
That auncient faders memorie,
Redith his bokis clepide confessionalle,
Wyth many anodir vertuous tretie,
Full of sentence sette so frutously
That them to rede shall yeue you corage,
So is he fulle of sentence and langage.[24]

Or Stephen Hawes, who praises Gower's "sentencyous dewe" which
cleanses our vices "wythe the fiery leames/ Of morall vertue." [25]
And, unless "sententious" and "moral" are taken as wholly pejorative, this is the value we must still look for in the works of Gower.

II

The allusions to Chaucer and Gower as fathers of English poetry
and wells of virtue—more or less defiled—continue. Beside them,
beginning in 1483 with Caxton's edition of the *Confessio Amantis*,
grows up the tradition of their personal association. Caxton's edition opens with the revised form of the Prologue, dedicated to

Henry of Lancaster instead of Richard II, then shifts to the earlier form of the text in the fifth book and continues with this text through the Chaucer greeting quoted above. In order to understand the significance of this shift we must here undertake a brief excursus on the manuscript tradition. In the third chapter the evolution of the text and manuscripts of the poems will be discussed more thoroughly. However, since the change in dedication and the omission of the Chaucer greeting are crucial to the evolution of Gower's critical reputation, it must be recalled that the *Confessio* exists in three versions. Although the loss of initial and final leaves makes it impossible to be certain of the number of manuscripts containing each version, there are internal differences which help to classify them, and we count here all forty-nine of those having and assumed once to have had the various prologues and conclusions.[26] Thirty-three manuscripts continue after line 23 of the Prologue:

> In oure englissh, I thenke make
> A bok for king Richardes sake,
> To whom belongeth my ligeance
> With al myn hertes obeissance
> In al that evere a liege man
> Unto his king may doon or can. (CA, Prol.23*)

And seven lines later, they go on to describe Gower's occasion for undertaking the *Confessio*:

> As it bifel upon a tyde,
> As thing which scholde tho betyde,—
> Under the toun of newe Troye,
> Which tok of Brut his ferste joye,
> In Temse whan it was flowende
> As I be bote cam rowende,
> So as fortune hir tyme sette,
> My lige lord par chaunce I mette;
> And so befel, as I cam nyh,
> Out of my bot, whan he me syh,
> He had me come in to his barge.
> And whan I was with him at large,
> Amonges othre thinges seid,
> He hath this charge upon me leid,

> And bad me doo my besynesse
> That to his hihe worthinesse
> Som newe thing I scholde boke,
> That he himself it mihte loke
> After the forme of my writynge. (CA, Prol.35*)

In fifteen manuscripts this dedication is replaced by exactly the same number of lines, 70, commencing:

> In oure englissh, I thenke make
> A bok for Engelondes sake,
> The yer sextenthe of kyng Richard.
> What schal befalle hierafterward
> God wot, for now upon this tyde
> Men se the world on every syde
> In sondry wyse so diversed,
> That it welnyh stant al reversed,
> As forto speke of tyme ago. (CA, Prol.23)

The revised Prologue continues lamenting the state of the world. Instead of the account of his meeting the King on the Thames, the poet states merely that he is going to write a book:

> After the world that whilom tok
> Long tyme in olde daies passed:
> But for men sein it is now lassed,
> In worse plit than it was tho,
> I thenke forto touche also
> The world which neweth every dai,
> So as I can, so as I mai. (CA, Prol.54)

The revised portion of the Prologue concludes:

> This bok, upon amendment
> To stonde at his commandement,
> With whom myn herte is of accord,
> I sende unto myn oghne lord,
> Which of Lancastre is Henri named:
> The hyhe god him hath proclamed
> Ful of knyhthode and alle grace.(CA, Prol.83)

Thirty-one of the thirty-three manuscripts with the dedication to Richard II in the Prologue conclude with the Chaucer greeting quoted above, a prayer and commendation of the King, and a final dedication of the book to Richard:

> But thogh me lacke to purchace
> Mi kinges thonk as by decerte,
> Yit the Simplesce of mi poverte
> Unto the love of my ligance
> Desireth forto do plesance:
> And for this cause in myn entente
> This povere bok heer I presente
> Unto his hihe worthinesse. (CA, viii.3044*)

Seventeen manuscripts conclude with a prayer for the state of England rather than for the King, and observations on the duty of a king. In these manuscripts there is no final dedication in the English verse, merely the statement:

> That y have do my trewe peyne
> With rude wordis and with pleyne,
> In al that evere y couthe and myghte,
> This bok to write as y behighte,
> So as siknesse it soffre wolde;
> And also for my daies olde,
> That y am feble and impotent,
> I wot nought how the world ys went,
> So preye y to my lordis alle
> Now in myn age, how so befalle,
> That y mot stonden in here grace:
> For though me lacke to purchace
> Here worthi thonk as by decerte,
> Yit the symplesse of my poverte
> Desireth forto do plesance
> To hem undir whos governance
> I hope siker to abide. (CA, viii.3121)

However, the Latin explicit mentions Henry of Lancaster, under the title Count of Derby: "Derbeie Comiti, recolunt quem laude periti,/ Vade liber purus, sub eo requiesce futurus." Of the seventeen manuscripts which omit the final dedication to Richard, sixteen omit the Chaucer greeting.

In summary: it appears that thirty-one manuscripts represent the original first version, dedicated to Richard II and containing the Chaucer greeting; thirteen, not all of the same version internally (the *intermediate* version is determined not on the basis of a revised dedication but of added lines), represent the final version dedicated to Henry of Lancaster, and omitting the Chaucer greeting. Five manuscripts are mixed. One, Bodl. 294 (37), has the early Prologue and revised conclusion. Two others (34–35) have lost so many leaves initially that their affiliations are difficult to determine but they are thought to have resembled 37. One manuscript, New Coll., Oxf., 326 (6), has the revised Prologue and original conclusion. Finally, one manuscript, Wollaton Hall (38), has both the revised Prologue and conclusion. However, it has textual borrowings throughout from the earlier version, and, in particular, has inserted the Chaucer allusion (CA, VIII.2941*), with the peculiar corruption "Cuther" for "Chaucer." The motive that produced this text might be nearly the same as that which produced Caxton's, to which we now return to our discussion of Gower's reputation.

Caxton's edition begins and ends following the text of the final version; however, from v.4500 to v.6400 it follows the fuller text of the intermediate version; and from v.6400 through the Chaucer allusion in VIII, the original unrevised version, inserting additional lines from the intermediate text. Obviously, since he had before him all three texts, Caxton knew both forms of the Prologue and conclusion. His practice appears to have been motivated by three considerations, all shrewdly practical: First, he clearly wanted the poem dedicated to a "good" king, Henry IV, rather than a "bad" one, Richard II. Second, he wanted to include as much material as possible, and the intermediate version supplied lines found in neither the first nor the last. And, finally, he recognized the publicity value of the Chaucer association and made sure that the lines referring to it were included. The earliest printed edition thus made a special point of including Gower's allusion to Chaucer.

The next edition, brought out by Thomas Berthelette in 1532, added to the picture. Macaulay suggested that Berthelette used a manuscript closely resembling 37, beginning with the dedication to

Richard and ending with the revised conclusion omitting references to both Chaucer and the King. For the dedication to Richard II, the Berthelette text substitutes the revised Lancastrian dedication, taken directly from Caxton as evidenced by the errors.[27] It adds other passages from Caxton, especially the Chaucer greeting. However, Berthelette was not satisfied with silent emendation. In his "address to the reader" he undertook the first editorial comment on the association, calling attention to the variant dedications and printing the original dedication to Richard II. The difficulties between the Yorkists and Lancastrians were now a half century in the background, and dedications to two kings were better than to one. Following the dedication to Richard II, Berthelette printed Chaucer's allusion to Gower and Strode from the *Troilus,* and then remarked that this "noble warke, and many other of the sayde Chausers, that neuer were before imprinted, and those that very fewe men knewe, and fewer hadde them, be nowe of late put forthe together in a fayre volume. By the whiche wordes of Chauser, we may also vunderstonde, that he and Gower were bothe of one selfe tyme, both excellently lerned, both great frendes to gether, and bothe a lyke endeuoured them selfe and imployed theyr tyme so wel and so vertuously, that they dyd not onely passe forth their lyfes here ryght honourably; but also for their so doyng, so longe (of lyklyhode) as letters shal endure and continue, this noble royalme shall be the better, ouer and besyde theyr honest fame and renowme."[28] The "fayre volume" mentioned is, as Tyrwhitt recognized, Thynne's edition of Chaucer published in the same year, 1532. After thus calling attention to the relationship between the two poets, Berthelette concluded with a description and woodcut of Gower's tomb in St. Mary Overeys Church in Southwark. This edition, reprinted in 1554 with no change save the excision of the reference to the "fayre volume" as no longer timely, was the guise under which Gower appeared to the reading public for three centuries—until the edition of the *Confessio Amantis* by Reinhold Pauli in 1857. By calling attention to the change in the dedication and the mutual allusions of the two poets, but not to the fact that the Chaucer greeting was omitted in the revised conclusion, Berthelette's edition helped shape Gower's reception until the 18th century.

John Leland, whose famous itinerary began four years after the Berthelette edition appeared, gave final shape to the pre-18th century view of Gower. In his *Commentarii de Scriptoribus Britannicis* (ca. 1540) [29] he wrote (I translate):

> Cap. cdxciii Concerning John Gower
> John Gower, a man of the nobility, came from Stittenham in Yorkshire, so I understand. He so pursued learned studies in his youth that among notable Englishmen of his age, at least among men of letters, he was easily outstanding. For the sake of money, he cultivated the courts and laws of his country; above all else, however, he cultivated the humanities and labored much in poetry. This is testified to by his poems of which he wrote many in Latin, zealous rather than felicitous in imitating Ovid. That should seem no wonder, especially in a semibarbarous age. With difficulty even in our so flourishing time can anyone imitate the overflowing beauties of Ovid's poetry, nothwithstanding that Eobanus Hessus has done so excellently, and that even earlier Jovianus Pontanus took the palm for pure honey and delight of the muses. Accordingly, we overlook certain infelicities in the poems of Gower, and we hold him up as the first refiner of our native language. For before that time the English language lay uncultivated and nearly wholly raw. Nor was there anyone who could write in the vernacular, works suitable for a discriminating reader. Thus the value of his works lies in their careful cultivation, that, the rude weeds stamped out, instead of thistles arise the pliant violet and purple narcissus. He wrote much satire on his nation, both in verse and prose, which is still carefully studied in our most flourishing age. Among his major works the first is *Speculum Meditantis*, next *Vox Clamantis*, and the third *Confessio Amantis*. These names, imposed by elegance upon the books, will not appear to the reader as a mistake. There is indeed a curious harmony, so to speak, among the names as one stems from another. But this appears clearly to no one unless they are collected together.
> Gower lived in the reign of Richard II to whom he dedicated his books and to whom he presented his poem *In Praise of Peace*,

full of virtue and good counsel, after he was blind. He lived to a ripe old age as revealed by the following lines:

> While I was able I wrote; but now because bent age
> Confuses the understanding, I leave writing to my followers.

I am not able to determine the exact time of his death. This, however, he established, that he should be honorably buried in London in the church of the Marian canons on the bank of the Thames, where his wife is likewise entombed, but more humbly. His tomb has an effigy adorned with two insignia, namely, a golden collar and an ivy crown interset with roses, the first the ornament of a knight, the second of a poet. I judge the reason that he had his tomb placed with the Marians to be as follows: A great part of the suburb by London Bridge burned in 1212, in the reign of King John. In this fire the monastery of the Marians was badly damaged, nor was it restored to its original state before the first years of Richard II. Then Gower, moved by such a calamity, partly through his friends, of whom he had many and powerful, and partly at his own expense, undertook the restoration of this church and its ornaments. Even today the Marians acknowledge the liberality of Gower towards them, although not to the extent that I have just stated. This, in my judgment, is the reason he commended his body to the Marians. But concerning Gower we say more in Chaucer.[30]

The relevant portion of the chapter on the life of Chaucer runs as follows:

> Cap. dv Concerning Geoffrey Chaucer
> ... In those times the most celebrated man among the advocates was John Gower, whose life we have already written. He was a man of reverent age and was taking wonderful pains to polish the English tongue. No sooner had he perceived and proved the genius and worth of Chaucer than he made him an intimate friend, took him to his embrace, looked upon him as one of his noblest delights—in short, honored him almost as if he were some divinity. Let this not rest upon my authority. Gower himself, in his work which bears the title 'Amantis', makes abundantly evident how high was his estimation of Chaucer. In addition to praise most intelligently bestowed, he calls him a distinguished poet, and constitutes him a sort of Aristarchus for his own labors. Behold for thyself, O reader, a most beauteous

contest of virtue! For as Gower, a man claiming little for himself, modestly submitted what he had done to the judgment of
Chaucer, so in turn Chaucer referred the 'Loves of Troilus' to
the criticisms of Gower and Strode. Who this Strode was I have
thus far been unable to learn from any author. But though he is
mentioned by no one else, I remember to have read creditable
things of a certain Strode, an alumnus of the College of Merton
at Oxford, as one most learned in poetry. He is enrolled in the
catalogue of Merton College in the last years of Edward III. So
much is evident from the lines of Chaucer that he had been a
student of philosophy. Add to this point that just as Chaucer
was at the same time an admirer and imitator of Gower, so
Scogan, a man given to all sorts of jocoseness and wit, whose
monument stands in Westminster Abbey, was likewise an admirer and imitator of Chaucer. But, on the other hand, by how
much the disciple Chaucer was greater than his master Gower,
by so much was Scogan inferior to Chaucer.[31]

In these two passages we have the fruits of the implications of
Berthelette's edition of the Confessio and of Leland's own surmises.
That Leland had Berthelette's printing of both the Troilus and
Confessio passages specifically in mind when he described the relationship between the two poets in the life of Chaucer is suggested
by the fact that his essay includes a poem eulogizing Chaucer's services to his native tongue which Leland says had been composed
some years before at the request of Berthelette. And Leland concludes his observations on a nonexistent Caxton edition of the
works of Chaucer by observing that "Nevertheless, our Berthelette
has surpassed this edition of Caxton through the exertions of William Thynne." Thynne's edition was published by Thomas Godfray, not Thomas Berthelette, but in the same year that the latter
published his edition of the Confessio. The confusion between the
editions in Leland's biography of Chaucer could be either the cause
or the result of his notions concerning the personal relationship
between the two poets. Or it may be that Berthelette actually did
have something to do with the Thynne-Godfray edition of Chaucer.
Not only does that edition make use of the woodcut border which
Berthelette had inherited from Pynson when he suceeded him as

Printer to the King, but the remarks on Thynne's *Chaucer* in the 1532 Berthelette edition of Gower hardly read like an advertisement for a rival printer. It could have been upon the basis of the Chaucer greeting in Berthelette's edition, if not the earlier Caxton edition, that Thynne inserted the *Testament of Love* into his edition of Chaucer's works. The interrelationships suggest that Berthelette, Thynne, and Leland were in communication while these two editions and Leland's *Commentaries* were being prepared.[32]

Leland's version of the relationship between the two poets, not printed until 1709, reached the public little changed in the second edition of John Bale's *Catalogus Scriptorum Illustrium Maioris Brytannię* (Basle, 1557). Bale's first edition (1548) had contained no biography of Gower, but when he came to insert it, he devoted as much space to it as he had to Chaucer's, quoting the opening paragraphs of Leland's account practically verbatim until he came to the names of the three major works at the end of the second paragraph. Here he inserted a full and very accurate list of Gower's works.[33] He concluded with a statement about Gower's blindness that gave rise to the long-standing error about the date of his death, concerning which Leland had professed ignorance: "Vixit Gouerus ad iustam usq3 senectutem, fuitq3 caecus, anno a Christi natiuitate 1402, & tandem est Londini sepultus in templo Mariae de Oueres . . ." (Bale, p. 525). This, which I take to mean "Gower lived to a ripe old age, and he became blind in the year of Our Lord 1402, and finally *(tandem)* was buried in London in the church of St. Mary Overeys," was taken by all the biographers until Todd to mean that he died in 1402.[34] At the end of his life of Chaucer, Bale inserted from Leland's life of Chaucer the discussion quoted above of the relationship between the two poets.

The Leland-Bale account of the relationship between Chaucer and Gower reappeared in the introduction to Speght's *Chaucer* (1598) as "This Gower in his booke which is intituled *Confessio Amantis*, termeth Chaucer a worthi Poet, and maketh him as it were, the Iuge of his workes." [35] This sentence and a note repeating Leland's suggestions about Gower's Yorkshire connections, legal

profession, and association with St. Mary Overeys provoked
Thynne's reply in the *Animadversions:*

> In the title of Chaucers educati*o*ne, yo[u] saye that 'Gower, in
> his booke entituled 'confessio amantis,' termeth Chaucer 'a
> worthye poet,' and maketh hym as yt were the 'iuge of his
> woorkes': in the wh*i*iche Booke, to my knowledge, Gower dothe
> not terme hym 'a woorthye poet' (Althoughe I confess he well
> deseruethe that name, & the same may be gathered oute of
> Gower commendynge hym): nether dothe he after a sorte (for
> any thinge I canne yet see) make hym iudge of his Workes,
> (whereof I wolde be glad to be enformed,) since these be
> Gowers woords, vttered by Venus in that booke confessio
> amantis: [He quotes the Chaucer allusion, CA, VIII.2941*].
> These be all the verses wh*i*che I knowe, or yet canne fynde, in
> whiche Gower in that book mentionethe Chaucer, where he
> nether nemethe hym worthye poet, nor after a sort submyttethe
> his woorkes to his iudgemente. But quite contrarye, Chaucer
> dothe submytte the Correcti*o*n of his woorkes to Gower in
> these playne woordes, in the latter end of the fyfte booke of
> Troylus: [He quotes the *Troilus* dedication, TC, v.1856]. But
> this error had in you byn p*a*rdoned, yf yo[u] had not sett yet
> downe as yo*u*r owne, but warranted with the auctoryte of Bale
> in 'Scriptoribus Anglie,' from whence yo[u] have swallowed y[t].[36]

Thynne also found Bale mistaken in taking it from Leland that
Gower was a Yorkshire man. As a professional herald, he was sensitive to the fact that the arms on the poet's tomb were different from
those of the Stittenham house. And he corrected the description of
the crown of ivy and roses, pointing out that there were only roses
and that the roseate chaplet was not an emblem of knighthood.
Finally, he pointed out that Buckley's testimony[37] that Chaucer
was of the Inner Temple had no bearing on Gower—although he
does not appear to have doubted that both poets had had legal
training. All in all, Thynne did much to straighten out the Gower
tradition. But at the same time, he reinforced Leland's misreading
of the Chaucer greeting as an expression of Gower's own feelings,
and brought to final expression the notion that Gower was Chaucer's mentor.

At the beginning of the 17th century, the observations of Stow and Weever gave Gower biography its first documentary base, as we shall see in the next chapter. However, the Leland tradition continued to shape his critical reputation. It appeared without change, along with Bale's list of Gower's works, in John Pits' *De Illustribus Scriptoribus Britanniae* (1619),[38] and it was further amplified in Thomas Fuller's *Worthies* (1662): Gower was, "born, saith Leland, in Stittenham . . . bred in London a student of the laws. Bale makes him *equitem auratum & poetam laureatum*, proving both from his ornaments, on his monumental statue . . . Yet he appeareth there neither laureated, nor hederated poet . . . but only roseated . . . Stowe likewise unknighted him . . . though in my apprehension the collar SSS, about his neck speaks him to be more. Besides, the collar speaks *civil* rather than military relation, proper to persons in places of judicature; which makes me guess this Gower some judge in his old age, well consisting with his original education." [39] Fuller's introduction of the phrase *equitem auratum & poetam laureatum*,[40] shows how Leland's "vir equestris ordinis . . . hederacea corona rosis interserta" came in the 17th century to have implications not originally intended. With Ben Jonson and then John Dryden, the poet laureate had come to be thought of as a member of the royal household who received a stipend. Fifteenth-century allusions to Chaucer as "worthy the laurer to haue" and to Chaucer and Gower as "poetis laureate," and some awareness of their court connections, were interpreted to mean they occupied such official positions.[41] In the patent by which Dryden was created laureate in 1670, "Sir Geoffrey Chaucer, Knight, and Sir John Gower, Knight," were named as having held the office before him.[42] The notion, soon to redound seriously to his discredit, that Gower had been poet laureate, was clearly voiced in Edward Phillips' otherwise slight account (*Theatrum Poetarum*, 1675): "*Sir John Gowr*, a very Famous English Poet in his time, and counted little inferiour, if not equal to *Chaucer* himself; who was his Contemporary, and some say his Scholar and Successor in the Laurel: For *Gowr* was also both Poet Laureat and Knight." [43] With William Winstanley's *Lives* (1687), we come to the end of what might be called the *uncritical* phase of the Gower tradition. Winstanley's account is still substantially that of Leland. His misreading of the *Troilus* dedication is significant evidence of the prevailing view of the relationship between the two poets:

> O marvel [sic], *Gower,* this Book I direct
> To thee, and to the Philosophical *Strode* . . .[44]

Both poets are indebted to King Richard II for office and income. Poor Strode has been pushed aside. The younger Chaucer is expressing fulsome praise for his mentor. Such is the cosy picture with which this phase closes. When the new one opened nine years later, Gower's character was to fall immediately under a shadow from which it has never fully emerged, and by the end of the next century his reputation both for political integrity and as a friend of Chaucer was nearly as low as it was high with Phillips and Winstanley.

III

It is interesting to speculate about the influence of politics upon literary reputation. The Puritan controversies and the Revolution had revealed to Englishmen the power of the pen, and after 1660 writers occupied a position of influence and responsibility that they had not previously. Always there is a tendency to read back into history the tensions and obligations of the present. There were superficial similarities between the political situations at the end of the 14th century and at the end of the 17th. In both periods party politics were strong, serious religious differences divided the public, and abrupt shifts in power and depositions of rulers made the problem of integrity very real. While one man remained loyal to a lost cause and suffered, another might shift allegiance and appear to profit by it. Dryden was, of course, a conspicuous example of both kinds of behavior, and within a short time Defoe, Swift, Addison, and a host of lesser figures were to be subjected to similar pressures. Men themselves experiencing political temptation might well look back to see how their predecessors had fared under similar circumstances. The two prologues to the *Confessio* had been known since Berthelette's edition of 1532, and Gower's *Cronica Tripertita* to all who knew the manuscripts of the *Vox Clamantis* in the major libraries in England. The *Testament of Love* had likewise been assigned to Chaucer since Thynne's edition of 1532. Speght had deduced from it and from records he discovered of the king's taking Chaucer's lands into his protection in 1379 that Chaucer was in political difficulties during the reign of Richard II "for he doth greatly complain of his own rashness in following the multitude, and of their hatred against him for bewraying their purpose." But, as Lounsbury pointed out,[45] Speght's statement appears to have made not the slightest impression upon the men of his time. It remained for the 18th century to find new significance in both Chaucer's and Gower's political involvement with the court.

The first evidence of the new view is to be found in the remarks of William Nicolson, antiquarian historian and (in 1702) Bishop of Carlisle, in the *English Historical Library* (1696): "*Richard* the Second's good Success in *Ireland* was so far outbalanc'd by the other (more unlucky) Adventures of his reign, that I have not heard of any who thought it worth their while to write his Life, except only a poor knight of John Pits's Creation. That author says, that one *Sir John Gower* (a *Yorkshire* knight, and Contemporary with the famous Chaucer) died in the year 1402, leaving behind him a deal of Monuments of his Learning, and (amongst the rest) a *Latin* Chronicle of King *Richard* the Second. There was indeed one Mr. *John Gower*, a noted Poet, who liv'd about the time he mentions. This witty Person took the Liberty, that has always been allow'd to Men of his Profession to make Free with his Prince; and Mr. *Stowe* (or his continuer *Howes*) has done him the honour to translate the elegy he made on this king's untimely death which (it may be) contains the whole Chronicle."[46] The lines by Stow are a very free translation from the end of the *Cronica Tripertita*: "For God allotted him [Richard] such ende,/ . . . As such a life deserued: as by/ the Chronicles thou mayst know."[47] They had stood in Stow's *Chronicle* for a century without being taken as evidence of Gower's "making free" with his prince. One need know only a little about the turbulent political career of the venerable prelate, who began as a Tory, to be accused a little later of "courting ye figure of ye Loggerhead at Lambeth," and was eventually to clash with Queen Anne herself over the right to grant the deanery of Carlisle,[48] to understand that he might be sensitive to political opportunism where others might see simply a statement of fact.

But Nicolson's was merely a passing comment. The real interpretation—or misinterpretation—of the political careers of Chaucer and Gower may be traced, through the life of Chaucer prefixed to the 1721 Urry edition of Chaucer, to Thomas Hearne. Hearne came to Oxford as a student in 1696 already a nonjuror in principle, and after the death of Queen Anne could not be brought to take the oath to what he regarded as a usurping dynasty, the Hanoverian. After taking his degrees, he became underlibrarian of the Bodleian, where he remained until January 23, 1716, the last day fixed for taking the oath to the Hanoverians. On that morning he was prevented from entering the library, and he was soon dismissed from his post. He continued to live at Oxford and distinguished himself by his editions of medieval chronicles and other antiquarian research. In later years he might have had several important positions—Camden professorship of history, keeper of the archives, head librarianship of the Bodleian—if he had been willing to take the oath, but this he refused to do, preferring "a good conscience before all manner of preferment and worldly honour." [49] In 1709 Hearne paraphrased in his diary Speght's account of Chaucer's political misfortune:

> It appeareth from ye Testament of Love that G. Chaucer was in some Trouble in the days of Rich. 2^d. where he complains very much of his own Rashness in following the multitude, & of their hatred against him for bewraying their Purpose. And in that complaint wch he makes to his empty purse M^r. Speght found ten times more adjoyned in a Ms^t. of it in M^r. Stowes hands than is in the Print, making therein great Lamentation for his wrongfull Imprisonment, wishing Death to end his Dayes. And 'tis plain from a Record in ye Tower that the King took Geff. Chaucer & his Lands into his Protection in ye 2^d year of his

Reign, because there was much Danger from him by reason of his favouring some rash attempt of the common People.[50]

In 1711 Hearne reported that his good friend John Urry, a fellow of Christ Church and likewise a nonjuror, had been encouraged by the new dean of his college, Francis Atterbury, to undertake an edition of Chaucer, for which Hearne thought him eminently qualified.[51] Then in 1713 Hearne came upon a copy of Gower's *Cronica Tripertita*. In a letter of August 30, 1713, he wrote of it:

> I lately looked over a Ms[t]. called Chronica Joannis Gower de tempore Regis Richardi 2[1] ad annum 2[dum] Henrici 4[ti]. 'Tis written in Latin verse, but is very violent against that goodnatured, but very unfortunate Prince. I happened to mention it to M[r]. Tyrrell . . . when he told me that he had not so much as ever heard of it before, which I wondered at, considering the great Diligence he hath used in raking up all he could in defence of Republican Principles against those unfortunate Princes that have been deposed by their Subjects, & for w[ch] the Rebells stand condemned by the best of our own Writers . . . & the Contrivers . . . have left no better Characters behind them than those of being Traytors to their Sovereigns, & what they look'd upon as the most glorious Part of their Lives is spoken of in no milder Terms than wth a proh! nefas whenever their Actions are particularized by the most judicious Writers of our English History.[52]

Somewhat later (1729) Hearne remarked in the preface to his edition of the *Historia vitae et regni Ricardi II* by the Monk of Evesham that he would not include what Gower said in the *Vox Clamantis* (he must have had the *Cronica* in mind) because of its enmity toward Richard and its criticisms of the church.[53]

Urry died March 19, 1715 (Hearne's descriptions in the Diary of his friend's last warning concerning his—Hearne's—danger from his political enemies and of Urry's final illness are truly moving[54]), with the text of his edition substantially complete. His final illness was brought on by a trip to London to make arrangements for its printing. John Dart, a London antiquary, had been commissioned to prepare a life to be prefixed to Urry's text. After Urry's death the edition fell into bad hands, at least from the Oxford point of view.

To the distress of Hearne and the dons, Timothy Thomas agreed to print in roman rather than in the traditional black letter that Urry had planned, and his brother William's revision of Dart's life occasioned anguished wails in that worthy's *Westmonasterium* (1723).[55] Whether it was through Dart or through William Thomas that the interpretation of the *Testament of Love* and Gower's politics outlined in Hearne's diary got into the Life of Chaucer, it is impossible to say. Since the account of Chaucer's political misfortunes there developed is based upon Speght, it could have been independent of Hearne. But in view of Hearne's evident interest in the edition, his previous allusions to Speght's account, and his work in editing medieval chronicles which would have made him exactly the sort of authority to supply the historical details with which Speght's account was filled out, there seems good reason to look to him as the originator of the fully developed legend: that Chaucer was attached to Gaunt's party, was forced to flee from England when that party fell from power in 1386, traveled through France, and finally took refuge in Zealand, where he wrote most of his books (this from Speght), that he returned to England when the treachery of his friends deprived him of support, was promptly imprisoned, during which time he wrote the *Testament of Love*, and was finally freed only after he had exposed his confederates. This legend was exploded a century later (1844) when Harris Nicolas showed that Chaucer was receiving his pension in London during the years when he was supposed to have been abroad and was a member of Parliament when he was supposed to have been in prison,[56] and by Bradley's and Skeat's eventual discovery of the USK acrostic in the *Testament*.[57]

The denigration of Gower's character which accompanied the Chaucer legend is even more likely to have come from Hearne. After repeating the Leland inference that Gower and Chaucer had known one another at the Inns of Court, the Urry Life goes on to say that in spite of Chaucer's [supposed] Wycliffite leanings: "Nor was he less esteemed by Gower, tho' a violent Bigot to the Church of *Rome*, and a perpetual exclaimer against Wycliffe and his Followers." [58] Of Gower himself: "He was a Man of singular Learning, and great Piety; but much given to change with the turns of State"; [59] a little later that frequently-to-be-repeated condemnation: "The respect Chaucer retained for his former master *Richard,* and gratitude for the Favours he had received from him, kept him from trampling upon his Memory, and basely flattering the new King; as most of his contemporaries did, and particularly Gower, who, notwithstanding the obligations he had to *Rich. II.,* yet when old, blind, and past any hopes of honour or advantage, unless the view of keeping what he enjoyed, basely insulted the memory of his murdered Master, and as ignominiously flattered his murderer." [60] The obligation that Gower had to Richard is in the note merely cited as the King's kindness in asking him into the royal barge and commanding him to write the *Confessio,* but that the authors of the Urry Life had something more in mind becomes clear when they remark a little later that Chaucer was not poet laureate, but "if any poet bore that title it is more likely to be Gower." [61] Here, then, is the fully developed picture of Gower's supposed ingratitude and political opportunism.

An extenuation was not long in appearing. Three years later (1724), John Anstis, Garter King at Arms, pointed out what had not been previously noted in descriptions of the effigy on Gower's tomb, that the SSS collar is clasped by a swan between two portcullises.[62] Anstis observed that this was the emblem of Thomas of Woodstock, Duke of Gloucester, the *Cignus* of the *Cronica Tripertita,* whose party had dominated the King and government for a brief period after 1386. The emblem on the effigy and the references in the *Cronica* led Anstis to suggest that Gloucester was Gower's real patron. Anstis' suggestion notwithstanding, the tradition of Gower's political opportunism took firm hold. It was as with the later charge of dullness: those who took pains to examine the evidence nearly all came to Gower's defense, but authors of histories of literature and biographical dictionaries kept it alive. The *Biographia Britannica* (1757) is an interesting case in point. Like most of its other entries, the Life of Gower is judicious and informed, quite the best that had appeared until that time. Building on Anstis' suggestion, it argued that it was Gloucester's brutal murder which led the poet to turn so violently against the King,[63] a theory which could still be defended by Karl Meyer in an 1889 Bonn dissertation,[64] even though Harris Nicolas had in 1828 pointed out that the SSS collar was given to Gower by Henry of Lancaster in 1393 and that Henry himself assumed the swan emblem after the death of Gloucester in 1397.[65] The Life in the *Biographia* goes on to answer in detail the accusations of Nicolson, Hearne, and the Urry Life with evidences from other historians that "justify what J. Gower has written" concerning Richard II. And the *Britannica* biographer concluded that Gower's writings "shew him to have been a person of great integrity and true piety." Nevertheless, when the same or some other author came to discuss Gower in the Life of Chaucer (a discussion which would, of course, be seen far more often than that of Gower himself), he fell back upon a paraphrase of the Urry condemnation; "we do not find that Chaucer was at all eager in paying compliments to the new King, much less that he triumphed in the misfortune of his late kind master and gracious benefactor, as others, and particularly Gower, who had been more obliged to that unfortunate Prince, and who at that time was both old and blind, most shamefully did."

The indictments for political opportunism continued, but before we examine either the defenses or reiterations we must record the second indictment under which Gower entered the 19th century. As we have seen, Leland's view of the close friendship between the two poets was repeated and elaborated without a dissenting voice to the time of Johnson's *Dictionary* and the *Biographia Britannica*. This may have been due partly to the fact that there was no new edition of the *Confessio* after Berthelette's, and hence no examination of the manuscripts after 1632 until Tyrwhitt turned to them in connection with his edition of Chaucer (1775–78). He read them in the light of a growing Chaucer idolatry and the deprecation of Gower's political integrity already being expressed. When Tyrwhitt came to the Man of Law's headlink in the Introductory Discourse to his edition of the *Canterbury Tales* (where so many subsequent interpretations begin), he observed that "the compliments which Chaucer has introduced upon his own writings are modest enough and quite unexceptionable; but if the reflection upon those who relate such stories as those of *Canace,* or of *Apollonius Tyrius,* were leveled at Gower, as I very much suspect, it will be difficult to reconcile such an attack to our notions of the strict friendship, which is generally supposed to have subsisted between the two bards." [66] The footnote that he appended to this observation contains the seeds of much future debate:

> There is another circumstance, which rather inclines me to believe, that their friendship suffered some interruption in the latter part of their lives. In the new edition of the *Confessio Amantis,* which Gower published after the accession of Henry IV, the verses in praise of Chaucer are omitted. See Ms. *Harl.* 3869. Though perhaps the death of Chaucer at that time had rendered the compliment contained in those verses less proper than it was at first, that alone does not seem to have been a sufficient reason for omitting them, especially as the original date of the work, in the 16 of Richard II, is preserved. Indeed, the only other alterations, which I have been able to discover, are toward the beginning and end, where everything which had been said in praise of Richard in the first edition, is either left out or converted to the use of his successor.

The late date for the revised dedication, accepted by most scholars in the 19th century, has now been almost certainly disproved, but the ghost of the quarrel has hardly yet been laid. Finally, Tyrwhitt noted one other apparent reference to Gower, toward the end of the Man of Law's Tale: the fact that in Gower's version Maurice is sent upon the errand to the Emperor, which led Chaucer to remark:

> Some men wold seyn, how that the child Maurice
> Doth this message until this Emperour . . .

"We may therefore conclude," observed Tyrwhitt, "that in this passage Chaucer alludes to Gower, who had treated the same subject before him, as he insinuates, with less propriety."

Tyrwhitt's observations, although evidently tinged with admiration for a Chaucer whose remarks upon his own writings are quite unexceptionable and whose treatment of the Constance story is obviously more proper, are stated factually enough, and he was careful to point out how extraordinary it was for Chaucer to retell one of Gower's stories if his intention was to quarrel with him. His caution will be well for us to bear in mind as we come to the more critical interpretations of the next century, and when we turn in the last chapter to an examination of the relationship between the works of the two poets. The evidence for an association between the two men is external as well as internal. The evidence for a quarrel depends exclusively upon interpretations placed upon possible allusions in their works. In the light of the objectively proved relationship, the allusions cannot be ignored, but just how they are to be understood remains a tantalizing problem.

IV

There is no need for us to analyze in detail the comments pro and con the Urry political and the Tyrwhitt quarrel indictments after the beginning of the 19th century.[67] They are important only as evidence that in spite of repeated defenses, the accusations persisted and colored the reactions to Gower's works. The logic by which one proceeds from personal to literary denigration is well illustrated in "On Gower, the Kentish Poet, His Character and Works," by W. Warwick, Esq. (1866),[68] in which it is asserted that Gower was (1) a shady business man, (2) a bad friend, (3) a disloyal subject, (4) an inferior poet, and eventually (5) the model for the merchant in Chaucer's Merchant's Tale! The reputation of Gower in the 19th century is paradoxical. The cynic might observe that his reputation for dullness grew almost in direct proportion as his works became accessible; that so long as he was little more than a name he fared reasonably well, but that as soon as he could be read people began to find what he was really like. And there is no doubt some truth in such an interpretation. But Gower has never attracted a popular following and has in consequence been subjected more than most authors to "hearsay" criticisms. The difference is that before the 18th-century attacks on his character such hearsay criticisms were almost uniformly favorable, whereas afterwards they became increasingly unfavorable, and this in spite of the awareness on the part of those willing to read him of the genuine virtues and importance that called forth the new editions: Chalmers' reprint of the Berthelette edition of the *Confessio* in 1810, the first in nearly two centuries; Lord Gower's edition of the *Balades* in 1818; H. O. Coxe's edition of the *Vox Clamantis* in 1850; Reinhold Pauli's new edition of the *Confessio* in 1857; E. Stengel's re-edition of the *Balades* in 1886; Henry Morley's modernizations from the *Confessio* in 1889; and finally G. C. Macaulay's great edition of the complete works at the end of the century, 1899–1902.

The baldly antagonistic criticisms of Gower's political activity can be summed up quickly. Theophilus Cibber (1753) had been content to dismiss him as a timeserver.[69] Joseph Ritson (1802) observed that "his *Vox Clamantis* might have deserved publication, in a historical view, if he had not proved an ingrate to his lawful sovereign, and a sycophant to the usurper of his throne." [70] Charles Cowden-Clark, Keats's friend, added (1835): "yet this execrable baseness attaches to the memory of Chaucer's friend Gower, who with the callous selfishness that not unfrequently accompanies a blind old age, was among the first to welcome the new sovereign, spurning at the same time his fallen master and patron." [71] The same canard is repeated later by Sir Adolphus Ward (1879), who saw Gower as one whose wisdom was "the kind that goes with the times, who was a flatterer of Richard and (by the simple expedient of a revised second edition of his *magnum opus*) a flatterer of Henry." [72] T. Arnold (1881) repeated the timid and timeserver epithets.[73] And even after Macaulay's edition began to appear, Frederick Snell (1901) found Gower a "rigid legitimist" who "found no difficulty in supporting the opponents of Richard when those opponents were princes like the Duke of Gloucester and the Earl of Derby." [74]

The arguments of those who discussed the supposed quarrel with

Chaucer and sought to defend Gower's political behavior are not so easy to sum up. William Godwin in his *Life of Chaucer* (1803) sought to defend Gower along the Anstis line and on the ground that he was under no obligation to Richard (without, however, realizing that the laureateship was the obligation that the Urry biographers had had in mind), but Godwin was content to accept Tyrwhitt's account of the quarrel.[75] Henry Todd's *Illustrations of the Lives and Writings of Gower and Chaucer* (1810) was important on two accounts. First, its defense of the Stittenham claim to Gower's ancestry was what led to Harris Nicolas's examination of the documents and "the appeal to fact." And second, Todd clearly pointed out the traditional error, into which even Tyrwhitt had fallen, of taking the Chaucer greeting at the end of the *Confessio* as expressing Gower's own sentiments rather than those of an allegorical Venus.[76] It may be noted that after Tyrwhitt and Todd, Gower was no longer referred to as Chaucer's mentor; the greeting was cited only as a Chaucer allusion, not as evidence of any particular relationship; and the discussion of the quarrel turned upon the Man of Law's prologue, with the excision of the Chaucer greeting referred to merely as subsidiary evidence.

In his 1828 reply to Todd, Nicolas made no comment either on the quarrel or on the political question, although his discovery that the SSS collar was the gift of Henry rather than of Thomas of Gloucester had bearings on the Anstis argument. However, in his Life of Chaucer prefixed to the Aldine edition (1845), Nicolas did express himself on the quarrel, observing that "Tyrwhitt's grounds for supposing that their friendship . . . ceased, are very light," and, indeed, answered by Tyrwhitt's own suggestion that Chaucer "could not have meant to show disrespect to Gower in a piece in which, like the 'Man of Law's Tale,' almost every incident is borrowed from Gower; and that the omission of the lines alluded to in the late copy of the 'Confessio Amantis' may be explained by Chaucer being dead." He concludes, "Their friendship certainly endured until within seven years of Chaucer's death; and the probability is that it was never dissolved."[77] In the introduction to his 1857 edi-

tion of the *Confessio*, Reinhold Pauli succinctly stated the case for
the 1392–93 date for the revised dedication, and defended Gower's
change in politics on the grounds of perfectly understandable dissatisfaction with the administration of Richard II. He likewise
doubted that there was a quarrel, and accounted for the omission
of the Chaucer reference on the ground that Chaucer was in trouble
with the existing government in 1392–93 (the legend based upon
the *Testament of Love* persisting in spite of Nicolas' life), and that
"timid" Gower would not therefore want to mention his friend to
Henry of Lancaster.[78] The author of an admirable review essay on
the editions of Pauli, Coxe, and Lord Gower in the *British Quarterly
Review* (1858) found Gower's shift of dedication at a time when
Richard was firmly on the throne and Henry *non grata* with the
royal party evidence of the poet's courage rather than his timidity.
While he accepted the notion of a quarrel, here, too, he saw Gower
behaving the more creditably since he was content merely to omit
the Chaucer allusion whereas Chaucer "twice sarcastically alludes
to Gower's works." [79]

In suggesting that Chaucer might have precipitated the quarrel
because he was resentful of Gower's dedicating the *Confessio* to the
son of his early patron, the *British Quarterly Review* introduced a
variation upon a suggestion about the genesis of the quarrel that
had been put forward in 1842 by Elizabeth Barrett (Browning). In
an article in the *Athenaeum* [80] she praised Gower's technique, but
found his allusion to Chaucer "impertinent," as if to say "I have
done my poem, and you cannot do yours because you are superan-
nuated." This suggestion of a literary jealousy has likewise continued
almost to our own time, thanks to the support of such influential
critics as W. W. Skeat and J. S. P. Tatlock. Adolphus Ward denied
it on the ground that literary life in England had not in the 14th
century reached the stage where literary jealousy was likely to exist,
a point of view accepted by few except Karl Meyer.[81] Macaulay considered the notion that Chaucer might have been seriously offended
by Gower as "hardly worth discussion." The view that he finally
worked around to in the introduction to *Selections from the Con-*

fessio Amantis (1903), and repeated in the Gower chapter in the *Cambridge History of English Literature* (1909), that the disappearance of the Chaucer lines "may be reasonably explained in connexion with the rewriting of the conclusion of that work, without the assumption of an ill-feeling,"[82] has been called into question by both Heinrich Spies and J. S. P. Tatlock.[83] There is no discernible "mechanical" reason why the revision had to begin exactly where it did, and the omission of the Chaucer greeting must represent deliberate excision.

Macaulay's view was evidently influenced by that of W. W. Skeat, who in the *Oxford Chaucer* (III.413) had undertaken to reverse the indebtedness between the two poets from that which had been universally accepted to his time and which has been generally accepted ever since. Following Pauli and J. W. Hales,[84] Skeat asserted that the first version of the *Confessio* was complete and the first epilogue written by 1385, but his efforts to prove that Gower borrowed from Chaucer rather than Chaucer from Gower in the Man of Law's Tale betray him into (for him) astonishingly unreliable reasoning. On the slenderest of evidence, Skeat posited two versions of both Chaucer's and Gower's tales: Chaucer's first version about 1380; Gower's first version about 1382–85; Chaucer's second version about 1387; and Gower's second about 1393. "We can hence understand what happened," he opined. "After Chaucer had written his story, he doubtless lent Gower, then his particular friend, a copy. Gower took advantage of the occasion to introduce some expressions which certainly give the impression that he copied them . . . Lücke . . . draws what is, in my opinion, the erroneous conclusion, that it was Chaucer who copied from Gower; which is like suggesting that Tennyson was capable of borrowing from Martin Tupper." (Lücke's article merely formalized the impressions of Tyrwhitt, and has been supported in all subsequent discussions.[85]) And finally, "Taken together, these appropriations by Gower, though not in themselves very marked, must have been annoying to his brother-poet." As we shall see, the relationships between the works of the two poets, and particularly between the *Mirour de l'omme*,

Confessio Amantis, Legend of Good Women, and *Canterbury Tales* can be explained only by assuming that Chaucer and Gower were in constant communication, passing their manuscripts back and forth frequently at least up to 1386 and again after 1390.

To the influence of Skeat was shortly added that of J. S. P. Tatlock,[86] who likewise found that "Chaucer may have been more or less seriously nettled at a continuation or revival of the criticisms of him for mysogyny and cynicism which had evoked the *Legend of Good Women*" and that "these criticisms may have been echoed by Gower or accompanied by contrasting praise of him, . . . the one contemporary poet with whose versification Chaucer had reason to fear comparison." "One would hesitate," he concluded, "to suggest such an explanation as this of the *Man of Law's Prologue* if it implied anything like pettiness or malice or ill-temper on Chaucer's part, which it is impossible to attribute to him; but there is nothing here that is not perfectly just, and even delicate and good-humored. It seems also to suggest rather vividly how much to the same 'set' the two poets belonged." There seems to be some contradiction between the concepts of a seriously nettled and a perfectly good-humored Chaucer, and the latter is further abrogated by Tatlock's reintroduction of a variation of Anstis's earlier suggestion that the differences between Chaucer and Gower may have been political rather than literary. In 1387, he thought, Gower disapproved of Richard's favorite, the Earl of Oxford, to whom Chaucer was indebted for permission (in 1385) to perform the duties of his wool comptrollership by deputy.[87] Now, Chaucer's indebtedness to Oxford has been called in question.[88] It was at least two years before Oxford's defeat by Gloucester; and all we know about Gower's attitude toward these officials we learn from the *Cronica Tripertita,* written after Richard's deposition, when by hindsight his attitudes would be more definite than they might have been at that time. Although it is possible that during the period when Gower was moving into the anti-Richard camp and Chaucer was still a servant in the royal household, the two did not see eye to eye politically, there is nothing in Chaucer's writing after 1386 to indicate that he was not of Gower's mind concerning Richard's maladministration, and there are quiet suggestions (*Lak of Stedfastnesse* and the passage on "tirauntz of Lumbardye" in the *Legend of Good Women*) that in spite of his professional obligations, Chaucer was concerned about the drift of affairs.

Elizabeth Barrett Browning's suggestion has been most recently voiced by Aaga Brusendorff (1925),[89] who interpreted the reference to the testament of love in the Chaucer greeting as "a gentle hint that Chaucer might do worse than follow Gower's example and compose a great work treating of love—a hint which Chaucer seems very properly to have resented." And the latest variation (1948) on the political explanation for the excision of the Chaucer greeting is that of Margaret Galway[90] who suggested that the Venus of the *Confessio*, like the Alcestis of the *Legend*, was Chaucer's supposed patroness Joan of Kent, and that the Chaucer greeting, a joint tribute to the Princess and her poet, was canceled along with the tributes to Joan in Chaucer's works after her death in 1385. This is an ironic conclusion to the debate about the interpretation of the greeting, which from Leland to Todd turned upon the *failure* to recognize that the greeting was by Venus, not by Gower himself, and now finally turns upon the recognition of that very fact.

Since the time of Anstis and the *Biographia Britannica*, those who have known both Gower's writings and English political history at the close of the 14th century have come to the defense of Gower's political integrity. Reinhold Pauli asserted categorically in the preface to his edition of the *Confessio* (1857), and the assertion was at once repeated by the *British Quarterly Review* (1858) and Thomas Wright (1859),[91] that Gower was of neither the Gaunt nor the Gloucester factions and that his allegiance shifted gradually through the course of Richard's reign. Even more impassioned was the defense of Henry Morley (*English Writers*, 1889), who heard in Gower's reaction against political and social injustice "the voice that sustains the keynote of our literature, and speaks from the soul of our history the secret of our national success. It is the voice that expresses the persistent instinct of the English mind to find out what is unjust among us and undo it, to find out duty to be done and do it, as God's bidding" (4.197). Macaulay also felt that Gower's views evolved progressively through his works in response to the changing political scene (2.xxi; 4.xxix). But for more than a half century after Macaulay's recovery of the *Mirour de l'omme* and his edition of the complete works had made a full-scale study possible, the integrity of Gower's life and writings still rested upon assertion. In 1945 George R. Coffman pointed the proper direction for such a study: that "the social instead of the literary aspect of Gower's writings may form the basis for an interpretation of him in his most significant role." Coffman perceived that the guiding principle throughout all Gower's works was the inculcation of the ideals of a conservative medieval moral order, and he found him progressing with consistency and growing clarity toward his central thesis, that the use of "God-given intellectual power will result in a world of peace and harmony, in proper human relations, in worthy rulers, and in a prosperous England." [92] At the time of his death, Coffman was on the point of making a full study of Gower's moral philosophy. The direction this would have taken is suggested by his final article, on the minor Latin poems (1954). In this he found Gower's shift in loyalty reflecting the attitude and point of view of a conservative middle-class Englishman from the years 1381 to 1400. No other poet, Coffman felt, had ever devoted himself so consistently to the single theme of the responsibility of a king for the welfare, morals, and integrity of his country. This very emphasis, which led Gower in *Vox Clamantis* to hope for so much from the young Richard, was what led him to such bitter disappointment and violent rejection when he found his hopes unfounded. [93] In the meantime, Maria Wickert had published her *Studien zu John Gower* (1953), [94] subjecting the *Vox Clamantis*, and through it Gower's entire world view, to the most perceptive and detailed scrutiny it had ever received, and reaching the same conclusion as Coffman concerning the coherence and intelligence of his social criticism.

Yet, in spite of this continuous, though small, stream of sympathetic interpretation, Coffman still felt impelled to address his 1954

article to "the unresolved problem of Gower's ethical integrity."
Perhaps the problem can never be fully resolved, but it warrants a
more thorough examination than it has received. Out of the directions mapped in Coffman's studies and in Miss Wickert's has come
the following investigation into the relationship between Gower's
life and writings. A more thorough understanding of his character
and his philosophy has led to a reappraisal of his relations with
Chaucer and to a realization of the implications of the sense in
which he and Chaucer were linked by their contemporaries and for
three centuries thereafter. As it was put in the *Kingis Quair*:

> Vnto [the] Impnis of my maisteris dere,
> Gowere and chaucere, that oñ the steppis satt
> Of rethorike, quhill thai were lyvand here,
> Superlatiue as poetis laureate
> In *moralitee* and eloqueñce ornate,
> I recommend my buk . . .[95]

The moral foundation of Chaucer's world view has been emphasized by nearly all the great critics: Ten Brink, Kittredge, Lowes,
Tatlock, C. S. Lewis, not to mention the recent exegetical critics.
But the useful distinction between satire and complaint as literary
modes in which medieval social criticism could be treated was never
clearly drawn until 1956 by John Peter.[96] It remains to be shown
how directly Chaucerian satire builds upon Gowerian complaint.
To that we shall return in the last chapter. We may not end by
accepting Leland's view of Chaucer as the "admirer and imitator"
of Gower, but at least we will understand the basis for that view
and recognize the inadequacy of the stereotypes of the brilliant
Chaucer and dull Gower bequeathed us by Taine, Lowell, and the
superficial critical tradition of the 19th century.

Figure 1. Gower Arms in the Glasgow MS. (51)

Figure 2. Gower Arms on the Tomb in Southwark Cathedral

Figure 3. Arms of Sir Robert Gower of Brabourn

Figure 4. Arms of the Langbargh Gowers

Figure 5. Arms of the Stittenham Gowers

Figure 6. Gower's first seal (1373)

Figure 7. Gower's second seal (1382)

Figure 1. Glasgow MS. (51), f. 129

Figures 2 and 5. Canon Thompson, *Antiquities of St. Savior's* (3rd ed., London, 1910), p. 201

Figures 3, 6 and 7. W. Warwick, "On Gower," *Archaeologia Cantiana*, VI (1866), 85-86

Figure 4. William Flower and Robert Glover, *Visitation of the North in A.D. 1575*, Surtees Society, CXLVI (1932), 24-25

2. Life Records

The Gower life records are no more satisfactory than those of Chaucer and Shakespeare. The gaps are more interesting than the documents. For Gower, we must work outward from his tomb in St. Mary Overeys Priory Church, now Southwark Cathedral, since this is the only positive identification of John Gower the poet. Unlike the name Geoffrey Chaucer, which appears to have been unique in its time, the name John Gower was common in all parts of England during the last half of the 14th century. Sorting out the documents that refer to the poet is so hazardous that it led Macaulay practically to throw up his hands.[1] Nevertheless, the attempt has its own kind of fascination, and in spite of the tenuous and tangential quality of much of the material it does help to create a sense of actuality about the man and his society.

I

The present appearance of the Gower tomb is of little assistance. It has been moved twice since 1800, the chapel of St. John in which it was originally located is no longer in existence, and all of the painting and lettering have been restored since 1958 on the basis of earlier descriptions.[2] The most nearly complete early account of the tomb is in Stow's *Survey of London* (1598):

> [The church of St. Mary Overeys] was again newly built in the reign of Richard II. and Henry IV.
> John Gower, esquire, a famous poet, was then an especial benefactor to that work, and was there buried on the north side

of the said church, in the chapel of St. John, where he founded a
chantry: he lieth under a tomb of stone, with his image, also of
stone, over him: the hair of his head, auburn, long to his shoul-
ders, but curling up, and a small forked beard; on his head a
chaplet, like a coronet, of four roses; a habit of purple, damasked
down to his feet, a collar of esses gold about his neck; under his
head the likeness of three books, which he compiled. The first,
named *Speculum Meditantis*, written in French; the second,
Vox Clamantis, penned in Latin; the third, *Confessio Amantis*,
written in English . . . Beside on the wall where he lieth, there
was painted three virgins crowned [accompanied by couplets
which he quotes, evidently from Berthelette]. His arms a field
argent, on a chevron azure, three leopards' heads gold, their
tongues gules; two angels supporters, on the crest a talbot.[3]

In the *Annales of England* (ca. 1600), Stow added an important
qualification after describing the painting of the three virgins: "All
which is now washed out and the image defaced by cutting off the
nose and striking off his hands." [4] Evidently the tomb had suffered
defacement since the dissolution of the priory in 1539 (not surprising in view of Gower's popish reputation)[5] and Stow had taken
the readings from Berthelette's preface of 1532, to which they correspond exactly. Two other details with biographical significance
might be added to Stow's description. He did not quote, although
his first sentence paraphrases, the inscription on the upper ledge of
the tomb: "Hic iacet I. Gower, Arm. [for *Armiger* 'Esquire'] Angl.
poeta celebrerrimus ac huic sacro edificio benefac. insignis. Vixit
temporibus Edw. III et Ric. II et Henr. IV"; nor does he mention
the swan clasp at the end of the chain of "esses."

The three books under the head of the effigy identify John Gower
the poet with John Gower of St. Mary Overeys, and the coat of arms
painted on the shield above the tomb and found in the Glasgow
manuscript (51) of the *Vox Clamantis* (Figs. 1 and 2) offer a clue
to his genealogy. Leland's tentative identification of the poet with
the Gowers of Stittenham (Fig. 5) in Yorkshire and Thynne's chal-
lenging that identification on the basis of the difference in the arms
were mentioned in the last chapter.[6] In 1631 John Weever had

pointed biographical documentation in the right direction by observing, on the basis of the correspondence between the arms on Gower's tomb in St. Mary Overeys and those on the tomb of Robert Gower in the old Norman chapel at Brabourn in Kent, "From this familie *Iohn Gower* the Poet was descended."[7] In spite of Thynne and Weever, the Stittenham suggestion continued to be repeated until it culminated in Henry Todd's *Illustrations of the Lives and Writings of Chaucer and Gower* (1810), which included a 14th-century deed signed by a John Gower of Stittenham as proof of the poet's connection, and was dedicated to George Granville Leveson-Gower, Marquis of Stafford and first Duke of Sutherland, as the head of the Stittenham family.[8] This proved too much for Harris Nicolas, who went to the calendars of public documents then in existence and produced a deed of 1373 bearing a seal with the same arms as those on the tombs of John and Robert, by which John Gower (in a related, unsealed document called "esquire of Kent") conveyed to John Cobham and others his manor of Kentwell in Suffolk.[9]

This and the associated records persuaded Nicolas, and have persuaded all commentators since his time, that the poet was descended from a Kentish rather than a Yorkshire family. None of the authorities has taken into account that there was in the Wapentake of Langbargh in the Cleveland hills of Yorkshire North Riding another Gower family, more prominent in the 14th century than the Gowers of Stittenham, whose arms bear a much closer resemblance than those of the Stittenham Gowers to the arms of the Kentish Gowers. The family is represented in 16th-century heraldic visitations by Gower of Stainsby, descended from Nicholas Gower of Sexhow, son of John Gower of Sexhow, "qui in armis gentilitiis portabant signum capitale inter tres canes sagaces argentes in caelestino campo" (Fig. 4).[10] Translated, this is a chevron between three scent–hounds argent in a field of azure. In the 13th century such a sporting dog was called a "gower."[11] In the heraldic records of the northern counties, these arms appear in various forms, with the prevailing colors the same as those of the poet, argent and azure.

Outside of Yorkshire, again as on the poet's arms, the whole animals are reduced to heads and tinctured gold.[12] There is uncertainty about the designation of the animals: they are called gowers, hounds, talbots, and wolves; and there are examples in other coats of arms of wolves' and leopards' heads being interchanged.[13] Furthermore, there is variation as to the placement of the animals. In 1350 Nicholas Gower used a seal bearing "on a bend [a diagonal band] three dogs passant," which the learned editor, C. T. Clay, calls a variant of the usual device; and three dogs on a bend are the device of 16th-century Gowers of Surrey, perhaps related to the Kentish family.[14]

If three dogs on a bend may be taken as a variant of a chevron between three dogs; if a chevron between three dogs' heads *or* may be taken as a variant of a chevron between three dogs *argent* or *sable*; and if leopards' heads may be accepted as variants of wolves' heads, may we not conclude that the arms of the poet which Stow and Thynne described as argent on a chevron azure three leopards' heads or, are really a variant on the Langbargh arms? The authority for the statements that the heads were of leopards cannot be determined. The woodcut of the tomb at the end of Caxton's edition of the *Confessio* (1483) bears no arms, and Berthelette and Leland did not include them in their descriptions. By the end of the century, the tomb was in poor condition, but Thynne was a professional herald and Stow and Weever experienced observers. The presumption is that they would not have been misled. Furthermore, the heads on the arms in the nearly contemporary Glasgow manuscript of the *Vox Clamantis* (Fig. 1) seem clearly to be those of leopards. Yet a comparison with the Brabourn arms (Fig. 3) is not reassuring. In noting the correspondence Weever did not describe the two sets of arms, so we cannot tell what he took the animals to be. The Brabourn brass has disappeared since his time, but in the modern reproduction of John Philipot's 17th-century drawing the heads do not look like those of leopards,[15] but rather like lions or possibly the drooping ears and ruffs of *canes sagaces*—scent-hounds. There seems never to have been any question that the animal on the poet's crest and seals (Figs. 6 and 7) is a gower or talbot.

Heraldry finds it easier to discredit than to establish relationships. All that we can conclude from an examination of the arms is that if the correspondence between the Southwark and Brabourn arms confirms the poet's Kentish affiliation, the similarities between the Kentish and Langbargh arms would make it possible for Leland to have been half right. John Gower the poet may well have been descended from a Yorkshire family, as he suggested, only not from the Stittenham family prominent after the 16th century, but rather from the Langbargh family.

Two sets of links are missing from the documentation: those which would explain the relation between John and Robert Gower, and those which would explain the relation between the Kentish and Langbargh families. But the circumstantial evidence is strong in both cases, and the different bodies of material show Gower moving in the same two worlds as Chaucer, the upper middle class society of the franklin, merchant, and lawyer, and the aristocratic society of a trusted retainer in a noble household. The world of the nobility appears in the career of Sir Robert Gower, that of the upper middle class in the marriages of his daughter and the business transactions of the poet himself.

II

Sir Robert appears first in a record of 1329, in the company of Henry, Earl of Lancaster, and David de Strabolgi, Earl of Athol, in a company of some ninety men coming "to Bedeford with armed power contrary to the statute of Northampton." [16] In 1332, Strabolgi granted him the manor of Kentwell in Suffolk.[17] In 1335 Robert Gower and Thomas de Buston were named as "the earl's attorneys, having power by the earl's letters patent" in the conveyance of the manor of Westlexham.[18] In the same year, the sheriff of Suffolk was ordered to restore to Robert Gower the Strabolgi manor of Maydenwater.[19] We may therefore conclude that Robert

Gower was a retainer of David Strabolgi from before 1329 until the earl's death in 1335.

The Strabolgis were closely associated with the Baliol claimants to the throne of Scotland. David, 8th earl of Athol (d. 1270), married Isabel of Chilham Castle, Kent. After his death in Carthage on the Seventh Crusade, she married Alexander Baliol, brother of John Baliol, King of Scotland, and occupied Chilham. Her son John by her first marriage, 9th earl of Athol, adhered to the Bruce. In 1295, he was brought as a prisoner to London. Released in 1297, he again sided with Robert Bruce and assisted at his coronation in 1306. In the English invasion of 1307 he was captured and executed, and his title and his lands forfeited. Evidently his son David had been kept in England with his grandmother after John's release in 1297. In 1300 David was listed as a prisoner in England, and he was reputed to have been reared at Chilham Castle. In 1307, Ralph de Monthermer, Earl of Gloucester, was created 10th earl of Athol, but in the same year, for 5,000 marks, he surrendered the title to David de Strabolgi of Chilham, as 11th earl of Athol. King Robert Bruce named David de Strabolgi High Constable of Scotland in 1311, but in 1314 he rebelled against Bruce and his Scottish title and lands were confiscated. From this time through David de Strabolgi, the 12th earl (d. 1335), and David de Strabolgi, the 13th earl (d. 1369), the English continued to honor the Strabolgi title, while a new line of Scottish earls was created, beginning with Sir John Campbell in 1320.[20]

David, 11th earl, married the daughter of John Comyn and Joan, daughter of William de Valence, Earl of Pembroke. Through his wife and his wife's mother, he acquired rights to the Pembroke manor of Brabourn, eight miles south of Chilham in Kent. But neither he nor his son ever lived there. David, 12th earl, was born at Newcastle-on-Tyne in 1309 and reared for at least the first three years of his life at his father's estate in Ponteland, Northumberland. He acceded to the title upon the death of both of his parents in 1326, had livery of some of his English lands in 1327, and of all in 1330.[21] Robert Gower was in his company in 1329 on an expedition evidently seeking to enforce the provision of the Treaty of North-ampton (1328), by which the English lords were to have their lands in Scotland restored. When this failed, David Strabolgi ac-companied Edward Baliol on his invasion of Scotland in 1332, and after the victory at Dupplin in 1333, Baliol momentarily restored his Scottish title and estates. When Baliol was expelled from Scot-land in 1334, Strabolgi joined the Scots. All his English holdings were confiscated; Robert Gower fell under suspicion and his Stra-bolgi manors of Kentwell and Maydenwater were likewise seized.[22] However, when Strabolgi rejoined the English in 1335, everything was restored. He was killed fighting on the English side in the battle of Kilblane, November 30, 1335.

David de Strabolgi's wife Katherine, martial daughter of Sir Henry de Beaumont, Earl of Buchan, continued to hold the border castle of Lochindorb against the Scots for eight months after her husband's death—at her own expense, as detailed in a graphic peti-tion for recompense made to Parliament—until she was "rescued" in June 1336.[23] In 1337, with considerable difficulty, she secured possession of Brabourn manor, which had been assigned to her in dower,[24] and there she lived until 1368, dying only a year before her son David, last earl of the Strabolgi succession. Robert Gower con-tinued to support Edward Baliol, as had his lord. In 1337, Baliol asked the chancellor of England for special protection for Robert "going in his service to Scotland," and in 1346 he begged the chan-cellor to release Robert from distraint to find an archer for his lands in Sussex "as Sir Robert is constantly with him."[25] Nevertheless, we must suppose that Robert Gower's family moved to Brabourn in 1337 as part of the Countess's entourage. His elder daughter, Katherine (named for the Countess, her godmother), was born there in 1340, and he himself was buried in the Countess's chapel in 1349.[26]

Through his marriage, Robert Gower was related to the Strabol-gis, the earls of Pembroke, and the powerful Yorkshire house of Moubray, from which the dukes of Norfolk were eventually de-scended. His wife Margaret was the daughter of Sir Philip de

Moubray, constable of Stirling Castle in 1311–12 and otherwise prominent in Scottish affairs, who was descended from Philip de Moubray, a younger son of the Yorkshire family.[27] Sir Philip was likewise related to the earls of Pembroke, for in 1336 we find Robert Gower and Margaret his wife releasing to Marie de St. Pol, late wife of Aymer de Valence, Earl of Pembroke, "the third part which by the law of France came to said Margaret by inheritance of the lands of her brother, Sir John de Moubray, knight, late lord of Tours in Vymeu [Hainault]." [28] At nearly the same time, Margaret's sister Philippa and her husband, Anselm de Guyse, released their third. Since Anselm was, like Robert, a Strabolgi retainer,[29] there can be little doubt that Robert the husband of Margaret was the Robert of Brabourn. At the same time as Margaret and Philippa, David de Strabolgi released to Marie de St. Pol "his fourth of the Pembroke succession in France" (in right of his mother, sister of Aymer de Valence).[30]

The Moubrays provide the most direct link that can be established between Robert Gower and the Langbargh Gowers. The parent Moubray family originated in the North Riding of Yorkshire,[31] and the Langbargh Gowers had dealings with them throughout the whole of the 14th century.[32] We are again plagued by similarities in names. The two relevant members of the Yorkshire family were John de Moubray, born in 1286, and, like John de Strabolgi before him, arrested for treason and hanged at York in 1322.[33] His son John and Robert Gower's patron David were seised with their fathers' lands in the same series of royal orders of 1327, and received royal grants in the same order in 1333.[34] Much earlier than this (1307), "John de Moubray of Scotland" and Aymer de Valence had been securities for the 5,000 marks by which David, father of Robert's patron, recovered his title from the Earl of Gloucester.[35] This John was neither the grandfather nor the uncle of Margaret Gower; if he was her brother, the "lord of Tours in Vymeu" must have been a good deal older than his sisters. One would like to suppose that he was the elder Moubray of the Yorkshire family, and that the relationship of the fathers explains the association of the sons, save that such an interpretation is weakened by the specific designation "of Scotland" in the writ of 1307. In any case, David's companion of 1327 and 1333 was after 1332 "put on numerous commissions of array, *oyer* and *terminer*, etc." At least three of these commissions were to look into complaints against the Langbargh Gowers.[36]

On the problem of unraveling the genealogy of the Langbargh Gowers, we can do no better than to quote the *Victoria County History*:

> The pedigree of the Gower family is somewhat obscure. The Robert Gower who was tenant here [in Faceby] in 1284–85 and was the son of Robert must apparently be identified with the Robert Gower, husband of Christiana, to whom in 1314 John Gower of Faceby granted a third of the manor for life with reversion to his own heirs. Robert and Christiana had two sons John and Laurence, and it is probable that John Gower of Faceby was the elder of these. In 1316 John Gower was in possession. He died in 1346, leaving a son and heir, John. Laurence Gower, who was mentioned in the will of the elder John and was perhaps his brother, held the manor in 1360, when it was claimed against him by the descendants of Richard de Skutterskelfe under an alleged settlement by Robert Gower. This claim was renewed in 1371, when John son of Laurence was the defendant, though he cannot have been in actual possession at that date. The manor had been released in 1364 by Richard Gower of Marton to Gilbert de Wauton, Christiana his wife and Elizabeth her sister. Christiana and Elizabeth were daughters and heirs of Alice de Hapton, who was the widow in 1336 of John Gower. Half the manors of Faceby and Carlton in Cleveland were granted in 1368 to Donald de Hesilrigg and Joan his wife for the term of their lives, with reversion to the heirs of Christiana. Elizabeth, the second co-heir, married William, son of Adam de Clapham, and was her sister's heir. In 1377 the tenants of Faceby, Low Worsall, Skutterskelfe and Staindale Bridge were Roger de Fulthorpe in right of his wife, Gilbert de Wauton, William de Clapham and John Sturmy.[37]

The Gowers of Faceby and Sexhow would appear to be the family of John Gower the poet, although the "obscurity" has so far made final identification impossible. The names Robert and John are common in the family, and the Gowers of Clapham, Surrey, have been claimed as 15th-century relatives of the Kentish family. But the vital link is missing. All we can do is to infer that sometime in the 1320's an enterprising young Robert of the Langbargh family somehow took service with the English Earl of Athol. October 13, 1322, might be very near to the exact date. On that day, the King, encamped at Rievaulx Monastery (ten miles south of Faceby on the map), wrote "to the earl of Pembroke [Aymer de Valence]. Understanding from his spies that the Scots are around [North] Allerton, [he] commands the earl to collect his forces and raise the country towards Byland [7 miles south of Rievaulx; along with Birdforth an important seat of the Yorkshire Moubrays], reaching it by Thursday the 14th as early in the day as possible, where he will find the Earl of Richmond and Henry de Beaumont [father of Katherine de Strabolgi] with instructions how to act. The King is near at hand in safety collecting his forces." [38] There was a skirmish the next day in which the English lost some harness. It is easy to suppose that Robert Gower was among the forces collected at that time. David de Strabolgi, father of his patron, then Chief Warden of Northumberland, must have been on the scene along with Henry de Beaumont, Joint Warden south of the Forth to Berwick. He may himself have enlisted young Robert, found him useful, and passed him on to his son as a trusted retainer. When the Strabolgis went south in 1337, Robert Gower and his wife—as yet childless—might have taken with them a precocious (or orphaned, or favorite) nephew (or cousin, or conceivably even much younger brother) to give him the advantage of a genteel education.[39] If the traditional date of 1330 for the poet's birth were at all accurate, he would have been seven in 1337, nearly the right age for such a move. By the 1350's he could have been old enough to enter the Inns of Court, and by 1368 have made enough money to buy Kentwell Manor from Robert Gower's heir. This is all inference, but it accords well with the dates and documents.

III

As we turn from the history of Robert Gower to the history of his daughters and his lands, we move from the world of the higher nobility to that of small farmers and artisans. The only connection Robert had with the poet Gower's group is an acknowledgment of 1343 that he owed Sir John de Pulteneye 15£. This John was probably the London alderman connected in various ways with individuals with whom the poet Gower was involved.[40] But before embarking upon this chapter, it may be well to include an abstract of 1348 which suggests again how hazardous is the whole business of trying to identify individuals or families in the 14th century. In MS. Chancery Miscellanea, Bundle 88, is listed:

> Fine, 21 Edward III, Manors of Poulteneye and Miserton [Leicester], John de Pulteneye, knight, complainant [buyer], and John de Tilteye, clerk, deforciant [seller]. Settlement upon the former for life, with divers remainders to Robert de Pulteneye, son of William Oweyn, William de Pulteneye, son of William Erneys, and Thomas de Pulteneye, son of John Spigurnel, and others.[41]

From this we see that at least the surname de Pulteneye must be regarded with grave suspicion.

In 1349 Robert Gower died, and the Countess Katherine was given wardship of his lands during the minority of the heirs.[42] In 1355, at the age of 21, her son David was given seisin of his father's estates,[43] but the family situation was not good. In 1359 the Countess was released from her military obligations because her holdings were too small.[44] In 1363 the Strabolgis joined in abortive negotiations for the return of their Scottish holdings.[45] None of this would incline the young earl to release the lands of the two adolescent daughters of his father's dead retainer. Nevertheless, in 1357 proof of the ages of Katherine and Joan, daughters and heirs of Robert Gower, was duly held before William de Apulderfeld, escheator of Kent; and Guy de Seintclere, escheator of Suffolk, was ordered to deliver to the two heirs their father's lands. The account of the proceedings is worth quoting in full as the best indication we have of the society in which the poet may well have spent his formative years:

> Writ to the escheator to take the proof of age of the said Katherine and Joan, whose lands &c. are in the custody of Katherine countess of Athol. 24 March, 31 Edward III.

> *Kent.* Proof of age taken at Canterbury, Monday the feast of SS. Philip and James, 31 Edward III.

> Thomas de Tyntone says that the said Katherine is of full age and that she was born in the town of Brabourn on Sunday the feast of St. Katherine, 14 Edward III [1340], and was baptised in the church there. This he knows because at the same time he was servant to the prior of Horton and on the same day the said prior delivered his manor of Tynton to Stephen de Forsham to farm. He says also that Joan, Katherine's sister, is of full age, and that she was born at Brabourne on Saturday before St. John the Baptist, 16 Edward III [1342], and was baptised in the church there. This he knows because on the same Saturday his wife bore a son named John.

> Thomas Mersshere agrees and says that on the Sunday Katherine was born he carried to John Syward of London 100s. sterling in the name of Sir Edmund Passhelee; and on the Saturday Joan was born he was at Brabourne with Lady Joan de Passhelee, who was her godmother.

> John Lefsone agrees and says that on the Sunday Katherine was born, Richard, his brother, died; and on the Sunday after the Saturday on which Joan was born he married Alice Stopynes his wife.

> Stephen Andreu agrees and says that on the Sunday Katherine was born, Joan, his mother, was buried in the churchyard of Smethe; and on the Monday after the Saturday on which Joan was born, Robert Brus married Avis Kempes.

> Philip Pikehare agrees and says that on the Sunday Katherine was born his own wife bore a daughter Emma; and on the Saturday Joan was born he began his journey to the court of Rome.

> Thomas Stoutyng agrees and says that on the Sunday Katherine was born he plighted his troth (affidavit) to Custance his wife at Stoutyng; and on the Saturday Joan was born he sold all

his lands &c. at Stoutyng to Edmund de Passheless, knight.

Roger Edmund agrees and says that in the week after the Sunday Katherine was born he was made apprentice to the office (*ad officium*) of baker in Hethe; and on the Saturday Joan was born he purchased 4a. of land of John Lucas at Brabourne.

John Hamond agrees and says that on Monday after the Sunday Katherine was born his father sold him 5a. land in Westbrabourne; and on the feast of St. John the Baptist after the Saturday Joan was born he was made apprentice with a baker at Wye.

John Bisshop agrees and says that in the year Katherine was born his father, Thomas Bisshop, purchased of John Jacot 7a. land in Westbrabourne; and in the year Joan was born the said Thomas purchased of Peter Kempe his principal messuage.

Robert Westbech agrees and says that on the Sunday Katherine was born he went on a pilgrimage to Santiago and the Holy Land; and on the quinzaine of St. John the Baptist after the Saturday on which Joan was born he returned home.

William Wybarn says the like and this he knows because in that quarter of the year before Sunday on which Katherine was born, William his uncle became dumb from Michaelmas to Christmas; and on the Nativity of St. John the Baptist after the Saturday on which Joan was born Thomas Wybarn his father purchased of Niel Robert 4½a. land in Brabourne.

John Wybarn agrees and says that at Michaelmas before the Sunday on which Katherine was born he was apprenticed to a tailor at Canterbury; and on the feast of St. John the Baptist after the Saturday on which Joan was born he purchased a messuage at Brabourne and married his wife Joan.

All the aforesaid say that Bartholomew de Sallo, parson of Styvekeye, co. Norfolk [another Strabolgi holding], was godfather of the said Katherine, and Katherine countess of Athol and Elizabeth de Whitefield were her godmothers; and that John de Vylers was godfather of the said Joan and lady Joan de Passhelee and the aforesaid Elizabeth her godmothers.[46]

We are here in a world of five-acre purchases and bakers' and tailors' apprentices, but also of travelers to Rome and pilgrims to Santiago and the Holy Land. Katherine, the elder sister, died the next year (1358) and Joan was left sole heir, but within less than three weeks after Katherine's death David de Strabolgi took possession of the property and kept it until 1364. By that time, Joan was married to William Neve of Wetyng (in Grimshoo Hundred, Norfolk, just three miles from Feltwell, one of the manors John Gower held at the time of his death). In May, June, and December 1366, and February 1367, William and Joan sued for possession of Kentwell and an interest in Radwynter, Essex, that went with it.[47] On June 28, 1368, John Gower the poet acquired Kentwell from "Thomas Syward, late citizen and peutrer of London, and Johanna his wife, daughter of Robert Gower." [48] From this record, it would appear that Thomas was already dead. In 1369 and again in 1380 John Spenythorn, "citizen and tailor of London," and Johanna his wife released Kentwell to John Gower, and in 1385 John Spenythorn alone released Gower "from all actions, real and personal." An undated entry would seem to indicate that John Spenythorn and Joan also had some interest in the manor of Maydenwater which her father had acquired from the Strabolgis along with Kentwell.[49] The delay in recording the court actions make the sequence of events unclear. It was 1366 before Joan's suit of 1364 was recorded. We cannot tell when after 1357 she married William Neve, or when she married either Thomas Syward or John Spenythorn. It is hard to suppose that she had three husbands between 1367 and 1369, although as an heiress she was obviously not allowed to remain a widow for long, and her second marriage must have been brief. The John Syward mentioned in the proof of her age as receiving money from Sir Edmund Passhelee was a tenant of St. Mary Overeys property in Southwark and likewise a pewterer.[50] Thomas, of the same craft and surname, could have been his son or brother. It is possible that Joan at one time lived with Thomas in Southwark near the poet's residence in St. Mary's Priory. Indeed, she may still have been living there when Gower moved into the priory about 1377, for, though Syward was dead by 1368, there is no indication where she lived with Spenythorn. She must herself have died before 1385, since she is not mentioned in the final release by Spenythorn. As interesting as any of this is the possibility that John Gower himself was instrumental in persuading Joan to clear the title to her property so that she could transfer it to him. That this was the case is suggested by a related, and even more complicated, real estate transaction in which he was engaged at just the same time.

The Septvauns affair, as we may term this next transaction, has represented, since the appearance of Macaulay's edition, another black mark against the character of the moral Gower. Between Sittingbourne and Maidstone in Kent lies Aldington, in the 14th century divided into two manors. Aldington Cobham was in the possession of the Cobham family from the time of King John until that of Queen Elizabeth. Between 1340 and 1361 it was in the hands of the Reginald Cobham who had stood security for Robert Gower in 1334 when the Earl his master defected to the Scots. Aldington Septvauns, the other manor, was held by Sir William de Septvauns at the time of his death in 1351.[51] His lands passed into the wardship of Alice de Staunton during the minority of his son William. In the same month in which his mother died, September 1364, William proved his age before the escheator in Kent.[52] It was ascertained that he had been born in 17 Edward III on the Feast of St. Augustine the Doctor, or May 28, 1343. His guardian was warned but "had no reason to offer why the lands &c. should not be returned to said William as being of full age." In 1365, after inquiry as to whether it would be to the prejudice of the king, John Gower purchased Aldington Septvauns from the heir with more than the usual formality.[53] Evidently he knew that this was a sticky wicket.

So it turned out to be. On April 13, 1366, John de Cobham of Kent and other justices and a jury of knights were commissioned "to enquire as to the age of the said heir, the proof of his age made before the escheator being erroneous; and, if it be found that he is still a minor, to ascertain by whom the previous proof was made and by whose procurement, imagination, and information, who had been in possession of the lands since the said proof, in whose company the heir has been and by whom he has been counselled and led, what waste and destruction has been done in the said lands, and what profit the king has lost by reason of the incorrect proof of age." [54] The original testimony of age had been by ordinary folk; the new testimony was by knights who had known William's father, and they agreed that he had been born in 20 Edward III, not 17, and would not be 21 until May of that year. William de Chirche-hull was accused of having suggested to William that he prove his age; John Gower had purchased a moiety of Aldington and allied lands for 80 marks; Sir Nicholas de Loveyne and others had bought other properties. After these feoffments, "the heir continually dwelt in the company of Richard Hurst and the said John Gower, at Canterbury and elsewhere, until Michaelmas last, and during the whole time he was led and counselled by them to alienate his lands"; after Michaelmas he dwelt with Sir Nicholas, who counseled him likewise. There had been no waste. It was adjudged that the heir was under age, that any contracts made by him should be voided and his lands recovered. A writ to the Mayor of the Staple at Westminster ascertained that the heir had appeared before the Staple and acknowledged himself bound to John Gower for 60£. and Nicholas de Loveyne for 1000£. Writs were issued to the purchasers to be in Chancery on the octave of Trinity next to show cause why their grants should not be annulled. The account in *Inquisitions post mortem* ends here. The *Rotuli Parliamentorum*, however, adds after the judgment that the heir's writs should be annulled and his lands recovered:

> but not toward any to whom the said William is obligated through debts by law merchant or before the Staple, or through recognizances, charters, writings, or any other contracts; to have such come before Chancery to show what they hold or to say whether they know why William's possessions should not be taken back into the king's hands and his contracts abrogated; for the doing and receiving of such justice as will be in this office.

These exceptions in the Parliamentary action indicate that Gower knew what he was doing when he had the writs and charters concerning his purchase recorded in Chancery. That his claim was eventually adjudged just is indicated by a special license recorded on February 6, 1368, "for William, son of William de Septvanz, knight, to enfeoff John Gower with a moiety of the manor of Ald-yngton, Kent, except 6 acres of land therein, notwithstanding that said William is held to the king by a bond of 3,000£. not to alienate, remit, or quitclaim his inheritance to any person or persons in fee or for life." [55] Five years later, in 1373, Gower disposed of Aldington and Kentwell together to John de Cobham, Thomas de Brockhull, and others.[56]

Macaulay saw in this affair a John Gower who was "a villainous misleader of youth . . . encouraging a young man to defraud the Crown by means of perjury, in order that he might purchase his lands from him at a nominal price" (4.xv), and who therefore could not possibly be identified with the moral poet. But the identification seems beyond reasonable doubt. Unless we discount the Brabourn coat of arms and Southwark connections completely, it must have been John Gower the poet who acquired Kentwell from Joan. And since Kentwell and Aldington were sold together, there seems no doubt that the John Gower in the Septvauns inquisition was the same. Without more evidence, it is idle to speculate on the legal or moral issues of the case. Certainly at this distance it appears to be something of a mess. Gower's is just one item in a wholesale dispersal of young William de Septvauns' estates; and how a boy under twenty could have got himself in debt to the tune of 1,060£. in 14th-century currency is hard to imagine. Nevertheless, as to Gower's involvement certain facts seem clear. The inquisition of 1366 was undertaken not to ascertain whether the heir had been defrauded, but whether the king had suffered loss of income because the Septvauns holdings had been released prematurely. Gower had taken the precaution of recording an inquiry as to whether his purchase would be to the prejudice of the king. Furthermore, contrary to Macaulay's implication—"John Gower had given 24 marks only for property worth £12 a year, with a wood of the value of £100"—the record states clearly that Gower paid 80 marks and that the heir acknowledged himself bound to him for 60£. besides. The Parliamentary judgment makes explicit provision for those holding exactly the writs and charters that Gower had secured, and Chancery found his claim so sound that it allowed him to retain the property by special license. Finally, the other individuals involved in the sequence of events were eminently respectable. John de Cobham, evidently the distinguished 3rd Baron associated with Chaucer on royal commissions,[57] would have been something of an accessory when he later bought Aldington unless he felt that Gower's title was clear. The William de Apuldrefeld on the jury appears to be the former escheator of Kent before whom the Gower daughters' ages were proved. In 1377 Sir John Frebody, parson of the church at Bocton, who testified at the second proof of William de Septvauns' age, joined Gower in purchasing land from Thomas Brockhull of the family that came eventually to own both moieties of Aldington.[58] Sir William de Chirchehull who counseled the heir to prove his age was a chaplain and guardian of the temporalities of the bishopric of Chichester.[59] Simon de Burgh, who "at his own suit, caused himself to be retained with the said heir as of his counsel" may possibly have been the esquire of the king's household mentioned in five of the Chaucer Life Records.[60] And Nicholas de Loveyne, Gower's other partner in crime, was prominent in Kentish affairs, Seneschal of Ponthieu, and honorable enough to be ordered in 1364 to try an action for debt brought by Simon, abbot of Cluny.[61] Nothing in the records except the statement that he influenced the heir suggests anything nefarious in Gower's behavior; indeed the records indicate just the opposite, that he was unusually scrupulous in this case. Certainly there is nothing in the record of the first proof of age to suggest that it was in any way illegal, and William de Septvauns himself lived to have a distinguished career in military and public service.[62]

IV

By the end of the 1360's, then, Gower was engaged in at least two real estate transactions which involved court action. There is no indication as to the source of his capital. His appearance before the Staple in the Septvauns action is evidence that he had investment

in the wool trade.[63] However, by his own statement it would appear
that he held some legal or civil office during these years. Apologiz-
ing for criticizing the church so harshly, he says in the *Mirour de
l'omme:*

. . . *je ne suy pas clers,*	. . . *I am not a clerk,*
Vestu de sanguin ne de pers,	*clothed in red or in purple,*
Ainz ai vestu la raye mance,	*but I wear a garment with striped sleeves.*
Poy sai latin, poy sai romance.	*I know little Latin or French.*
(MO, 21772)	

The statement that he wears striped sleeves takes on special significance in the light of four mid-15th-century illuminations of the
courts at Westminster, in which all of the court officials except
judges and registrars wear "rayed" gowns. For example, the illumination of Chancery (see the frontispiece), the court with which we
know John Gower had dealings, shows "two judges in scarlet robes
trimmed with white badger or lambskin, one of them uncovered
and tonsured, and the other having on his head a sort of brown cap.
The former holds in his hand an open document with the great seal
appendant. On each side of the judges are two persons seated wearing yellow, or as they were called mustard-colored robes, three of
them evidently tonsured. Below them are the registrars and other
officers with rolls before them. On the table, which is covered with
a green cloth, stands one of the six clerks or a clerk in court reading
a record, and on his left an usher in a party-colored gown of green
and blue, *rayed* or striped diagonally. On the right, at the table, is
the sealer pressing down a matrix of the great seal with a roller on
the wax attached to a pendant, and before him lie a number of
writs folded up and sealed, with pendant labels, as subpoenas and
Chancery writs were prepared until a recent period. At the bar stand
three serjeants with coifs and wearing party-colored gowns of blue
and green and blue and brown; there are also two apprentices of the
law or barristers, clad in party-colored gowns of blue and light
brown and green and light blue. All these party-colored gowns are
striped or rayed, some vertically, and others diagonally, the divisions of the respective colors being separated straight down the front

and back." [64] These rayed gowns are said to have grown out of liveries, and at *Mirour* 24280 Gower criticizes lawyers for wearing their clients' liveries. At a later period, rayed cloth appeared in the liveries of the mayor and other corporation officials of London. Stow observes, "I read that in the year 1516, it was agreed by a common council in the Guildhall that the sheriffs of London should (as they had been accustomed) give yearly rayed gowns to the recorder, chamberlain, common sergeant, and common clerk, the sword-bearer, common hunt, water-baliff, common crier, like as to their own offices." [65] We may here observe that Ralph Strode was Common Sergeant during the 1370's, and so would have been covered by such a custom, if it extended back into the 14th century—but more of him in a moment. Also, in the *Cronica Tripertita* (1.140) the impeachment of Sir Simon Burley by the Merciless Parliament of 1388 is described as "Corruit in fata gladii vestis stragulata" (The striped garment fell to the fate of the sword). Clearly striped garments connoted a civil livery of some sort.

In his real estate transactions, Gower was engaging in what he himself criticized as one of the principal vices of the legal profession. We may recall Chaucer's Man of Law in connection with Gower's canny handling of the Septvauns affair:

> So greet a purchasour was nowher noon;
> Al was fee simple to him in effect—
> His purchasyng myghte nat been infect. (CT, Prol.320)

According to Gower, lawyers were so successful in their profession that they were soon able to purchase largely:

Ensi ly pledour orendroit	Thus the lawyer now,
Combien q'il povre au primer soit,	however poor he may be at first,
Bien tost apres avera du quoy	soon will have so much of everything
Si largement, que tout q'il voit	that everything he sees
Luy semble a estre trop estroit	will seem too constricted for him
De pourchacer soulein a soy.	to purchase for himself alone.
(MO, 24535)	

One would not have to press Gower's criticisms very hard to make them fit the Septvauns case. He quotes Isaiah 5:8–9 condemning foolish men who set dwelling to dwelling and field to field (MO, 24541): the final effect of the Septvauns purchase was to add Aldington Septvauns to Aldington Cobham. The lawyer's foolish heir sells in the moment of a day what it had taken his father thirty years of hard labor to amass (MO, 24584): young William Sept-vauns may not have been a lawyer's son, but he certainly dispersed his father's holdings in little more than a moment of a day. Sheriffs wink at bribed juries enpaneled to help deprive victims of their inheritance (MO, 24892), and fail to render true accounts to the Exchequer after a death (MO, 24940): the findings of the first proof of young William's age were dismissed because the jury was not properly sworn. At least nine times Gower mentions "purchas-ing" as the special vice of the legal profession,[66] and he speaks at length of "Les beals manoirs . . . ,/ Qui sont semblable au Paradis" (MO, 24735) which judges acquire with their ill-gotten gains.

The bitterness of these and the other denunciations led Macaulay to conclude that Gower could not possibly have been a lawyer. However, the specific allusions bespeak a firsthand knowledge of the Septvauns case and many others like it, the reference to rayed sleeves suggests a professional involvement in the law, and the criti-cisms of the profession might just as well come from an outraged member of the fraternity as from an outsider. Leland's tradition that Chaucer and Gower met at the Inns of Court cannot be sub-stantiated since no records of the Inns survive from before 1422. However, Gower's description of the training of the lawyer, the de-gree of coif, and the privileges of serjeancy (MO, 24373), and his technical descriptions of the functions of *plaidour, client, tort, deslayment, cas* (MO, 24206), *advocat* (24258), *president, ap-prentis, attourné* (MO, 24794) accord well with the early state of the profession. As Macaulay observed, a Gower appears in Tottil's publication of the legal yearbooks (1585) several times in 1355 and 1356.[67] He appears usually as a counsel, but on some occasions he speaks apparently as a judge. Macaulay felt that this Gower was in too high a position by 1355 to have been the poet. The lack of in-formation about the date of Gower's birth and his education merely compounds the difficulty. We must probably concede that barring some fortunate discovery, we know all we are likely to about the poet's professional activity. However, the data in hand are sufficient to indicate that Gower had some sort of legal connection, and that is sufficient to support the interpretation of his writings offered in the fourth chapter.

V

From the 1360's date the first records of Gower's financial and legal transactions. From the 1370's date the first records of his acquaintance with Chaucer and his association with St. Mary Overeys Priory. We know that by 1398 Gower was occupying his own quarters in St. Mary's Priory, probably a house in the close, for on January 2 of that year, license was granted by the Bishop of Winchester for the marriage of John Gower and Agnes Groundolf, both parishioners of St. Mary Magdalene, Southwark, without further publication of banns, outside their parish church, in the oratory of the said John Gower, within or beneath (infra) his lodging in the priory of St. Mary Overeys in Southwark.[68] In 1377 the church and priory were being restored from a fire that had ravaged Southwark a century and a half earlier. Leland held that this was the time at which Gower, "partly through his friends, who were numerous and powerful, and partly at his own expense, repaired the church and restored its ornaments." [69] What would have been more natural than that he be granted permission to build personal apartments in the priory as part of his restoration?

Like so many of the details of his biography, this one can only be inferred. We know that in the 1370's Gower was doing business with individuals who owned property on or near London Bridge. Beginning in July 1378 are a series of five entries relating to Gower's purchase of lands in Throwley and Stalesfield, Kent (again within eight miles of Brabourn), from Isabel, daughter of Sir Walter de Huntyngfeld. As with other transactions, this one has connections stretching back to Sir Robert Gower. In 1339, one of the witnesses in the final Strabolgi quitclaim of Kentwell had been Geoffrey de Say, who was in 1355 given custody of Isabel, fourteen-year old daughter of Walter de Huntyngfeld. In 1378 John Gower turns up buying land near Brabourn from the heiress. Later (1396), a Sir Walter de Huntyngfeld is listed in the Bridgemaster's Account Rolls as owning property on the London Bridge.[70] In 1367 a John Gower, presumably the poet, bought interest in lands in London and Kent from John Gravesende, citizen and draper of London, with such witnesses to the transaction as John de Tornegold, fishmonger and alderman of London, and John de Stodeye, vintner, alderman, and eventually mayor (and close associate of John Chaucer, Geoffrey's father).[71] It is noteworthy that these purchases both included Kentish holdings. As late as 1382, John Gower was still identified in the Close Rolls as "esquire of Kent."[72] Perhaps, as we shall see in the next chapter, there were financial advantages in refusing knighthood and citizenship. He may even have lived part of the time in the country, although where we cannot tell since his most important holdings were never in Kent. Yet the supposition that he was in residence at St. Mary's Priory much of the time after 1377 accords better with his association with Chaucer and allusions to Southwark, the Thames, and the Court in the *Vox Clamantis* and *Confessio Amantis* than the supposition that he continued to live out in Kent until the 1390's.

The middle seventies marked a change in Gower's way of life, perhaps a retirement from strenuous professional activity. If he was born about 1330, he would have been more than forty-five by 1377, a ripe age in that day. The colophon appended to many manuscripts of the *Vox* and *Confessio* asserts that "John Gower, desirous of lightening somewhat the account for the intellectual gifts God gave to his keeping, while there is time, between work and leisure, for the knowledge of others, composed three books of instructive material."[73] At the end of the first book of the *Vox Clamantis*, the dreamer wishes with all his heart to be at leisure to write what he has seen ("ex toto corde vacare volo," VC, 1.2148). The composition of such works as the *Mirour, Vox,* and *Confessio* required not only leisure, but also a library of sorts, which would have been available at St. Mary's. And the priory would have provided the scriptorium the poet needed for the many sumptuous gift manuscripts of his works. All of this leads to the conclusion that from about 1377 until his death in 1408, John Gower lived a semiretired life in St. Mary's Priory, devoting his time mainly to his books and his friends.[74]

The tradition of St. Mary Overeys goes back to the time when a convent of nuns was established before the Norman Conquest on the endowment of the proceeds from a ferry across the Thames at the site of London Bridge, beside which their house was built.[75] After the Conquest, the house was reconstituted a college of Marian Canons and so continued into the 16th century. After the dissolution it was purchased by the Montagues, and it came down into the 18th century as Montague Close. In the early 19th century, remains of the old brick vaulting were still being used as stables and bins. In a drawing of ca. 1550 by Antony Van den Wyngaerd, cloister-like windows facing the river are visible beside the bridge.[76] On the west side, the priory close adjoined the city residence of the Bishop of Winchester, known as Winchester House. With Winchester House, St. Mary's shared water stairs [77] from which Gower could take a boat directly across to the Temple at the bend in the river, or on up to Westminster, as he could have been doing when King Richard urged him to undertake the *Confessio*. On the east side of the priory close, a gate opened out onto Pepper Lane which led to High Street or Old Southwark, the scene of the peasants' attack upon London Bridge in June of 1381 and of the citizens' grand reconciliation with Richard II in August 1392, both of which were so important in Gower's literary career. Lining both sides of the thoroughfare were the inns, later famous as the resorts of the actors and roisterers of Elizabethan times. As one came south off London Bridge, to the right on the west side of the street, lay the priory close, Pepper Lane, and St. Mary's chained gates. To the left, or east, diagonally across from the church, set among a row of seven or eight inns (among them the Mermaid, to judge from a 16th-century map), was the Tabard.

Across the bridge, Chaucer's London stretched for a mile along the north bank. The Wool Quay, where much of the time from 1374 to 1386 Chaucer kept the customs accounts "in manuo suo," lay downriver from St. Mary's water stairs. In May 1374 Chaucer had been granted by the Corporation of the City of London his dwelling over Aldgate.[78] About 1377, presumably, Gower moved into St. Mary's Priory. In May 1378, when Chaucer went on a four-month trip to Italy, he gave his power of attorney to John Gower and Richard Forester, a lawyer who turns up frequently in the records until 1405 and who may have succeeded Chaucer in the lease on Aldgate.[79] Sometime after 1382, Chaucer dedicated *Troilus* to "moral Gower" and "philosophical Strode." Chaucer's and Gower's circle must therefore have included Ralph Strode, and may well have included other civil servants with clerical and legal training and literary interests such as Thomas Usk and Thomas Hoccleve.

Ralph Strode is himself a tantalizing figure. Recent scholarship accepts the identity of the fellow of Merton College (1359–60), the scholastic friend and opponent of John Wyclif, and the London lawyer (1373–87).[80] If this is so, many of the philosophical generalizations in Chaucer's and Gower's works that we shall be considering in the following chapters could have originated with him. Furthermore, since Merton was the home of 14th-century English astronomical calculation, it could have been with Strode's help that Chaucer began "a product of this Oxford school," his *Treatise on the Astrolabe*, and possibly, also, *The Equatorie of the Planetis*.[81] However, there has been no study of the possible relations between the writings of Chaucer and Gower and Strode's works on syllogistic reasoning that have been preserved; there is no record of mathematical or social-philosophical treatises by Strode's hand; and Gollancz's tentative identification of his *Fantasma Radulphi* with the *Pearl* cannot be supported.[82] Furthermore, the transition from Oxford logician to London lawyer was an unlikely one.[83] The offices of Common Serjeant (i.e., public prosecutor) for the Corporation of London, which Ralph Strode of London occupied from 1373 to 1382, and Standing Counsel, which he occupied from 1386 until his death in 1387, were lay positions requiring a political acquaintance with the London courts and citizens, acquirable, one would suppose, only through the usual training in the Inns of Court. In any event, the London Strode was in 1375 granted an apartment over Aldersgate corresponding to Chaucer's over Aldgate, and throughout the next decade he prosecuted victuallers, vintners, and artisans on behalf of the Corporation for exactly the sort of fraud that Gower criticized in the *Mirour de l'omme*.[84]

Thomas Usk likewise bridged the careers of cleric, lawyer, and civil servant. In 1375 he was called "clerk" in the records, and in 1376 he was mentioned as an attorney prosecuting in behalf of John Bere, haberdasher.[85] By 1381 he was secretary to John de Northampton, whose election to the mayoralty cost Strode his office of Common Serjeant in 1382. When Northampton was defeated by Brembre, Usk fled the country; but receiving no help from his fellow party-members, he returned and was committed to Newgate Prison (August 1384). He then entered Brembre's party, testified against Northampton, and received the King's pardon (September 1384). In October 1387 he was appointed Under-Sheriff of London. But again he found himself on the wrong side, for he was soon arrested along with Brembre by the Lords Appellant, and tried for treason and executed in 1388. His *Testament of Love* was written between 1384 and 1387. Its relations to Chaucer's *Boece* and *House of Fame* have been detailed by Skeat.[86] Its moral philosophy shows marked parallels with Gower's, and Gower's admonition at the end of the *Confessio* that Chaucer should get on with his own "testament of love" resembles somewhat the allusion to the *Troilus* in Usk's *Testament*.[87]

Thomas Hoccleve was a generation younger than the other two. He entered the office of the Privy Seal in 1387–88, when he was nineteen or twenty years old. In 1392 he went surety for Guy de Rouclif, a fellow clerk in Privy Seal from whom Gower bought the manors mentioned in his will. Like the others, he was both clerk and civil servant. In 1394 he was given maintenance at the convent on Hayling Island in Hampshire; by 1398 he was designated "king's clerk"; and he served in the Privy Seal office until 1424 when he was given maintenance in the convent of Suthwyke in Hampshire.[88] His references in *The Regement of Princes* (1412) to the death of his "maistre deere" Chaucer led Furnivall to believe that he was at Chaucer's deathbed [89] (as a clerk in the Privy Seal, he would have been working in Westminster). But his apostrophe on the death of Gower is nearly as pointed:

> Hast þou nat eeke my maistre Gower slayn
> Whos vertu I am in sufficient
> For to descreyue . . . (*Regement*, 1958, 75)

These allusions, the excellent portrait of Chaucer in MS. Harleian 4866 of *The Regement*, and the parallels between his and Gower's views on kingship suggest that Hoccleve knew the two poets personally.

These associations cluster about the Inns of Court, Chancery, and Guildhall, reaching out into the Staple and the Custom House. The list of names and legal and business interrelationships could be extended almost indefinitely. Richard Forester and Guy de Rouclif have been mentioned already. From 1381 to 1383 Brembre was with Chaucer as Collector of Customs. In 1381 Chaucer and Strode together went surety for a prominent merchant, John Hende,[90] who was mayor of London in 1392 at the time of Richard's quarrel with the citizens that evidently led Gower to change the dedication of the *Confessio Amantis*. And so on. But in 1386 Chaucer moved away from Aldgate and the Custom House; in 1387 Strode died; in 1388 Usk was executed. So the middle of the 1380's made great changes in Gower's and Chaucer's literary circle, bringing to an end a decade in which Gower had written the *Mirour de l'omme* and *Vox Clamantis*, and Chaucer nearly everything except the *Book of the Duchess* and parts of the *Canterbury Tales*. In the last chapter we shall assay the literary implications of this decade of association.

VI

The only other Gower business transaction of which we have records is the purchase of the two manors mentioned in his will. On
August 1, 1382, Guy de Rouclif, clerk, sold John Gower, esquire of
Kent, the manors of Feltwell in Norfolk and Multon in Suffolk.[91]
As usual, there are prior connections. Feltwell and Multon were
Arundel property in which the Pembrokes had an interest, as they
had in the Strabolgi holdings.[92] And Guy de Rouclif was a York-
shireman from a family in the cloth trade similar to the individuals
with whom the poet transacted his London business.[93] This purchase may offer indirect evidence both of Gower's retired status and
his legal connections. It is obvious that he did not buy the property
with any idea of taking part in its management since five days after
the purchase he leased it for the duration of his life to a group
headed by the parson of the church in Feltwell. The lessees were
to render "yearly 40£. in the abbey church of the monks at Westminster during John Gower's life." [94] This stipulation might appear
to indicate that Gower was living in Westminster at the time, but
in view of the other evidence it seems more likely to be simply an
arrangement made by a lawyer associated with the royal courts in
Westminster. Gower continued as legal owner and maintained
some interest in the property. In 1396 John Cook of Feltwell was
pardoned for not appearing to answer John Gower, esquire, touching a debt of 10 marks, and in 1401–02 the *Inquisitions Concerning
Feudal Aids* listed John Gower as the owner.[95] The 1396 entry
scotches once and for all a suggestion put forward in 1889 by Henry
Morley that the poet is to be identified with the John Gower, clerk,
who held the church at Great Braxted, near Witham, Essex, from
1390 to 1397. Macaulay discounted this on various grounds, including the "arm." on his tomb; and the discovery that he was called
"esquire" in the very middle of the period when Morley would have
had him in minor orders makes it certain that two different individuals were involved.[96]

On January 23, 1398, the bishop of Winchester granted a license for the marriage of John Gower and Agnes Groundolf outside their parish church, in the oratory connected with his lodgings in the priory of St. Mary Overeys. So far as the records are concerned, this appears to be his first marriage. At the beginning of the 1380's he had written concerning the corruption of the clergy, "Sufficit vna michi mulier, bis sex tamen ipsi" (One woman is enough for me, that one needs twelve, VC, iii.1615). However, this had the ring of a rhetorical generalization rather than an autobiographical statement, and one might suppose that Gower would not have chosen an apartment in a priory if he wanted a normal domestic establishment. About 1400, in the letter transmitting a copy of the Vox *Clamantis* to Thomas of Arundel, Archbishop of Canterbury, he described himself as "senex et cecus . . . corpus et egrotum, vetus et miserabili totum" (old and blind, infirm of body, decrepit and totally miserable).[97] If this can be taken at all literally, we must assume that Gower, now about seventy, would have been in need of constant care. The introduction of a woman into a monastic establishment would have caused difficulties, and then as now the kind of devoted care the old man needed would have been hard to hire. A wife would have been by all odds the best solution. We hear nothing of Agnes's family—the name of Groundolf is itself suggestive. Such a marriage of convenience between an elderly invalid and his nurse would explain the permission to perform the wedding in Gower's lodgings. The epitaph which Gower composed for her tomb, once beside his own in St. Mary's, shows something of his regard for her:

> Quam bonitas, pietas, elemosina, casta voluntas,
> Sobrietasque fides coluerunt, hic iacet Agnes.
> Uxor Amans, humilis Gower fuit illa Ioannis:
>   Donet ei summus celica regna Deus.

> (Her faith enhanced by goodness, piety, charity, willing chastity, and sobriety, here lies Agnes. She was the loving wife of humble John Gower. May God grant her the heavenly kingdom.)

The terms *elemosina* and *casta voluntas* speak volumes.[98]

Presumably Agnes cared for Gower until he died. His will, proved

October 24, 1408, is a recapitulation and confirmation of the events and associations of the previous life records.[99] He left special bequests to the prior, canons, and servants in the priory; established the chantry which Berthelette described as still in existence in 1532; and made special provisions of vestments and chalices for the Chapel of St. John the Baptist where his body was to be buried, and for the oratory in his lodgings. In addition, he left the prior a large book "newly composed at my expense," a *martilogium* or calendar in which to enter the names of saints, benefactors, and obits, on condition that it should have recorded in it each day his own name as a benefactor. This was a final evidence of his employment of a scriptorium in connection with St. Mary's. He left bequests to the churches of Southwark and to various hospitals in Southwark and about London. To his wife he left 100£. in cash, three cups, one "coverlet" (*cooperculum*, possibly a tablecloth), two saltcellars, twelve silver spoons, and all his furniture and utensils of bedroom, hall, pantry, and kitchen. He specified also that she should receive all rents due from his manors of "Southwell in Com. Notth. [or North.] quam de Multon in Com. Suff.," as he had more fully determined in other writings under his seal. Agnes his wife was executrix, and the witnesses were shades from his past and present existence: Sir Arnold Savage was of a family in Bobbing, Kent, "Under the Blee, in Canterbury Weye." The father of that name died in 1410 after a distinguished career in Commons, on the King's Council, and as an ambassador to France. The son of that name died in 1420 after being knight of the shire from Kent in 1414. The Savages owned an "inn" or city residence near London Bridge in 1391–92, and in 1405 evidently assisted with the glazing of the Chapel of St. Thomas of Canterbury on the bridge, which had been rebuilt between 1384 and 1396.[1] Sir Arnold's daughter married first Sir Reginald Cobham, of the Kentish family, and afterwards William Clifford, son of Chaucer's friend Lewis. The *Dictionary of National Biography* for some reason identifies the son as the witness to Gower's will, although the career of the father actually accords better with the poet's own experiences and writings in the 1390's.[2] We can hardly hope to identify the second witness, "Roger esquire"; and I have been able to find nothing about the third, William Denne, except what is stated in the will, that he was "canon of the King's Chapel." Presumably this was a chapel in St. Mary Overeys, and he was one of the brethren among whom Gower had been living. John Burton, clerk, the final witness, was the clerk in Chancery who had recorded John Spenython's final release of Kentwell to Gower in 1385.[3] So here among the witnesses, we have representatives of the Kentish gentry among whom Gower was reared and with whom he did business, his Chancery professional associates, and the residents of Southwark, lay and ecclesiastical, among whom he passed his last years.

The error in the designation of the manor in Gower's will is cleared up by a final reference to his wife. On February 16, 1410, Hugh Lutterall, a knight associated with Sir Arnold Savage and others of Gower's circle, granted Agnes Gower, late the wife of John Gower esquire, 20£. yearly rent from his manors of Feltwell, Norfolk, and Multon, Suffolk.[4] The manors were in the Lutterall fee, and Dame Elizabeth Lutterall had had to quitclaim them when Gower bought them in 1382. Here it would appear that her son or a relative had repurchased them, granting Agnes half the income that her husband had been getting. Perhaps these were the arrangements "more fully determined in other writings" mentioned at the end of Gower's will. This record makes it clear that the "Southwell in Com. Notth." or "North." in the will was a clerical error in the recording for "Feltwell in Com. Norff."

The three life records that remain to be mentioned are the only ones except for the Chaucer power of attorney that can possibly be associated directly with Gower's literary career. In the next chapter we shall turn to an examination of the evolution of Gower's social and political convictions through the history of his literary career. It will be sufficient now merely to set down the high points as a context for these last records. The balades and the *Mirour de l'omme* precede his political involvement. The *Vox Clamantis*, dating from near the time of the Peasants' Revolt, contains in Book VI Gower's first address to the young King, in which bad counsel is blamed for his mistakes. The original Prologue and conclusion to the *Confessio Amantis*, dating from about 1386, dedicate the work to Richard II in the same tolerant and laudatory tone. But in 1392–93 Gower altered the dedication of the *Confessio* to Henry of Lancaster. In the autumn of 1393, Henry, then still Earl of Derby, ordered his clerk of the wardrobe to pay one Richard Dancaster 26s.8d. for a collar to replace one given to "un Esquier John Gower."[5] This would appear to be the collar of S's depicted on the effigy and in the portrait at the beginning of the Fairfax manuscript (40). Henry is known to have had made for himself and others collars of S's and in the *Cronica Tripertita* is designated as he "qui gerit S" (1.52).[6] No swan pendant like that found on Gower's collar is mentioned in the record. In the *Cronica*, Thomas, Earl of Gloucester, is designated *olor* and *cignus* (1.49, 62), and Anstis, who first discussed the significance of both the S's and the swan pendant, suggested that this pendant was an acknowledgment of Gower's support of Gloucester and the Lords Appellant. At any rate, the fact that Gower received the collar in the fall of the year he revised the dedication makes it likely that it was in return for a presentation manuscript of the *Confessio* with its altered dedication. As we shall see, the *Cronica* is a straightforward defense of Henry's usurpation; hence it is no surprise to find that five weeks after his coronation, on November 21, 1399, Henry made Gower a grant of two pipes of wine of Gascony yearly, at the port of London.[7] This substantial grant Gower acknowledged in a complimentary poem repeating his insistence that the major responsibility of the king is safeguarding the rights of all classes by maintaining justice and the law—a major theme of all his writing from 1377 until the end of his life—and referring to both the wine and the *Cronica*. "O recolende, bone, pie rex, Henrice, patrone," he begins, "O be mindful, good and pious King Henry, my patron, of your responsibility for what you have wrested from Pharaoh." After admonishing the King to pursue virtue and law, the poem continues, "Thus, as loving he can, Gower will write for you, gracious King. . . . While he drinks his pious respects, your fame cannot dry up. . . . If you will pursue virtue, your Chronicle will show an equal perfection." [8]

This climax in Gower's relations with the court follows a curious episode which may or may not be connected with it. On December 11, 1397, John Frenche, Peter Blake, and Thomas Gandre, all of London, and Robert Markle, serjeant at arms, undertook mainprise for Thomas Caudre, canon of the priory of St. Mary Overeys in Southwark, that he would do or procure no harm to John Gower. Of these, Thomas Gandre was a "purser" or "pouchmaker" with a shop near London Bridge and Robert Markle an official with the London Corporation or Parliament.[9] This may have been simply a private quarrel, or it may have had some connection with Gower's legal and financial transactions. Yet one wonders whether Gower's open advocacy of Henry might not be what got him into trouble at the end of Richard's reign.

The life records bring us thus finally to questions such as those raised by Gower's reputation in the 18th and 19th centuries: How is Gower's changing political allegiance to be understood, and what relation does his political involvement bear to his writing? It will take two chapters to deal with these questions. In the next we shall explore the textual evolution of his works and what they reveal concerning his relations with the court. In the fourth, we shall explore the coherence and authority of the themes of his major poems.

3. Literary Career

The biographical evidence suggests that the middle seventies marked a turning point in Gower's career. By 1377 he had assisted with the restoring of St. Mary Overeys and presumably moved into his apartment in the priory, where he could have leisure and access to the sort of library he needed for the composition of the *Mirour de l'omme,* or *Speculum Meditantis* as he renamed it when he became aware that this initial effort would grow into an imposing trilogy. Toward the end of the *Mirour,* after a conventional apology for his sinful life, he comments on this change in his mode of living and indicates that it was accompanied by a change in the form and subject matter of his writing:

Jadis trestout m'abandonoie	Formerly I abandoned myself
Au foldelit et veine joye,	to foolish delight and vain joy,
Dont ma vesture desguisay	in which I disguised my dress
Et les fols ditz d'amours fesoie,	and composed foolish love poems,
Dont en chantant je carolloie:	which I sang dancing.
Mais ore je m'aviseray	But now I shall take thought
Et tout cela je changeray,	and change all that;
Envers dieu je supplieray	I shall pray to God
Q'il de sa grace me convoie;	that by His grace he direct me;
Ma conscience accuseray,	I shall examine my conscience,
Un autre chançon chanteray,	and sing another kind of song
Que jadys chanter ne soloie.	which I was not accustomed to sing.
Mais tu q'escoulter me voldras,	But you who would hear me,
Escoulte que je chante bass,	listen to what I sing so low,
Car c'est un chançon cordial;	for it is a heartfelt song.
Si tu la note bien orras,	If you listen well to the tune,
Au commencer dolour avras	you will feel sorrow at the beginning
Et au fin joye espirital:	and in the end spiritual joy;

Car Conscience especial,	for Conscience especially,
Qui porte le judicial,	which pronounces judgment,
Est de mon consail en ce cas,	is of my opinion in this matter;
Dont si tu voes en communal	wherefore if you should desire
Chanter ove moy ce chançonal,	to sing this song with me,
Ensi chantant dirrez, Helas!	you must begin by singing "Alas!"

(MO, 27337)

Later, in the *Confessio*, he speaks again of having written lyrics:

> And also I have ofte assaied
> Rondeal, balade and virelai
> For hire on whom myn herte lai
> To make, and also forto peinte
> Caroles with my wordes qweinte,
> To sette my pourpos alofte;
> And thus I sang hem forth fulofte
> In halle and ek in chambre aboute. (CA, 1.2726)

The only ones of Gower's pieces that could possibly fit the designation "fols ditz d'amours" or "rondeal, balade and virelai" are his two balade sequences designated by Macaulay *Cinkante Balades* and *Un traitié selonc les auctours pour essampler les amantz marietz.*[1] Neither of these sequences has come down to us in a form that could precede the *Mirour.* The *Cinkante Balades* are preserved in only one manuscript, in 1900 kept at Trentham Hall in Staffordshire, but now in Dunrobin Castle in Sutherland.[2] This small volume has a curious history, fraught with the same sort of interesting biographical associations as many of the other Gower manuscripts. From the hand and illumination, it would appear to emanate from the scriptorium that produced most of Gower's other gift manuscripts, and it contains a notation by Sir Thomas Fairfax, its 17th-century owner, that it was presented by Gower himself to King "Edward ye fourth att his coronation." "Edward" has been corrected to "Henry," and "or before" has been inserted above "att," after which "att" and "or" were struck through. On the verso of the second leaf is a name which has been taken to be "Rychemond" and a notation in a 16th-century hand: "Liber Hen. Septimi tunc comitis Richmond manu propria script." Thomas Warton, who first called attention to the existence of the *Cinkante Balades*, sug-

gested that the Trentham MS. might have been a present from the
poet to King Henry about the year 1400. He described it as "ele-
gantly written and illuminated." Macaulay judged that while the
book may have been arranged for presentation to the King, the
manuscript must be a copy the author kept by him, as the presentation copy "would probably have been more elaborately orna-
mented." [3] Although it does not have the overelaborate illumination
of some of the later manuscripts, both the script and initials appear
to be up to the standard of the best Gower manuscripts. But if this
was a presentation copy, it had got out of royal hands by 1656, when
it was presented to Fairfax by Charles Gedde, Esq., of Aberdeen. [4]

Whether the Trentham manuscript is the original presentation
volume or a copy, the nature and purpose of its contents are clear.
Only a few of the pieces could have been recent compositions: *In
Praise of Peace*, [5] addressed to Henry after his coronation; the two
fulsome French balades dedicating the *Cinkante Balades* to Henry;
the fifteen lines of Latin between these two balades, pieced together
from two Latin poems defending the legitimacy of Henry's coronation; [6] and the concluding lament for Gower's blindness. [7] *Rex celi
deus*, the second piece in the book, is a revision of lines originally
addressed to Richard in the *Vox Clamantis* early in the 1380's. [8] The
eighteen balades of the *Traitié* are found in nine manuscripts in
addition to the Trentham, and they conclude with verses likewise
adapted from the *Vox*. Only the two dedicatory balades of the
Cinkante Balades and the fifty-two balades in that sequence are
unique to this manuscript. What we have, then, is a collection
bringing together samples of Gower's poetry in all three languages
to make a complimentary volume for the King. Appearance of a
piece in the collection provides no evidence at all for the date of its
composition. Warton judged that the *Cinkante Balades* were from
the poet's youth. [9] Kittredge, quoting the references in the *Mirour*
and the *Confessio*, likewise judged them early. [10] Macaulay argued
on the basis of their impersonality and universality that they were
produced for Henry, "Por desporter vo noble Court roial" as asserted in the second dedicatory balade. He evidently thought that

although some of the balades may have been written earlier, some dated from as late as 1399, after Henry had assumed the throne.[11]

Now, there are other possible explanations for the tone of the *Cinkante Balades*. They do not sound like the productions of an aged, half blind moralist. In spontaneity and lyric emotion they compare with the conclusion of the *Confessio*, so highly praised by C. S. Lewis. Some of them utter the conventions of the troubadour *planh* very gracefully. For example:

Sicome l'ivern despuile la verdure	*Just as winter despoils the lovely*
Du beal Jardin, tanque autresfoitz Estée	*garden of its verdure, until summer*
L'ait revestu, ensi de sa mesure	*reclothes it again, so in its measure*
Moun coer languist, mais il s'est esperée	*languishes my heart; but it is hopeful that*
Q'encore a vous vendrai joious et lée.	*I shall return again to you joyous and glad.*
(CB, vii.15)	

Others address the loved one with appealing sincerity:

O tresgentile dame, simple et coie,	*O gentle lady, unaffected and quiet,*
Des graces et des vertus replenis,	*so full of virtues and of graces,*
Lessetz venir merci, jeo vous supploie,	*be merciful, I beg you,*
Et demorir, tanqu'il m'avera guaris;	*and stay until I am healed,*
Car sanz vous vivre ne suis poestis.	*for without you I cannot live.*
(CB, ix.33)	

The conventions are charged with idealistic, youthful emotion, as in this final example:

Au solail, qe les herbes eslumine	*To the sun which shines upon the plants*
Et fait florir, jeo fai comparisoun	*and makes them flower I compare*
De celle q'ad dessoubtz sa discipline	*her who has beneath her discipline*
Mon coer, mon corps, mes sens et ma resoun	*my heart, my body, my senses, and my reason,*
Par fin amour trestout a sa bandoun:	*in pure love, completely in her fealty:*
Si menerai par tant joiouse vie,	*Thus shall I lead a joyful life*
Et servirai de bon entencioun,	*and serve her with good intentions,*
Sanz mal penser d'ascune vilenie.	*without evil thought of any churlishness.*
Si femme porroit estre celestine	*If a woman created of human flesh*
De char humeine a la creacion,	*were able to be divine,*
Jeo croi bien qe ma dame soit devine;	*I think my lady would be divine,*
Q'elle ad le port et la condicion	*for she has the manner and condition*
De si tressainte conversacioun,	*of such sainted conversation,*
Si plein d'onour, si plein de courtoisie,	*so full of honor and of courtesy,*
Q'a lui servir j'ai fait ma veneisoun,	*that it is my whole pursuit to serve her*
Sanz mal penser d'ascune vilenie.	*without evil thought of any churlishness.*
(CB, xxi.1)	

This is far from Catullus, and one might argue that Gower could have written such lines at any time in his life. However, the personal pose and ingenuous sentiment of the first forty of the *Cinkante Balades* are most attractive thought of as the expression of an idealistic, young poet. The disillusionment and tendency toward moralization in XLI–XLIII of the *Cinkante Balades* and the didactic tone of all the balades in the *Traitié* betray the preoccupations of the *Mirour* and *Vox Clamantis*. One might therefore infer a chronological development through the two sequences—although who is to say that a young man may not have his moments of disillusion and an old man his moments of sentimentality?

The most interesting difference between Gower's balades and Chaucer's early poems is that whereas Chaucer wrote in English and Gower in French, it is Chaucer who reveals a profound influence from the French court poets, whereas Gower shows little, if any, knowledge of them. Chaucer began his career as "grant translateur," in Deschamps' words, transforming the polished and highly stylized poetry of the French court into an equally brilliant English equivalent. The range of court poetry had been extended by mid-14th century to include far more than the love lyric and the political sirventes of the troubadours. Furthermore, alongside their independent lyrics, which the French poets were standardizing into balade, rondel, and the like, Machaut and others in their *dits* and *lais* were fond of stringing lyrics on a thread of narrative, akin to the *chante fable* of the *trouvère*. In pieces like Machaut's *Jugement dou Roy de Behaigne* and *Dit dou lion*[12] (which so influenced the *Book of the Duchess*), the lyric appeals and complaints do not differ in form from the narrative, whereas in Froissart's *Le tretié de l'espinette amoureuse* or *Le joli buisson de Jonece*,[13] the octosyllabic couplets of the narrative are frequently interspersed with balades, rondels, and virelays. Chaucer was never particularly drawn to the independent love balade. *To Rosemounde* and the less successful *Womanly Noblesse* are his only original balades in this vein. Among the doubtful pieces, *Against Women* and *A Balade of Complaint* may be added to the list. The three balades in *The Complaint of Venus* were translated from Oton de Grandson. The four "Complaints" and *Merciles Beaute* are not balades. The other seven balades very probably by his hand are didactic or occasional. Chaucer showed a distinct preference for dealing with love in a narrative frame and allowing the complaint of the Black Knight in *The Book of the Duchess*, the rondel at the end of *The Parliament of Fowls*, or the balades in *Troilus* and *The Legend of Good Women* to stand as separate lyrics within the frame. In sum, we may say that Chaucer was influenced by contemporary French court models in his early poetry in three ways: in verbal borrowings so familiar that they need not be recapitulated; in turning the balade to philosophical and didactic topics (e.g., *Fortune, Lak of Stedfastnesse*); and in the practice of imbedding the lyrics formally or thematically within a romantic narrative.

Gower reveals these influences in much lesser degree. The balade tradition came to maturity with Machaut, Deschamps, and Frois-sart,[14] who wrote scores of independent balades and might imbed as many as 128 balades in a larger sequence (e.g., Froissart's *Le livre du tresor amoureux*). But if Gower's *Cinkante Balades* were com-posed as a sequence before 1380, his is the earliest sequence uncon-nected with other verse and prose now known. The mere fact of priority means little. Balades and balade sequences were in the air in France and England at the end of the 14th century as sonnets and sonnet sequences were two centuries later. But Gower's inde-pendence of the French court poets, his priority in composing a balade sequence, his concentration on the theme of love, and par-ticularly his treatment of this theme, all suggest an inspiration other than the French contemporaries who so influenced Chaucer.

The absence of formal and verbal influence is hard to demon-strate in any succinct way. In the last half of the century, the balade was still in flux as to meter, stanza form, and the presence or absence of the envoy. Its firmest feature was that it had three stanzas ending in a common refrain. Most of the poems in Grandson's collection that are called balades are in stanzas of nine and ten lines, but the lines are prevailingly decasyllabic and the three stanzas are occasionally followed by an envoy of four lines. Machaut's stanza lengths and rhyme schemes are more nearly like Gower's, but he still wrote frequently in the older short lines of six to eight syllables. He never ended his regular balade with an envoy, although he usually did his five-stanza chante royal.[15] On the whole, Deschamps' balades—and Chaucer's—are most nearly like Gower's in their regular employment of the envoy, their prevailingly decasyllabic meter, and their employment of the *ababbcc* "rime royal" (used also in *In Praise of Peace*) and *ababbcbc* "Monk's Tale" as the most frequent rhyme schemes. Half (twenty-seven) of the *Cinkante Balades* are in seven-line "rime royal," and half in eight-line "Monk's Tale" stanzas. All of the balades in the *Traitié* are in "rime royal." All but one of the *Cinkante Balades* have envoys and none of the *Traitié*. But none of this tells us much about Gower's inspiration.

Nor are the verbal parallels any more helpful. "Simple et coie," the familiar romance collocation by which Chaucer characterized the Prioress, appears twice in Gower; [16] and "coer et corps" was likewise a favorite with Gower, Deschamps, and Grandson.[17] The refrain of Gower's xxv, "Car qui bien aime ses amours tard oblie," used by Chaucer in the rondel at the end of the *Parliament of Fowls*, and by Machaut and Deschamps, was proverbial.[18] Deschamps' refrain, "Telle dame estre empereis de Romme," reappears in Gower's xliii, spoken by the lady, "Si jeo de Rome fuisse l'emperesse." [19] The refrain to Gower's xliii, "C'est ma dolour, qe fuist ainçois ma joie" resembles Machaut's "C'est ma dolour et la fin de ma joie." [20] The technique of alluding to the names of great lovers, found in Grandson's "Ho! doulce Yseult, qui fus a la fontaine/ Avec Tristan, Jason et Medea" is used in Gower's xliii, "Plus tricherous qe Jason a Medée," etc., and in most of his balades in the *Traitié*, as well as in the envoy to Chaucer's "Hyd, Absolon" and elsewhere.[21] But, in the context of the tradition, such verbal echoes as these are trifling. When one considers the multitude of exact lines and extended passages from French court poetry that have been identified in Chaucer's poems, the contrast with Gower is obvious.[22]

Gower's fondness for the term *fin amour* is a first clue to a more direct inspiration. In my reading of Machaut's balades I have not found the term used once, nor have I found it in Grandson's poems, and only once in Deschamps'. Doubtless the term does occur in 14th-century French court poetry, but it is safe to say that Gower's eight uses [23] are more than is common in poetry derived from Guillaume de Lorris' portion of the *Roman de la Rose* in which the troubadour distinction between *fin* and other types of *amour* had been blurred. Furthermore, we never find in Gower's balades the personifications popularized by the *Roman*, such as "Faulx Parles," "Dangier," "Envie," "Doulx Regart," "Male Bouche," "Raffus," and the host of others that spring from Guillaume's flowery garden into the lyrics of Deschamps and Grandson.[24] Finally, the claim has been made that the parallels between Gower's balades and the troubadour poetry of Provençe are more frequent and direct than between the troubadours and Chaucer. Jean Audiau, who listed the parallels in both,[25] has thirteen from all of Chaucer's works, some as commonplace as "Youre eyn two wol slee me sodenly" and "my hertis wounde," from the doubtful *Merciles Beaute* or "The herte in-with my sorrowful brest yow dredeth" from the *Legend of Good Women*. By contrast, Audiau listed fifty parallels in the *Cinkante Balades*, some of which he considered so striking that he was led to infer "une connaissance personnelle, directe, de la poésie meridionale. Et je demande enfin s'il est un autre moyen d'expliquer les passages de Gower (assez rares, il est vrai) ou l'imitation du texte provençal est particulièrement évident." I must confess that I am not so impressed as Audiau by the direct similarity. The readings he cites are so common to the whole troubadour-derived convention that I would hesitate to conclude, "Gower n'a-t-il pas en entre les mains, comme Pétrarque, un chansonnier des troubadours?" Nevertheless, I believe that Audiau's impression is sound: that Gower's debt to the troubadours and their immediate successors is greater than Chaucer's, just as Chaucer's debt to the French court poets is greater than that of Gower.

The reason for Chaucer's orientation is clear. As a page boy in a French-speaking court, he must have grown up hearing and reading the poetry of the French court poets. The reason for Gower's troubadour orientation is less clear. But there is a tantalizing possibility that deserves to be considered, even though the documentary evidence is too early and too meager to make possible a definite conclusion. In the Record Room of Guildhall in London, in the *Liber Custumarum,* are recorded a series of regulations for governing a religious, charitable, convivial, and musical organization called the "Pui." [26] At each feast, the entertainment consisted of songs composed and sung by members, and a member was exempted from the 12-pence dues at a meeting to which he came provided with a new song. The elected ruler of the group, called the Prince, decided upon the merit of the songs and awarded a crown for the best. The fraternal and charitable functions of the group are detailed at length, but its principal function was clearly regarded as musical and literary: "And whereas the royal feast of the Pui is maintained and established principally for crowning of a royal song, inasmuch as it is by song that it is honoured and enhanced, all the gentle companions of the Pui by right reason are bound to exalt royal songs to the utmost of their power, and especially the one that is crowned by the assent of the companions upon the day of the great feast of the Pui. . . . And although the becoming pleasance of virtuous ladies is a rightful theme and principal occasion for royal singing, and for composing and furnishing royal songs, nevertheless it is hereby provided that no lady or other woman ought to be at the great sitting of the Pui, for the reason that the members ought hereby to take example, and rightful warning, to honour, cherish, and commend all ladies, at all times, in all places, as much in their absence as in their presence." [27]

The institution of the Pui came into existence in southern France in the 13th century as merchants and artisans of the *haute bourgeoisie* began to imitate the refinements of the troubadours.[28] The original name, Confrérie de Notre Dame du Puy, suggests that the inspiration for the fraternity came in the first place from the celebrated, miracle-working statue of the Virgin in the cathedral at Le Puy en Velay in Auvergne, but before the end of the 13th century societies were to be found throughout southern France, and in Picardy, Normandy, and Flanders. From which area the institution was imported into England cannot be ascertained. However, H. T. Riley, editor of the *Liber Custumarum,* suggested that since the mercantile relations with northern France were interrupted at the end of the 13th century and beginning of the 14th century by the French interference in Edward I's wars of the Scottish succession, the merchants who established the English Pui probably came from areas subject to the English Crown in Bordeaux, Gascony, Guienne—neighbors to Auvergne and in the *langue d'oc* area, which was the historic home of the troubadour poetry. In support of this conjecture is the record in the Letter Books (probably entered in the 1320's) that Henry le Waleys, who had been mayor of both London and Bordeaux and had been granted castles in Gascony, in 1299 granted "unto the Brethren of the Pui 5 marks of yearly quit-rent, to be received from all his tenements in London, towards the support of a chaplain celebrating divine service in the new chapel at the Guildhall of London." A possible connection with St. Mary Overeys at this early date is the fact that from 1283 to 1306 its prior was "William Wallys." [29]

How the regulations of the Pui came to be inserted among the City records is unknown. They are on twelve interpolated folios (ff. 174–186) which include, along with the undated regulations of the Pui, a list of the city benefices and their benefactors, likewise without any indication of date, and the succession of mayors and sheriffs between 4 Edward I (1275) and 14 Edward II (1320). If these three items have any connection in time, the regulations of the Pui and the lists of benefices must both have been still current in 1320. How much later than this the Pui flourished it is impossible to say. Riley detects the germs of dissolution in the second series of regulations which, besides reaffirming the original constitution, insert extensive new directions for the treatment of those who fail to attend the great feasts or default in their payment of dues. Those who default for seven years together are to be expelled from the company. I am not sure that the revision of a constitution and the provision of machinery for handling delinquents is not as probably a sign of maturity as of decay. At least, the new regulations purport to be "trove e establi a tenir cum Estatuz a tuz jours." One interesting evidence they provide is the difficulty the brethren encountered in encouraging song as distinct from verse. Two or three who understood singing and music were to be appointed specifically to evaluate the music, "For without singing no one ought to call a composition of words (*une resoun endite*) a song, nor ought any royal song be crowned without the sweet sounds of melody sung." "Resoun endite" might well describe what Gower had to offer, since there is no evidence that his balades were composed to be sung.

For Gower to be a member, the Pui would have had to continue into the 1350's, the period of the French and English wars, when, according to Riley, the songs, alms-deeds, processions, and festivities of an organization of French merchants would likely have met with rude interruptions amid the anathemas launched against the perfidious enemy. Riley's argument overlooks the fact that the Pui was a cultural organization and that the period of the Hundred Years' War marks the high point of French influence in England, on language, literature, dress, and manners. There is no reason to suppose that an organization so thoroughly naturalized that by 1299 it could be endowed with income from London real estate, and whose third Prince—indeed the only individual named in the regulations—was evidently an Englishman, Johan de Chesthounte (John Cheshunt), should not have survived into the middle of the century. Furthermore, although there is no reason why the Pui had to be coexistent with St. Mary's Chapel in Guildhall, it is a fact that the first mention of the chapel is found in connection with Henry le Waleys' grant of 1299 and its connection with the Pui is detailed in the regulations. The chapel is referred to sporadically throughout the century, and by 1430 it had fallen into disrepair and had to be rebuilt.[30] In the final volume of *Guildhall Plea and Memoranda Rolls,* Mr. P. E. Jones associates John Carpenter's 15th-century bequest founding a chantry college and choir school in the chapel with the tradition of the Pui.[31] None of this is proof, but it is certainly some indication that the Pui existed long enough for Gower to have been present at its feasts. Even proving that the Pui still existed would not prove that Gower was a member. On that score, we have only the fact of his friend Strode's employment by the City, which would have made Guildhall his headquarters, and the possibility of Gower's own civic employment as indicated by his rayed sleeves. In addition, it may be worth mentioning that in 1370 one Thomas Chesthunte, goldsmith, of the same surname though a half century later than the "Prince" of the Pui in 1320, sold some land in partnership with John Gravesende, draper, from whom Gower had bought property in 1367.[32] Such is the evidence to which the literary historian of the 14th century must resort!

The regulations of the London Pui are the most complete in existence, but it is noteworthy that they call the pieces to be performed merely "chauncon" and "chauncon reale." These are not names of specific poetic forms like balade or rondel, but merely the equivalent of *song*, generally *love song*. Evidently throughout the 13th century, the songs composed for the Puis were as unsystematized and varied in form as those of their troubadour models, in which the origins of the later specific prosodic and stanzaic arrangements are all to be found. These were formalized by court poets in the 14th century.[33] Once such literary arbiters had legislated the classic forms, however, the Puis turned their attention to them, using such types as the balade or rondel for poetic contests. There is no evidence for the exact date at which any Pui took up the balade as an exercise, but the fad began, evidently, after the middle of the 14th century. The guess of the scholar who has had most to say about the London Pui is that "It is not unlikely that both the ballade and the *chant royal* may have figured in its latest contests, if not in English, perhaps in French." [34]

Some of the characteristics of Gower's *Cinkante Balades* support the possibility that they were prepared either for recitation before the Pui or directly influenced by the practice of the Pui. For one thing, the convention of adding an envoy grew out of the poetical contests in the Pui. In these, the envoy was usually addressed directly to the "Prince" who was to judge the productions, and as a result of the convention many balades by court poets never intended for a Pui contest were likewise addressed to the Prince. So circular an affair is literary influence: the Pui takes up the balade because it has been popularized without the envoy by the court poets (e.g., Machaut) and gives it back to later court poets (e.g., Deschamps) with an envoy addressed to the Prince. In his use of the envoy in the *Cinkante Balades*, Gower was following the convention of the Pui, but the fact that his envoys are always addressed to love or to the lover who is the recipient of the whole balade, never to an arbiter-Prince, indicates his independence of the convention. This independence could be taken as evidence that he was not directly influenced by the tradition of the Pui. However, in view of the fact that he was one of the first to envision and create a balade sequence, as well as the technique of integrating the envoy with the poem, of making it a capstone for the whole like the concluding quatrain or couplet of a sonnet, rather than a formal salutation, may be part of his own contribution to the technique of the balade.

The prevailingly cheerful and philosophical treatment of love may be another evidence that most of the *Cinkante Balades* were prepared "to honor, cherish, and commend all ladies in their absence" at the great festivals of the Pui. As Macaulay has observed, they are "only to a very limited extent, if at all, expression of the actual feelings of the author towards a particular person. As an artist Gower has set himself to supply suitable forms of expression for the feelings of others, and in doing so he imagines their variety of circumstances and adapts his composition accordingly." Macaulay would contend that this impersonal tone was because the poems were intended for recitation before the court of Henry IV. But the fact that Gower's balades generally avoid the languorous, sentimental pose of the broken heart that was conventional for courtly love lyrics would have made them appropriate to the situation of the Pui. A middle-class, male audience at a convivial, semireligious festival might well have reacted to patently false sentiment like the common fowl in Chaucer's *Parliament*, "Com of! . . . allas, ye wol us shende!"

A final indication that Gower's balades may have been written for a merchant Pui rather than for the Court is their advocacy of married love. A marginal notation at the end of v says "Les balades d'amont jesqes enci sont fait especialement pour ceaux q'attendont lours amours par droite mariage." And at the beginning of vi, "Les balades d'ici jesqes au fin du livere sont universeles a tout le monde, selonc les propretés et les condicions des Amantz, qui sont diversement travailez en la fortune d'amour." Actually the first note is applicable only to the two balades numbered iiii, and the fifth, which have constancy as their theme. The conjugal tone is not found in the first three balades, which breathe unsatisfied love ("D'ardant desir celle amorouse peigne/ Mellé d'espoir me fait languir en joie," iii.1), but it is found in several later balades, for example viii, which might just as well be a husband's farewell; xv with its refrain, "Mon coer remaint, que point ne se remue"; xxi on the ennobling effect of love; such balades in praise of his lady's beauty and character as xxxviii, xliii, xlv; and especially the third balade from the end, which gives

Le tierce point dont amour ad la vois,	The third point concerning love,
Amour en son endroit ceo nous aprent	Love itself reveals to us
Soubtz matrimoine de les seintes lois,	in the holy laws of matrimony,
Par vie honeste et nonpas autrement.	in honest life, and not otherwise.
(CB, xlix.15)	

Although the *Cinkante Balades* do not address themselves directly to marriage, that is the principal subject of the eighteen balades in the collection Macaulay entitled *Traitié*. Gower had come eventually to think of them as an addendum to the *Confessio Amantis*. In seven of the ten manuscripts in which they occur, they are joined to the *Confessio* by a headnote stating, "Puisqu'il ad dit ci devant en Englois [i.e., in the *Confessio*] par voie d'essample la sotie de cellui qui par amours aime par especial, dirra ore apres en François a tout le monde en general un traitié selonc les auctours pour essampler les amantz marietz, au fin q'ils la foi de lour seintes espousailes pourront par fine loialté [cf. "fin amour" in *Cinkante Balades*] guarder, et al honour de dieu salvement tenir."[35] Their eventual association with the *Confessio* was no doubt because of the way in which they summed up its major themes, and indeed the continuous theme of all three major poems as we shall trace it in the next chapter. The first balade in the *Traitié* takes as its theme the superiority of reason over sensuality and the transience of the flesh and permanence of the spirit:

Le creatour de toute creature,	The creator of all creatures,
Qui l'alme d'omme ad fait a son ymage,	who made the soul of man in his image,
Par quoi le corps de reson et nature	so that the body, by reason and by nature,
Soit attempré per jouste governage,	would be tempered by just governage,
Il done al alme assetz plus d'avantage;	gives the soul the greatest advantage;
Car il l'ad fait discrete et resonable,	for he has made it discreet and reasonable,
Dont sur le corps raison ert conestable.	wherefore reason will be guardian of the body.
En dieu amer celle alme ad sa droiture,	In love of God the soul has its authority,
Tant soulement pour fermer le corage	only in order to strengthen the heart
En tiel amour u nulle mesprisure	in such a love that no false concern
De foldelit la poet mettre en servage	with foolish joy can enslave it to
De frele char, q'est toutdis en passage:	the frail flesh, which is always passing away;
Mais la bone alme est seinte et permanable;	but the virtuous soul is holy and everlasting,
Dont sur le corps raison ert conestable.	wherefore reason will be the guardian of
(T, I.1)	the body.

The second balade takes as its theme the superiority of divine over human love:

De l'espirit l'amour quiert continence,	Spiritual love seeks continence,
Et vivre chaste en soul dieu contemplant;	to live chaste, contemplating God alone.
Li corps par naturele experience	The body by natural experience desires
Quiert femme avoir, dont soit multipliant;	to have a wife in order to multiply.
Des bones almes l'un fait le ciel preignant,	The one impregnates the heaven with virtuous souls;
Et l'autre emplist la terre de labour:	the other fills the earth with labor.
Si l'un est bon, l'autre est assetz meilour.	If the one is good, the other is even better.
(T, II.1)	

The sexual urge is regarded as lawless emotion and marriage as its lawful restraint. In the third balade, as at the beginning of the last

book of the *Confessio* (VIII.51), Adam and Eve are cited as the origi-
nators of legitimate marriage, and in succeeding balades the misfortunes of lovers who did not respect "seintes espousailes" are cited as
horrible examples: VI, Nectanabus and Ulysses and Circe; VII, Her-
cules and Deianire; VIII, Jason and Medea; IX, Agamemnon and
Clytemnestra;[36] X, Helen of Troy and Mundus and Pauline; XI,
Albinus and Rosemond; XII, Prochne and Philomena; XIII, Pharaoh
and Sarah; XIV, David and Bathsheba; XV, Lancelot and Tristan; XVI,
Valentinians; and XVII, Gawain. All of these except Pharaoh, whose
lust for Abraham's wife Sarah brought the plagues upon Egypt, and
Gawain, "courtois d'amour, mais il fuist trop volage," are treated
at greater length in the *Confessio*. Furthermore, even in the three
manuscripts in which they occur apart from the *Confessio*, each
balade is provided with the same sort of Latin sidenote explaining
its moral implications. The final balade reemphasizes the themes of
virtuous love and social order:

Des trois estatz benoitz c'est le seconde,	Of the three estates, the second is most blessed,
Q'au mariage en droit amour se ploie;	which submits itself to marriage in legitimate love;
Et qui cell ordre en foldelit confonde	and whoever should confound this order by foolish joy
Trop poet doubter, s'il ne se reconvoie.	might greatly doubt whether it could be restored.
Pource bon est qe chascun se pourvoie	Hence it is well that everyone should so conduct himself
D'amer ensi, q'il n'ait sa foi blemie:	in love that his faith be not blemished.
N'est past amant qui soun amour mes-guie.	He is no lover who misdirects his love.

(T, XVIII.8)

These three estates would appear to be the virginal, married, and
widowed, in the same unusual order that Chaucer gives them in the
Legend of Good Women (G 282, 295).

In theme, subject, and treatment, the balades in the *Traitié* appear to belong to the period of the major works, and more precisely
to the period of the *Confessio Amantis*, after 1386. Just as the coronation of Henry IV provided the occasion for the composition of
the two dedicatory balades and the final arrangement of the *Cin-*

kante Balades, Gower's own late marriage offered the occasion for
the collection and final form of the *Traitié.* This is to be inferred
from the Latin moralizations at the end, the first nine lines ("Quis
sit vel qualis sacer ordo connubialis," etc.) on the virtues of holy
marriage, the next nineteen ("Carmen de variis in amore passion-
ibus," etc., adapted from *Vox Clamantis* v.53ff) against the vices of
courtly love, and finally:

> *Lex docet auctorum quod iter carnale bonorum*
> *Tucius est, quorum sunt federa coniugiorum:*
> *Fragrat vt ortorum rosa plus quam germen agrorum,*
> *Ordo maritorum caput est et finis amorum:*
> *Hec est nuptorum carnis quasi regula morum,*
> *Que saluandorum sacratur in orbe virorum.*
> *Hinc vetus annorum Gower sub spe meritorum*
> *Ordine sponsorum tutus adhibo thorum.*

(The law of good authors teaches that the fleshly journey is
safest for those who have the bonds of marriage upon them.
The cultivated rose is more fragrant than the field plant. The
estate of marriage is the chief end of love. Hence marriage is to
the body as regulation is to custom, which is intended for
salvation in the world of men. Thus I, Gower, prudent and
aged in years, in hope of merit, undertake the ordinance of
marriage.)

Quixley's translation of the *Traitié* into English in about 1400
gives Gower secondhand credit for the longest sequence of balades
in Middle English, as well as for one of the earliest in French. The
English verses are interesting chiefly as examples of the northern
dialect and of the influence of French prosody and vocabulary.[37]
Gower's French meter has been called unorthodox because of the
influence upon it of English syllabic stress. Quixley's English meter
almost defies analysis because he, on the other hand, pays no attention to syllabic stress, being content merely to count the syllables.
He translates the balades line for line, practically rhyme for rhyme.
His only additions are a seven-line introductory stanza and a final
nineteenth balade. The introductory stanza gives some notion of
the quality of the verse:

Who þat liste loke in þis litel tretice
May fynde what meschief is of auoutrie
Wherfore he þat will eschewe þat vice
He may see here to beware of folie.
Gower it made in frenshe with grete studie
In balades ryale whos sentence here
Translated hath Quixley in this manere.

The final balade, based upon a possible allusion to the *De Concupis-centia* of St. Augustine, comments on the punishment due the adulterer. The last of its three stanzas takes for its first line the first line of Gower's envoy:

Al université de tout le monde
Johan Gower ceste Balade envoie;
Et si jeo n'ai de François la faconde,
Pardonetz moi qe jeo de ceo forsvoie:
Jeo sui Englois, si quier par tiele voie
Estre excusé; mais quoique nulls en die,
L'amour parfit en dieu se justifie.

To the community of the whole world
John Gower directs this balade;
and if I have no eloquence in French
pardon me where I go astray.
I am English, if I may seek so
to be excused; but nothing more of that.
Perfect love justifies itself in God.

(T, xviii.22)

To all þe worldes vniversitee
This balade be ensample and myrrour:
Any whoo lyst nat to stonde in this degree,
Rather or þat he fall into errour
Of flesshly lust, I rede he chese þat peramour
That is, was, and euer schall be lastyng,—
God of heuen, our blys without endyng.

H. N. MacCracken in his edition suggested that the translator was John Quixley, lord of the manor of Quixley, ten miles northeast of York and twelve miles from Stittenham, who might have made the translation in 1402 in honor of the marriage of his daughter Alice, on the precedent of Gower's composition of the original in honor of his own wedding. This is entirely possible, although the discovery of a Frater John de Quyxley after 1382 in the Dominican convent at York[38] raises the question as to whether this and the other pieces in the manuscript (a translation of John of Hildesheim's *Historia Trium Regum* on the Magi, and William of Nassyngton's *Speculum Vitae*)[39] would not have been an appropriate exercise for a Dominican friar. MacCracken's second suggestion—that this early translation helps confirm an early connection, if only through admiration, between the poet and the Gowers of Stittenham—is less attractive. Actually, what we appear to have here is the first of several instances of the poet's sending gift manuscripts of his works to prominent families in the North Riding or with North Riding connections. In 1328, the manor of Quixley was purchased by John de Mauleverer, whose arms bear three hunting dogs; whose relative (? daughter) married Nicholas Gower of Sexhow, one of the most important of the Langbargh family; who in 1345 engaged in business with John Rouclif, relative of the Guy de Rouclif from whom the poet later purchased Feltwell and Moulton. In the 15th century and afterwards, the chief seat of the Mauleverers was Ingelby-Arncliff, on which the Langbargh Gowers were tenants.[40] In 1693 Sir Richard Mauleverer owned MS. Morgan M. 126 (16) of the *Confessio* (not one of those containing the *Traitié*, alas), either as a gift to the family from the poet himself, or through the John Darcy whose name likewise appears in it and who himself had or was related to someone of the same name who had close associations with the Langbargh Gowers.[41] Hence, we may assume that the French *Traitié* came to the translator through the poet's Yorkshire relatives and associates.

II

But this is all much later in his career. We must now return to the middle seventies and follow Gower's development from the casual composition of love balades for an audience such as the Pui to literature in a more serious vein. The development from the contemplative spirit in which he entered upon this activity to his political involvement in the 1390's is accurately chronicled by the successive changes in the colophon he composed about 1390 upon finishing the first version of the *Confessio Amantis* (I translate):[42]

> Because anything should be shared with others in proportion
> as one receives it from God, John Gower, desirous of lightening

somewhat the account for the intellectual gifts God gave to his keeping, while there is time, between work and leisure, for the knowledge of others, composed three books of instructive material as follows:

The first book, written in French, is divided into ten parts; treating of the vices and virtues and the various classes of this world, it undertakes to teach by what right path the sinner who has transgressed ought to return to a recognition of his creator. The title of this book is *Speculum Hominis*.

The second book, composed in Latin hexameter and pentameter verses, deals with those remarkable events which occurred in England in the fourth year of the reign of King Richard II, when the peasants rebelled against the nobles and freemen of the realm. Declaring the excusable innocence of the aforesaid king, then a minor, the evidence reveals that because of faults of other kinds, and not because of fortune, outrages fell on men. And the title of this volume, which contains seven pages (*cuius ordo Septem continet paginas*), is *Vox Clamantis*.

The third of these books, written in English and divided into eight parts, *which was made at the instance of his most serene highness, the* aforesaid *king of England, Richard II,* following the prophecy of Daniel concerning the mutability of earthly kingdoms, marks out the time from Nebuchadnezzar to the present. Following Nectanabus and Aristotle, it also treats of those things by which King Alexander was trained, as much in his governing as in other things. The principal subject matter of this work is founded on love and the promises of lovers, where *the meanings of various chronicles and stories and also the writings of poets and philosophers* are inserted for the sake of example. And, more particularly, the name of the present work is *Confessio Amantis*. [The italicized phrases are paralleled in the sidenote of the first version of the *Confessio*, Prol.40*.]

This colophon appears in at least fifteen manuscripts of the earliest versions of the *Vox* and *Confessio* (1–2, 10, 13–22, 25, 58). There are two later forms. In the manuscripts Gower had prepared immediately after Henry's accession (40–41, 43, 50–51) the important changes are as follows:

First paragraph: "intellectualiter" is replaced by "sensualiter," perhaps in recognition of the fortunate physical endowment which carried the poet through nearly eight decades.

Second paragraph: the title *Speculum Hominis* is changed to *Speculum Meditantis*.

Third paragraph: "when the peasants rebelled against the nobles and freemen of the realm. Declaring the excusable innocence of the aforesaid king, then a minor, the evidence reveals that because of faults of other kinds, and not because of fortune, outrages fell on men" is replaced by "whence torments grieved not only the nobles and commons of the realm, but the most cruel king himself, falling from on high for his own crimes, was cast into the pit which he dug."

Last paragraph: "which was made at the instance of his most serene highness, the aforesaid king of England, Richard II" is replaced by "which was made in honor of his most valorous lordship, Henry of Lancaster, then count of Derby"; and from the description of the contents the clause "where the meanings . . . example" is omitted.

A third version of the colophon is attached to four manuscripts of the interim version of the *Confessio* (36–39).[43] These manuscripts all date from the 15th century although copied from a version of the *Confessio* as it stood ca. 1392–93. The more important readings are as follows:

First paragraph: "intellectualiter" to "sensualiter" as above. But more important, "dum tempus instat" (while there is time) is replaced by "dum vixit" (while he lived), and "between work and leisure" is omitted. Certainly the first of these changes, and perhaps both, appear to betoken the hand of the scribe writing after Gower's death.[44]

Second paragraph: the name of the *Mirour* is changed, as above, and the description paraphrased in a pointless, but typically Gowerian fashion: "It undertakes to teach by what right path the sinner who has transgressed ought to return to a recognition of his creator" becomes "especially the way by which a sinner in penance can find the mercy of Christ is finally reviewed with complete devotion of mind."

Third paragraph: the reference to Richard II falls between the exoneration in the first version and the condemnation in the final, or Fairfax, version. Here the statement is noncommittal: "it deals with the various misfortunes with which England was afflicted in the time of Richard II, where the author prays for the prosperity of the realm."

Last paragraph: the *Confessio* is attributed to Henry and its contents described much as in the Fairfax.

We shall consider shortly the revisions in the *Vox* and *Confessio* that account for—or accompany—the changes in the colophon. Our present concern is with the state of mind implied by "while there is time, between work and leisure" in the first paragraph of the earliest version. These remarks suggest that Gower turned to the *Mirour* mainly to occupy his time during retirement. We know little about the evolution of the *Mirour* in comparison with the two later pieces. No manuscript of it was known to Bale or Stow, and Warton identified the *Speculum Meditantis* with the *Traitié* in the Trentham manuscript.[45] The recovery of the text by G. C. Macaulay ranks with the most important landmarks in English medieval scholarship. On the basis of the first version of the colophon, he guessed that it would be found under the title *Speculum Hominis* rather than the *Speculum Meditantis* of the later colophons, by which it had been designated in all notices after Leland's. In the course of his search for manuscripts of the *Confessio* at Cambridge in 1895, Macaulay mentioned this title to the librarian, Mr. F. J. H. Jenkinson, who called his attention to a manuscript in French with the heading "Cy apres commence le livre François q'est appellé Mirour de l'omme," which he himself had lately bought at auction and presented to the University Library (MS. Cambridge Univ. Library, Additional 3035). Upon examination it proved to be Gower's lost poem.[46] The table of contents is preserved with the division into ten parts, which are mentioned in the colophon but are not marked off in any distinctive way in the text. However, after the contents four leaves are lost and an indeterminate number of leaves are lost at the end so that we have no dedication, prologue, epilogue, or colophon by which to learn the date or special purpose the author may have had in mind for the piece. We have only to consider how much less we would know about the evolution of the *Confessio* if it had reached us in only one manuscript in this mutilated condition to realize that we are at a disadvantage in discussing the external history of the *Mirour*. Furthermore, the *Mirour* manuscript has none of the personal associations of the Trentham or other manuscripts which would make it possible for us to hazard a guess about its history. The binding is from the 18th century and the only marginalia seem to indicate that it lay in some manor house about 1745, perhaps near Gloucester.[47]

The negative evidence may itself have some significance, however. The manuscript bears a family resemblance in hands and illuminated initials to the manuscripts supposedly produced in Gower's scriptorium between 1390 and 1408, and the correctness of the text led Macaulay to infer that it was written under Gower's own direction.[48] One reason that so many good texts of the *Vox* and *Confessio* have come down appears to be that Gower took the initiative in having them copied for presentation to important individuals or institutions with whom he had connections. This would appear to be the way that manuscripts got into the hands of Richard Mauleverer, John Thwaites, and Thomas Neville, for example, and into the abbeys of Fountains and Bury St. Edmunds. Once manuscripts passed into such responsible hands as these, their chances of survival were pretty good. The history of Gower manuscripts is to this extent—perhaps unflatteringly—different from the history of Chaucer manuscripts or collections of romances which early got into the hands of booksellers who turned them out in inferior copies and sold them across the counter to people who read them to pieces rather than carefully laying them away in a press. If we have not lost many Gower manuscripts, the reason we have only one of the *Mirour* is that Gower had very few copies of that piece made. This, in turn, supports the view that he did not think of himself as speaking to the public, as he did when he wrote his later poems, but rather that he undertook it more or less for his own edification. Only as he progressed through it did he become inflamed with the reformer's zeal and feel called upon to address himself to the King and to the English nation.

The *Mirour* is composed of three parts once described by G. L.

Kittredge as the cause, condition, and remedy of man's situation on earth.[49] The first part (lines 37–18420), after a short introductory allegory on the origin of sin, uses the framework of the books of vices and virtues; the second (lines 18421–27360) uses the framework of complaint on the estates; and the last (lines 27361–29945) is a life of the Virgin Mary. All of this matter, whose themes and substance will be considered in the next chapter, was drawn from clerical sources, for which we may assume Gower made good use of the library at St. Mary Overeys, just as he must later have made good use of its scriptorium. One of the three manuscripts surviving from the priory, "The Book of St. Mary Overes" (British Museum, Cotton, Faustina, A.viii) suggests the sort of reading that would have been available to Gower.[50] It is a bookbinder's compilation of various manuals and registers once belonging to the priory, of which the first forty folios are a typical penitential, dealing with the ways of making confession, doing penance, and securing absolution. Folios 44–49 then give brief characterizations and proper penances for the major sins: f. 44 "De parricidio," f. 44^v "De matricidio," and so on with fornication, lying, sacrilege, etc. Then after seventy leaves of priory business, ff. 119^v–145 contain historical material. The first section, from the Incarnation to 1065, is indebted to such authorities as Eusebius, Jerome, Hugh of Fleury, Isadore of Seville (on meteors); the second section, 1066–1207, has some close parallels to the *Imagines Historiarum* of Ralph de Diceto; the final section, 1208–1240, is a contemporary chronicle. Many of the entries consist simply of lists of names of popes, emperors, Saxon and Norman kings, illustrious writers from Trogus to Hugh of St. Victor, and the like. But there are short expository accounts of such matters as the Danish settlements in France, the deeds of the Normans, a version of the prophecies of Merlin, and extracts from Bede relating to the marvels of Britain. While I have not been able to discover that Gower made any direct use of the materials in this manuscript, parts of it must have been in the priory in his time, and it suggests the sort of reading that gave bent to all his major writing after 1377. The vices and virtues, the sins of the estates, and confession provided him with the framework for his three major poems, and he made increasing use of historical and fabulous allusion from each work to the next.

The references to lovers and love at the beginning make it appear that Gower began work on the *Mirour* fresh from his French balades:

Escoulte cea, chascun amant,	*Listen to me, each lover,*
Qui tant perestes desirant	*who appears so desirous*
Du pecché, dont l'amour est fals: . . .	*of sin, whose love is false. . . .*
He, amourouse sote gent,	*Ha, foolish, amorous people,*
Si scieussetz le diffinement	*if you knew the end*
De ce dont avetz commencé,	*of what you have commenced,*
Je croy que vostre fol talent	*I believe that your foolish inclination*
Changeast, qui muetz au present	*would change, which now perverts*
Reson en bestialité.	*reason into bestiality.*
Car s'un soul homme avoir porroit	*For if a man could have*
Quanq'en son coer souhaideroit	*whatever his heart desired*
Du siecle, pour soy deliter,	*of the world, to delight him,*
Trestout come songe passeroit	*like a dream it would all pass away*
En nient, et quant l'en meinz quidoit,	*into nothing, just as he thought it in his*
Par grant dolour doit terminer:	*hands—it would end in great sorrow.*
Et puisque l'amour seculer	*And since secular love*
En nient au fin doit retorner,	*must in the end return to nothingness,*
Pour ce, si bon vous sembleroit,	*therefore, if it please you,*
Un poy du nient je vuill conter.	*I shall tell a little about nothing.*

(MO, 1)

This is the theme of the *Traitié* and the theme which was to underlie the argument that Gower was to develop through his three major poems: the degradation and transience of temporal love, which turns reason into bestiality. Its appearance here is merely preliminary evidence of the quality of mind which was to emerge through the next decade, for Gower had probably not yet written the *Traitié* and he can hardly have envisioned the grand plan which was to evolve from these opening lines through nearly 74,000 lines of French, Latin, and English verse. The larger scheme evolved gradually along with his developing conception, but also under the pressure of the momentous national events already foreshadowed in 1377, which were to rise to a shattering crescendo in 1381, to another climax in 1388, and to a final catastrophe at the end of the

1390's. Since there is no mention in the *Mirour* of the youth of Richard II, which weighed so heavily on Gower's mind in the *Vox* and in the colophon, it has been assumed that the piece was substantially complete before Richard came to the throne in 1377. Lines 22297 ff appear to refer to the Good Parliament of 1376, and at line 18825 ff there is a clear allusion to the Great Schism of 1378, when rival popes were elected in Rome and Avignon. Since Gower was an inveterate reviser it is possible that the allusion to the Schism was a later interpolation. All that the dates indicate is that Gower was at work on the poem from before 1376 until after 1378.[51]

The fact that the *Mirour* proceeds from an abstract allegory on the origin of sin, through a generalized discussion of the vices and virtues, to a very specific criticism of the London scene in the 1370's is part of its inheritance from clerical tradition, influenced, as we shall see in the next chapter, by Gower's legal training and point of view. But the literary tradition and external political events reinforced one another in such a way that the *Mirour* ends in a vein quite different from that in which it begins. For example, at the beginning of the poem the role of the King in the war with France is defended. Edward III's claim to the French crown in the right of his mother, Isabella, is upheld. The French are accused of the sin of "inobedience":

De ce q'encontre leur ligance
Chascun par guerre se defent
De faire hommage et obeissance
A celluy qui de sa nescance
Le droit depar sa mere prent.
(MO, 2144)

Of those who, despite their fealty,
by war resist
offering homage and obeisance
to him who by his birth, through
his maternal line, has the right to rule.

But by the time Gower comes to kingship in the catalog of the estates, his view has changed. He criticizes the King for taxing the clergy to support war (MO, 22297), taking the opposite from the popular Wycliffite side in this controversy. After a break in the manuscript (MO, 22359), the text picks up with a story from I Esdras 3:4. The king asks what is the strongest thing in the world, and his chamberlains reply a king, a woman, wine, and truth in ascending order (MO, 22765). In Esdras and in Gower's later, fuller retelling (CA, VII.1783), the order is wine, king, woman, truth, and the reference to woman is complimentary: she is stronger because both drunkard and king are born of her. The changed order in the *Mirour* is pejorative: wine is stronger because it overcomes both king and woman. Macaulay's note suggests that the *Mirour* order is simply the result of misremembering, but Gardiner Stillwell has pointed out that it echoes the current criticisms of Alice Perrers, whose petticoat rule is condemned more directly in succeeding lines: [52]

Voir dist qui dist femme est puissant,	He speaks truth who says woman is powerful,
Et ce voit om du meintenant:	and that may be seen today.
Dieus pense de les mals guarir,	May God heal the ills,
Q'as toutes loys est descordant,	for it is contrary to all laws
Qe femme en terre soit regnant	that a woman should rule the land
Et Rois soubgit pour luy servir.	and a King be subject to serve her.
Rois est des femmes trop deçu,	The King is much deceived by women,
Qant plus les ayme que son dieu,	when he loves them more than his God—
Dont laist honour pour foldelit:	then he abandons honor for foolish joy.
Cil Rois ne serra pas cremu,	That King will not be feared
Q'ensi voet laisser son escu	who will thus forfeit his shield
Et querre le bataille ou lit.	and seek the battle of the bed.
(MO, 22807)	

In the Good Parliament of 1376, Alice and several of the King's other bad advisers were impeached. The same Parliament may have been in Gower's mind when he interpreted two of the six qualities which made David a good king. As a shepherd, David devoted himself to separating the good sheep from the bad (MO, 22887), and as a harper:

Pres du pastour ore om verra	Near the shepherd may be seen
Berbis ruignous, dont trop y a;	mangy sheep, of which there are many.
Et del harpour diont François,	And the French say of the harper:
La harpe est en discord pieça	the harp has been in discord for some time;
U est qui bien nous harpera?	where is he who will harp us well?
Je ne say dire a ceste fois.	I cannot say at this time.
(MO, 22963)	

Stillwell reads this enigmatic passage as: the King's counselors are tainted sheep; it is they who create discord. The French, aware of

Edward's ambition, say in effect, "If he wants to rule our country hadn't he better clean his own up first?" Ironically they ask, "Where is he who will harp us well?" Gower, thinking they have a point, replies gravely that he cannot answer their question at the present time.

The treatment of kingship (MO, 22225–23208) is interesting because it early shows Gower's political interest. He begins this passage with the sort of generalized, impersonal comment that has characterized the *Mirour* up to this point, but the abstract discussion of the responsibilities of kingship brings to his mind the problems of England in his own day and his treatment suddenly becomes pointed and specific. From here on, in the discussion of the great lords and lesser estates, the sense of immediacy obtrudes more and more often upon the abstract moralization. Gower's reactions mirror the social and economic changes under way about him. In the first half of the poem the vices and virtues cited are almost exclusively clerical or aristocratic. The Seven Deadly Sins had originated in the monastery and by the 12th or 13th century they had been pretty thoroughly adapted to the court. Gower's emphasis upon *gentilesce, savour, gouvernance,* and *prouesce* for the conduct of the good life was, therefore, an inheritance from the sources of the first half of his poem, as well as from the environment in which he had been reared. But this aristocratic prejudice came to be tempered by other influences, and his treatment of the lesser estates shows the respect for wealth, trade, and the business-boosted nationalism which Marxist philosophy has come to find typical of a rising bourgeoisie.[53] Gower is an excellent subject for Marxist analysis because on the one hand he subsumes so much that is most characteristic of the medieval mind, while on the other hand his understanding of the function of the entrepreneur and his spirited defense of the reward due risk capital read like something out of Adam Smith.[54] Nowhere does his patriotism ring out more roundly than in his forty-seven-line paean to the wool trade:

O leine, dame de noblesce,   O wool, noble lady,
Tu es des marchantz la duesse, . . .   you are the goddess of merchants, . . .
Car les marchantz de tous paiis   for the merchants of all lands,
En temps du peas, en temps du guerre,   in time of peace, in time of war,
Par grant amour te vienont querre; . . .   come seeking you with a passion. . . .
En Engleterre tu es née.   You are born in England.
                    (MO, 25369)

The same patriotic reaction leads him to lash out against the Lombard bankers (MO, 25417) whose "eschange, usure, et chevisance"
control international monetary exchange. He could no more understand the principles of credit and interest than could most of
his English contemporaries,[55] and he aligned himself with the merchants and tradesmen in blaming the "seignourie de nostre terre"
for permitting the Lombards to despoil English merchants (MO,
25484), for giving special privileges to foreigners (MO, 26377),
and for general malfeasance:

Mais qant vient que la governal   But when it comes that the rulers
Est capitous et desloial   are headstrong and disloyal,
Et se delite es faitz vileins,   and delight in doing evil things,
Il porra faire trop de mal.   they can do much ill.
            (MO, 26383)

What drew Gower most forcibly out of the role of Mr. Spectator, however, was his awareness of the growing unrest among the
peasants. In earlier portions of the poem he had taken a benign,
seignoral attitude, criticizing the feudal lords for oppressing the
peasants (MO, 4735), showing a real appreciation of the joys of
vagabondage, "Ove l'aise q'est appartenant" (MO, 5801), and taking more than one occasion to repeate the commonplaces of natural
equality and the virtue of glad poverty.[56] His criticisms of both the
tyranny of the rich and the rebelliousness of the poor were typical
of responsible critics in his own day, and have been repeated by
later historians of the period.[57] The startling clarity with which he
foresaw the Peasants' Revolt was sober fact:

Mais certes c'est un grant errour   But certainly it is a great error
Veoir l'estat superiour   to see the higher class
El danger d'un vilein estant.   intimidated by the peasant class.
    Me semble que la litargie   It seems to me that lethargy

Ad endormi la seignourie,	has so put the nobility to sleep
Si qu'ils de la commune gent	that they do not guard against
Ne pernont garde a la folie,	the folly of the common people,
Ainz souffront croistre celle urtie	but permit that nettle to grow
Quelle est du soy trop violent.	which is so violent in its nature.
Cil qui pourvoit le temps present	He who observes the present time
Se puet doubter procheinement,	may soon fear that,
Si dieus n'en face son aïe,	if God does not give help,
Qe celle urtie inpacient	this impatient nettle
Nous poindra trop soudainement,	will very suddenly sting us,
Avant ce q'om la justefie.	before it can be brought to justice.
Trois choses sont d'une covyne,	There are three things of such nature
Qui sanz mercy font la ravine	that they perform merciless destruction
En cas q'ils soient au dessus:	when they get the upper hand:
L'un est de l'eaue la cretine,	one is flood water,
L'autre est du flamme la ravine,	another is wild fire,
Et la tierce est des gens menuz	and the third is a mob
La multitude q'est commuz:	of common people led by instigators—
Car ja ne serront arrestuz	for they will not be stopped
Par resoun ne par discipline.	by reason or by discipline.
(MO, 26482)	

On the basis of such internal evidence we may conclude that between 1376 and 1378 Gower finished writing the *Mirour*, which he had begun in a withdrawn, devotional mood but finished thoroughly concerned about the political and social unrest he perceived about him. In his next piece, he addressed himself directly to these national issues.

III

The eleven manuscripts of the *Vox Clamantis* fall into several categories.[58] All Souls (50), Glasgow (51), Cotton Tiberius A.iv (52) and Harleian 6291 (53) are fine presentation manuscripts of the kind that Gower apparently had made to give away. All four contain not only the *Vox* but its continuation, the *Cronica Tripertita*, and the three Latin poems that we may refer to as the "laureate" group: *Rex celi deus* and *H. aquile pullus* (Macaulay 4.343) which must have been composed to be read or presented at the coronation of Henry on October 13, 1399, and *O recolende* (Macaulay 4.345), thanking Henry for the grant of wine made five weeks later. Since none of these pieces could have been composed until the end of 1399, it is safe to assume that any manuscript containing them was still in process of completion in 1400. Furthermore, MSS. 51, 52, and 53 contain *Presul, ouile regis* (Macaulay 4.368), identified by "Nota de primordiis Stelle Comate in Anglia." This has been taken as a reference to the comet which appeared in March 1402 and excited comment in the records.[59] Two of these manuscripts (50–51) contain the Fairfax colophon, and two (52–53) have replaced the first paragraph of the Fairfax with the first paragraph of the intermediate version, i.e., "dum tempus instat" with "dum vixit."

The evolution of the All Souls manuscript (50) suggests the history of the other presentation manuscripts. It is prefaced by a dedicatory epistle to Thomas of Arundel, Archbishop of Canterbury and embattled supporter of Henry's claim to the throne. But Macaulay judged (4.369) that the handwriting of the epistle is "distinctly later" than that of the text of the Vox. The epistle is full of erasures, and the corrections nearly all refer to the loss of the author's sight. From this it would appear (1) that the Vox was written first in a fine, firm hand. (2) Later the dedicatory epistle and Latin and French poems and colophon were added before and after the Vox in two different hands. (3) Still later lines in the epistle were scraped out and new lines speaking of Gower's blindness inserted in the same hand. In the meantime, changes in both the second and third hands had been made in the body of the Vox. The indications as to date are that (2) would be after 1399, since the laureate group are in the later hand; hence (1) would be before 1399, and (3) after 1400 but before 1402 since the manuscript does not contain *Presul, ouile regis*.

The history of the Glasgow manuscript (51) can be worked out in nearly the same way. The text of the Vox is in one hand. The text of the *Cronica*, colophon (Fairfax version), and laureate and other poems, ff. 109–131, is in a second hand. But in the midst of this continuation, on f. 129, are the miniatures of Gower's arms and a tomb, and epitaphs that appear on Gower's tomb. Presumably, since the Fairfax colophon is used, the additions were being made while Gower was still alive. But the tomb and epitaphs must have been inserted at the time of his death, in 1408, and the final pieces (including *Presul, ouile regis*) then added in the same hand that had been at work while Gower was alive. We could hardly ask for better evidence than this that the scribes turning out these manuscripts were very intimately associated with Gower at the time of his death—that they were, indeed, the brothers in St. Mary's Priory. MSS. Tiberius A.iv (52) and Harleian (53) must not have been quite so far along as Glasgow when Gower died, and so the scribes were able to substitute the "dum vixit" paragraph in the colophon for "dum tempus instat."

MS. Huntington, Hm. 150 (54) is apparently an independent copy from the same authority as MSS. 50–53, but made before the *Cronica Tripertita* was added to the text. Its readings agree closely with, but are independent of 52. Although it is a fine manuscript, there are no corrections as in the other four to suggest that it was in the hands of the author. Like 51 and 52, it contains the miniature of the archer shooting at the world, well executed but in a pose quite different from the other two. It does not contain the colophon, the laureate group, or *Presul, ouile regis,* so it could date from any time between the revision of the *Vox* (ca. 1392) and the accession of Henry IV in 1399.

Aside from MSS. 50–53, MS. Trinity College Dublin, D.4.6 (58), is the only manuscript of the *Vox* that contains the colophon. This manuscript is in a 15th-century hand, with only the simplest initials and without erasure or correction. Yet it lacks the *Cronica,* and both text and colophon are the earliest versions.[60] Clearly, this is a late, commercial copy of a version of the *Vox* dating from about 1390 after the colophon describing all three works had been composed, but before either the *Vox* or the colophon had been revised in the light of Gower's changed political opinions. The Hatfield manuscript (59), which likewise presents the unrevised text, may be a more sumptuous copy of the same original.

Another variation is to be found in MS. Laud 719 (56). Like 58, it is in an early 15th-century hand, but it is noteworthy in that it omits not only the *Cronica* but also the text of Book I on the Peasants' Revolt, numbering the books I–VI instead of I–VII. As we shall see, there is internal evidence that the *Visio* of the Peasants' Revolt was added after Books II–V had been written. The picture of the archer, crudely drawn but following the pose of 51–52, is here prefaced to Book III. The text is mixed; some of the readings are original and others revised, and at one point (VI.1159–1200) it includes both versions, the second written right after the first. Hence, if this manuscript is by any chance a late copy of a ca. 1380 version of the Vox, it was partially revised from a post-1392 text, and one of the laureate poems, *H. aquile pullus*, was added in the same hand that wrote the rest of the manuscript. Part of the problem is that Laud presents substantially the same text as MS. Digby 138 (55), likewise of the mid-15th century, but including all of the Vox. Digby does not include the drawing of the archer, but the "Ad mundum mitto" epitaph that accompanies it is jotted down among cooking recipes and aphoristic lines from the Vox on the blank pages at the end. This shows that a later reader had an opportunity to compare 55 with 51, 52, or 56. Macaulay's conclusion (4.lxviii) is quite safe. The source of 55 and 56 either had the first book and 56 chose to suppress it, or else did not have the first book and 55 took it from another copy. MS. Lincoln Cathedral 72 (57) is copied from 56, and MS. Cotton Titus, A.xiii (60), from 55.

The versions of the *Vox Clamantis* may, therefore, be identified as **a, b,** and **c** (see the stemma in Appendix A). Version **a** would represent a hypothetical pre-1381 version composed essentially of Books II–V of the present text. Version **b** is that produced between 1381 and 1386 in which the *Visio* of the Peasants' Revolt and the Epistle to the King in Book VI were added. Version **c** is a revision of **b** begun after 1390 and not completed until after 1399, in which the *Cronica Tripertita* was added and the allusions to Richard II revised.

The only external evidence for the existence of a version of the Vox lacking the *Visio* is the Laud manuscript (56) discussed above, whose testimony is impeached by its revised readings and kinship to Digby (55). Yet it is a fact that the structure of the poem suggests that Book I is a later addition.[61] The initial heading, "Incipit cronica qui Vox Clamantis dicitur" (Macaulay 4.20), was evidently composed under the influence of the *Cronica Tripertita* addition of the c version. The headnote proper does not mention the title. That first appears in the headnote to Book II, which even though it has been adapted to refer back to the *Visio* has the tone of a preliminary announcement: "et vocat libellum istum Vox Clamantis, quia de voce et clamore quasi omnium conceptus est" (and he calls the book *Vox Clamantis*, which is composed as by universal voice and clamor, Macaulay 4.82). The name appears first in the text at II, Prol. 83, set again in a passage that was composed or adapted to refer to visions, presumably the *Visio*, as the motive for the rest of the book. The length of the various books is likewise significant. I is 2150 lines; II, 630; III, 2142; IV, 1232; V, 1016; VI, 1366; and VII, 1481. In this series, II appears to be more nearly the length of a prologue than of a book. Only Books I, II, and III have prologues as they now stand, and the tone of the prologue to III is that of the opening of the whole discussion. Furthermore, it is noteworthy that after the impassioned emotionalism of Book I, the Peasants' Revolt is not mentioned throughout the rest of the poem.

Book III presents the first revised passage in the poem. In the unrevised version (MSS. 58–59), the book begins by naming the Three Estates and then launches directly into general criticism of the vanity of prelates. In the revised version (MSS. 50–57, including 56—Laud—which is one of its problems), immediately after the Estates, the Great Schism of 1378 is cited as the first example of the corruption of the clergy. At the conclusion of the discussion of the clergy, end of Book IV, the revised version again returns to the Schism, while the first version does not.[62] As Maria Wickert has pointed out, it is inconceivable that Gower, with his passion for social unity and order, could have failed to mention the Schism in the first version if he had been writing after it occurred. Thus, on the basis of several kinds of evidence, we are led to conclude that Gower was writing his criticisms of the estates in Vox II–V and the *Mirour* at nearly the same time.

What possible motive could he have had for composing the two discussions in different languages simultaneously? As we observed before, the *Mirour* began as a private, devotional document and only gradually led Gower into social criticism. Although several times he asserted that he was not speaking from firsthand experience, but reporting common knowledge,[63] he did not in the *Mirour* adopt the role of universal spokesman implied by the title *Vox Clamantis*, asserted in the headnote to Book II ("de voce et clamare quasi omnium") and repeated again and again throughout the text:

> I write of present-day evils of which the common
> voice of mankind outwardly complains in this country.
> . . . I intend my words of good to bring evil to light.
>   (VC, III.Prol.55)
> Nothing I write is my own opinion. Rather I shall
> speak what the voice of the people has reported to me.
>   (VC, IV.19)
> I cry out what the voice of the people cries out.
>   (VC, VI.15) [64]

In the *Mirour* (12725) he quoted the proverb *Vox populi, vox Dei*, but when he returns to it in the *Vox*, after repeated assertions that he is voicing universal complaint, it falls with a different effect:

> *Vox populi cum voce dei concordat, vt ipsa*
> *In rebus dubiis sit metuenda magis.* (VC, III.1267)

> (The voice of the people agrees with the voice of God, so that in critical times it ought to be held in greater awe.)

And again at the conclusion of the poem:

> *Quod scripsi plebis vox est, set et ista videbis,*
> *Quo clamat populus, est ibi sepe deus.* (VC, VII.1469)

> (What I have written is the voice of the people, but you will also see that where the people cry out, God is often there.)

This universal voice, the voice of the Old Testament prophets, is the mode of perception and expression that distinguishes medieval complaint from classical satire. In the next chapter we shall observe the way in which it connects Gower's writings with the medieval homiletic tradition, and in the fifth chapter the generalized voice of complaint and the individualized voice of satire will help account for Gower's and Chaucer's different treatment of similar materials. In addition to its stylistic significance, however, the notion of the universal voice had political overtones in the 14th-century struggle toward parliamentary sovereignty. In the *Historia Anglicana*, Walsingham reported that when Edward III replaced the deposed Edward II on the throne, the Archbishop of Canterbury preached on the text Vox *populi, vox Dei*,[65] and Gower's own *Cronica Tripertita* emphasizes that popular and parliamentary opinion played an important part in the fall of Richard II. In O *Deus immense*, Gower warned Richard just before his fall, "Ad vocem plebis aures sapienter habebis" (You should have wiser ears for the voice of the people, Macaulay 4.363). The repeated assertion of this idea throughout the Vox *Clamantis* would appear to indicate that this piece represented the public counterpart to the contemplation in the *Mirour*.

This purpose helps to account for the fact that the Vox was written in Latin. Gower was not, like Langland or the Lollards, a demagogue. He was adopting the opposite role, that of transmitting popular complaints to influential authority. This authority could hardly be either the unsound King or his child successor. There is no evidence that Gower as yet had any direct contact with the court. In 1377, he would have been more likely to address his admonitions to such influential clerics as William of Wykeham, Bishop of Winchester and a leading figure in the opposition to John of Gaunt, whose London palace, it will be recalled, adjoined St. Mary Overeys; William Courtenay, Bishop of London, Wykeham's ally; Simon Sudbury, Archbishop of Canterbury, whose murder Gower condemned so violently in the Vox; Thomas Brunton, Bishop of Rochester and royal confessor; Ralph Erghum, Bishop of Salisbury and Gaunt's chancellor and ally; and others of the "Caesarian" clergy.[66] The All Souls manuscript of the Vox went eventually to just such a recipient, Thomas of Arundel, in 1373 Bishop of Ely, active on the side of the Appellant Lords in 1386, made Archbishop of Canterbury in 1396, banished from England by Richard in 1397, only to return in triumph with Henry whose coronation he engineered and performed in 1399.[67] Even if Gower could not speak directly to the great prelates, he might at least hope to communicate with their underlings. The bitter invective in the *Mirour* (20250ff) against the way clerks swarmed to monopolize offices in court is probably a fairly accurate picture of a time in which "of the two great departments of government the Chancery was entirely clerical, while the Exchequer was rapidly tending in the same direction." [68] The fact that the shortcomings of the clerics themselves receive such disproportionate attention in the *Vox* (two books, III and IV, vs. one, V, for knights, peasants, merchants, and artisans, and one, VI, for lawyers and the king) is merely another evidence of its clerical audience. Latin was to be for a long time yet the language of serious political discussion as well as of theology and philosophy. Gower's audience for the *Vox* would have been the same as that for Wyclif's Latin tracts, or for John of Salisbury, Henry of Bracton, Thomas Favent, and Sir John Fortescue.

If we hypothesize that the criticism of the estates in the *Mirour* and *Vox* dates from nearly the same time, around 1377, we find less surprising the close resemblances between their treatments of all of the estates except that of the king. Indeed, the warning against a possible uprising of the peasants, quoted above from the *Mirour*, is virtually repeated in the *Vox* with no indication that it is any more imminent:

> [The serf and the day laborer grumbles] that he doesn't like cooked foods much, unless you give him some roast. Neither weak beer nor cider is of any use to him, and he will not return tomorrow unless you provide something better. O why should a man whom water drawn from a well has nourished since birth demand such delicious drinks? Born of a poor man's stock and a poor man himself, he demands things for his belly like a lord. The established law is no help to one, for there is no ruling such

men, nor does any one make provision against their misdeeds. This is a race without power of reason, like beasts, for it does not esteem mankind nor does it think God exists. I believe that in a short time the lords will submit to them, unless justice shall have been obtained by means of fear. (VC, v.641)

Such lines must have been written before the event. They echo the reason and beast arguments of the *Mirour* directly. But before Gower had brought his Latin poem to conclusion, the event he so direly predicted came to pass, and the piece had to be altered to take account of it. The heading of the Prologue of Book 1 echoes the language of the predictions in both the *Mirour* and the Vox:

In the begining of this work, the author intends to describe how the lowly peasants violently revolted against the freemen and nobles of the realm. And since an event of this kind was as loathsome and horrible as a monster, he reports that in a dream he saw various throngs of the rabble transformed into different kinds of domestic animals. (VC, 1.Prol. headnote)

Presumably in the part of the poem composed before 1381, Gower had not got to the estate of kingship in Book VI, or if he had he discarded it in favor of a more timely discussion. His criticism of lawyers at the beginning of the book echoes in detail their criticism in the *Mirour*, although their context here betrays the emergence of the thematic development which will be traced in the next chapter. But the Epistle to the King appears to ride upon the national approbation of the young monarch's behavior at Mile End and Smithfield. "Stes magis, o pie Rex, domito sublimis in orbe" (May you stand sublime in a vanquished world, O blessed King, VC, VI.1183*), Gower exclaims in the peroration. Whether the fact that the Epistle has its own introduction (VC, VII.viii headnote) and conclusion (VC, VI.xviii end) is evidence that it was composed to stand alone it is impossible to say, but it seems clearly to mirror the public reaction to Richard's rule foreshadowing the Parliament of 1386, just as the criticism of the peasants in the *Mirour* and Book v of the Vox foreshadow the Peasants' Revolt. "A mob of flatterers proceeds to the forefront of the royal court," the Epistle commences, "and the court banishes those who dare speak the truth . . . No greediness ought to have power to tarnish your reputation; instead all people should rejoice in your generosity" (VC, vi.551*, 1807). After 1382, Richard's grants to his favorites, such as the effeminate Robert de Vere, Michael de la Pole, and Simon Burley, brought his treasury to bankruptcy. The crown itself and other jewels were pledged to the city of London for a loan. The efforts of the Lancastrian chancellor, Richard Scrope, to put a brake on Richard's ill-advised generosity resulted only in his dismissal from office.[69]

"O king, banish your indolence, withstand your carnal passions, and stoutly take the path of righteousness . . . It is also your concern to be your people's defender in arms. And in order to defend justice with valor, remember your father's deeds as a model for this" (VC, vi.841, 917). "Richard possessed a sensitive, and far from unintelligent, but at the same time lazy and profoundly conventional mind," writes Anthony Steel, and he goes on to infer that one of the psychological problems that eventually led to his breakdown was his being admonished that to be a great king, he must be a great knight like his father when he was physically incapable of becoming a great knight.[70] Line for line, the facts and opinions in Gower's Epistle can be paralleled in the chronicles and histories of the period between 1382 and 1386; and the actions of the Parliament of 1386 in dismissing Suffolk as chancellor and John Fordham, Bishop of Durham, as treasurer indicate that they agreed with Gower that "The boy is free of blame" (VC, vi.555*), having been led astray by bad counsel.[71] Chapter xii against letting himself be corrupted by lust and petticoat rule reflects the conventional accusation that tyrants violated the wives and daughters of their subjects,[72] but also the very real experiences of the last years of Edward III.

The **b** version of the Vox may, then, be taken to date from about 1386. It includes Book i in reaction to the Peasants' Revolt, and the Epistle in Book vi addressed to the young monarch in terms of affection and hope.[73] As we shall see, the Confessio Amantis must have been begun about the same time and completed by 1390. When the *Confessio* was done, or nearly done, the first version of the colophon was composed to go with both it and the *Vox*. The allusions to the King in the first version of the colophon echo closely the first version of the Epistle:

> *Innocenciam tamen* dicti domini *Regis tunc*
> *minoris etatis causa* inde *excusabilem* pronuncians.
> (Colophon, Bodl. 902)

> De erroribus *tamen* et iniuriis modo contingentibus
> *innocenciam Regis* nostri, *minoris etatis causa,*
> quantum *ad presens excusat.* (VC, vi.vii headnote)

IV

When the first version of the colophon was composed, the Peasants' Revolt loomed in Gower's mind as the most important feature of the *Vox*. When the Fairfax version was composed, all mention of the Revolt had disappeared, and the piece was instead described as dealing with the bad rule and fall of Richard. Since there is nothing in the *Vox* proper about the fall of Richard, this final version of the colophon must have been composed with the *Cronica Tripertita* principally in mind. The *Cronica* is Lancastrian propaganda under the guise of history. The first part, treating the events of 1387–88 just after the *Vox* had been finished, commences by voicing one of the major themes of Gower's political philosophy as we shall see it unfolding in the next chapter, "the causes of the kingdom's being divided against itself" (*Cron.* i headnote). In about 1387 Gower was making the evils of divisiveness the major theme of the Prologue to the *Confessio*, but the estimate of Richard expressed in the *Cronica* is very different from that of the first versions of the *Vox*, the *Confessio*, and the colophon.

"The king always had an obdurate heart" the *Cronica* begins (1.13), and it goes on to give the political struggle with the Appellant Lords an interpretation completely prejudicial to Richard. Again, the parallels in the contemporary chronicles and modern

histories document every detail in the poem. The livery and cog-
nizance by which the Appellants are identified resemble those in a
popular lampoon of 1398 printed in Wright's *Political Poems*.[74]
In both the lampoon and the *Cronica*, the Swan is Thomas of
Woodstock, Earl of Gloucester and leader of the Appellants; the
Bear, Thomas Beauchamp, Earl of Warwick; and the Horse, Richard, Earl of Arundel (brother of Thomas to whom the All Souls
manuscript was presented and *in capite* owner of Gower's manor of
Feltwell). Gower adds the Wreathed Feather, Thomas Moubray,
Earl of Nottingham (scion of the Yorkshire house with whom Robert Gower and the Langbargh Gowers were connected); "he who
wore S," the Earl of Derby, future King Henry IV; and the Northern Moon, Henry Percy, Earl of Northumberland. Only the two
leading figures on the King's side are given figurative designations:
Richard himself, "the shadowy one who bore the sun"; and Robert
de Vere, Earl of Oxford, the Boar. The King's other supporters are
referred to directly: Michael de la Pole, Simon Burley, John Beauchamp, Nicholas Brembel (Brembre), Richard Tresilian, and un-
named bishops and judges. The familiar events of the rebellion of
the Appellants are reviewed: the raising of the Cheshire archers,[75]
the battle of Radcot Bridge,[76] the interview between the Lords
Appellant and Richard in the Tower,[77] and the proceedings of the
Merciless Parliament of 1388 [78] are summarized fully. The King's
party are throughout called greedy, treacherous plotters, and the
Appellants model Englishmen.[79]

The second part of the *Cronica* skips to 1397, when Richard took
his revenge for the Merciless Parliament. Again the account, although couched in hyperbolic praise and blame, is circumstantial.
The Swan, the Horse, and the Bear are loyal supporters of the
Crown, but "the King, more cunning than a fox, plotted tricks with
constant deceitfulness in order to entrap the nobles through an
agreement of feigned peace." [80] The betrayal of Arundel and Warwick,[81] the seizure of Gloucester at Pleshy,[82] the proceedings of the
Parliament of 1397,[83] the murder of Gloucester,[84] the execution of
Arundel,[85] the banishments of Warwick, Cobham, and the Arch-

bishop of Canterbury,[86] and the excesses of Scrope, Bushy, and Green [87] are all recounted.

The last part of the *Cronica* begins by deploring the tyrannous "committee" rule of Richard's last year; [88] and then it goes on to recount the exile and return of Henry,[89] the Lancastrian slander of Richard's flight to Ireland,[90] Henry's triumphant reception,[91] the capture of Richard,[92] and the Parliaments of September 29–30 and October 6 at which Richard was deposed and Henry elected king.[93] Gower's acute awareness of the legal implications of the struggles of both 1388 and 1399 is of especial significance in view of the political theory underlying the argument of his major poems. The central issue as deduced by later historians was the extent to which the courts and parliament were independent of the king. The constitutional theory embodied in the sermons by Thomas of Arundel to the two Parliaments makes even more significant the dedication of the All Souls manuscript. Anthony Steel has observed that the second sermon shows something approaching a true understanding of parliamentary sovereignty.[94] Bracton had asserted that justice, respect for law, and respect for property were essential to kingship, but that if the king breaks the law only God can punish him. Arundel went beyond this to assert that Parliament can make and unmake law against the king's will, as it had in 1388 and was doing again. Therefore, by implication more than by direct assertion, the king was under God and Parliament. As we shall see in the next chapter, Gower expressed Bracton's point of view on kingship in the *Vox* proper, and progressed a little beyond it at the end of the *Confessio Amantis.* Here at the end of the *Cronica* he came closest to expressing the significance of the legal situation in his emphasis upon the continuity of the Parliament before and after Henry's election,[95] and its "declaring fully valid those things which the Bear, the Horse, and the Swan had recently done [in 1388], and rejecting those things which Richard had done through perverse, overbearing, and treacherous guile" (*Cron.* III.365). This is as far as he went. The *Cronica* concludes with the version of Richard's death found in the St. Albans Chronicle, that, melancholy at the failure of the rebellion of Kent, Salisbury, and others at Cirencester in January of 1400, he deliberately starved himself to death.[96]

All of this is what Gower had in mind when he wrote the version of the colophon found in the All Souls and Fairfax manuscripts. Since the condemnation of Richard begins in the first lines of the *Cronica,* it could not have been begun much before 1399, nor could it have been completed until after Richard's death in February 1400. This in turn raises the question of the date and motive for the changes in the *Vox* proper. Aside from the introduction of the references to the Great Schism, these changes are the rewriting of the introduction and conclusion to the Epistle to the King (VI.545–580, VI.1159–1200), and of three lines at the very end of the poem (VII.1479–81). In the earlier version of the introduction and conclusion to the Epistle, the young king is personally absolved and the misfortunes of the nation blamed on the "curia maior" (high court, VC, VI.547*), presumably the "continual council" of twelve appointed to carry on the government after 1377, or the two guardians, Arundel and Suffolk, and their great council which succeeded the continual council after 1381.[97] "If the King were of mature age, he would set right the scale which is now without justice" (VC, VI.559*), Gower asserted hopefully. At the end of the Epistle, the headnote to Cap. xviii states that "he prays devoutly in behalf of the King's position, that God may preserve his bloom of youth in all abundance," and the text of the chapter itself was revised into the cloying *Rex celi deus* of the laureate group when it was removed from the *Vox.*

Here, as with the *Confessio Amantis,* the mechanics of Gower's revision are curiously akin to those in revising a printed book. In the four presentation manuscripts (50–53), in the introduction thirty-six lines were scraped out and replaced by thirty-six lines of new text in another hand. In three of the manuscripts (51–53), the first eight or ten lines of the new text are written in a distinctly smaller script than the regular text, as though the scribe were not sure that he could get it all in, and after that the reviser's hand grows as large or larger than the hand in the regular text. At the end of the Epistle, forty lines of text were erased and replaced by forty-two new lines. To accommodate the extra two lines, the heading of Cap. xix had to be erased and rewritten in thirty-five words instead of the original forty-nine. None of the other manuscripts containing the revised text (54–57) shows this sort of revision in process.

The sentiments of the revised passages are much like those of the *Cronica Tripertita*. The Epistle had originally shown real feeling for the young monarch. "O you of tender years," Gower had then written, "your age does not allow of your being capable of deceitfulness, and your noble birth is opposed to your debasing yourself" (VC, vi.845). But the *Cronica* takes as its text: "Rex induratum cor semper habet . . . Stultorum vile sibi consilium iuuenile/ Legerat . . ." (The King always had an obdurate heart . . . He took the base, youthful advice of fools . . . . , *Cron.* 1.13), and the revised introduction to the Epistle begins: "Rex, puer indoctus, morales negligit actus" (The King, an undisciplined boy, neglects moral behavior, VC, vi.555). The revision increases from five to twelve the number of references to the youthful counsel by which the King is misled.[98] In addition, "there are older men who in pursuing their gains tolerate many scandals for the boy's pleasure" (VC, vi.565). This has the ring of Oxford, Suffolk, and Simon Burley again, but viewed from the perspective of 1397 rather than from the perspective of 1381. The revised introduction concludes with enigmatic warnings as to the King's fate. To a boy misbehavior "is not wrongdoing but joking, not dishonor but glorious sport, but his destiny springs out of this wrongdoing" (VC, vi.571). "A mother does not know the fate designed for her child, but in the end every secret is clearly revealed" (VC, vi.575). This latter suggests the one sentence preserved from the lecture Joan of Kent gave her son in January 1385, which will be discussed in the last chapter in connection with the date and inspiration for the *Legend of Good Women* and *Confessio Amantis*. According to Adam of Usk's report: "The King . . . promised that he would willingly be guided by the counsel of the twelve. To whom his mother replied, 'At thy coronation, my son, I rejoiced that it had fallen to my lot to be the mother of an anointed king; but now I grieve for I foresee the fall which threatens thee, the work of accursed flatterers.' " [99] The conclusion to the Epistle has been changed from a warm prayer for the prosperity and long life of the young king to a stern warning that unless he mends his ways, he cannot expect to continue his rule. "The royal majesty is venerated above all as long as the king governs the affairs of his kingdom honorably . . . [but] there is a cry nowdays among the people that because the law is failing, wrongdoing is becoming its own justification" (VC, vi.1159, 1179).

In its final form, as Macaulay observed,[1] the Vox Clamantis and Cronica Tripertita thus become a unified commentary on the tragic course of Richard's rule from 1381 to 1400, with a prologue (the Visio), a midpoint (the Epistle), and an epilogue (the Cronica). Gower was evidently aware of this unity when he revised the last lines of the Vox, replacing "Every man alive should withstand evil. I am the worst of all, but may the Maker of the World grant me relief through His spirit" by "Every man alive should withstand evil. Indeed, when the great guilt by which virtue is corrupted is not purged but is instead continued, it deserves the bad fate which in the end is given it." And in the four presentation manuscripts he added a colophon connecting the Cronica with the Vox in which the full scheme is outlined:

> Here ends the book which is entitled Vox Clamantis issued especially concerning the period of great misfortune in England, which, as you have heard, befell the unfortunate Richard II at the beginning of his reign, ostensibly as from the rod of God. And furthermore, since he was not remorseful for this, but was instead hardened to the tyrant's ways, he did not desist from incessantly scourging his kingdom with constant oppressions until he deservedly underwent the scourge of divine vengeance, even to the extreme of his own deposition. (Macaulay 4.313)

The optimistic view of Richard in the first version of the Epistle had not shown him "hardening into the tyrant's ways," and so it had had to be altered to reflect the tone of the prologue and to foreshadow the conclusion.

There is no doubt that in 1400 Gower intended the *Vox* and *Cronica* to be viewed as a continuous work. But this does not date for us the evolution either of the two pieces or of the point of view they embody. Maria Wickert argues convincingly that the similarity between the judgments on Richard in the revised Epistle and in the *Cronica* indicate that the revisions in the *Vox* were made in 1400 when the *Cronica* was written. But against this chronology stands the evidence of manuscripts 54–55, which have the revisions in the Epistle and last three lines of the *Vox* without the prose transition or the *Cronica,* and of the Hatton manuscript (61) which contains the *Cronica* without the *Vox.* The two pieces were not regarded as inseparable, and we have evidence enough of Gower's prescience concerning the Peasants' Revolt to suppose that he might have written lines predicting some sort of bad end for Richard several years before the event. As we shall see in the next chapter, the architectonic development of Gower's major themes embraces the *Mirour, Vox,* and *Confessio.* Into this broad, philosophical discourse, the very specific account in the *Cronica* will not fit. At best, it is an exemplum or addendum. However, since this thematic development is independent of the passages that Gower altered, it offers no evidence concerning the dates of the revisions in the *Vox.* All that we are entitled to conclude is that by the time of Richard's deposition, Gower had become thoroughly disillusioned about his reign. Reflecting this disillusionment and predicting his fall, Gower made changes in the *Vox.* To defend the Lancastrian usurpation, he wrote the *Cronica.* In the four manuscripts that we know were in his hands between 1400 and 1408, he provided a prose transition explaining Richard's rule from 1381 to 1399 as a cumulative catastrophe in exactly the terms Henry would most have liked to have it viewed.[2]

V

The question as to whether Gower's view of Richard altered before the cataclysm of 1399 must, therefore, turn upon the textual history of the *Confessio Amantis* rather than of the *Vox Clamantis*. The *Confessio* comes down to us in forty-nine manuscripts in three versions, whose most distinctive features were quoted in the first chapter for their bearing on Gower's reputation. The first version, attributing the poem to the meeting with Richard (CA, Prol. 24–92*) and ending with the allusion to Chaucer and final dedication to the King (CA, VIII.2941–3114*) is actually found in eleven manuscripts.[3] Presumably, although by no means certainly, it was found in twenty other manuscripts now lacking the leaves on which one or both of the passages would be found.[4] Of these thirty-one manuscripts, fourteen conclude with the earliest version of the colophon,[5] and nine others now lacking the final folios may once have done likewise.[6] Six manuscripts which appear to be complete have no final colophon.[7] Most copies of this version have beside line 331 of the Prologue a Latin sidenote dating a criticism of the Schism as "Anno domini Millesimo CCC° Nonagesimo," or 1390. This would appear to set a date before which the first version cannot have been completed. However, a poem so long must have been some time in process, and, as we shall see in the last chapter, the account of the meeting with Richard in the Prologue and the allegorical portions of Book I (lines 1–288) and Book VIIII (lines 2149–2940) are closely related to Chaucer's *Legend of Good Women* and appear to date from about 1385.

None of the manuscripts of the first version have been considered contemporary with Gower. They are dated by Macaulay and the catalogs as from "early" to "mid" and even "late" 15th century. Most of them are handsome, expensive manuscripts, illuminated in the same style as those prepared under Gower's own supervision. Presumably they were copied from an exemplar or exemplars produced shortly after 1390. Just how or why so many of this early, politically embarrassing, version should have been produced after

Richard's deposition remains a question. Indeed—and this generalization applies to the manuscripts of all three versions—if the Trentham, *Mirour,* and six manuscripts of the *Confessio* and *Vox Clamantis* so identified by Macaulay (33, 40, 50–53) can be taken as
products of Gower's own scriptorium (that is, surely, the scriptorium of St. Mary Overeys), there seems to my untutored eye no
reason why a good many of the other manuscripts that do not have
the marks of authorial revision which characterize the latter six,
and are dated purely on the basis of script and illumination, could
not have been produced in the same scriptorium between 1390 and
1399.[8] I do not urge this point in the face of more competent pale-
ographical authority; I merely suggest it as a solution to an otherwise embarrassing question. At any rate, the manuscripts of the
early version of the *Confessio* (1–32)[9] resemble those of the
early version of the *Vox* (55–59) in that they were produced in a
situation more independent of the author's supervision than the
later versions. Around 1390, it would appear, Gower was making or
releasing copies of his poems more casually than he did later in the
decade, when he had become politically involved with the Lancastrian cause.

On the evidence of corrections in the text and revisions which
smooth the meter, Macaulay distinguished three stages of the first
version, indicating that the manuscripts were copied from three exemplars, or the same exemplar in three stages of correction.[10] These
changes, important for the establishment of a good text, have no
bearing on Gower's literary career. The first substantive revision
appears to have occurred within a year or so after the completion
of the first version. The allusion to Chaucer and praise of Richard
at the end of the poem were excised (164 lines) and replaced by a
generalized conclusion to the dream allegory and a prayer for the
state of England (232 lines). This last is dated by a Latin sidenote
found in some manuscripts of both the second and third versions:
"Hic in anno quarto-decimo Regis Ricardi orat pro statu regni"
(CA, VIII.2975 margin).[11] The fourteenth year of Richard's reign
extended from June 21, 1390, to June 21, 1391. This is the period

when Gower would have had least cause to change his opinion of
the King. Tout stresses that "sound government, domestic and external peace, and remission of taxation seemed at once to flow from
the assumption by the young king of the duties of his office" in
1389.[12] The honeymoon lasted through 1390 and 1391. But in 1392
came Richard's famous quarrel with the city of London.[13] In February of that year, more hard pressed than usual for money, he tried
to enforce the law compelling every citizen worth 10£. or more in
real property to take up knighthood. This the citizens were reluctant to do because of the feudal obligations the honor carried
with it (we recall the defiant "armiger" on Gower's own tomb).
Their sheriffs replied that the statute was impossible to enforce because of the fluctuations in property values. The King next re-
quested a "voluntary" loan. This, too, the city refused. Then,
according to the chroniclers, the King turned for money to a Lombard merchant, only to learn that the citizens were willing to
advance the Lombard the money they had refused him. Whatever
the cause, as Tout says, "Richard lost both his temper and his
sense of proportion." In May the Chancery, Exchequer, and Common Bench were ordered to York, where they remained until the
following January. On June 25, 1392, at the beginning of "the yer
sextenthe of Kyng Richard" (CA, Prol.25) the mayor of London,
the sheriffs, and aldermen were arrested and fined 3000£., and the liberties of the city were suspended until it should pay the enormous
fine of 100,000£. The citizens were forced to capitulate. An elaborate reception was given for Richard as he moved north in August.
Through the intercession of the Queen and the promise of a "gift"
of 10,000£., the liberties of the city were restored on September 19.
All seemed to be well, but it is certain that this episode gravely
prejudiced the Londoners against Richard. In the crisis of 1397–99,
unlike that of 1386–88, he had no party whatever in the city on his
side, and seventeen of the citizens who were sentenced in 1392 were
among the aldermen who welcomed Henry of Lancaster in 1399.

This would seem ample reason for Gower to have altered the
conclusion to the *Confessio*. His sympathies would have lain en-

tirely with his personal and business associates, the London citizens. The mayor who was suspended in June was of the Gower-Chaucer circle. He was the draper John Hende, for whom Chaucer and Strode had acted as securities a decade before.[14] The pageantry of the grand reconciliation between Richard and the citizens began just outside St. Mary Overeys, at Bridge Gate in Southwark.[15] Gower could hardly have escaped sharing the lingering distrust the episode engendered. How then could he continue to speak of

> Richard by name the Secounde,
> In whom hath evere yit be founde
> Justice medled with pite,
> Largesce forth with charite . . .
> For he yit nevere unpitously
> Ayein the liges of his lond,
> For no defaute which he fond,
> Thurgh cruelte vengaunce soghte. (CA, viii.2987*)

The epitome of a responsible state which Gower substituted in the revision caps the impressive coherence of his trilogy much more effectively than did the encomium on Richard. Undoubtedly there were sound artistic reasons for the change, as there were to be for the changes in the Prologue. But it is in keeping with Gower's method that his literary design should grow directly out of his re-actions to the political events of his day.

The same political tensions provide an explanation for the excision of the Chaucer allusion along with the praise of Richard. It may strike us as odd for Tout to cite Chaucer as an example of an "ejected favourite creeping back into office" or "an old courtier being cautiously given preferment" when he was appointed Clerk of the King's Works in 1389.[16] But this may well be how it appeared to the King's parliamentary opponents. In January 1391 Chaucer relinquished the clerkship, but he obviously continued in the expectation of royal favor. In January 1393 he was granted 10£. "for good service rendered to the king in the year now present." [17] There was no reason for Gower to endanger Chaucer's position with the King by associating him even remotely with his own decision to excise the fulsome praise of Richard at the end of the *Confessio*. Viewed in this light, the excision was an act of consideration.

The only difficulty in taking Richard's quarrel with London as the occasion for the change in the conclusion to the *Confessio* is that it conflicts with the date attached to the revision. The fourteenth year of Richard, June 21, 1390–91, is a year before the events that occurred in the summer of 1392. No other event in this period satisfies the internal and external requirements nearly so well as this, and I am reluctant to relinquish it as an explanation. One possibility is that the date in the revised conclusion was intended to correspond with the 1390 in the Prologue rather than with the date of the time of the revision. If Gower intended to expunge the former conclusion, he might have predated the revision to make it appear to correspond in time with the Prologue. It is noteworthy that in the final version the date in the Prologue is eliminated.[18]

Furthermore, the whole notion of a distinct version of the *Confessio* with the original Prologue and revised conclusion is ill supported by the manuscripts. Only one manuscript of the second version (37) is so constituted; two others (35–36) may once have been. On the other hand, four manuscripts of this version (33–34, 38–39) agree with the final version in containing both the revised Prologue and conclusion. Indeed, the distinguishing characteristics of the intermediate version are not the introduction and conclusion, but internal additions and changes,[19] specifically (1) the addition of a passage on chastity at v.6395–6438*; (2) the addition of the tale of Lucius at v.7086–7210*; (3) the addition of the tale of the Jew and the Pagan at vii.3207–3360*;[20] (4) the omission of forty-six lines from the discussion of largesse, v.7701–46; and (5) the transposition of vi.665–964 to just after vi.1146. Since there is no discernible thread connecting these various changes, the best guess is that the manuscripts of the second version were copied from an exemplar in the midst of general revision (like the Fairfax, see below), for it is clear that Gower could not for long have intended the revised conclusion to stand with the unrevised Prologue.

So far, the question of Gower's relations to Henry of Lancaster has not needed to be raised. But unlike the revised conclusion, which reflected no more than displeasure with Richard, the revised Prologue announced a new allegiance. This revision is dated both in the text and in a Latin sidenote as the sixteenth year of King Richard (CA, Prol.24), or the year of June 21, 1392–93. It does not repudiate but simply omits reference to the meeting on the Thames at which Richard asked Gower to undertake the poem. In the ensuing lines, the purpose of the *Confessio* is pointed up more directly than it had been in the original. Again, whatever other motives Gower may have had for rewriting these lines, one of them was certainly the same as that for rewriting the conclusion: to make unmistakably clear the place of this final work in the coherent pattern evolved through the *Mirour* and *Vox*. The heart of this alteration is the substitution of these lines in the revision:

> Whan the prologe is so despended,
> This bok schal afterward ben ended
> Of love, which doth many a wonder
> And many a wys man hath put under.
> And in this wyse I thenke trete
> Towardes hem that now be grete,
> Betwen the vertu and the vice
> Which longeth unto this office. (CA, Prol.73)

for these lines in the original version:

> My kinges heste schal nought falle,
> That I, in hope to deserve.
> His thonk, ne schal his wil observe;
> And elles were I nought excused,
> For that thing may nought be refused
> Which that a king himselve bit. (CA, Prol.70*)

The revision is loftier and more assured in tone, and it emphasizes the *regimine principum* motif which underlies not only the structure of the *Confessio* proper, but Gower's entire trilogy. The revised passage concludes:

> This bok, upon amendment
> To stonde at his commandement,
> With whom myn herte is of accord,
> I sende unto myn oghne lord,
> Which of Lancastre is Henri named. (CA, Prol.83)

This was in 1393. We have already had two examples of Gower's prescience, in his accurate prognostication of the Peasants' Revolt and the fall of Richard. So we see him behaving characteristically as he transfers his dedication from Richard to his successor in the middle of the period of Richard's "good rule," when there could have been virtually no indication that Henry would succeed him on the throne. The behavior of Henry through the early nineties does not suggest that he was grasping for the crown. The house of Lancaster had from the beginning of his reign been Richard's staunchest support; Henry's adherence to the Appellants had evidently been patched up and he was on good terms with Richard. But Henry was the antithesis of Richard in the chivalry and largess that made a popular idol. Ever since he had led the Appellant forces from the battle of Radcot Bridge to camp in triumph in the fields outside Clerkenwell at Christmas in 1387, he had been the hero of the Londoners. By including him in the dedication of the *Confessio*, Gower was again merely displaying the sentiments of a London citizen.

Henry was out of the country during both of the years specified in the *Confessio Amantis*.[21] From June 20, 1390, to April 30, 1391, he was away on his first crusade in Prussia. And he left England in July 1392, at the height of Richard's quarrel with London, for another campaign in Prussia. But instead of providing assistance, his troops this time quarreled with the Germans, and by September Henry had given up the idea of a Prussian crusade. Sending most of his troops home, he embarked instead on a triumphant tour through eastern Europe and into the Holy Land, returning to England in July 1393. As we have seen, the order for the collar to replace the one Henry gave Gower is found among papers in the Duchy of Lancaster Miscellanea dated October and November 1393. We may therefore conclude that Gower wrote the revisions to the Prologue in the winter after Richard's quarrel with the Londoners and greeted Henry with the new dedication upon his return in the summer of 1393. The new dedication cannot in itself be considered an act of disloyalty to Richard since Henry had shared with Richard the dedication of the first version by being named in the explicit of at least eight manuscripts. To the four lines of Latin found in seven manuscripts of the first version,[22] expressing the hope that Gower's pages will prove a perpetual blessing to his countrymen, these eight add two lines later paraphrased in the text:

> *Derbeie Comiti, recolunt quem laude periti,*
> *Vade liber purus, sub eo requiesce futurus.* (Macaulay 3.478)
>
> (Go, dear book, to the Count of Derby, well considered by those versed in praise; upon him rest your future.)

These lines have been added to an exemplar of the first version dating from before June 1392. Double dedications are by no means uncommon in literary history. Karl Holzknecht called this one merely "the most notable case of a double dedication in England, at least in the early time." [23] But the fact that it was at once caught up in the partisan emotions surrounding the deposition of Richard has brought Gower's double dedication into question.

Macaulay suggested (2.xxvi) that the occasion for the change in dedication was the sending of a presentation copy of the *Confessio* to Henry, and that this would hardly amount to publication. "The author probably did not feel called upon publicly to affront the King by removing his name and praises, either at the beginning or end, from the copies generally issued during his reign." He goes on to remark, "Whether or not this conduct justifies the charge of time-serving timidity, which has been made against Gower, I cannot undertake to decide. He was, however, in fact, rather an opposite character, even pedantically stiff in passing judgment severely on those in high places, and not bating a syllable of what he thought proper for himself to say or for a king to hear, though while the King was young and might yet shake himself free from evil influences he was willing to take as favourable a view of his character as possible. Probably he was for some time rather of two minds about the matter, but in any case, 'timid and obsequious' are hardly the right epithets for the author of the Vox Clamantis." The tenor of this whole volume must stand as my support of the judgment that there was nothing timid or obsequious about Gower's alterations in either the Vox Clamantis or Confessio Amantis. The existence of thirty-two manuscripts of the first version as against seven of the second, and nine of the third all ultimately derived from the Fairfax (40), supports Macaulay's belief that the first continued to be the official version throughout Richard's reign. I have already indicated my belief that a good many of these thirty-two manuscripts were produced in the scriptorium of St. Mary Overeys during the decade of 1390–99.

The most interesting manuscript of the second version is Huntington El. 26. A.17 (33), illuminated with a version of the lion crest and ostrich feather recognizances of John of Gaunt and the swan that came to be associated with his son Henry. The absence of royal emblems indicates that it was prepared before the accession of Henry to the throne, but its actual recipient is not clear. The swan was the recognizance of Thomas, Duke of Gloucester, until his death in 1397, as indicated by Gower's use of that emblem for him in the Cronica. Henry is not supposed to have assumed the swan until after Thomas's death. But a combination of Lancaster and Gloucester markings in the same manuscript would be unusual. One would like to think that Henry had some claim upon the swan before 1397 and that this is the actual mauscript presented to him in the summer of 1393. In any case, it ranks with the Fairfax in elegance and correctness, and Macaulay lists it as one of the manuscripts prepared under Gower's own supervision.[24] From the same exemplar as 33, although not directly, came MSS. 34, 38, and 39. MS. 34 now lacks both the beginning and end, but it is in close textual agreement with 33. MS. 38 is greatly contaminated; not only does it insert the Chaucer allusion (*Chaucer* corrupted to *Cuther*) before the revised conclusion, but many of its individual readings are first version unrevised. MS. 39 is equally hard to classify, in that while it has the revised Prologue and conclusion, its treatment of the internal additions and transpositions is not at all clear.[25]

The "specialness" of MS. 33 is further indicated by the difference of its textual history from that of the other three manuscripts of the second version. On the one hand, MSS. 35, 36, and 37 present a version of the *Confessio* that must date before MS. 33 and the summer of 1393; on the other hand, they cannot have been completed before 1397, or possibly even 1408. MS. 37 has the revised conclusion and unrevised Prologue of the *Confessio* as it must have stood in the fall of 1392, after Richard's quarrel with London had led Gower to eliminate the praise of the King at the end but before he had rededicated the Prologue to Henry. MSS. 35–36, which now lack their opening folios, probably agreed with 37. Yet MSS. 36–37 and the contaminated MSS. 38–39 all four contain the version of the colophon which is most noncommittal about the contents of the *Vox* (i.e., dating from the mid-nineties, after the loss of faith in Richard but before his fall), but prefaced by the *dum vixit* paragraph suggesting that it was actually written down after his death.[26] The same four manuscripts add to the *Confessio* two of Gower's later poems, the *Traitié* followed by the Latin verses on his marriage (Macaulay 1.391), which could hardly have been written before late 1397, and the Latin *Carmen super multiplici viciorum pestilencia* (Macaulay 4.346) dated "anno regni Regis Ricardi Secundi vicesimo" or 1396–97. These pieces are likewise found in the Fairfax manuscript (40) and in MSS. 50–51 of the *Vox*. It cannot be without significance that MSS. 1–35 appear to have been copied from exemplars which contained the *Confessio* alone, and MSS. 36–49 from exemplars which contained pieces composed after 1397. In terms of composition as opposed to text, the manuscripts of the *Confessio* fall into three categories: 1–32, first version from three progressively revised exemplars of the period 1390–92; 33–35

from a special exemplar prepared for Henry's presentation manuscript; and 36–49 directly or ultimately from exemplars still lying
around Gower's scriptorium after 1400 when he was making a final
effort to organize and anthologize his collected works.

This final flurry of activity was probably precipitated by Henry's
accession to the throne. For some reason, the base text chosen for
the final version of the *Confessio Amantis* was the version of 1390–
92, without the additions of 1393. Any attempt to explain why is a
guess. Mine is that we have nothing more than the result of an
accident. Copies of the first version were plentiful; copies of the
second, as we have seen, scarce and full of problems; Gower himself was ill and blind. Some scribe or amanuensis simply grabbed
the copy that came first to hand, which became in due course the
Fairfax manuscript (40). Macaulay has given a full account of the
erasures and substitutions of leaves by which this manuscript was
converted from a first to a third version text.[27] Only he apparently
felt that both the Fairfax (40) and presentation manuscripts of
the *Vox* (50–51) underwent progressive revisions throughout the
1390's. This appears to me highly unlikely, for in none of these
cases are we dealing with an author's holograph—the work copy on
which he actually scratched over and wrote down. These manuscripts are all handsomely written, well illuminated, fair copies
made by professional scribes. The fact that several handwritings
can be discerned means no more than that several compositors
were involved. It is more reasonable to suppose that immediately after Henry's accession, Gower determined to produce new
versions of his French, Latin, and English works. He apparently
did not reissue the *Mirour*, but he prepared the Trentham manuscript of the *Cinkante Balades* and saw that the *Traitié* was attached to most of the other manuscripts. The new version of the
Latin involved writing and attaching the *Cronica* to the *Vox*, along
with the laureate and other shorter poems, and the version of the
colophon signalizing Richard's fall. The new version of the English
involved making an official edition of the text with the revised Prologue and conclusion which had been in existence for about seven

years. The small last-minute changes such as erasing the 1390 date
by Prol. 331 (but missing the one by vɪɪɪ.2972), improving the
famous lines "The beaute faye upon her face/ Non erthly thing it
may desface" (CA, ɪv.1321), changing a *Cuius* to *Eius* after vɪɪ.
1984, and the like are the sort that neither an author nor editor
ever finishes making. As with the V*ox Clamantis,* shorter French
and Latin poems and the version of the colophon signalizing Richard's fall were then added. That this was intended as the final official version is indicated by the fact that whereas only ᴍs. 33 of the
second version came out unequivocally with the new dedication to
Henry, at least five manuscripts (41–45) take their texts directly or
ultimately from the Fairfax (40). ᴍs. 46, evidently written expressly
for John Dedwood, in 1483 mayor of Chester, is a contaminated
text agreeing mainly with 40 but containing individual readings
from the first version unrevised. ᴍs. 47 is likewise of the Fairfax
version, but its independent readings and marginal collations with
the first version show exactly how contamination occurred. Any
later scribe using this as an exemplar would produce an impossibly
mixed text. ᴍs. 48 was copied from Caxton's edition (based upon
all three versions). And the Clumber manuscript (49), described
in Maggs Catalog 691 (May 1940) as the third version, I have been
unable to trace.

VI

The next chapter will be devoted to a consideration of the themes
and structure of Gower's major poems, and we have had occasion
already to say something about the French balades and the *Cronica
Tripertita.* We may here round out the discussion of Gower's works
by a brief comment on *In Praise of Peace* and the short Latin
poems that found their way into the manuscripts compiled about
1400 when Gower was setting his literary house in order. Of the
latter, the *Carmen super multiplici viciorum pestilencia, vnde tempore Ricardi Secundi partes nostre specialius inficiebantur*[28] is
dated in its headnote 20 Richard II, or June 21, 1396–97. George

Coffman, the only scholar who has given serious attention to the minor Latin poems,[29] suggested that it may be incomplete because, of "the many vices with which England was poisoned in the time of Richard II," only Lollardy, pride, concupiscence, and avarice are treated. But if Gower was up to his old tricks and intended once again to go through all the Deadly Sins, we have no indication of the fact, for in its present version the poem has a sound conclusion. Its immediate occasion would appear to have been the outbreak of Lollard activity which brought Richard back from his first Irish expedition in 1395 and the subsequent parliamentary efforts to suppress the movement in 1396 and 1397.[30] Gower's 17th-century reputation for religious bigotry may well have grown out of his re-actions to Lollardy in this poem, which would have been accessible to anyone who knew the *Confessio* or the *Vox* in fourteen of their best manuscripts in the colleges at Oxford and Cambridge and in such well-known collections as the Cottonian and Harleian.[31] In many of his opinions Gower saw eye to eye with the Wycliffites: in his criticism of the corrupting effect of temporal possessions upon the church, the vices of the mendicant orders, the injustices of the ecclesiastical courts, even the authority of the pope. But as the studies of Owst, Pantin, and others have made clear in recent years, Wyclif and the Lollards had no corner on criticism of the corrup-tion of the clergy.[32] There is not one of their social criticisms that cannot be paralleled by dozens of papal and episcopal decrees. Wyclif's central doctrine of dominion by grace is itself merely the development of a papalist argument. Gower was not a theologian. When he wrote "Papa potest falli" (the pope may err, VC, IV. 923), he was speaking, as we shall see in the next chapter, on an entirely different level from Wyclif in *De Potestate Papae* and *De Eucharistica*—on the level, that is, of *lex positiva*, or human law, as opposed to eternal natural law. He would never have dreamed of questioning the doctrine of papal infallibility properly understood as the final authority in matters of faith and doctrine. In the *Mirour* he had written:

L'estat du pape en sa nature	The estate of the pope by its nature
Ne porra faire forsfaiture	cannot make a mistake
En tant comme pape, ainz Innocent,	in anything papal, but Innocent,
Qui tient l'estat papal en cure,	who holds the papal estate in trust,
Cil puet mesfaire d'aventure.	he may perhaps do wrong.

(MO, 18781)

The horror he felt of the Lollards was the same as that he felt of the Peasants' Revolt, the antipathy of one whose whole world view was founded upon the concept of an ordered universe toward anything which would appear to disturb this order. The third line of the *Carmen* indicates that order, not theology, is the real concern of the poet: "Nescio quid signat, plebs celica iura resignat" (I don't know what it signifies that the common people reject heavenly law). When Wyclif is called a new Jovinian (line 32), it is because, like Satan in heaven, he sows seeds of rebellion against the authority of the church in the realm of faith and doctrine. In recognizing the concurrent authority of the church and state, Gower was speaking like Dante and St. Thomas Aquinas from the mainstream of medieval dualism. Actually there is little that is new in the poem, either in conception or expression. Wyclif had been likened to Jovinian at the end of the Epistle to the King in Vox, vi.1267, and the argument for faith over reason is a pastiche of lines in Vox, ii. ix. Pride is the root of all evil; the flesh is fragile and revolting; money has overcome justice—so run the last three sections of the poem.

De lucis scrutinio, found in three of the Latin presentation manuscripts and two others,[33] is an abstract of the criticism of the Estates just as the *Carmen* is of the criticism of the Deadly Sins. It is as though having given so much of his life to elaborating these patterns, Gower could not now leave them alone, but found himself recapitulating in a desultory way. Like the begettal of Sin and Death and the Infernal Parliament at the beginning of the *Mirour*, the "scrutiny" of light (there is no synonym), which destroys the evils that grow in the shadows, is to the lover of English poetry almost unbearably Miltonic in conception. Gower blends the figures of light and sight with that of the anthropomorphic state, entreating the light to search out and cleanse Rome of its two popes and enlighten the simoniac prelacy:

> *Sic caput obscurum de membris nil fore purum*
> *Efficit, et secum sic cecus habet sibi cecum.* (*De lucis*, 11)

> (A dark head does not make for bright limbs; the blindness of the one causes blindness in the other.)

No translation will do justice to the play upon light, sight, virtue, and their contraries in the 103 lines. When we recall that at the time he was writing, Gower was losing his own sight, we are reminded even more forcibly of the author of "When I consider how my light is spent" and "At our heels all Hell should rise/ With blackest Insurrection, to confound/ Heav'n's purest Light . . ." Gower begs light to illumine the clergy, king, political rulers, knighthood, lawyers, merchants, and the common people. The dark sins of each class again incorporate lines lifted directly from the *Vox*. But the whole is nonetheless effective in its employment of the fresh figure.

Ecce patet tensus ceci Cupidinis arcus,[34] thirty-six lines of Latin (most of them lifted from *Vox*, v.147ff), which break off incomplete at the end of the *Cinkante Balades* in the Trentham manuscript, belong to an earlier period, although their juxtaposition to *De lucis scrutinio* in the Macaulay edition emphasizes the play upon Cupid's blindness, the blindness of lovers, and the blinding of reason by love in the opening lines (1–8). "Sic amor omne domat, quicquid natura creauit" (15), the sexual drive as a recalcitrant but indispensable facet of divine creativity, links these lines with one of the major themes that we can trace from the opening balades of the *Traitié* to the appearance of Genius and Venus as central figures of the *Confessio Amantis*. "O natura viri," the fragment concludes in a four-times-repeated apostrophe: O human nature, compounded of contraries which must always be at war; Cupid inflames this war; nothing can escape his bolt.

O deus immense,[35] found in three of the presentation manuscripts, is a final address to Richard on the responsibilities of kingship. "The malice and cunning with which Richard carried through his acts of revenge, his mounting recklessness, his dark suspicions, and the evident disquiet aroused in the minds of many who had been his friends, all suggest a sudden loss of control, the onset of mental malaise. If Richard was sane from 1397 onward, it was the sanity of a man who pulls his own house about his ears." So writes May McKisack in our day.[36] Gower's poem begins in the same vein: "O immeasurable God, under whom by the sword captious and vicious kings ("Quidam morosi Reges, quidam viciosi") are overcome according to their various merits . . ." Then follows a Horatian proverb, used previously as an introduction to the Epistle in the *Vox*, which epitomizes both admonitions: "Quicquid delirant Reges, plectuntur Achiui" (VC, vi.497, *O deus* 5, Whatever folly their kings commit, the Achaeans must suffer).[37] In the *Vox* it had been explicated, "Nam caput infirmum membra dolere fecit" (498); here "Quo mala respirant, vbi mores sunt fugitiui" (6, For they fare badly where morality has departed). The "Nam caput" line is used near the end of the poem, at line 85. The piece continues: a king should observe his coronation oaths, seek good counsel and avoid the bad, not plunder his subjects' gold, listen to the voice of the people. A good king's glory will live forever, but where the head is infirm, the body will suffer. Law, not fate, governs the health of kingdoms. Finally a pointed warning:

> *Rex igitur videat cum curru quomodo vadat,*
> *Et sibi prouideat, ne rota versa cadat.* (101)

> (A king should therefore see how the cart is running and take care not to fall under its wheels.)

The similarities between these admonitions and the charges brought against Richard at the time of his deposition are evident:[38] his violations of his coronation oaths, taking exorbitant taxes on account of his avarice and pride, giving gifts to flatterers, failure to take good counsel, failure to do justice and maintain the laws. Presumably the poem was written before the deposition proceedings of 1399 and the reason for its similarity to the articles there charged against Richard is that both reflect the popular sentiments of the country after 1397.

In Praise of Peace, found in the Trentham manuscript and from a separate source in Thynne's edition of Chaucer,[39] is concerned directly with the parliamentary proceedings leading to Henry's accession.[40] It begins by detailing his claims to the throne: fortune and God's grace, lineage, and popular election (stanzas 1–2). At the Parliament of September 30, 1399, Henry had challenged the crown on the grounds of his descent from Henry III "and through the right that God of his grace hath sent me, with the help of my kin and my friends to save it." He did not accede to Archbishop Arundel's desire that he accept, if not a parliamentary title, at least one deriving from some form of national consent, but he did submit to some form of acclamation by the lords spiritual and temporal *cum toto populo.* At the same Parliament, Henry had proposed that he claim the throne by conquest, but Chief Justice Thirning had objected on the ground that a conqueror is under no obligation to respect the laws, lives, and property of his subjects. At the end of the *Complaint to His Purse* Chaucer epitomized Henry's own claims: "O conquerour of Brutes Albyon,/ Which that by lyne and free eleccion/ Been verray kyng." In view of the legal basis for the political philosophy developed through his major works, it is significant that Gower adopted the Chief Justice's position rather than Henry's own. Succeeding stanzas warn Henry against presuming upon the right of conquest and contrast the good end of Solomon with the bad end of Alexander (stanzas 5–7). In his reply to the Chief Justice and the Estates on September 30, Henry had disclaimed the intention of depriving any man of his heritage, franchises, or rights. Gower reminded him of this promise: "The lawe of riht schal noght be leid aside" (line 56). The next ten stanzas on the king's responsibility for maintaining peace develop again the argument that runs throughout the major poems. The concluding plea to Henry to "Ley to this olde sor a newe salve,/ And do the werre awei" (line 122) reveals again how directly Gower's theorizing is related to England's discouragement after thirty years of reverses in the Hundred Years' War. In the next three stanzas (19–21), the King is advised to seek good counsel. Then Gower returns to the subject of peace by admonishing him to maintain domestic tranquillity (stanzas 22–28). As the first responsibility of knighthood is to maintain the rights of the church, so the king's responsibility is to maintain the rights of Christianity against the pagans (recall Henry's own crusades)—a responsibility that Christian kings are neglecting in their internecine struggles (stanzas 29–32). The church itself can give no leadership because it is leaderless; so nations must turn to their own laws for accord. This assertion of the superiority of civil to canon law is a significant final echo of the legal basis for Gower's grand pattern:

> If holy cherche after the duete
> Of Cristes word be nought al avysed
> To make pes, acord and unite
> Among the kinges that ben now devised,
> Yit natheles the lawe stant assised
> Of mannys wit to be so resonable,
> Withoute that to stonde hemselve stable. (PP, 232)

The Schism is the main cause of war between and within nations, but Gower realizes that it may be beyond Henry's power to mend it (stanza 37). Nevertheless, he repeats, "evere y hope of King Henries grace/ That he it is which schal the pes embrace" (line 272). The poem concludes with final exhortations to the King to seek peace and rule with pity (stanzas 38–55).

In Praise of Peace was Gower's last important poem. It sums up the final twenty years of both his literary career and his literary achievement. The former is obsessed with the king, the latter with the idea of kingship. In his career, we see Gower drawing ever closer to the person of the king: viewing Edward from a distance in the *Mirour*, addressing Richard at the end of the *Vox*, actually meeting him at the beginning of the *Confessio*, receiving tangible rewards from his successor in 1393 and 1399, revising his works and ending up an apologist for the Lancastrian usurpation of Henry. Has there ever been a greater sycophant in the history of English literature?

But such a reading of Gower's literary career must assume that a human being cannot act upon disinterested principle. It is this principle, the place of kingship in his view of an ordered society, which must in the end determine whether Gower was merely an opportunistic timeserver or a poet-philosopher of depth and integrity. To the elucidation of this principle we turn in the next chapter.

4. Major Themes

The most striking characteristic of Gower's literary production is its single-mindedness. The similarity in the method, structure, and content of his major pieces was what made it possible for Macaulay to identify the *Mirour de l'omme* as Gower's work when it turned up in a defective, anonymous manuscript.[1] This external similarity is the outgrowth of an inner consistency in purpose and point of view. In a very real sense, Gower's three major poems are one continuous work. The *Mirour de l'omme* he renamed *Speculum Meditantis*, presumably to harmonize with *Vox Clamantis*, and he called his English poem *Confessio Amantis*. As self-conscious as the verbal harmony in the titles is the linkage between the texts.

In the two balade sequences as they now exist, there is movement from the courtly tone of the *Cinkante Balades* to the moral and philosophical tone of the *Traitié pour essampler les amantz marietz*. In the latter group, as pointed out in the previous chapter, the first balade takes as its theme the superiority of reason over sensuality and the transience of flesh and permanence of the spirit. These themes are developed in the eighteen balades in the *Traitié*, through illustrations of false and incontinent lovers, nearly all of whom reappear in the *Confessio Amantis*. The same themes introduce the *Mirour*, whose opening lines warn "chascun amant" against the degradation and transience of temporal love which turns reason into bestiality. At the end of the *Mirour* proper the contrast between reason and bestiality is applied to the rebelling peasants, who are said to be transformed by passion and error from human beings to beasts (MO,26482). This concluding motif is

then brilliantly dramatized as an opening to the Vox *Clamantis*, in
the vision of the Peasants' Revolt. After developing his criticism of
society in a deeper and more philosophical fashion through that
poem, Gower began the last book of the Vox by lamenting the decline of social morality in terms of the traditional figure of the
statue in the dream of Nebuchadnezzar. In light of the previous
linkage, we are hardly surprised to find the social complaint in the
Confessio Amantis introduced by the same statue (Prol.585), emphasized by a miniature in many of the authoritative manuscripts
and a statement in the colophon.[2] Finally, the last thirty-four lines
of the *Confessio*, rejecting temporal love in favor of love eternal,
take the reader directly back to the sentiments at the beginning of
the *Traitié*, which Gower attached to the end of the *Confessio* in
the manuscripts he prepared after 1400.

The history of the revisions of the Vox and *Confessio* indicates
that this linkage did not come about accidentally. Having finished
the lament on the estates in the *Mirour* and Vox, Gower later
added the connecting vision in Book 1 of the Vox. Dissatisfied with
the Prologue and conclusion of the *Confessio*, he altered both to
improve their connections with the themes of the other poems.
These revisions are the product of mingled motives: the reactions
of the man to twenty years of political turmoil, the uncompromis-
ing world view of the moralist, and the esthetic sense of the poet.
However, when all is said, our judgment upon the structural coherence of the three major works must be the same as that of Leland
upon the verbal harmony of the titles: "Est tamen . . . utpote unius
ab altero pendentis"—that is, that the three works were intended to
present a systematic discourse upon the nature of man and society.
For this they do. In spite of their length and involution, they provide as organized and unified a view as we have of the social ideals
of England upon the eve of the Renaissance. This view may be
subsumed under three broad headings: individual VIRTUE, legal
JUSTICE, and the administrative responsibility of the KING. The
three works progress from the description of the origin of sin and
the nature of the vices and virtues at the beginning of the *Mirour*

de l'omme, through consideration of social law and order in the discussion of the estates in the *Mirour* and *Vox Clamantis*, to a final synthesis of royal responsibility and Empedoclean love in the *Confessio Amantis*. But while this evolution provides a pattern, the social consequences of individual sin are kept constantly in view at all times, and the importance of law and the functions of the king are given specific attention in all three works. That is to say that in addition to linear development through three stages we must recognize the possibility of interest in two or three levels at any given point.

Four streams fed this argument. The first and most easily recognizable is the penitential tradition associated with the books of vices and virtues; the second, nearly as evident but more difficult to explore, is the popular sermon; the third is the belletristic poetry from which Gower borrowed not only stories and allusions, but (in the *Vox*) actual passages of verse; and the fourth is the political doctrine underlying medieval civil and canon law. What Gower did was to mold the materials of the moralistic and belletristic traditions, using the sentiments and techniques of the popular sermons, to express a medieval publicist's view of man and society.

I

There is no reason to recapitulate in detail Gower's relationships to the penitential tradition, since this is the aspect of his sources that has been studied most fully. The growth of this literary tradition from the requirements laid down by the Fourth Lateran Council of 1215–16 is by this time a familiar story.[3] The Council crystallized earlier local and individual promulgations concerning religious observance by requiring every Christian to confess at least once annually to his priest. The key lines of this canon for the association of social criticism with the ecclesiastical sacrament are those which recur to an analogy already established in the earlier penitentials, that the priest was, like the physician, to adjust the cure to the disease: "The priest, moreover, shall be discreet and cautious, so that in the manner of the skillful physician he may pour wine and oil upon the wounds of the injured, diligently searching out the circumstances both of the sinner and the sin, that from these he may prudently understand what manner of advice he ought to offer him and what sort of remedy he ought to apply, employing various measures in order to heal the sick." [4] The implication that sins were dependent upon the situation of the sinner led to the classification of sins according to professions and estates.[5] These classifications appeared first in handbooks intended to give confessors the information they needed to diagnose the ills of their parishioners, and eventually in popular discussions written to enable devout laymen to examine their own consciences and direct their own behavior. These two lines of development were established by two of the first and most influential of the treatises which followed the Lateran Council, St. Raymond of Pennafort's *Summa de casibus* (ca. 1235), which set the pattern for the confessional manuals, and Guilielmus Peraldus' *Summa de vitiis et virtutibus* (ca. 1260), which set the pattern for the moralistic "examination of conscience." Pennafort wrote in the tradition of the older penitentials, couching his work partly in the catechetical form of the confession: "*Quid sit confessio. Confessio est legitima coram sacerdote peccatorum declaratio. . . . Cui confitendum est . . . Quae sunt necessaria ad veram confessionem . . .*" [6] From this tradition, by the way of later confessional manuals and such popular adaptations of the form as Robert Mannyng of Brunne's *Handlyng Synne*, came the frame Gower adopted for his *Confessio Amantis*. Genius, the priest of Venus, sets the situation in the catechetical tradition very explicitly:

> Tho he began anon to preche,
> And with his wordes debonaire
> He seide to me softe and faire:
> '*Thi schrifte to oppose and hiere,*
> My sone, I am assigned hiere
> Be Venus the godesse above, . . .
> For that belongeth to thoffice
> Of Prest, whos ordre that I bere,

So that I wol nothing forbere,
That I the vices on and on
Ne schal thee schewen everychon;
Wherof thou myht take evidence
To *reule with thi conscience. . . .*
Thogh I ne conne bot a lyte
Of othre thinges that ben wise:
I am noght tawht in such a wise;
For it is noght my comun us
To speke of *vices and vertus,*
Bot al of love and of his lore.
                    (CA, 1.230)

In the ensuing text the questioning and answering are maintained through exchange between Genius and the lover, identified by marginal notes:

Opponit Confessor   What seist thou, Sone, as of thin Ere?
Respondet Amans   Mi Fader, I am gultyf there . . . (CA, 1.558)

However, Genius's speech shows that Gower was working in more than one tradition. The references to "reule with thi conscience" and "vices and vertus" bespeak the tradition of the "examination of conscience," which Gower had employed even more directly in the *Mirour,* as indicated by the use of the term *Mirour* or *Speculum* in its title,[7] and in the *Vox,* which concludes with the explanation that the piece was written "that every man might examine himself within" (VC, vii.1458). The classic example of this tradition, the *Summa* of Peraldus, is an expository treatise of more than a thousand pages of scriptural, classical, and patristic citations and scholastic development of the *significationes* of the vices and virtues, intended for the examination of one's own conscience. Peraldus himself compared this process to a mirror: "Specula sunt dei precepta quibus anima sancte semper aspeciunt" (God's precepts are mirrors into which holy spirits are always looking).[8]

The most important vernacular adaptation of Pennafort and Peraldus in a treatise for private moral instruction was Frère Laurent Gallus's *Le somme le roi,* dedicated to King Philip of France in 1279. This influential work likewise gave rise to two different sorts of treatment, each of which had its influence upon Gower. It was adapted unembellished in other French versions, especially the *Miroir du monde*, and into several English versions including the *Ayenbite of Inwit* and the *Book of Vices and Virtues*.[9] On the other hand, its adaptation by William of Waddington in the *Manuel des péchés* began the tradition of introducing exempla to illustrate the sins, a practice developed even more brilliantly by Robert Mannyng of Brunne, whom F. J. Furnivall called "the worthiest forerunner of Chaucer."[10] Gower's *Mirour* and *Vox Clamantis* tend toward the straightforward moralistic discussion of Frère Laurent[11] whereas the *Confessio* resembles the more entertaining elaborations of William of Waddington and Robert Mannyng.

In the preface to his edition, Macaulay called attention to some of the similarities and differences between Gower's *Mirour* and the *Somme le roi*, *Manuel des péchés*, *Ayenbite of Inwit*, and Parson's Tale.[12] In 1905 Mlle. Elfreda Fowler published a lengthy study of the parallels between Gower's *Mirour* and the *Somme le roi* tradition,[13] arguing for a closer relationship between Gower and a later form of the *Miroir du monde*, while tending to lose sight of the differences Macaulay had pointed out. More recently Father J. B. Dwyer brought forward parallel quotations and treatments of material in Gower's *Mirour* and Frère Laurent's *Somme* which he felt drew Gower's work closer to that version.[14] No one who is familiar with the texts can fail to perceive that Gower was deeply indebted to the penitential tradition for the idea of the Seven Deadly Sins and for much of the material employed in their elucidation. But Macaulay's observation that Gower's three major works do not belong properly to the penitential tradition must be reiterated. Quite aside from the literary characteristics upon which Macaulay based his distinction, there are differences of theme and treatment. As indicated by the canon of the Lateran Council and illustrated by Chaucer's Parson's Tale, confession was the *raison d'être* for the whole tradition. It is relegated in Gower's *Mirour* to 263 lines (MO, 14835–15096) under the virtue *Science*, the fifth daughter of

Prouesce; it is not mentioned in the *Vox Clamantis,* but is used to provide an artistic frame for the *Confessio.* Nowhere did Gower treat sacramental confession as a major theme. Furthermore, the synods and episcopal decrees which sought to enforce the Lateran canon established a fairly definite body of knowledge in which the priest was to instruct and examine his parishioners. This included the Creed, the Ten Commandments, the Two Precepts of Love (*dei et proximi*), the Seven Works of Mercy, the Seven Sacraments, the Seven Cardinal Virtues, and the Seven Deadly Sins.[15] The fact that Gower chose to treat only the last is another evidence that he was not attempting to cover the same ground as the *Somme le roi* or *Handlyng Synne.*

II

Linking the Seven Deadly Sins with criticism of the social classes had been made easy by the directive of the Lateran Council that the priest adapt the penance to "the circumstances both of the sinner and the sin." This directive was expanded in subsequent decrees and led finally to the detailed expositions of the failings of men and women of all classes found in the penitentials. But in doing so it merged with the second stream that fed Gower's works, the popular sermons. This stream likewise had its origin in the decrees of the Fourth Lateran Council that instituted a program of preaching in the vernacular vigorously pursued by the friars, which produced a great efflorescence of homiletics in the 13th century.[16] We have mentioned that William of Waddington and Robert Mannyng introduced exempla and realistic social commentary into the penitential tradition. These features had appeared earlier in the sermons. Even more than the confessor, the preacher who wanted to hold his audience had to make his message attractive and direct it to the special interests of his hearers. A searching scrutiny of social classes and their customs came to be so typical in the 13th century that special collections, *sermones ad status,* were designed with this purpose in mind.[17] The thread connecting the ancient penitential tradition, the canon of the Lateran Council concerning confession, and the popular sermons is nowhere better illustrated than by the persistence of the medical analogy. In the prologue to one of the most famous collections of *sermones ad status*, Jacques de Vitry (d. ca. 1240), explained that he had written sermons addressed to prelates, to priests in synod, to monks and nuns and other regulars, to scholars, to pilgrims and crusaders, to soldiers, to merchants, to farmers and mercenaries, to servants of both sexes, and to virgins, widows, and married women because "the remedy does not suit every illness." [18] Gower himself used the medical analogy in the *Vox* (II, Prol.20).

Lists of sins grew out of the penitential tradition and categories of the estates out of political theory and social reality. They were brought together, personified, dramatized, and elaborated in the sermons. G. R. Owst's statement of the relationship between Gower's *Mirour* and the technique and material of the sermons is not extravagant:

> In all the literature that has been published, it would be difficult to find a more perfect mirror of the social gospel as presented by the pulpit, its artistry as well as its doctrine, within a single frame, than his *Mirour de l'omme*, or *Speculum Meditantis*. Mr. G. C. Macaulay, although all too painfully silent again concerning the influence of contemporary English preaching upon the mind of his poet, must be allowed to speak for what he calls "as regards subject matter, the most valuable part of the *Mirour*. It is that which contains the review of the various classes of society . . . He describes for us meetings of city dames at the wine-shops, the various devices of shop-keepers to attract custom and to cheat their customers, and the scandalous adulteration of food and drink. The extravagance of merchants, the discontent and luxury of labourers, and the corruption of the law courts are all vigorously denounced; and the Church, in the opinion of our Author, is in need of reform from the top to the bottom. Gower's picture is not relieved by any such pleasing exception as the parish priest of the Canterbury Tales." The significance of all these features for our main thesis will be apparent when we turn to the sermons and discover them there. However,

our interpreter goes on, "The material which we find in the *Mirour de l'omme* is, to a great extent, utilized again, and in particular, the account given of the various classes of society is substantially repeated in Gower's next work, the Latin *Vox Clamantis*." Here the traditional homiletic view of the social organism, divided into clergy, knights, and labourers, is maintained; and the sins of each group are attacked in detail, those of the Orders, the secular clergy, and the lawyers receiving special atten. Finally, the Prologue to Gower's third great work, the *Confessio Amantis*, where the poet turns in despair to sing of Love "is nothing but an abstract of the line of thought pursued in the *Vox Clamantis*." Rehearsing the vices and corruption in Church and State once again, the poet decides not only that the days are evil, but that "the end of the world has come." Clearly the preacher's message had weighed all too heavily upon his mind.[19]

It is to be noted that although the sermons provide no unifying principle, they do touch upon ideas underlying Gower's integrated world view that find no place in the penitentials. For example, Owst shows that the theoretical socialism usually associated with Wyclif finds wide expression in the sermons; and that sin is treated as the cause of dissension in society and as having social and national as well as merely individual significance.[20] But such ideas appear in the sermons only as isolated pronouncements, whereas in Gower's treatment they form parts of a coherent pattern. Leaving this pattern for fuller discussion in a moment, we can observe the difference between Gower and the homilists in their handling of a patristic analogy. Bromyard's *Summa predicantium* and the sermons make use of a comparison between society and a harp whose strings, representing the different classes, must be kept in tune. This figure, taken from Cicero's lost *Republic*, is preserved in St. Augustine's *De civitate Dei* (II.21) as an explanation of how reason should produce harmony in a republic. In the sermons it shows no particular relevance to political theory. The vagueness of Bromyard's conception is indicated by the passive constructions: "sicut patet quando illa [chorde] quae debet tangi non tangitur," i.e., "things" aren't going right.[21] In Gower's *Mirour*, however, the analogy appears in a discussion of David as an exemplary king. Among his accomplishments, "Ly Rois David estoit harpour" (MO, 22877), and as a good harper must bring his upper and lower strings into harmony, so must the king bring accord among his greater and lesser subjects:

Le seignour soit en sa puissance	Let the nobleman be in his power
Et la commune en obeissance,	and the common people in subservience,
L'un envers l'autre sanz mesfere:	the one without misdeed toward the other:
Rois q'ensi fait la concordance	the king who brings about this accord
Bien porra du fine attemprance	is well able with delicate tuning
La harpe au bonne note trere.	to coax good notes from the harp.
(MO, 22915)	

Here the analogy supports a theory of order in society and of the office of the king. Such an organic use of the figure is in turn found in a discussion of political theory, Nicholas of Cusa's *De concordantia catholica*: "Therefore the king ought to be a lute-player and one who knows how to preserve harmony among all the strings, great and little, and not stretch them too little or too much: that the common concord may resound through every chord." [22] Which is simply to say that when Gower uses political figures or ideas, he is likely to show affiliations with publicist literature rather than with the sermons.

Mlle. Fowler and Father Dwyer argued for a direct influence of the penitential tradition upon the form and content of the *Mirour*. Maria Wickert has proposed an equally profound influence of the sermon upon the form and content of the *Vox Clamantis*. The text of John 1:23, "Ego sum vox clamantis in deserto," contains a recognized typological allusion to both the preacher and the penitential sermon. For example, John Waldeby in a contemporary sermon on the text observed: "not only of John but of any fitting preacher by the voice of one crying is meant the voice of Christ." [23] John the Baptist was prescribed in the Liturgy as the subject for one of the penitential sermons of Advent, and St. Bonaventura in a commentary on the Advent sermon decreed that it should be handled *ad status*: "The sermon of John is recommended to meet the need of the people in three ways, inasmuch as it delivers different instructions to three different kinds of hearers: first to the unruly throng who constitute the parishioners, second to the publicans who constitute the minor officials, and third to the military who constitute the leaders and rulers." [24] The *Vox Clamantis* is addressed even more directly than the *Mirour de l'omme* to different classes, and in the *Vox* more than in any of his other pieces, Gower adopts the apocalyptic tone of the inspired preacher. Furthermore, instead of being structured like the *Mirour* about a sequence of sins, virtues, and classes, the *Vox* shows some evidence of being structured about the *increpatio* (scolding), *exhortatio* (exhortation), and *comminatio* (warning) which St. Bonaventura set forth as a pattern for the penitential sermon. The first and last of these elements are clear: the various classes are scolded throughout the first six books, and the *memento mori* and despair over the plight of the English nation in the seventh book appears a sufficient warning. It is less easy to name any significant section of the poem *exhortatio*.

The picture of the archer found in four manuscripts of the *Vox* [25] may likewise be connected with its homiletic background. In the clearest copies there is a man in a brown hat and a blue coat with a brown lining, with three arrows in his belt, shooting an arrow at a globe divided into three sections. Macaulay suggested that the threefold division corresponded to three elements, air, earth, and water. But Wickert suggests instead that they represent the Three Estates, and points to the similarity in sentiment of the four lines of verse accompanying the painting and the four lines at the beginning of Book III describing the Estates:

> *Ad mundum mitto mea iacula, dumque sagitto;*
> *At vbi iustus erit, nulla sagitta ferit.*
> *Sed male viuentes hos vulnero transgredientes;*
> *Conscius ergo sibi se speculetur ibi.* (VC, p. 19)

(At the world I shoot my darts and arrows, but what is just will receive no arrow. However, I shall severely harm the transgressors; conscious of myself I shall keep my eye on them.)

> *Nouimus esse status tres, sub quibus omnis in orbe*
> *More suo viuit atque ministrat eis.*

Non status in culpa reus est, set transgredientes
A *virtute status, culpa repugnat eis.* (VC, III Prol.23)

(We recognize that there are three estates. In his own way
everyone in the world lives under them and serves them. No
estate is accused of being at fault, but when estates transgress
against virtue, their fault declares against them.)

The probability that the banded orb represents the Estates is enhanced by the fact that in MS. Laud 719 (53), which lacks the
Visio of Book I and may have connections with the original form
of the *Vox*, the picture immediately precedes Book III in which discussion of the Estates is ushered in by these lines. Like the "vox
clamantis," the archer and arrows were figures for the preacher and
sermon. Beginning with the scriptures (Hebrews 4:12; Psalms 44:6,
119:4; Ephesians 6:11), through Gregory the Great who interpreted
the text of Habakkuk 3:11 as "Jacula Domini sunt verba sanctorum,
quae corda peccantium feriunt," to Gower's contemporary, John
Bromyard, who found "Sermo namque domini quandoque in sacra
scriptura sagittae comparatur" (The divine message is sometimes
compared in sacred scripture to an arrow), the analogy may be
amply demonstrated.[26] Hence, the painting supports the notion
that in writing the *Vox* Gower thought of himself as criticizing the
Estates in the tradition of *sermones ad status.*

Miss Wickert has argued for a more intimate influence of the
artes praedicandi upon at least the prologues of Books II and III of
the *Vox.*[27] For example, she finds the prologue to Book II divided
into the four *causae* prescribed for introductions in the handbooks
on homiletics:

1. causa materialis	—	lines 1–2 and 75–84
2. causa efficiens	—	lines 3–8 and 65–74
3. causa finalis	—	lines 9–20 and 43–46
4. causa formalis	—	lines 21–30

These divisions are real and might well have been conscious, but
like attempts to squeeze Chaucer and other medieval writers into
rhetorical patterns, this one does not quite fit. To be precise, it does

not account for thirty lines (31–42 and 47–64). It is the same with the other homiletic formulas such as *invocatio, gratia sermonis, gratia auditas, correctio, adulatio,* and the like. If the instances cited by Miss Wickert are conscious, all that can be concluded is that they are employed very loosely and sporadically.

III

The case for influence of sermon rhetoric, as contrasted with theme and tone, would be more convincing if so much of the *Vox* were not a mosaic of lines drawn from Ovid, Peter Riga, Nigel Wireker, and other known sources. A close analysis of twenty lines from the *Visio,* Book I, which seem particularly personal, has broad implications for Gower's relations to all of his sources. The passage expresses what one would expect a resident of Southwark, just beside London Bridge, to have felt during the fateful days of June 12–14, 1381, when the peasants were swirling through the borough and over the bridge into the city. The unitalicized words in Gower's lines and in the Ovidian parallels suggest the extent of Gower's verbal indebtedness: [28]

1501   *Qui prius attulerat* verum michi semper amorem
      nam cum praestiteris verum mihi semper amorem
                               (*Ex ponto,* 4.4.23)
   Tunc tamen aduerso tempore *cessat* amor:
      hic tamen adverso tempore *crevit* amor (*ibid.,* 24)
   Querebam fratres *tunc fidos, non tamen ipsos*
      quaerebam fratres, *exceptis scilicet illis,* (*Tristia,* 3.1.65)
   Quos suus optaret non genuisse pater.
      quos suus optaret non genuisse pater. (*ibid.,* 66)
   Memet in insidiis semper locturus habebam,
   Verbaque sum spectans pauca locutus humum:
      verbaque sum spectans pauca locutus humum (*Fasti,* 1.148)
   Tempora cum blandis absumpsi vanaque verbis,
   Dum mea sors cuiquam cogerat vlla loqui.
   Iram multociens frangit responsio mollis,
1510   *Dulcibus ex verbis tunc fuit ipsa salus;*
   Sepeque cum volui conatus verba proferre,

Torpuerat gelido lingua retenta metu.

  torpuerat gelido lingua retenta metu. (*Heroides,* 11.82)

Non meus vt querat noua sermo quosque fatigat,

Obstitit auspiciis lingua *retenta* malis;

  substitit auspicii lingua *timore* mali. (*ibid.,* 13.86)

Sepe meam mentem volui dixisse, set hosti

Prodere me timui, linguaque tardat ibi.

Heu! miserum tristis fortuna tenaciter vrget,

  An miseros tristis fortuna tenaciter urget, (*ibid.,* 3.43)

Nec venit *in fatis* mollior hora *meis.*

  nec venit *inceptis* mollior hora *malis* (*ibid.,* 44)

Si genus est mortis male viuere, *credo quod illo*

  Si genus est mortis male vivere, *terra moratur*

(Ex ponto, 3.4.75)

1520   *Tempore vita mea morsque fuere pares.*

One must always allow for the probability that the text of Ovid Gower had before him varied in words and phrases from those we use today. Nevertheless, we can see something of the way he cut and fitted the bits he culled from his sources into the lines he composed himself. The passage begins with a reference to a friend who evidently differed from him politically. To express this idea, Gower reverses a distich from Ovid's verse letter "To Brutus." For the more emphatic *praestiteris* he substitutes the milder *attulerat;* Ovid's *hic* is replaced by *tunc* since Gower's dream is cast in the past tense; and most important, the verb *crevit* (increased) is replaced by *cessat* (ceases). Next Gower speaks of seeking faithful brothers, altering slightly two lines from *Tristia* in which Ovid's poem speaks of coming to Rome "in fear, an exile's book" and seeking its "brothers," i.e., Ovid's other books, in a library in the temple of Apollo. In *Vox,* IV.1113, Gower adapted *fratres,* the brothers Simeon and Levi in the *Aurora,* to mean monks, and so we may possibly understand by this that he sought the faithful brothers of St. Mary Overeys. *Exceptis scilicet illis* in Ovid refers to those erotic books like the *Ars amatoris* which had brought about his exile. Since this was inappropriate to Gower's meaning, he replaced it with filler, *tunc* and *non tamen ipsos.* The ensuing line, perfectly clear in the *Tristia,* is enigmatic in Gower's context. Who were the faithful and who the misbegotten brothers? The reference to being ambushed or trapped in line 1505 has been traced to no source. It might appear to describe what Gower conceived to be the situation of a loyalist in Southwark during the troubles; and the line describing his consequent speechlessness, although it comes out of a context of Ovid humbly addressing the god Janus, fits Gower's context very well. Then five lines which (assuming they are his own) show that Gower could compose perfectly coherently in Latin, followed by a line of Canace's lament from the *Heroides* quoted verbatim. Evidently the word *lingua* in this line suggested another occurrence in Laodamia's complaint two chapters later, which Gower included after a rather lumpish line of his own. The Ovidian line, which in the original implied fear, he revised by the substitution of *obstitit* (withstood) for *substitit* (stood still) and *retenta* (restrained) for *timore* (fear). Then two fairly smooth lines of his own composition, followed by three more adapted from Ovid. In the first, a conjunction is replaced by an interjection to effect an appropriate transition. In the second, the differences may well reflect a different text. At least the Loeb edition gives *meis* as a manuscript variant for *malis*. This change would demand some change of *inceptis* to make sense. *In fatis meis* would do as well in Ovid's context as *inceptis malis*—perhaps even better in view of the reference to *fortuna* in the preceding line. Finally back to *Ex ponto* for the opening clause of the next to the last line, an epigrammatic statement of the sort that a writer with Gower's mind would have found it easy to remember, and then on to the final original line, itself a rather pithy statement.

What are we to make of this performance? Do the twenty lines in question describe any personal experience or express any personal sentiment? Of one thing we may be sure: they do not express an experience or sentiment taken from Ovid. The seven quotations from four texts come from such a variety of contexts and are so tailored to fit their positions that if the passage has any meaning, it must be that of the immediate author. And the passage does have meaning. It is typically Gowerian in the ambiguity of the refer-

ences to the friend and the brothers and in the absence of specific
details which produce the verisimilitude of a born poet or novelist
such as Chaucer. Yet, in spite of its generality, we are left with a
vivid impression of what it must have been like to live through a
popular revolution, when, terrified to express himself on any subject, one could not tell friend from foe and found existence a waking nightmare.

Most of all we must wonder at the method of an author who
wrote in this manner. I have deemed it worthwhile to tabulate only
the first book of the Vox. In some ways this is not typical of the
other six books in that it quotes more extensively, particularly from
Ovid, and appears to be more imaginative, a more "literary" production, than the Mirour or the rest of the Vox. Yet its very dependence makes it a prime example of Gower's use of his sources. Of the
2150 lines of Book I, 247 are taken or adapted from Ovid (Metamorphoses 140, Fasti 30, Ex ponto 29, Heroides 25, Ars amatoris
9, Amores 8, and Remedia amoris 6), 37 are from the Aurora of
Peter Riga, 26 from the Speculum stultorum of Nigel Wireker, and
17 from the Pantheon of Godfrey of Viterbo, for a grand total of
327 lines borrowed, or approximately one in seven.[29] Aside from
these, only one source shows up in later books, De vita monachorum. As an example of the order of quotations from any one
source, those from the Heroides run:

VOX	HEROIDES	VOX	HEROIDES	VOX	HEROIDES
1.4	17.112	1.1442	5.14	1.1564	14.52
1.1188	3.4	1.1485	14.37	1.1564–66	10.111–113
1.1224	5.68	1.1496	5.46	1.1612	19.52
1.1283	8.77	1.1512	11.82	1.2001–02	11.27–28
1.1385–86	20.91–92	1.1514	13.86	1.2003–04	14.29–30
1.1420	3.24	1.1517–18	3.43–44	1.2033–34	2.123–124

The inference would appear to be that we have here an author so
thoroughly steeped in a few books that their words came readily to
mind to express his own ideas, and having on his desk copies of
the books, through which he was riffling constantly.

Gower's relation to the Aurora tells the same tale. Father Paul
Beichner has identified 446 lines from this popular Biblia versificata

in various books of the *Vox,* and four more in the *Carmen super multiplici viciorum pestilencia.*[30] As with Ovid, the lines are incorporated into Gower's own discussion. For example in Book vi. 937–967, when he calls upon young King Richard to emulate the illustrious deeds of his father, the description of the deeds is a mosaic of lines from the *Aurora* describing Judas and Simon Maccabaeus, Saul, Judah, and David. Again, of the twenty-two lines of a passage describing the hypocrisy of the friars (iv.1059–80), seventeen are taken from various places in the *Aurora.* Beichner's view of the relationship between the borrowings from *Aurora* and the theme of the *Vox* supports the conclusions voiced above concerning the use of sermons and penitentials:

> Although Gower's reading of the paraphrases of Scripture in the *Aurora* must have refreshed and supplemented his knowledge of the Vulgate, he was much less interested in the Biblical content of Peter Riga's poem than in the moral interpretation of the matter. Whether he created a mosaic from slightly changed passages separated by hundreds or thousands of lines in the *Aurora,* or whether he used a long excerpt from one place, his context is original. And the general context of *Vox Clamantis*—conditions within the various orders of society at the time of the Peasants' Revolt—gives originality even to passages borrowed without change by removing them from the plane of the exegete's timeless moral interpretation of Scripture to the reformer's criticism of his own day and counsel for improvement. To develop his Latin craftsmanship, Gower read and reread *Aurora,* memorized passages as models of elegant writing, plagiarized and imitated them; he even borrowed some of the few Classical allusions with which Peter Riga had ornamented his writing. When to his use of the *Aurora* is added that made of Ovid, of the *De Vita Monachorum,* of the *Speculum Stultorum,* and the *Pantheon,* one is overwhelmed by Gower's industry. And yet I believe that he felt he was honestly presenting his views on his own day even though he expressed himself in words and criticisms borrowed from his predecessors.[31]

The difference between Gower's use of Ovid and the *Aurora* on the one hand, and of Latin verse satires such as the *Speculum stul-*

torum and *Vita monachorum* on the other, further betrays his purpose and interest. Two exempla, that of the revengeful cock who prevents a young priest from securing a benefice because he had earlier broken its leg, and that of the herd of cows attacked by flies, gave Gower two thirds of his ninety-eight lines of quotation from the *Speculum stultorum*.[32] The quotations from the *Vita monachorum* come in even more sustained bursts, with little change in meaning from the original.[33] For example in Vox, IV.395–480, fifty lines are taken from passages in the *Vita* warning monks against pride, luxury, and other temptations of Satan, and placed in the same sort of context as that from which they were taken. In Vox, V. 335–428, twenty-three lines from the middle of the *Vita* in which monks are being warned against the wiles of women are placed in a commentary on the temptations of sex. In Vox, VI.313–398, fifty-six lines picked from various parts of the *Vita* are adapted as advice to judges: since the judges are here being warned against avarice, the meanings of the lines adapted are again appropriate. In Vox, VI. 1019–1116, sixteen lines from the *Vita* are included in the address to the king, good ascetic advice which fits well in context—VI. 1019–24, all men are born equal; VI.1085–86, physical beauty may retard spiritual development; and so forth.

Gower's acquaintance with the *Pantheon* is of particular interest since it shows him fitting into a tradition. Godfrey of Viterbo was chaplain to Conrad III and Frederick I and a staunch adherent of Emperor Henry VI in the disputes between the Empire and the Papacy at the end of the 12th century. The catalog of his writings bears at least a superficial resemblance to the *Vox Clamantis* and its continuation, the *Cronica Tripertita*, and to parts of the *Mirour* and *Confessio*. Godfrey's *Speculum Regum*, on the genealogy of the Germanic kings, was dedicated to young King Henry and intended for his instruction; *Pantheon* begins with a sort of *de natura rerum* and then undertakes a universal history; *Gesta Frederici* and *Gesta Henrici VI* are continuations of the history in the *Pantheon* as the *Cronica* is of the *Vox*. The contents of the first part of the *Pantheon* suggest the sort of information Gower might have gleaned there: "Particula I, De divina essentia ante omnem creaturam; Particula II, De angelis et de diabolo et de animabus sanctorum et de questionibus diversis inde movendis et earum solutionibus secundum sanctos; Particula III, De celis et de planetis et de stellis et natura et motu eorum; Particula IV, De elementis; Particula V, De anima hominis diversas sententias habens divorsorum philosopharum en quibusdam auctor est contra; Particula VI, De creatone Adem primi hominis"—and on into biblical history.[34] But since the direct quotations from the *Pantheon* apparently amount only to some eighteen lines, and the story of Apollonius of Tyre, which Gower attributes to the *Pantheon*, shows wide divergences from that version,[35] we can tell little about how extensively Gower was influenced by the work.

Undoubtedly further reading would uncover more sources for individual lines,[36] but there is no reason to pursue the process any further here. It has seemed worthwhile to carry it this far in connection with the *Vox Clamantis* only because there, if anywhere, the identifiable sources might have been expected to cast some light on Gower's purpose and structure. But they do not. They reveal only how completely his poems embody the literary genre of "complaint" as formalized by the promulgations of the fourth Lateran Council.[37] The recurring, virtually unchanging, motifs of this genre from the 13th century through the 16th were, first, the fall of man which brought sin and misery into the world, man as a microcosm whose sin taints the cosmos, lament over the lost felicity of the Golden Age, and *memento mori*; second, analysis, exemplification, and personification of the Seven Deadly Sins and their subcategories; and, third, criticism of the estates of society, in particular the clergy, lawyers, merchants, usurers, doctors, women, and the rich. The appearance of these three themes individually or together reveals nothing save that an author was of his time. It is their special handling that is significant. Chaucer's achievement, as we shall see in the next chapter, was stylistic. In medieval English literature, he alone managed to treat these themes with the wit and specificity that converted them from complaint to satire. Gower's achievement was intellectual rather than stylistic. As derived from the penitentials and sermons and treated in the complaints, these three themes bore no *organic relationship* to one another. They were merely differing expressions of the continuing estimate of the discrepancy between biblical injunctions and contemporary practice. What Gower managed to do was combine the traditional themes of complaint with political theory so as to create a meaningful pattern of human society regulated by law and love under the leadership of the king.

IV

The Leland tradition of Gower's legal profession and the slender biographical evidence to support it were treated in the first and second chapters. Whatever the truth about that may be is of little importance in our consideration of the legalistic fabric of his works, since medieval thought in general, be it social, moral, or theological, was saturated with the commonplaces of civil and canon law. We should not be surprised, either, that Gower deals largely in legal commonplaces rather than in the specific allusions one would expect of a trained lawyer. We may recall the total absence from Petrarch's writings of any trace of his legal training. Gower did refer at least thirteen times [38] to "la loy civile" or "civilia iura," which meant technically the *Corpus juris civilis* of the later Roman Empire, the foundation for canon law and political philosophizing from the 12th century on. In the *Mirour* he went so far as to translate the famous opening sentence, "Iustitia est constans et perpetua voluntas ius suum cuique tribuens":

De ceste vertu bonne et fine	Of this good and fine virtue
La loy civile ensi diffine,	civil law gives this definition
Et dist: 'Justice est ferm constant	and says: "Justice is a firm determination
Du volenté que ja ne fine,	of the will that never ends,
Q'au riche et povre en jouste line	which justly to rich and poor
Son droit chascun vait donnant.'	gives each his right."

(MO, 15193)

This quotation was, however, a staple of collections of legal aphorisms, and the addition of the reference to the rich and poor—not found in the *Corpus*—shows its transmission to Gower through the English common law.[39] Other references to civil law likewise find their closest parallels in the principles of common law. The statement at *Mirour* 14138 that civil law will assist only the waking man, not him who sleeps, echoes the precept in the *Digest* that ignorance of the law injures those who demand their rights. But Gower's wording resembles more closely the popular doctrine of laches: "equity does not encourage stale claims nor give relief to those who sleep upon their rights." [40] The argument from civil law at *Mirour* 23748 that knights should not engage in trade echoes numerous prohibitions in the *Justinian Code* against decurions' and soldiers' engaging in trade and manufacture, but it again has contemporary applications.[41] Usually "la loy civile" means simply secular law. At *Mirour* 26365 burghers are accused of employing trickery against "loy civile"; at *Mirour* 9093, concerning the fornication of monks and nuns, it is observed "Les tient Incest sans loy civile." Elsewhere civil law is contrasted with other kinds of law, as when ignorance of kings is condemned:

Qui sciet ne latin ne romance,	*Who knows neither Latin nor French,*
Du bible ne de Concordance,	*nor Bible nor concordance,*
Ne de Civile ne decré,	*nor civil nor canon law,*
Pour governer sa digneté.	*to guide his high position.*
(MO, 22264)	

The terms for secular law may vary. At *Mirour* 21463 it is asserted that "la loy commune" has no power over friars; at *Mirour* 17536 that women are subject to men "en loy judicial." A reference in the *Vox Clamantis* to the subjects a clerk studies as "civilia iura et logicam" (VC, III.2015) may be slightly more technical. But the reference to "Civile" in the *Confessio Amantis* again offers evidence that Gower's knowledge of civil law came to him through popular channels:

> Write in Civile this I finde:
> Thogh it be noght the houndes kinde
> To ete chaf, yit wol he werne
> An oxe which comth to the berne,
> Therof to taken eny fode. (CA, II.83)

As Macaulay pointed out, this passage reflects a misreading of "De lege Furia Caninia sublata" from the *Institutions*, concerning the repeal of a law which restricted the power of owners of slaves to manumit at will "quasi libertatibus impedientem et quodammodo invidiam." John Bromyard and other medieval commentators read "Caninia" as "canina," in the light of "invidiam," as meaning that the law compelled men to imitate the dog in the manger by with-holding liberty from slaves for whom they no longer had use.[42]

Just as "civil" was a general term for secular law, "decretal" ap-pears in Gower's works as a general term for ecclesiastical law rather than as a specific reference to Gratian's *Concordantium discordantium canonum*, the foundation of canon law.

> *In re consimili, sicut decreta fatentur,*
> *Iudicium simile de racione dabis.* (VC, IV.347)

> (Like decisions should be rendered in similar cases, as prescribed in the decretals.)

Gower goes on to criticize canons who take their name from canon law but do not observe its usage (VC, IV.360). A similar charge is made at *Mirour* 21158, and papal laws are called "decretals" at *Mirour* 20291.

The fact that most of the references to civil law occur in the *Mirour* may be additional evidence that that piece was composed for the legal-mercantile society in which Gower appears to have moved before retiring to St. Mary's. The reference to the "decreta" and the coupling of civil law with clerical education support the evidence of the language and dedication that the *Vox* was intended for a clerical audience. And the virtual absence of specific legal allusions and dependence upon the *de regimine principum* material for political ideas support the notion that the *Confessio* was more specifically intended for the King.

Gower shows more concern for the legal profession than he does for law in the abstract. Its members receive disproportionate at-tention throughout the three works. In the *Mirour* they have 996 lines, as compared with 1423 for emperors and kings, 1251 for bishops and deans, 945 for monks and friars, 870 for the nobility and knights, 802 for merchants and artisans, 623 for the pope and cardinals, and 574 for curates and annualers. In the *Vox*, as is consonant with its being addressed to the clergy, ecclesiastics have two books (iii for the secular clergy and iv for the regulars); knights, peasants, merchants, and artisans have one (v); and lawyers and the king have one (vi). In the *Confessio*, lawyers and the king are the only classes treated directly, both in Book vii. In the Middle Ages, and indeed as late as Dickens' *Bleak House* and *Great Expectations*, lawyers bore the brunt of the strain produced by privilege's giving way to equity. No doubt much of Gower's criticism of the avarice and venality of the profession was conventional,[43] but much of the convention was based upon fact. In a day in which secular courts were but a step away from the manorial system in which the lord was frequently both judge and party, when such conflict of interest was still a prominent feature of the ecclesiastical courts (as Gower himself complained, MO, 20140), and when lawyers appeared in court wearing the liveries of their noble retainers, there can be no doubt that injustice was rife. It is noteworthy that whereas Gower disqualified himself in the *Mirour* when discussing the corruption of the church, he claimed personal knowledge of the law:

Car ce n'est pas de mon savoir	*For it is not in my knowledge*
D'escrire ou dire ascunement	*to write or say anything*
De les Evesques au present:	*of today's bishops;*
Mais ce q'om dist, ne say si voir,	*but what people say, I will tell—not know-*
Dirrai.[44] (MO, 19059)	*ing whether it is true.*

But—of lawyers:

Je prens tesmoign a celle gent,	*I bear witness concerning these people,*
Si tort puet donner largement,	*if wrong is able to pay well*
Le droit ne gaignera que poy.	*right gains but little.*
(MO, 24190)	

Ten specific charges are made against lawyers in the *Mirour* (24254ff): 1) their confederacy prevents them from pleading wholeheartedly; 2) they are lowborn; 3) they wear the liveries of their rich clients; 4) like physicians, they rejoice in the difficulties of others and delay their recovery since this means profit; 5) they wriggle out of taxes; 6) they advance in their professions by purchasing their positions; 7) they will not talk until paid; 8) they sell their integrity for money; 9) they plot the downfall of their neighbors; 10) they acquire wealth by trading in real estate, are great "pourchasours." Judges and minor officials are accused of the same greed and venality, and Book VI of the Vox begins with nearly the same criticisms.

This condemnation is so violent that it led Macaulay to conclude (1.lxii) that Gower could not possibly have been a lawyer himself. But one may question the validity of this psychological inference. Gower's condemnation of the profession appears to grow directly out of a profound respect for its responsibility. At the beginning of the diatribe in the Mirour he asserted:

La loy de soy est juste et pure	The law itself is just and pure
Et liberal de sa nature,	and liberal in its nature,
Mais cils qui sont la loy gardant	but those who are guardians of the law
La pervertont et font obscure.	pervert it and make it obscure.
(MO, 24601)	

The ideal for judges is equally high (MO, 24690, 24793). At the beginning of the discussion of lawyers in the Vox:

> Qui tamen ad veras leges vacat, et sine fraude
> Iusticiam querule proximitatis agit,
> Vt psalmista canit, est vir magis ille beatus. (VC, VI.9)

Shortly afterward:

> Gens sine lege quid est, aut lex sine iudice quid nam,
> Aut quid si iudex sit sine iusticia? (VC, VI.481)

These two lines are echoed in a eulogy on the law in the Confessio:

> What is a lond wher men ben none?
> What ben the men whiche are al one
> Withoute a kinges governance?
> What is a king in his ligance,
> Wher that ther is no lawe in londe?
> What is to take lawe on honde,
> Bot if the jugges weren trewe? (CA, VII.2695)

The author who wrote such lines into every one of his major works had a profound regard for the potential of the profession. The tone of his criticisms may be better accounted for by supposing that he was adopting the familiar medieval convention of basing legal commentaries upon the pretext of attacks upon false judges.[45]

The treatment of the church courts provides a transition from conventional complaint to moral philosophy. As custodians of ecclesiastical law, the clergy were subject to the same corruptions as lawyers (MO, 18457). The Roman curia was simply another court, suffering from the same corruptions as the civil courts (VC, III.1220). The organization of the ecclesiastical courts was specifically criticized because in them the clergy were both parties and judges (MO, 20140). Gower was very conscious of the impropriety of a layman's criticizing the clergy and at *Vox,* III.1675, he took refuge in a quasi-legal defense ("quasi" because in it "law" refers to Scriptural as well as legal precept): "The law wills that the abuser of justice leave off the vice which has been adjudged against him. We are all brothers in the Church of Christ and always stand in one another's need; however, the law says if your brother errs correct him and thus make him return to God." Later, speaking of the friars, he is even more directly legalistic: "Doubtful things should be treated cautiously not so much for the world's sake as for God's. If anyone usurps worldly authority, however, the powers of law restrain him from abusing it. One cannot take another's valuable personal property unless he denies the validity of the law. But when a friar steals what belongs to the soul, I do not know by what law he justifies it. Certainly not by papal dispensation. The pope may err—*Papa potest falli*—but he who sees within knows whether it is for love of money or for love of God" (VC, IV.907).

Gower's criticism of the ecclesiastical courts is based upon one of the basic concepts of medieval moral philosophy. This is the distinction, inherited by canon law from Roman legal theory, between "natural" and "human" law. The latter Gower referred to as "positive" law (*lex positiva*), an unfortunate designation for the modern reader since the term "positive" has undergone a semantic shift away from its original connotation of "changeable" (from *positus*, something placed or set down, and hence removable). The Thomistic distinctions are clear and sufficiently general.[46] St. Thomas defined the "principle by which things are governed, which exists in God" as "eternal law," the "participation of a rational creature in eternal law" as "natural law," and "particular determinations of the law of nature" as "positive human law." Gower was caustic in his criticism of the motive behind the positive law of the church. In the Vox (III.227, 263) he asks: "Does Christ grant me indulgence for wicked deeds? I think not; but he shows mercy afterwards. Or does Christ prohibit what is not a sin? He does not do so. But now with their many new decrees they prohibit what is not prohibited by the law either of Moses or of Christ. But if I paid, they would remit tomorrow what they call a sin today. . . . Thus it is that the positive law which the clergy has established has become big business—*grande figurat opus*. Just as the more birds the fowler wants to catch, the more nets he spreads, so the clergy increase their positive laws and make more narrow the pathway of people in the world." The discussion in the *Mirour* (18451) is almost identical, even to the figure of the fowler (a common figure for the devil),[47] save that there positive law is called "la loy papal," but in the briefer comment in the *Confessio* it is again referred to as "lawe positif" (Prol.247).

The concept of natural and human law played a much more important part in Gower's world view than merely as a stick with which to beat clerical corruption, however. It provided the explanation for law in the first place, and for order in both human society and the universe. In the final analysis, Gower's great trilogy may be said to take its structure and meaning from this concept. Both the *Institutions of Justinian* and the *Decretum* begin by distinguishing three kinds of law, *lex naturali*, *lex gentium*, and *lex civili*—natural law, the law of peoples, and civil law.[48] Natural law was an involved and ambiguous concept, but, among other things, it was (to quote from the opening lines of the *Decretum*), "that held everywhere by *instinct of nature*, not by enactment; as, for instance, the union of man and woman, the generation and rearing of children." Natural law was thus first exemplified by the universal sexual instinct which man shares with animals. On this level it could be identified philosophically with the deterministic impulse to procreation whose history A. O. Lovejoy has traced from Plato's *Timaeus*, through the naturalism of the school of Chartres, into modern scientific thought under the designation, "the principle of plenitude." [49] Nowhere did the conflict in medieval thought between the heresy of considering God's creative energy scientific determinism, and the orthodoxy of trying to invest it with some sort of moral responsibility, manifest itself more than in the problem of sex.[50] On the one hand, Gower saw sex as a blind instinct. In the *Traitié*, he paraphrased the doctrine of the *Institutions*: "Li corps par naturele experience/ Quiert femme avoir, dont soit multipliant" (II.3). In the *Confessio*, he was even more emphatic:

> Bot yit the lawe original,
> Which he hath set in the natures,
> Mot worchen in the creatures,
> That therof mai no obstacle,
> Bot if it stonde upon miracle. (CA, VII.660)

But reason and the soul invest man with greater responsibility than animals. He has the privilege of misusing his instincts. In the incestuous relationships of Machaire (CA, III.170, 350) and Cain and Abel (CA, VIII.68), Gower shows the sexual manifestation of natural law working at cross purposes with reason and human law.

Gower's two different personifications of Venus and Genius betray the ambiguity of the medieval view of the natural law of sexual love. Jean de Meun's presentation in the *Roman de la rose* is largely deterministic: Nature is God's vicar on earth. Genius, her priest, is potency. Venus is sexual passion. In their amoral view, the only sin is shirking Nature's work.[51] In the *Vox Clamantis*, this symbolism is given an almost pornographic reading:

> Venus and Genius do not teach the cloister cells, which they now govern in their fashion, to keep laws concerning the flesh. Genius is the convent's protector and confessor, and sometimes

he holds the rank of bishop. He visits the ladies in their cloister under the guise of righteous authority, but when he comes to their bedchambers, he casts righteousness aside, and wields his power over them. Although he may be in a fur-lined cape while he is giving instruction, he nevertheless administers his naked authority to them forcefully. By Genius's decision they are stoned [?pun] for their sins, but no mortal blow injures these women. (VC, IV.595)

All this is changed in the *Confessio Amantis*. Genius is reduced to the role of the priest of Venus and made to give advice on courtly love (the sins of love, CA, I–VI), conventional love (marriage, CA, VII.5351–VIII.270), and ascetic love (CA, VIII.2908)—not to mention general moralistic and political advice which, as we shall see, is the real burden of the *Confessio*. The anomaly is that instead of urging the Lover on to sexual intercourse and procreation, in the *Confessio* Venus and Genius are made the advocates of their mortal enemies, reason and self-discipline. According to Genius, man's reason must modify natural law (CA, VII.5375) and marriage is ordained by God that "bothe lawe and kinde be served" (CA, VII.5364).

It is important to understand that whatever his adaptation of the conventional symbols, Gower understood the philosophical implications of the principle of plenitude. Otherwise the brilliant thematic tie between the beginning of the *Mirour* and the end of the *Confessio* goes unperceived. If, as Lovejoy argues, the procreative urge was by the school of Chartres and Jean de Meun regarded as the emanation of the creative energy of divine love, then the opposite is sterility—nothingness.[52] It is surely not by chance that the *Mirour* begins:

Un poy du nient je vuill conter . . .	I will tell a little concerning nothing . . .
Dont saint Gregoire sagement . . .	for St. Gregory says wisely . . .
Disant que nient en soy comprent	that nothingness comprises within itself
Le noun du pecché soulement,	simply the term for sin,
Car pecché tous biens anientist.	since sin annihilates all good.

(MO, 34, 54, 58)

Pagan stoicism had equated evil with the mere absence of good;[53] but the Patristic authority upon which Gower drew had equated this nothingness with the active forces of evil, the Antichrist. Structurally, Gower's trilogy progresses from the opposite to the divine creative energy at the beginning of the *Mirour,* nothingness and chaos represented by Satan and Sin, to its affirmation in the personifications of Venus and Genius in the *Confessio.*

However, the allegorical account of the origin of sin, always an integral element in the literature of complaint, is likewise the starting point for medieval legal theory. Sex became a sin in the Fall which brought about the law of peoples, "wars, slaveries, captivities," the "might makes right" of primitive man. In order for man to become civilized, all the depraved human instincts, sexual, avaricious, and pugnacious, had to be ordered and controlled under civil law, the product of human reason and Empedoclean love. On these concepts, Gower established the pattern of sin-law-love which he traced through his three major poems. In this pattern, sin is the starting place for law; as stated in the *Vox Clamantis,* "Pro transgressore fuerant leges situate" (VC, vi.469), and repeated in the *Confessio Amantis,* "Propter transgressos leges statuuntur in orbe" (CA, vii.2695).[54] So it is that Gower's trilogy begins with an account of the origin of sin, and that two of the most boldly imaginative and poetically effective passages in all his work are the allegorical accounts of the cause and effect of sin at the beginnings of the *Mirour* and the *Vox.*

v

The account in the *Mirour* begins with the fall of Lucifer (MO, 74), based ultimately upon the many New Testament allusions which develop the concept of the universal struggle between God and Satan. Then comes a brief description of the Temptation and Fall "Selonc que truis en genesi" (MO, 112). The account of the origin of Sin and Death which follows (MO, 205) is interesting both intrinsically and for its possible relation to Books i and ii of Milton's *Paradise Lost.* Gower and Milton use much the same allegory: the Devil himself conceived and bore the maiden Sin, then became enamored of his own creation and upon her begot Death.

This concept may be traced ultimately to James 1:15, "Then when lust hath conceived, it bringeth forth sin: and sin, when it is finished, bringeth forth death." This verse was allegorized in the *Hexameron* of St. Basil, and the figure makes its appearance in a sermon by Robert Grosseteste.[55] Neither of these, however, combines this allegory with the infernal parliament in which the devil and his followers plot the overthrow of mankind. Antecedents for the parliament, too, can be easily found: if not the Olympian councils in the *Aeneid* (cf. the opening of Book x), then the satiric *debat* before the courts of love, in the beast fables, and in clerical satire. In the *Mirour* (MO, 417) as in the *Roman de la rose*, the retainers are called "ly baroun." It has been supposed that Gower and Milton were making use of a similar tradition, since it seems unlikely that Milton would have had access to a manuscript unknown to Bale and Stow. Yet until a treatment combining the incestuous begettal of sin and death with the infernal parliament makes its appearance, the influence of the *Mirour* upon *Paradise Lost* remains an open question.[56]

Gower combines the accounts of the origin of sin and death and the infernal parliament with that of the marriage of the daughters of the devil to various classes of society. This allegory likewise has a venerable history, from the analagous treatment in *De Nuptiis Philologiae et Mercurii* of Martianus Capella to the more direct antecedent in *Le mariage des neuf filles du diable*, likewise attributed to Grosseteste.[57] In the *Mirour*, Death engenders upon Sin the Seven Deadly Sins (MO, 235). Dispatched by their grandsire, the Devil, the Sins take over all the World's affairs:

Orguil sa gloire maintenoit,	*Pride maintained his glory;*
Envie ades luy consailloit,	*Envy continually counselled him;*
Et d'Ire fist son guerroier,	*he made Wrath his warrior;*
Et d'Avarice tresorer,	*Avarice his treasurer;*
Accidie estoit son chamberer,	*Sloth was his chamberer;*
Et Glotonie de son droit	*Gluttony was by right*
Estoit son maistre boteller,	*his chief butler;*
Et Leccherie en son mestier	*and Lechery for her special office*
Sur tous sa chiere amie estoit.	*was above all others his mistress.*

(MO, 292)

Having caused Man's banishment from Paradise, the Devil calls a parliament of the Sins and the World, before which he speaks after the fashion of Amor in the *Roman de la rose* and Satan in *Paradise Lost*, asking counsel of the company as to how Man may be brought finally to hell. Sin promises to deceive the Body; the World promises to delude Man by means of worldly vanities; Death confesses his impotence with regard to the Soul but promises to bring the Body to subjection. A messenger, Temptation, is sent to bring Man to the parley. The Devil, Sin, and the World promise him pleasure and power, while "par commun assent" (MO, 489) Death is kept discreetly out of sight. The Body succumbs to the blandishments, but the Soul stands firm, presenting the opportunity for a conventional debate between body and soul (MO, 529): "Remembre aussi que tu la loy/ Primer rompis en cel estage" (MO, 536)—Remember, says the Soul, that you are breaking the first (original or natural) law at this point. When the Soul finds that it can make no headway by argument, it calls on Reason and Fear "Qui sont sergant de sa covine" (MO, 663). Reason has no success, either; so Fear searches through the rooms until it finds the horrible figure of Death which it displays to the Body. This makes the Body turn away from Sin:

Paour ensi la Char rebroie,	Fear thus forces the Body
Q'au Conscience la renvoie,	to return to Conscience;
Et Conscience plus avant	Conscience in turn
Au bonne Resoun la convoie,	conveys it to right Reason;
Et puis Resoun par juste voie	then Reason justly
A l'Alme la fait acordant.	makes accord between it and the Soul.
(MO, 733)	

Perceiving that they have lost this round, Sin hatches the scheme for her seven daughters to marry the World, that through their progeny the attack upon Man may be renewed.

Now this allegory, which is not badly handled, is a significant starting point for Gower's criticism of man and society, since it provides a graphic exposition of the theological foundations for medieval legal doctrine. We may turn again to St. Thomas for a summary:

Three things are necessary for man's well-being, the knowledge of
what to believe, of what to desire, of what to do. The first is
taught in the Creed, the second in the Lord's prayer, the third
by Law. Of this we intend to treat. We begin by distinguishing
four kinds of law.

The first is called the law of nature. It is no other than the
light of intelligence set in us by God, showing us what we should
do and what avoid . . .

But on top of this law the devil has sown another, the law of
concupiscence. At the beginning the soul was subject to God,
and so the flesh was subject to reason. Since the devil's suggestion withdrew us from our obedience, the flesh has become rebellious . . .

Nature being in ruins, the law of Scripture now enters to recall men to deeds of virtue away from vice. Two influences are
at work here, fear and love. First fear: a man begins to avoid sin
by the prospect of judgment and hell. *The beginning of wisdom
is the fear of the Lord.* And again, *The fear of the Lord casts out
sin.* Though a man who avoids sin from motives of fear is not
righteous, nevertheless righteousness starts here where the Mosaic Law lays its emphasis. Yet its force is not enough, the hand
may obey but the mind is not held, and therefore the Gospel
Law sets another measure to keep men away from evil and bent
on good, namely the power of love.[58]

St. Thomas's summary casts a revealing light on Gower's structure.
Throughout the *Mirour* and *Vox* the fearful effects of sin and death
are displayed. The *memento mori* note is sounded frequently, but
nowhere more profoundly than at the end of the *Vox Clamantis*.
And the *Confessio Amantis*, which concludes the trilogy, is an exposition of the laws of love, both human and divine. The fact that
St. Thomas casts his discussion in the framework of law is the more
interesting in view of Gower's own preoccupation with legal solu-
tions. This is not to suggest that Gower was influenced by St.
Thomas, whom he never mentions. Furthermore, St. Thomas was
speaking of Scriptural law and leading up to a discussion of the
Creed and Lord's Prayer, whereas Gower is preoccupied with legal
justice and regal responsibility. What is important is the evidence
of the contemporary thought underlying Gower's plan. Justice

and love represent the objective of man's struggle and—structurally
—the conclusion of Gower's trilogy, just as sin and the fall represent
the beginning. The intermediary between these two is reason expressing itself in law.

The function of reason has been suggested by the transition between the first balade in the *Traitié*, quoted in the previous chapter,
and the opening lines of the *Mirour*. In the balade, man's soul is
fashioned in the image of God "Par quoi le corps de reson et
nature/ Soit attempré per jouste governage" (T, 1.3), and in the
Mirour the effect of sin is that it turns "reson en bestialité" (MO,
24). In the allegory on the origin of sin, we have seen that Fear
works through Conscience and Reason to reconcile the Body with
the Soul.[59] These are but glimpses of the broader scheme in the
scholastic conception of order in the universe which saw reasoning
intellect as the distinguishing characteristic of a human being.
Rufinius in his commentary on the distinction between natural and
human law in the *Decretum* presents the legal theory which underlies Gower's treatment:

> The dignity of man before sin was lofty, hanging as if on cords
> of these two qualities: Namely, rectitude of justice and clarity
> of knowledge; through the one he controlled human affairs,
> through the other he approached divine matters. However, as
> the wickedness of the devil grew within him, the rectitude of
> justice was depressed by the weight of perverse malice and by
> the mist of error the light of knowledge was made dim. There-
> fore, since through the lameness of ill-will he came to his blind-
> ness of ignorance, yet still retained the natural order imprinted
> on his mind, it was necessary that the integrity of knowledge be
> repaired through the exercise of justice. And therefore, since the
> natural force deep within him had not been extinguished, he be-
> gan to bestir himself that in some way he might differ from the
> brute beasts, as by his prerogative of knowing and living by law.[60]

The *Mirour de l'omme* is a working out of the implications of reason and personal virtue in preparation for the legal and political
discussions that come later. Yet this *psychomachia* between the
vices and virtues is itself set in a legalistic frame. After the long

description of the Seven Deadly Sins and their progeny (MO, 949–9720), the allegory is resumed. The Devil and his cohorts make one final assault on Man. When Avarice comes into battle brandishing a satchel of florins, Man succumbs at once and allows himself to be led to the castle of Accidie (Bunyan's Wanhope) where he is imprisoned out of the reach of the Soul, Reason, and Conscience. Reason and Conscience then take the case to a superior court:

Enmy la court superiour	In the superior court,
Devant dieu firont leur clamour	before God, Reason and Conscience
Ensi Resoun et Conscience:	thus made their clamor.
Leur advocat et procurour,	Their advocate and proctor
Et sur tout leur coadjutour,	and above all their coadjutor
C'estoit Mercy, qui d'eloquence	was Mercy, who by her eloquence
Tous autres passoit du science.	surpassed all others in knowledge.
(MO, 10045)	

God ordains a marriage between Reason and the Virtues to offset that between the World and the Sins. The allegorical struggle is referred to again at the end of the account of the Virtues, where the Body consigns itself to the Vices and the Soul vows itself to the service of Reason alone (MO, 18409). The discussion of the estates begins with the frame of the legal debate:

Si nous parlons de ces prelatz	If we speak of those prelates
Qui sont sicomme de dieu legatz	who are like God's ambassadors
Ove la clergie appartienant,	taking the part of the clergy,
Ils sont devenuz advocatz	they have become the advocates
Du Pecché pour plaider le cas	of Sin, to plead her case
Encontre l'Alme.	against the Soul.
(MO, 18421)	

After this the judiciary frame is not referred to, but this has been enough to indicate that the parliament and law court were employed as frames for the *Mirour* much as the confessional was later to be employed for the *Confessio Amantis*.

The glorification of reason as the distinguishing feature of human nature is yet another medieval inheritance from Roman legal theory.[61] In the *Summa*, St. Thomas had designated Freedom of Will, Conscience, and Reason as the qualities which raised man above beast.[62] Beast symbols for man's lower nature were familiar in sermons, moralistic treatises, and beast fables. Not the least interesting precedent for Gower is the sermon by Robert Grosseteste already referred to as detailing the ancestry of sin and death. It goes on to emphasize the soul's loss of its divine semblance through sin, and its distortion to the likeness of a beast. The list of animal symbols there included—pig for gluttony, a goat for lechery, dog for wrath, wolf for avarice, and lion for "tyrannical oppression of one's subjects"—is typical of the tradition of the Seven Deadly Sins. The list of animals on which Gower's Sins were mounted on the way to their wedding is but another example of the genre. Gower's Sins also carry birds on their wrists: Pride on a lion, bearing an eagle; Envy, dog and sparrowhawk; Ire, boar and rooster; Accidie, ass and owl; Avarice, horse (*baucan*) and hawk (*ostour*); Gluttony, wolf and kite; Lechery, goat and dove.[63]

The identification of the Sins with bestiality and the marriage of Reason to the Virtues leads to the glorification of reason as the uniquely human attribute at the end of the discussion of the estates in the *Mirour*. Everyone blames the world for man's plight, but its elements are not at fault (MO, 26605). The sun and moon are not at fault, and one good man's prayers surpass the power of all the stars.[64] Trees and animals do not sin. Whence, then, comes evil into the world? "Beste une y ad, comme je suppose,/ A qui dieus ad resoun donné" (MO, 26789). This beast, whom God formed in his own image and called man, is responsible for the evils in the world (MO, 26820). Then follows the paraphrase of a quotation from St. Gregory that reappears later in both the *Vox Clamantis* and the *Confessio Amantis*: "Omnis autem creaturae aliquid habet homo. Habet namque commune esse cum lapidibus, vivere cum arboribus, sentire cum animalibus, intelligere cum angelis." [65] Man is a microcosm of the chain of being. With lower creation he shares existence and sensation; with the angels he shares intelligence—reason (MO, 26919). The significance of the nativity scene at the end of the *Mirour* is sensitively interpreted as "L'umaine essance ove la divine/ Entre les bestes le posa" (MO, 28053). Through his free will, man can choose good or evil (MO, 26977). He differs

from other beasts in that he enjoys the prospect of eternal joy or
damnation (MO, 27100, 27160). He has only himself to blame
when the world injures him (MO, 27200). This extended discussion of reason as the basis for the natural hierarchy of beast and
man ends with a direct reference to the popular discontent that was
soon to explode into the Peasants' Revolt:

Quant pié se lieve contre teste,	*When the foot rebels against the head*
Trop est la guise deshonneste;	*the behavior is wholly illegitimate;*
Et ensi qant contre seignour	*thus when the people rise up*
Les gens sicomme salvage beste	*like savage beasts in tempestuous*
En multitude et en tempeste	*multitude against the nobleman,*
Se lievent, c'est un grant errour;	*it is a great mistake.*
Et nepourquant la gent menour	*And notwithstanding, the inferior people*
Diont que leur superiour	*say that their superiors*
Donnent la cause du moleste,	*give the cause for their injury—*
C'est de commune le clamour:	*this is the common cry.*
Mais tout cela n'est que folour,	*But all this is but folly*
Q'au siecle nul remede preste.	*for which there is no immediate remedy.*

(MO, 27229)

These lines echo the conclusion of the treatment of the peasants
at the end of the discussion of the estates 700 lines earlier, quoted
in the previous chapter to illustrate the linkage between the *Mirour*
and the *Vox*. Both passages represent the practical application of
the theories of law and order emerging at the end of the *Mirour*.
Reason and human law supported the social hierarchy just as natural law supported the natural hierarchy. Rebellion against the
social hierarchy represented rebellion against reason and law, and
ultimately against the divinely instituted universal order, and it
reduced the rebels to the level of unreasoning beasts.

VI

Against such a background, the vision of the Peasants' Revolt
which introduces the *Vox Clamantis* may be recognized as an exemplum of the fearful effects of rebellion against universal order.
The allegory turns upon the ideals of reason and the law, represented by the obverse of the bestial shapes and behavior. It begins
with a description of springtime nature with its conventional over-

tones of the peace and fecundity of the Golden Age (VC, 1.1).
Night and storm bring the beautiful day to an end, and in his sleep
the dreamer in the first of three visions sees the churls rebelling.[66]
The curse of God flashes upon the rascally bands, and they are
turned into beasts: "Qui fuerant homines prius innate racionis,/
Brutorum species irracionis habent" (They who before had been
men of *innate reason* [so nearly Rufinius' phrase] had the appearance of irrational beasts, VC, 1.177). This is the thesis of the vision.
There are seven bands of rebels. The first band, burden bearers
transformed into asses, refuse to bear their loads and take on pretensions of dress and manner: "Their asinine behavior, however,
labeled them as stupid and rude because they had no reason" (VC,
1.237). The second band, peasants transformed into monstrous
oxen with the feet of bears and tails of dragons, refuse to draw the
plow: "Only a lawless course remained to the farmers, and they,
too, became ungovernable by reason" (VC, 1.287). The third band,
transformed into monstrous swine, are led by "the wild boar of
Kent" (?Roger Cave) on a bloody rampage. The fourth band, outside servants transformed by the devil himself into dogs (VC, 1.
440), mingle with the fifth band, household servants in the shape
of cats. With them come criminals in the shape of gray foxes who
break into the city and steal because "no law prevents them" (VC,
1.486). The rustics undergo two degrees of metamorphosis—into
the shapes of domestic animals, symbolizing their servile status, but
domestic animals with the natures of wild beasts, symbolizing their
lawless frenzy. So it is that the dog "which was formerly gentler
than a sacrificial animal became a swift wolf" (VC, 1.491). The
twofold transformation is represented even more dramatically when
the rebels of the sixth band are transformed into domestic fowl,
and the cock and the goose then transformed into a raven and a kite
(VC, 1.527). Domestic fowl and birds of prey mingle and usurp
one another's functions "since law and order were banished" (VC,
1.524). The final band of peasants takes the shape of frogs and
flies, the plagues of Egypt, fierce and noxious as the rest. Last of
all comes the Jay, Wat Tyler, who preaches lawlessness:

> O you servile wretches, whom the world has long subjugated
> by its law, now comes the day when the peasants will triumph
> and drive the freeborn from their lands. Let all honor come to
> an end, let justice perish, let no virtue which formerly existed
> endure further in the world. Let the law which formerly held
> us in check with its justice give over and from here forward let
> our court rule. (VC, 1.693)

The final line may be a criticism of the unauthorized peasants'
courts, but to Gower the law of the peasants is anarchy:

> The foolish populace did not know what its "court" was. How-
> ever, he ordered them to adopt the laws of force—*iura vigoris*.
> He said, "Strike," and one man struck. He said, "Kill," and an-
> other killed. He said, "Commit crime," and everyone committed
> it, nor did anyone oppose his will. (VC, 1.713)
>
> What king or law might be was unknown to those mad crea-
> tures; no rule or order restrained them. (VC, 1.769)

The animal bands bring utter chaos with them as they swirl
toward London in the famous eleventh chapter of Book 1, vowing
"with savage rage in the woods that they would trample on justice
in a mad frenzy by overthrowing all laws" (VC, 1.895). The sack
of London by the peasants is recounted in the five chapters following, in what is described as the second vision. The use of the familiar eponym New Troy, and the echoes of the sack of Troy in
Book II of the *Aeneid* (although curiously there are no verbal
echoes of Virgil) give the details an epic heightening. Some of the
events of the attack upon London and the Tower can be identified
beneath the rhetoric and the Homeric nomenclature. The treacherous surrender of London Bridge is referred to (VC, 1.904). The
burning of the Lancastrian Savoy Palace is identified by the same
word play Chaucer used in the *Book of the Duchess:*

> *Que via salua fuit, furit ignibus impetuosa,*
> *Quo longum castrum ductile nescit iter.* (VC, 1.929)
>
> (What had been the Savoy burned fiercely with fire,
> so that Lancaster did not know which way to take.)

The burning of the priory of St. John of Jerusalem at Clerkenwell,

Baptisteque domus (VC, 1.931); the invasion of the apartments of
the Princess of Wales in the Tower (VC, 1.997); the murder of
Simon Sudbury, Archbishop of Canterbury (VC, 1.1001); the attack upon the Inns of Court (VC, 1.1173); and perhaps other
actual events can be recognized. Macaulay accuses Gower of transmitting calumny when he accuses the peasants of pillaging the city;
but he allows that "it is certain that dishonest persons must have
taken advantage of the disorder to some extent for their own private
ends," and Tout has since produced evidence that the rebels plun-
dered the privy wardrobe in the Tower for arms.[67] However, to become overly concerned about the historical versimilitude in the
second and third visions, after observing the technique of the first,
is to miss the point. Presumably if Gower had wanted to write a
chronicle, he would have done so. The first book of the *Vox Clamantis* is not history but a poet-philosopher's meditation on the
meaning of history. That meaning is clearly that when order is not
maintained, chaos ensues. The poet's intention is to paint the chaos
as vividly as possible, with the help of every fact, figure, exaggeration,
vituperation. The city is the symbol of order, and, as the ones ravaging it, the peasants are subjected to the severest criticism, but this is
as much a doctrinaire reaction as the bigotry of which Gower has
been accused. As a matter of fact, he elsewhere expresses deep concern for the peasants in their place,[68] and he here voices his disappointment at the failure of the aristocracy to live up to its obligation
to maintain order: "The peasant attacked and the knight in the city
did not resist. Troy was without a Hector" (VC, 1.991). The murder of the archbishop is the culminating horror of the lawless frenzy,
because the archbishop is the symbol not only of the love and peace
which characterize an orderly society (VC, 1.1010), but also of
order and authority: "Qui pater est anime, viduatur corporis expers.
. . . Qui fuerat doctor legum, sine lege peribat" (He who is father
of the soul is seen to be without body. . . . He who was doctor of
law perished without law, VC, 1.1083). The city becomes a scene
of carnage (VC, 1.1163). Death knocks at the courts of justice
(VC, 1.1173). All that the King can do is lament (VC, 1.1155);

he is no longer respected (VC, 1.1180). With the breakdown of order, the dreamer fears that mankind itself is threatened with extinction: "Now mankind is coming to an end, since beasts and warfare have seized control of men, and since there is no justice in their laws" (VC, 1.1370).

The second vision ends when the rioting has destroyed the dreamer's home (VC, 1.1380). He abandons the city, the symbol of humanity and civilization, and flees to the woods and caves where he lives like a hunted animal (VC, 1.1360).

> The enemy was close at hand on the right and pressed hard from the left, and each side terrified with like fear. Alas! How many times did I retreat into the shadows when I saw the maniacs, and my ear was always wide open. Alas! How many times did I hide in the woods, hardly daring to go into caves. Late at night, I despaired over what the early morning might bring. Alas! How many times did fear, striking terror into my wits, say to me, "Why do you run away? You will remain alive only a short time here." (VC, 1.1413)

Man's relation to nature and his fellow men here is the very opposite to that of the Golden Age. Since sin had destroyed nature's beneficence, man's only hope of security lies in social organization, in reason, order, law, and the king. Gower makes it quite clear in this and in ensuing chapters that he is writing "quasi in propria persona," that the flight to the woods is imaginary. It represents a key point in his social argument, the nadir of the exposition that had begun with the description of the origin of sin at the beginning of the *Mirour*, that if sin is allowed to destroy individual virtue and social order, man cannot exist upon the earth. From this nadir Gower goes on painfully to reconstruct a positive theory of society.

Up to this point in the *Mirour* and the *Vox*, the state as an organism has not occupied a prominent place in Gower's discussion. But the events of the Peasants' Revolt (speaking biographically) or the progress of his own argument (speaking critically) now brought him to a heightened awareness that man does not survive by individual virtue alone, and that social organization must underlie the achievement of order and justice. This awareness makes its appearance in the third version of Book I, that of the ship in a storm, to which Gower makes a reasonably successful, dreamlike transition by having the dreamer simply run out of the woods and board the ship (VC, 1.1600). The ship as an image for the state was familiar from classical literature. John of Salisbury had used it in the Prologue to the eighth book of the *Policraticus*. In *De Regimine*, St. Thomas had again adopted it, like Gower calling the king the "gubernator." [69] Of more immediate relevance are a macaronic sermon in MS. Bodley 649 and an elegy in the Vernon MS. on the death of Edward III. In the elegy, the ship is likened to the chivalry, the rudder to the king, the mast to the commons, and the wind to prayers which provide the motive power for the whole:

> Whyl schip and reþer togeder was knit,
> þei dredde nouþer tempest, druyʒe nor wete;
> Nou be þei boþe in synder flit,
> þat selden seyʒe is sone forʒete.[70]

In the sermon, the ship image is connected directly with the Peasants' Revolt and dissension among the aristocracy: "nostra navis was so hurlid and burlid inter ventos et freta quod erat in grandi periculo et sepe in puncto pereundi. ffuit in grandi periculo quando communes surrexerunt contra dominos. ffuit iterum in grandi periculo quando domini litigabunt inter se." [71] Both elegy and sermon join the images of ship and tower:

> Sumtyme an Englische ship we had,
> Nobel hit was and heih of tour.

> *ffuit etiam adeo fortis quod fortissima navis of*
> *toure super mare . . .*

These two images Gower associated with the events of the peasants' attack upon the Tower of London to produce the striking—if verbally derivative—storm description of Caps. xvii-xx. In the interest of developing the thematic connection between individual sin and social chaos, Gower violated his narrative chronology.

The sack of London had been dealt with in the first vision, 500 lines earlier, but he now returned to it, using the new figure. The attack by the peasants upon the Tower of London (with which the ship is specifically identified, VC, 1.1743) stands for the attack of bestial disorder upon the state itself. The occupants of the ship are the nobility (VC, 1.1603). The helmsman is the king (VC, 1.1727). The storm all but overwhelms the ship. "In this flood water, the owl swam among the larks, the wolf among the sheep, the wicked among the upright. The furrowing keel suddenly sank from the force of this water, which advanced upon the bridge and forecastle" (VC, 1.1647). There is no point in trying to identify the great whales that tremble before the storm, nor the monsters that come out of the storm to attack the ship, when Gower does not do so. We are dealing again with figurative generalities. By a combination of Christian prayer and pagan propitiation of Neptune through the sacrifice of the Jay (the killing of Wat Tyler by William Walworth), the storm is caused to subside. Now the figurative ship is transformed into something more literal, or perhaps, to adopt Miss Wickert's reading,[72] into the poet's mind. It bears the dreamer to the "Insula Bruti" (VC, 1.1963), whose inhabitants are a wild, quarrelsome people of mixed stock, but the poet thinks "there is not a worthier people under the sun if there were mutual love among them" (VC, 1.1981). A divine voice tells him that "a quarrelsome island where peace seldom lasts long has received him" (VC, 1.2024), that he should be cautious, cease to struggle, and write down what he heard in his dream. Waking, he perceives that "the madmen have been subdued under the law of old, and that a new mode of law has repaired the broken course of events" (VC, 1.2061):

> The peasantry had been bound in chains and lay patiently under our feet . . . Similarly Satan's power lay prostrate, overwhelmed by divine might, but nevertheless it lurked in hiding among the ungovernable peasantry. For the peasant always lay in wait to see whether he by chance could bring the noble class to destruction.
>
> (VC, 1.2093)

The aristocratic tone of this conclusion was what offended Taine, Jusserand, and the other liberal historians of the 19th century, who saw in the Peasants' Revolt a popular democratic movement. Their enthusiastic views of Wyclif, Langland, and Chaucer as levelers are, however, being revised, and we may conclude that Gower's position with regard to social hierarchy was typical of his time. Patristic authority and all medieval political theory supported the notion of a hierarchy of ranks and orders, and it was to be several centuries before John Ball's kind of socialism was to appear even theoretically respectable to the educated classes.[73] For only one parallel to Gower's position, we may quote Master Thomas Wimbleton preaching at Paul's Cross in the middle of the century:

> And therefore, saith clerke Avicenne, that every unreasonable best, if he have that that kind hath ordeined for him, as kind hath ordeined it, he has suffisance to live by himselfe without any help of other of the same kind . . . But if there ne were but o man in the world, though he had all that good that is therein, yet for defaut he shuld deie, or his life shuld be wors than if he were naught . . . Herfore evrich man see to what state God hath cleped him, and dwell he therein by travile according to his degree. Thou that art a laborer or a crafty man, do this truelly. If thou art a servant or a bondman, be suget and lowe, in drede of displesing of thy Lord. If thou art a marchaunt, deceive nought thy brother in chaffering. If thou art a knight or a lord, defend the poore man, and needy fro hands that will harme them. If thou art a iustice or a iudge, go not on the right hand by favour, neither on the left hand to punish any man for hate. If thou art a priest, undernime, praye, and reprove, in all maner patience and doctrine. Undernime thilke that ben negligent, pray for thilke that ben obedient, reprove tho that ben unobedient to God. So every man travaile in his degree.[74]

Beside this could be put the observation in Chaucer's Parson's Tale that "sith the time of grace cam, God ordeyned that som folk sholde be moore heigh in estaat and in degree, and som folk moore lough, and that everich sholde be served in his estaat and in his degree" (CT, x.770).

What distinguishes Gower's views from those of many of his contemporaries, and places him among the progressive thinkers of his day, is his emphasis upon legal justice and regal responsibility for all the estates, defined in terms of "le bien commune," "bonus communi," or "the comun good," depending on the language in which he happened to be writing. Like so many other social and political concepts, this one is of classical origin and was naturalized into Christian thought by the early church fathers.[75] In Aristotle's *Politics*, it represents a normative concept, the sort of good which a virtuous man would desire.[76] It forms the basis for the Roman concept of the *res publica*. Passages from Cicero's lost *Republic* preserved in St. Augustine's *De civitate Dei* (II.21) define *the people* as being "not every assemblage or mob, but an assemblage associated by a common acknowledgment of law and by a community of interest" (*juris consensu et utilitatis communione*). John of Salisbury, William of Occam, St. Thomas Aquinas, and other civilists and canonists made important use of this concept, and by the 14th century it had become a commonplace.[77] In the hands of John Ball and the Lollards, it might be radical—"a favourite phrase of fourteenth century socialism, both in England and France"—but it was used even more frequently as a synonym for the responsible state in which each class performed its proper function.[78] Gower emphasized this concept more than any of his English contemporaries. In the *Miour*, ingratitude of both the rulers and subjects destroys "l'amour commun" (MO, 6727); joy in the good fortune of others promotes "le commun proufit" (MO, 12905); concord guards "la pes commune" in the cities (MO, 13871); the failure of friars to bear their burden in society is contrary to "la commune pes" (MO, 21540); covetousness on the part of the king militates against "la commun profitement" (MO, 23178); knights are supposed to defend "le commun droit" (MO, 23610, 23784); lawyers' fees taken from the "bien commun" should be returned to the same (MO, 24341, 24345); bailiffs and other minor officials are instituted by "la loy commune" for "le proufit de communalté" (MO, 24823); merchants employ fraud for their own ends rather than serving "le commun proufit" (MO, 25260); artizans are necessary to "le bien commun" (MO, 25503).

The theory that each estate "est ordiné par son endroit/ De faire au siecle ascun labour" (MO, 23618), implied throughout, but mentioned only briefly in the *Mirour,* becomes the principal subject of the *Vox Clamantis.* In its final form, that work begins with the example of the peasants' failure to perform their duties (Book I). The Boethian discussion of fortune in Book II is a logical introduction to a discussion of the estates, since, according to Roman political theory, one's estate, either as slave or emperor, was the result of fortune.[79] This conception St. Augustine had modified by arguing that slavery, at least, was the result of sin and war, indirectly implying greater virtue on the part of freemen than of slaves, and even greater virtue on the part of the Christian prince.[80] So in Book II of the *Vox* Gower combats the "common view" that the misfortunes of the day were the result of fortune, and argues that they are the result of sin (Caps. i–vi). He concludes the book by arguing that "since man does not understand the circumstances of the world" (VC, II.451), which would certainly include the disposition of the Three Estates, he should have faith and accept its divine order (VC, II.467, esp. 600ff). The Three Estates cited at the beginning of Book III are thus part of the "ordo munde." The only question is as to how well they are fulfilling their designated roles. After this introduction, Gower launches into a criticism of the clergy which frequently echoes the criticism in the *Mirour* save that it is much more legalistic in tone. Not only does their corruption involve misuse of "lex positiua," as discussed above, but their condition is so hopeless that, in the interest of justice, the laws of laymen (*laici jura,* VC, III.1680) must be forced upon them and "laymen must try to hold them in check" (VC, III.1700). The secular clergy and most of the regulars are granted their place in society, but mendicants who live in a disorderly fashion are again dismissed as of no service to the common good (VC, IV.936). And just as "le commun droit," "le loy civile," and "le commun loy" had defined the obligations of knighthood in the *Mirour,* so "commune

bonum," "lex," and "iusticia" define their obligations at the beginning of Book v of the Vox. After a diatribe against courtly love
as a motive for knightly behavior, Gower concludes that "a knight
who is worthy battles in Christ's name and defends the common-
wealth—*rem communem*—with his arm" (VC, v.491). Peasants
likewise "should be bound to their various tasks for the common
good"—*pro bono communi* (VC, v.628). And finally,

> Since no single region produces all the various kinds of things
> necessary for human use, merchants, among others, have been
> appointed to assist the world's citizens. Through their agency
> the goods of all regions are mutually shared.
>
> (VC, v.655 headnote)

VII

By the sixth book of the Vox Clamantis, Gower has reached
the point where he can attempt his first synthesis of the ideas of
law, the common good, and kingship. A comparison of the treatments of kingship in the Mirour, Vox, and Confessio provides a
touchstone for the evolution of Gower's thought. In the first, evidently written in the last years of Edward III, the conception of the
king tends to be primarily personal and sacerdotal; in the second,
written shortly after the accession of young Richard II, it tends to
be judicial, although it again devolves into a series of exhortations
to personal virtue; in the last, written when Richard had begun
to demonstrate his weakness both in character and policy, the discussion is of the education of a prince. The nature of the discussion
in each of the three works was no doubt influenced by the drift of
national affairs and by Gower's growing involvement with the
court, but it likewise follows the development of his theoretical
argument from the consideration of individual sin and virtue to the
consideration of social chaos and order.

The emphasis upon the character of the king in all three treatments had social significance since in the ecclesiastical tradition
authority was considered dependent in the last analysis upon personal virtue.[81] In an ordered state, reason must rule and not bestial

passion. St. Thomas, commenting upon Aristotle, had summed it thus in *De Regimine*:

And thus the Philosopher speaks wisely when he suggests in III *Politics* [cap.11], that in a right government not a beast, but God and the understanding should rule; for a beast rules when a king tries to rule others not by reason, but by passion and lust, in which we share with the beasts; but God rules when in ruling others the king does not deviate from right reason and from natural law.[82]

In this respect the good king and good aristocracy differed from tyrants of Lombardy, whom Gower described some half dozen years before they appeared in the Prologue to Chaucer's *Legend of Good Women*: [83]

Ascuns diont q'en Lombardie	They say that in Lombardy
Sont les seignours de tirandie,	there are tyrannous lords
Qui vivont tout au volenté	who live without restraint,
Sanz loy tenir d'oneste vie,	without law to hold their lives in check;
Ainçois orguil et leccherie	instead pride and lechery
Et covoitise ont plus loé.	and covetousness are greatly admired.

(MO, 23233)

Even though virtue and divine grace form the basis for authority, the classic role of fortune is recognized in all three of Gower's poems.[84] The section on kings in the *Mirour* is preceded by one on emperors composed of two parts: a lost leaf commenting on Nebuchadnezzar (a type of the ruler whom passion and pride reduced to bestiality),[85] and a Boethian lament against inconstant fortune and the mutability of temporal kingdoms (MO, 22021), both topics to be developed more fully in the *Vox* (Book II and elsewhere) and the *Confessio*, which speaks specifically of "a king, which on the whiel/ Fortune hath set aboven alle" (CA, VIII.3172).

According to medieval theory, however, the true king was divinely ordained to make and maintain justice for all. As Bracton described his function a century earlier:

The king was created and chosen for this: that he should make justice for all, and that in him the Lord should sit, and that he himself should decide his judgments, and that he should sustain

and defend what he has justly judged, because if there were no
one to make justice, peace could easily be wiped out, and it
would be vain to establish laws and to do justice if there were
no one to protect the laws.[86]

Gower emphasized this admonition in the *Mirour*. In addition to
protecting the church, the king must maintain justice:

Et puis doit de sa Roialté	And thus should royalty,
Selonc justice et equité	with justice and equity,
Guarder la loy dedeinz sa bonde.	preserve the law within its boundaries.
(MO, 22234)	

"Justice" is cited as the king's responsibility eleven times more in
the *Mirour*, and "lois" or "droit" five times more in the 599 extant
lines on the king (two more leaves have been lost following line
22359, evidently ending with another allusion to Nebuchadnezzar).
In addition to these references to the judicial, which become the
substance of Book VI of the *Vox*, emphasis in the *Mirour* is placed
directly on the sacerdotal role of the king. King David is cited as
an example:

Ly Rois David, comme dist l'auctour,	King David, as writers say,
Estoit des six pointz essamplour,	was an example in six ways
Dont chascun Roy puet essampler:	which each king should exemplify:
Ly Rois David estoit pastour,	King David was a shepherd,
Ly Rois David estoit harpour,	King David was a harper,
Ly Rois David fuist chivaler,	King David was a knight,
Ly Rois David en son psalter	King David in his psalter
Estoit prophete a dieu loer,	was a prophet who praised God,
Ly Rois David en doel et plour	King David in sorrow and tears
Estoit penant, et pour regner	was a penitent, and to rule
David fuist Rois, si q'au parler	David was king, which is as much as to say
As autrez Rois il fuist mirour.	that to other kings he was a mirror.
(MO, 22873)	

Each of these roles is developed at length. Although three of them
may be interpreted politically ("harpour," "chivaler," "rois,"),
three are sacerdotal ("pastour," [87] "prophete," "penant"), and none
is judicial. Private morality and personal salvation appear to be
the substance of such arguments as that in death the king fares no
differently from the poor laborer (the *memento mori*, MO, 23105)
and that the king's soul can suffer more than those of lesser degree

(MO, 23125). However, throughout the discussion, in accordance with medieval political theory in general, the king is viewed as at the summit of society ("Rois, qui tous estatz surmonte," MO, 23117), with only his fear "d'infernal gaiole" (MO, 23145) to keep him virtuous.

In the *Vox Clamantis*, emphasis is placed largely upon the judicial role of the king. He is grouped with lawyers rather than with the chivalry. Book VI begins by praising law in the abstract. Then it goes on to criticize the corruption of lawyers, judges, and minor officials in terms closely paralleling those in the *Mirour*. In Cap. vii it returns to the theme of the opening lines, the need for law in society, stating that it is the responsibility of the king to make sure that the legal machinery operates without fraud and corruption—only the English King is still a boy and unable to fulfill his responsibility. This leads in turn to a reiteration of an idea which had appeared at the end of the first book of the *Vox*, and which was to provide the central thesis for the *Confessio*, the danger of divisiveness on either the domestic or national level (VC, vi.487). The solution in the *Confessio* was to go beyond that here proposed and to advocate justice within the frame of Empedoclean love. Here the responsibility is laid directly on the king: "Therefore, all who govern kingdoms can see that the greatest part of our fate depends upon them" (VC, vi.495). As in the *Mirour*, the first criterion is still the personal virtue of the ruler: "Peoples have perished because of the king's sin . . . but royal goodness brings the joys of peace to the people" (VC, vi.501). And the glory and honor of the king are the national unity maintained by law (VC, vi.521).

The introduction to the Epistle to the King in the *Vox Clamantis* emphasizes that his chief shortcoming is poor counsel.[88] In the first version of the Epistle, written early in the 1380's, blame for plight of the nation is placed upon the Council: "The high court which should be our guide is lawless, and, as the voice says, it commits high crime. No voice now speaks for the common good, but instead each man seizes upon the opportunities for his own profit" (VC, vi.547*). In the revision, the King is blamed directly, first

for his undisciplined behavior, then for choosing bad companions
(VC, vi.555). But however Gower's opinion of Richard may have
altered as a result of the progress of events, the Epistle that follows
is unchanged. It is a collection of commonplaces from the *Secretum
Secretorum* and the *speculum regale* tradition, permeated with legal
argument. As the headnote to the first chapter of the Epistle states:
"However much the royal power may be exalted above the laws,
it is nevertheless only proper that his royal highness, by persevering
in good behavior, zealously govern himself under the laws of justice
as if he were a free man, and his people as if in the presence of
the Almighty King." There follows an earnest exhortation to the
King to submit himself to law and self control.[89] Cap. ix begins
and Cap. x ends with the proper selection of counsellors, but in
between it is devoted to matters of policy: the King should be
swift and stern in meting out justice (VC, vi.690); he should not
allow his minions to extort from the poor (721, 741, 811); he
should place his reputation above money (733); he should support
the church (739); he should see to it that noble and peasant bear
equal burdens (747). Cap. xi warns the King against pride and
gluttony; Cap. xii against lechery, using the exemplum of Balaam
and Balak as it was to be used again in the *Confessio*. Cap. xiii
extols his military responsibility, holding up to the youthful Richard
the exploits of his father, the Black Prince. The account of the
earlier English successes on the Continent takes on a heroic ring
(VC, vi.937), but Gower concludes that the Black Prince's real
accomplishment was that he kept the peace at home: "The land
was quiet under that great prince; no sword terrorized those whom
his hand protected" (VC, vi.961). So, while "there is a time for
war and a time for peace" (VC, vi.973), love is a king's best
weapon: "Omnia vincit amor, amor est defensio regis" (VC, vi.999).
Cap. xiv is devoted to extolling love as the basis for authority and
as the binding force in society (VC, vi.1027). Cap. xv praises wisdom as the chief virtue of a ruler and winds up the political exhortation in the Epistle with a repetition of familiar ideas: "Per-

form your duties to your law," "be a lover of justice," "be dutiful and govern your people according to law" (VC, vi.1065).

We observed in connection with the beginning and end of the *Mirour* how Gower appealed to the traditional clerical arguments that fear of the Lord and fear of death are the beginnings of wisdom and justice. At the end of the Epistle to the King and in the final book of the *Vox* these concepts receive fuller development (VC, vi.xvi–xvii, vii.x–xix). They lead to another lament for the passing of godly clerics, heroic rulers, and chaste lovers (vi. xix–xxi). And while the final diatribe against lovers might appear at first glance disproportionate and unrelated to the Epistle to the King, it turns out, like the *memento mori*, to provide a transition to the last book, which in turn provides a transition to the *Confessio Amantis*.

The *Confessio Amantis* has been traditionally regarded as a poem whose chief subject is courtly love. Set as it is in the frame of the lover's confession to Genius, the priest of Venus, and concluding with a renunciation of earthly love, it begs for such an interpretation. Yet there is always the problem of relating this obviously courtly theme to the political theory set forth in the Prologue, Book vii, and the conclusion—a feat usually accomplished by the simple expedient of denigrating Gower's art. The last book of the *Vox Clamantis*, however, indicates the intended connection. For here adulterous, carnal love is taken as the principal reflection of selfish, temporal love (*cupiditas*, if one will, although the term is not mentioned), which brings all suffering into the world, and contrasts with selfless, divine love (*caritas*, again not so named), which leads to personal salvation, social justice, unity, and peace. The first evidence of cupidity in Book vii is that *largitas* has departed from the world (VC, vii.i); the second that adulterous love (*Gallica peccata*, vii.156) has poisoned human relations and put justice to flight. Characteristically, Gower can elicit from the lament that adultery has overthrown law in England one of his clearest statements about the legal basis for social accord:

For law is well established [in other countries], judges for all men in common, and decides all cases without trickery. Neither rank, sex, bribes, entreaties, fear, nor anything else can withhold rights from the least of men. And so, to a certain extent, justice redeems their sin of the flesh, which fails because of its frail nature. But in this country, not only are we mastered by the goad of the flesh, with which man is spurred on, but indeed the law, ignorant of what is right, oversteps its boundaries. And so our native land goes astray with crooked steps, to such an extent that men say there is no longer law and order in our realm.

(VC, VII.1319)

The universal implications of this complaint against the decay of society are figured in an adaptation of popular interpretations of the statue of Nebuchadnezzar's dream (Daniel 2:37). At least since the time of Alcuin,[90] the empires mentioned in Daniel's own interpretation had been identified as Babylonian (the golden head), Persian (the silver breast and arms), Macedonian (the brass stomach), Roman (the iron legs), post-Roman (the clay feet). But an equally common moral interpretation drew upon the Ovidian figure of the four ages (*Metamorphoses*, I.88): the Golden Age of the Earthly Paradise, the Silver Age when nature grew unkind and men had to seek shelter, the Bronze Age when men grew fierce and warlike but were still free from any taint of evil, and finally the Iron Age when honesty and generosity gave way to treachery and greed. Richard of St. Victor generalized the moral interpretation by identifying the golden head of the statue with intelligence, the silver breast with truth, the brass stomach with dissension, the iron legs with cruelty, and the clay feet with fragility.[91] Jean Gerson gave it a political turn by combining the Platonic figure of golden leaders, silver auxiliaries, and iron and brass artisans and husbandmen (*Republic*, III) with the anthropomorphic figure of the state: the golden head of the state is the king; the silver breast and arms are the chivalry; the brass stomach, merchants; the iron legs and clay feet, laborers.[92] At the end of the *Vox Clamantis*, Gower combined the moral and political interpretations: "The golden head of the statue has been cut off, yet the two feet of iron and clay still stand. The noble, golden race has departed and a poor one of iron has sprung forth" (VC, vii.5). The glorious rich who dispensed gold have disappeared, leaving behind a race of mercenary misers hard as iron (VC, vii.i–ii). Both clerics and laymen are as feeble clay before the temptations of the flesh (VC, vii.iii–v). In the Prologue of the *Confessio*, Gower returned to the identification of the parts of the statue with the empires of the world. But the figure of the statue and the identification of adultery with lawlessness both form bridges between the *Vox Clamantis* and the *Confessio Amantis*.

VIII

To assert that the major theme of the *Confessio Amantis* is a completion of the sin-law-love pattern of Gower's moral argument is not to deny that the matter is courtly love nor that one of its purposes was to bring together a collection of stories for the delectation of an aristocratic audience. Our problem is to see how legal and political preoccupation molded Gower's treatment of the material in this piece as we have seen it molding the penitential and belletristic materials in the *Mirour* and *Vox*. We must begin by observing that the real context of the piece is not courtly love, but Empedoclean love as a social cement.[93] C. S. Lewis has pointed out that the Prologue is esthetically a transition from the "ordinary world" into the allegory of love. But it must be emphasized that the allegory exists for the light it throws on the ordinary world. It is in the Prologue that we find the chief continuity with Gower's previous poems. Its mood picks up just where the *Vox* leaves off, in total discouragement about the chaotic, disunited state of the English nation. Two of the most specifically patriotic passages in Gower's three major poems are at the end of the *Vox* (vii.xxiv) and in the revised dedication at the beginning of the *Confessio* (CA, Prol.24ff). One can almost see the poet turning from the one to the other. Both patriotism and discouragement are more pronounced in the revised dedication than in the original dedication of the *Confessio*, which—problems of chronology now aside—in-

dicates the harmony of mood in the form in which Gower finally
intended the two pieces to be read.

The revised Prologue goes on to set the book in the tradition
of the *speculum regale*:

> If noman write hou that it stode,
> The pris of hem that weren goode
> Scholde, as who seith, a gret partie
> Be lost: so for to magnifie
> The worthi princes that tho were,
> The bokes schewen hiere and there,
> Wherof the world ensampled is;
> And tho that deden thanne amis
> Thurgh tirannie and crualte,
> Right as thei stoden in degre,
> So was the wrytinge of here werk.
> Thus I, which am a burel clerk,
> Purpose forto wryte a bok. (CA, Prol.41)

This is as good a point as any to observe that the emphasis of the
Confessio upon politics and the conduct of kings can be demonstrated statistically. It is relatively easy to count the stories which
have kings or princes as their central figures; and even though no
two people will agree on all the ascriptions, most of the stories can
be assigned the categories of love, or general morality, or political
instruction. The fifteen which seem to me to overlap have been
assigned to both categories and counted twice in the subtotals.

Total of all stories without overlapping 141
Total of stories in all categories about kings . . 98

Stories about	Love	General Morality	Politics
Book i	5	4	5
Book ii	5	2	5
Book iii	8	2	6
Book iv	12	7	4
Book v	12	7	4
Book vi	3	2	4
Book vii	8	2	36
Book viii	4	–	–
Total	57	26	64
Stories repeated	15	1	15

The connecting links, the introductions and conclusions of Genius, and the questions and confessions of the Lover all attempt to set the sins and their illustrations in the context of love, but aside from them, the subject of the *Confessio Amantis* is moral and political instruction in a ratio of about eight to five.

Such an analysis makes particularly significant the conclusion to the revised Prologue:

> Whan the próloge is so despended,
> This bok schal afterward ben ended
> Of love, which doth many a wonder
> And many a wys man hath put under.
> And in this wyse I thenke trete
> Towardes hem that now be grete,
> Betwen the vertu and the vice
> Which longeth unto this office. (CA, Prol.73)

"This office" could simply mean love, but it can equally mean the responsibilities of "greatness." If we are not entitled from this to conclude that the allegory of love is merely a sugar coating, we are at least entitled to assume that the virtues and vices therein examined pertain quite as much to the governance of a ruler as to that of a courtly lover. And it should be remembered that the political is the aspect of the poem Gower himself chose to emphasize in the colophon describing his three major works.

The unrevised portion of the Prologue picks up with the now familiar theme of the virtue, prosperity, and stability of the good old days: "Justice of lawe tho was holde" (CA, Prol.102). Now everything is different:

> The world is changed overal,
> And therof most in special
> That love is falle into discord. (CA, Prol.119)

The reason is divisiveness. The "comun vois which mai noght lie" cries out:

> And sein the regnes ben divided,
> In stede of love is hate guided,
> The werre wol no pes purchace,

> And lawe hath take hire double face,
> So that justice out of the weie
> With ryhtwisnesse is gon aweie. (CA, Prol.126)

Such peace as the world can expect is attributed to the hope that the power of "hem that ben the worldes guides" will, with good counsel, be kept "upriht":

> That hate breke noght thassise
> Of love, which is al the chief
> To kepe a regne out of meschief. (CA, Prol.148)

Finally, Gower would have the French wars ("In which non wot who hath the werre [worse]," CA, Prol.175) brought to an end, and nations reconciled to love "which is king sovereign/ Of al the worldes governaunce" (CA, Prol.185). In this context is love introduced in the *Confessio Amantis*. The remainder of the Prologue goes on to detail the catastrophic effects of divisiveness within the clergy, the commons, and (using the statue in Nebuchadnezzar's dream) the empires of the world. The cause of all evil is division through lack of love, here finally properly designated charity (CA, Prol.851, 892, 903).

The two patterns that we have discerned in Gower's presentation through the three works have been the movement from sin through justice to love and the movement from individual sin and social chaos to individual virtue and social order, particularly in connection with the treatment of the king, but also in the treatment of the clergy, peasants, and other classes. This second pattern asserts itself at the end of the Prologue of the *Confessio* and becomes the controlling idea throughout the poem. Already of the clergy it has been said:

> And ech of hem himself amendeth
> Of worldes good, bot non entendeth
> To that which comun profit were. (CA, Prol.375)

The concept of the individual instance as an exemplum of the universal truth is introduced at the end of the Prologue by the third presentation of the Gregorian figure of man as a microcosm, himself composed of diverse humors and elements that are always at war: "And whan this litel world mistorneth,/ The grete world al overtorneth" (Prol.957). Would that another Arion (not this time David) might appear whose harping would bring peace into the world. In this context, again, as in the *Visio*, "as if in the person of another whom love holds fast, pretending himself to be a lover" (1.60 Latin sidenote), the author presents the Lover's education.

It is unnecessary, after C. S. Lewis, to analyze the love allegory itself. The May landscape, the dream, Venus and the God of Love —all so curiously parallel to the Prologue to the *Legend of Good Women*—are strictly in the French dream convention. There is verisimilitude here in the depiction of the dreamer's behavior and emotions in love, as there was in the depiction of his terror in the *Visio*. But the moralistic comment which Professor Lewis took as peripheral is central, the allegory of love which he took as central is peripheral. The allegory and the final palinode of "love cured by age" are very nearly as moving as Lewis's eloquent exposition makes them out to be. Yet his misgiving that he was giving the allegory a more conceptual form than is justified by the text is well founded. For it is clearly the Prologue and the moralistic digressions that are the heart of Gower's matter. It is they which connect with and carry to a conclusion the theme that he has been developing since the first lines of the *Mirour*. And it is J. A. W. Bennett who has more correctly perceived that the real point to the conclusion of the poem is not "love cured by age," but Venus's order that the Lover eschew the "singuler profit" of romantic love and devote himself to the "common profit": i.e., he is to pray hereafter for peace, have reason for his guide, and go where "vertu moral" dwells (CA, VIII.2913–25).[94]

What Lewis called the "long and unsuccessful coda" after the lover's rejection of love, Book VIII.2971ff, balances the Prologue and puts the discussion back into the context of universal truth. Again, the revised conclusion points this up more directly than the original, showing that the larger pattern became clearer in Gower's mind as he revised. It begins with the familiar statement of the

responsibilities of reasonable human creatures (CA, VIII.2971).
Then it recapitulates the responsibilities of each estate to promote
unity and the common good through Empedoclean love. The
clergy:

> Hem oughte wel to justefie
> Thing which belongith to here cure,
> As forto praie and to procure
> Oure pes toward the hevene above,
> And ek to sette reste and love
> Among ous on this erthe hiere.
> For if they wroughte in this manere
> Aftir the reule of charite,
> I hope that men schuldyn se
> This lond amende. (CA, VIII.2996)

The chivalry should "defende and kepe/ The comun right and the
fraunchise/ Of holy cherche" (CA, VIII.3023). The people complain that "brocage" is overthrowing the "lawis of oure lond" (CA,
VIII.3031) and that pursuit of "singuler profit" (3039) has caused
much division in town and city. All hope for peace and unity lies
with the king:

> Ther is a stat, as ye schul hiere,
> Above alle othre on erthe hiere,
> Which hath the lond in his balance:
> To him belongith the leiance
> Of clerk, of knyght, of man of lawe;
> Undir his hond al is forth drawe
> The marchant and the laborer;
> So stant it al in his power
> Or forto spille or forto save. (CA, VIII.3055)

This repetition of the familiar theme of national peace and unity
promoted by love under the leadership of the king is the real conclusion to the Confessio Amantis, not the withdrawal from romantic love. And this is the context in which the Lover's confession
must itself be viewed.

The Latin headnote and sidenote at the beginning of Book 1
reveal the plan. Having just concluded in the Prologue that divi-

sion through lack of charitable love is the cause of social disorder,
Gower begins:

> *Naturatus amor nature legibus orbem*
> *Subdit, et vnanimes concitat esse feras:*
> *Huius enim mundi Princeps amor esse videtur,*
> *Cuius eget diues, pauper et omnis ope.*
> *Sunt in agone pares amor et fortuna, que cecas*
> *Plebis ad insidias vertit vterque rotas.* (CA, 1.headnote)

> (Nature-embodied love furnishes the world with laws, and in-
> cites all to be wild beasts. The prince of the world may be seen
> to be love . . . Love and fortune are equal in agony, which lure
> the blind people to the trap or the wheel.)

Naturatus nature, nature "in being," was a technical scholastic term
in contrast with *natura naturans,* nature "becoming." Michael
Scotus had designated the former "elementaris," and the latter
"divina." [95] Gower is therefore beginning his discussion with the
physical aspects of love "to which not only human beings, but also
all living creatures are naturally subject" (sidenote, again echoing
so closely the first canon of the *Institutes of Justinian*). Genius
outlines the progressive nature of the argument:

> Ferst that myn ordre longeth to,
> The vices forto telle arewe,
> Bot next above alle othre schewe
> Of love I wol the propretes,
> How that thei stonde be degrees
> After the disposicioun
> Of Venus. (CA, 1.254)

The Lover—and the reader—are to be instructed first in the degrees
of love, beginning with the vices of animal love and ending with
the virtues of spiritual love. Animal love begins, quite naturally,
with the senses, and having love enter through the eyes is one of
the firmest conventions of the courtly tradition. Yet, as evidence
of Gower's blending of different traditions, we may observe that
discussion of the five senses was likewise part of the tradition of
the *Secretum Secretorum* [96] from which Gower takes material for

Book VII. Gower does not return to this material in Book VII, and he is content here to treat only the first two, seeing and hearing.

It is both impossible and unnecessary for us to attempt to assay the erotic versus the political implications of each tale. One difficulty about making any statement about Gower's "attitudes" or "treatments" is that he is so voluminous that any conclusion or demonstration involves counting thousands of lines or referring to scores of instances. Aside from the bare statistics listed above, we must be content with an analysis of the first book. In it, neither the stories of Acteon nor Medusa (CA, 1.333, 389) illustrating the dangers of seeing, nor the accounts of the serpent or the sirens (CA, 1.462), illustrating the dangers of hearing, bear directly upon romantic love. Immediately after these two, Gower falls back into the familiar pattern of the Seven Deadly Sins to structure his work, and, as has often been observed, the fit between the ensuing stories and either the Seven Sins or courtly love varies from mediocre to poor. In spite of the supposedly erotic situation, the frame is infused with political allusions of one kind and another. In the *Mirour*, for example, Pride was personified as a female with five daughters (MO, 1057); in the *Confessio*, Pride is a male and has five ministers (CA, 1.583). In the *Mirour*, the first minister, Hypocrisy, is restricted largely to the clergy, following the tradition of the *Roman de la rose*. In the *Confessio*, the hypocrite's "malice/ Under colour of *justice*/ Is hid" (CA, 1.605), and "Ipocrisis secularis" is given independent treatment:

> This vice hath ek his officers
> Among these othre seculers
> Of grete men, for the smale
> As for tacompte he set no tale,
> Bot thei that passen the comune
> With suche him liketh to comune. (CA, 1.647)

The story of Mundus and Paulina has its own interest for the implicit blasphemy of lines 917–920, but its elaborate seduction plot is actually no more appropriate to hypocrisy in love than to hypocrisy in public affairs; and the taking of counsel and appeal to the emperor at the end (990ff) are clearly political—at least an emperor punishes both a duke and priests for their seduction of the wife of a "worthi Romein." The second story illustrating hypocrisy, that of the Trojan horse (CA, 1.1077), is purely military and political.

Discussion of "Inobedience" turns upon the law (CA, 1.1239, 1243, etc.). Murmur and Complaint, his "secretaries" and "ministers" (CA, 1.1345 sidenote), although adapted to love, betray their political lineage. The Tale of Florent—to anticipate the comparison to be made in the next chapter—betrays its legal connection when Florent, unlike his opposite in Chaucer's Wife of Bath's Tale, asks "to have it under Seales write,/ What questioun it scholde be" upon which his life was to depend (CA, 1.1474, CT, III.912). The first two stories illustrating Surquidry have no erotic associations: the destruction of Capaneus by the gods for pride (CA, 1.1977), and the Trump of Death (CA, 1.2021) which ends in a vivid *memento mori* associated with kingship in the same way that we saw it associated in the *Mirour* and the *Vox*. The third tale, that of Narcissus, does have a slight bearing on presumption in love.

Avantance is Pride's herald (CA, 1.2403), but the tale of Albinus and Rosemund which illustrates it is a genuine love tragedy in spite of its clerical descent. On the other hand, while the comment under Vain Glory on the dress and behavior of lovers does bear on love (CA, 1.2704), the story of Nebuchadnezzar's punishment which illustrates this sin (CA, 1.2785) is, as we have seen, a staple of moralistic and political discussions of kingship. The final story in Book I, The Tale of the Three Questions (CA, 1.3067), is a general illustration of the virtue of humility with neither romantic nor political implications.

Time and again the links and tales in the other books of the *Confessio* touch directly on the themes of the previous pieces. Note, for example, complaint against the Lombard bankers under False Semblant (CA, II.2100) and the passage on supplantation in great offices at court (CA, II.2337). In the Tale of Constantine and Silvester there is a fine passage on the equality of all men before

Fortune and the "lawe of kinde," which states "The povere child is
bore als able/ To vertu as the kinges Sone" (CA, II.3258) and
repeats again one of Gower's favorite adages, ultimately from Cassiodorus' Varia, xii.3, that authority rests upon pity or love (II.
3300).

Book III begins with the observation that wrath is "A vice forein
fro the lawe" (CA, III.5), and in the first tale, the incest of Canace
and Machaire is attributed to the natural instincts. The next tale,
of Tiresius and the snakes, illustrates the all-embracing virtue of
legitimate sexual intercourse, since Tiresius is transformed into a
woman for striking the serpents in the act of coupling.

> And for he hath destourbed kinde
> And was so to nature unkinde,
> Unkindeliche he was transformed. (CA, III.373)

Incidentally a nice example of *adnominatio*. Following the Tale of
Orestes, there is a brief discourse on the need for a judge or ruler
to be ruthless in performing justice. Such an admonition as

> Lo thus, my Sone, to socoure
> The lawe and comun riht to winne,
> A man mai sle withoute Sinne, (CA, III.2230)

reads strangely in the midst of the allegory of love, as does the
ensuing discourse on the evil of killing in wars (III.2582). The discussion of the prowess necessary for knighthood, and of gentilesse
in Book IV (1615, 2190) are quite as appropriate to the *speculum
regale* as to the *speculum amoris*. The education of Achilles in the
same book (IV.1963) foreshadows the education of Alexander in
Book VII. In Book V, the long tale of Jason and Medea is fraught
with political overtones, such as the reception by the "nobles and
comun" and the "parelement" to which they are welcomed (CA,
V.3758). Among the kings who illustrate sacrilege at the end of the
book we find our old friend Nebuchadnezzar (V.7009).

Up to Book VII, the sins are treated to a book each: I pride; II
envy; III wrath; IV sloth; V avarice; VI gluttony. At Book VII where
the king or another reader might logically expect to find a discus-

sion of the sin of lechery—particularly in a lover's confession—
Gower introduced his most direct advice on the education of a
prince. It would thus appear that the whole framework of the
Confessio, the whole manipulation of expectation, was intended to
focus attention upon this "digression." The protests of Genius at
vi.2420 and vii.1 are the same as his protest at 1.235, that as the
priest of Venus he has no competence except in her lore, yet he
intends more:

> Bot natheles for certein skile
> I mot algate and nedes wile
> Noght only make my spekynges
> Of love, bot of othre thinges,
> That touchen to the cause of vice. (CA, 1.237)

> Bot natheles to knowe more
> Als wel as thou me longeth sore;
> And for it helpeth to comune,
> Al ben thei noght to me comune,
> The scoles of Philosophie,
> Yit thenke I forto specefie,
> In boke as it is comprehended. (CA, vi.2429)

The only times that Genius comes alive, as a kind of hemmed in,
straitjacketed Nun's Priest longing for a wider mission, are in
these two passages and in his final address to the Lover (viii.2063)
which devolves into another expression of the legal and regal
themes. His final personal advice to the Lover, again expressed
apologetically because he is the priest of Venus and the advice is
therefore heresy, is that since "Of every lust thende is a peine" he
should "Tak love where it mai noght faile," i.e., spiritual love
(CA, viii.2096). This advice passes on to a reiteration of the contrasts between individual and social love, using for the microcosmic
analogy this time not the universe but a kingdom. Unless love is led
by good counsel, it should beware:

> For conseil passeth alle thing
> To him which thenkth to ben a king;
> And every man for his partie

> A kingdom hath to justefie,
> That is to sein his oghne dom.
> If he misreule that kingdom,
> He lest himself. (CA, viii.2109)

Set in the matrix of the political moralization of the Prologue and coda, pointed up by the organization of the sins, prepared for by repeated direct and indirect allusion in the first six books, Book vii of the *Confessio Amantis* appears not as a digression but as the heart of the discussion. Gower makes his transition to it neatly, as usual. The account of the conception of Alexander by Nectanabus which concludes Book vi leads nicely to the familiar tradition of Aristotle's education of Alexander at the beginning of Book vii. This introduction led earlier scholars to surmise that the "boke" Genius had just referred to (vi.2435, above) must have been the famous *Secretum Secretorum* which is introduced by the same tradition. However, Macaulay pointed out that the *Trésor* of Brunetto Latini provided the material for the Aristotelian classifications of knowledge which follow the introduction.[97] It is less important to try to decide whether Gower was referring to the *Trésor* or making use of some expanded version of the *Secretum* than to see that he is again molding his sources to express his own message. As Macaulay observed, Gower's method of treating the principles of government under "Policy" is independent of the *Trésor*, and it merely borrows material, not organization or viewpoint, from the *Secretum*. According to Gower's scheme, Policy is a subhead under a three-fold classification of what a prince should know, "Theoretique," "Rethorique," and "Practique." But everything up to Policy takes only the first 1679 lines of the book, while Policy has the remaining 3859 lines (CA, vii.1680–5438), of which the last 1200 (4210 on), dealing with chastity, provide a transition to Book viii, and together with the treatment of marriage and incest at the beginning of that book form the expected discussion of lechery, which completes the scheme of the Seven Deadly Sins.

Policy comes straight to the point of the conception which more than any other distinguishes the postmedieval social order from the stratified, hierarchical medieval view of society:

> A king schal sette in governance
> His Realme, and that is Policie,
> Which longeth unto Regalie
> In time of werre, in time of pes,
> To worschipe and to good encress
> Of clerk, of kniht and of Marchant,
> And so forth of the remenant
> Of al the comun poeple aboute,
> Withinne Burgh and ek withoute,
> Of hem that ben Artificiers,
> Whiche usen craftes and mestiers,
> Whos Art is cleped Mechanique.
> And though thei ben noght alle like,
> Yit natheles, hou so it falle,
> O lawe mot governe hem alle,
> Or that thei lese or that thei winne,
> After thastat that thei ben inne. (CA, vii.1682)

The concept of one law for a various population is the shadow line that divides the modern world from the medieval. As Holdsworth has observed:

> Whether we give this or that class special status, it is, I think, clear that in the Middle Ages there were a number of persons who occupied special positions of their own. We should perhaps be guilty of an anachronism if we called them abnormal persons; for it is to be doubted whether early law recognizes such a thing as a normal person. It recognizes rather various ranks and groups and classes, each occupying its own legal position in a loosely organized society. The very idea of a normal person is the creation of a common law which has strengthened the bonds of this society by administering an equal justice to all its members.[98]

We shall comment in the next chapter on the close parallel between Gower's statement and the sentiment in Chaucer's Prologue to the *Legend of Good Women* (F.380) and the possible influence of these ideas on the social criticism in the *Canterbury Tales*. Here we may observe merely that the passage introduces "fyf pointz" of Policy. Of these the first two demand little comment. Truth as good policy for a ruler is extolled and illustrated (CA, vii.1711). Liberality, originally a pagan and heroic concept of kingship,[99] had been treated before in the Epistle to the King in the Vox *Clamantis* (vi.811), where it was Christianized by being identified with alms-giving. It was treated even more extensively in the fifth book of the *Confessio* as an antidote to avarice, without any direct reference to the principles of kingship. Here it is first linked with the concept of common ownership before the Fall (vii.1991) and then extolled as a royal virtue. There lurks the possibility of topical allusion to Richard II in the fact that warning against prodigality is linked with warning against flattery.[1] At least in the various versions of the *Secretum*, prodigality is not usually linked with flattery, although in John Yonge's—a caution against any generalization about Gower's or any other medieval writer's relation to his sources—warning against flatterers does immediately precede discussion of largess.[2]

However, it is the third point of Policy, Justice, that most deserves our attention. The 400 lines treating and illustrating this topic represent a climax in Gower's treatment of the themes of law and order—of the dependence of the common good upon personal virtue, legal restraint, and royal authority. The passage begins by returning to the underlying conception of sin as the reason for law, recalling the allegory on Sin at the beginning of the *Mirour* (MO, 205) and echoing closely the opening lines of Vox *Clamantis*, vi.vii:

> Pro transgressore fuerant leges situate,
> Quilibet vt merita posset habere sua: . . .
> Gens sine lege quid est, aut lex sine iudice quid nam,
> Aut quid si iudex sit sine iusticia? (VC, vi.469, 481)

> Propter transgressos leges statuuntur in orbe,
>   Ut viuant iusti Regis honore viri.
> Lex sine iusticia populum sub principis vmbra
>   Deuiat, vt rectum nemo videbit iter.

> What is a lond wher men ben none?
> What ben the men whiche are al one
> Withoute a kinges governance?
> What is a king in his ligance,
> Wher that ther is no lawe in londe?
> What is to take lawe on honde,
> Bot if the jugges weren trewe? . . .
> For wher the lawe mai comune
> The lordes forth with the commune,
> Ech hath his propre duete. (CA, vii.2695)

The ensuing lines offer Gower's most lucid and earnest comment on the interdependence of the king, the legal system, and a peaceful nation. The king is above all men and all estates:

> For his astat is elles fre
> Toward alle othre in his persone,
> Save only to the god al one,
> Which wol himself a king chastise,
> Wher that non other mai suffise.
> So were it good to taken hiede
> That ferst a king his oghne dede
> Betwen the vertu and the vice
> Redresce, and thanne of his justice
> So sette in evene the balance
> Towardes othre in governance,
> That to the povere and to the riche
> Hise lawes myhten stonde liche,
> He schal excepte no persone.
> Bot for he mai noght al him one
> In sondri places do justice,
> He schal of his real office
> With wys consideracion
> Ordeigne his deputacion
> Of suche jugges as ben lerned,
> So that his people be governed
> Be hem that trewe ben and wise. . . .
> Wher as the lawe is resonable,
> The comun poeple stant menable,
> And if the lawe torne amis,
> The poeple also mistorned is. (CA, vii.2732)

There follow two brief exempla on honest judges, concluding that those who now "deme and jugge comun lawe" are no longer friends "to comun riht" and no longer seek the "comun profit" (CA, vii.2821, 25, 28).

The concept of the common good is reiterated through the subsequent illustrations. Under the laws of "Prince" Lycurgus, Athens exemplified an ideal society:

> Ther was withoute werre pes,
> Withoute envie love stod;
> Richesse upon the comun good
> And noght upon the singuler
> Ordeigned was, and the pouer
> Of hem that weren in astat
> Was sauf. (CA, vii.2927)

When Lycurgus saw how well the city was faring, he called a Parliament to make his system permanent. He explained that the laws were of divine origin. Mercury had brought them "To do justice and equite/ In forthringe of comun profit" (2957). Lycurgus had the people swear never to change the laws in his absence. When they had done so, he disappeared:

> So that Athenis, which was bounde,
> Nevere after scholde be relessed,
> Ne thilke goode lawe cessed,
> Which was for comun profit set.
> And in this wise he hath it knet;
> He, which the comun profit soghte,
> The king, his oghne astat ne roghte;
> To do profit to the comune,
> He tok of exil the fortune,
> And lefte of Prince thilke office
> Only for love and for justice. (CA, vii.3004)

This is the most eloquent statement in all Gower's writing of the legal foundation of society and the ideal relationship of the king to the law. The repetition of the subject of the second sentence ("He . . . the king . . .") is an indication that Gower was consciously striving for rhetorical effect, the same effect he achieved by direct statement a few lines later:

> Do lawe awey, what is a king?
> Wher is the riht of eny thing,
> If that ther be no lawe in londe? (CA, vii.3075)

The last two points of Policy, pity and chastity, are anticlimactic, but they serve to round out the treatment and to put the political discussion back into the erotic frame that Gower had fashioned for it. Pity echoes the *Secretum's* exhortation to mercy, and illustrates with stories from that source and elsewhere the political advantages of mercy over cruelty.[3] Its central tag, quoted twice before in the *Mirour* and later in *In Praise of Peace*, is from Cassiodorus' *Varia*: "Pietas siquidem principum totum custodit imperium." [4] The final point of chastity reveals Gower's concern for gathering up all loose ends and for effecting smooth transition. If there were a separately set off treatment of lechery, to complete the treatment of the Seven Deadly Sins, it could not differ much from the commentary and illustration which ends Book vii (lines 4215–5438) and begins Book viii (lines 1–2216). The reference to the fall of Lucifer and the creation of Adam and Eve at the beginning of the last book rounds out the trilogy by again recalling the beginning of the *Mirour*. The reiteration of the contrast between the laws of marriage and the amoral, natural sexual urge which led primitive man "as a cock among the Hennes,/ Or as a Stalon in the Fennes" to take "what thing comth next to honde" (CA, viii.159), reinforces the contrast between the bestial and the reasonable which has pervaded all three works, and even more directly recalls the theme of the *Traitié pour essampler les amantz marietz*.

The most impressive feature of Gower's moral philosophy that emerges from careful study of the text of his works, therefore, is not its high idealism, nor its concern over the relations between the individual and society, nor even its progressive views on social justice under the rule of law. It is rather the unity and coherence of Gower's world view and the success with which he managed to infuse into a heterogeneous mass of conventional material a personal vision capable still of commanding our respect.

5. Gower and Chaucer

With some awareness of Gower's literary career and the coherent evolution of his moral philosophy, we are finally in a position to consider the relationship between his writings and those of Chaucer. But first we must come to some agreement as to what constitutes literary influence. Like so much other Chaucer criticism, the study of the relations between Chaucer and Gower has foundered upon the rock of verbal parallels. Poets, even poor poets, are not likely to imitate slavishly the tone or idiom of their immediate contemporaries. One can share something of W. W. Skeat's righteous indignation at the suggestion that Chaucer borrowed phrases from Gower—"which seems like suggesting that Tennyson was capable of borrowing from Martin Tupper" [1]—even though, like all of Skeat's references to their possible relationship, this one is colored by Chaucer idolatry and the conventional 19th-century denigration of Gower, whose *ad hominem* basis was traced in the first chapter. But there are other kinds of relationships besides verbal and stylistic. These may be grouped together under the anthropologist's designation, "stimulus diffusion." A society need not necessarily borrow another society's alphabet or architecture. It may borrow the *idea* of writing or of building in stone. Similarly, authors who converse together and read one another's writings over a period of years need not borrow one another's very words, but they are likely to show concern for the same themes and experiment with the same forms. So it is that we have a series of revenge tragedies on the Elizabethan stage, and essays on related topics in the *Tatler* and *Spectator*. So it is that Wordsworth and Coleridge strike similar chords in "Intimations of Immortality" and "Dejection: an Ode," and Pound and Eliot express similar concern for the wasteland of modern culture.

At the time their association began, Gower was on the point of turning to a new medium, virtually unrelated in either style or content to his love balades, whereas Chaucer was to continue developing the style and material of the *Book of the Duchess* into such masterpieces as the Knight's Tale and *Troilus and Criseyde*. It is a commonplace of Chaucerian criticism, however, that after 1369, along with increasing artistry, Chaucer's poetry reveals a deepening philosophical insight and a quickening social conscience. This has in the past been attributed largely to the experience of his Italian journeys. As R. K. Root put it, "In 1373 and again in 1378 Chaucer was sent on diplomatic missions to Italy, and came for the first time into vital contact with the great intellectual movement of the early Renaissance. He felt the power of Dante's divine poem; he breathed the atmosphere of humanism which emanated from Petrarch and his circle; he found in Boccaccio a great kindred spirit, an author of keen artistic susceptibility, who in character and temperament had much in common with himself. He found in Italy not only a new set of models, superior in art and depth to those of France; he received as well a new and powerful intellectual stimulus, which set him to thinking more deeply on the problems of philosophy, and gave him a keener interest in the intricacies of human character." [2] In particular, his inspiration is thought to have been Dante. "Dante did for Chaucer," says Lowes, "what Greek a century later did for Europe." [3]

Undoubtedly Chaucer's glimpse of the Italian Renaissance was a liberating experience, but we are now on the verge of revising the exaggerated estimates of the generation of Lowes and Sir Mungo MacCallum concerning Chaucer's debt to Italy.[4] Skirting the question of how much Italian he could read without the help of a French pony, we may agree with Canon Looten and Mario Praz that to Chaucer Dante was a mine of learned information and local reference rather than a shaping intellectual influence.[5] A more immediate source for Chaucer's broadening perspective and deepen-

ing moral intensity were the traditions and documents of medieval
moralism with which he had been familiar all of his life—the sermons, penitentials, treatises, and poems of Robert Mannyng, John
Wyclif, John Bromyard, William Langland, and especially John
Gower. In this tradition and the writings of these authors are to be
found the moralistic materials of social criticism that figure increasingly in Chaucer's poetry until they come finally to occupy a
central place in the *Canterbury Tales*. However, while Chaucer's
general relations to the moralistic tradition have been frequently
referred to,[6] the special resemblances between his works and Gower's have occasioned little comment.

One reason that these resemblances have not been examined
chronologically and in detail is probably, again, the low estimate
into which Gower's writings have fallen. To modern readers, Chaucer's and Gower's treatments of the same material are so different
that comparison appears fruitless, if not downright wrongheaded.
Since the 18th century, literary taste has so shifted away from the
generalized moralistic mode which John Peter terms "complaint"
that all literature in this vein—not only medieval, but much of
Spenser, Milton, and Bunyan—has declined in popularity. Literature employing the sharper, more specific mode of satire has enjoyed a corresponding rise in critical estimation, as witness the
revivals of Donne, Swift, and Pope. Gower's poetry fits exactly the
criteria which Peter establishes for complaint, whereas Chaucer
strives constantly toward, and finally in the *Canterbury Tales*
achieves, all the characteristics of satire.[7] To begin with, Gower's
treatment of the vices and virtues and the estates is conceptual and
allegorical, while Chaucer works increasingly in the concrete peculi-
arity of real life. Second, Gower's "voice" is deliberately impersonal.
He is forever protesting that he is speaking not his own opinion
but *in vocem populi*, whereas Chaucer has one of the most distinctive voices in all literature. Third, one of the most striking
features of Chaucer's highly individual style is its use of such variations as urbanity, malevolence, raillery, scurrility, cynicism. This
variety contrasts with the monotone of Gower's complaint, which

"like the Christianity it espouses, strives always to be sober and reasonable, if occasionally severe." Fourth, Gower's complaint is essentially hortatory. Since it castigates the shortcomings of all mankind, including the reader, it can hardly be read for pure "enjoyment." Chaucer's satire betrays no such desire for reform; it is addressed to a reader not himself being subjected to criticism, who can therefore sit back and appreciate the satirist's shrewd hits on the faults of others. Finally, Peter observes, satire is a comparatively sophisticated mode and complaint is not. Chaucer's wit and sophistication have come to be appreciated more fully by each succeeding generation, whereas few readers today can tolerate Gower's humorless and iterative moralism.

These differences between the styles of the two poets have diverted attention from the similarities in their writings obvious to commentators in the 15th and 16th centuries.[8] The biographical details that have survived support the Leland tradition that Gower was Chaucer's senior and mentor; their allusions to one another and the evolving pattern of the parallels in their works suggest that Gower was a sort of conscience to his brilliant but volatile friend, encouraging him by both precept and example to turn from visions of courtly love to social criticism. During the decade from 1376 to 1386, when they appear to have been living close together, the references proceed from Chaucer towards Gower. It was Chaucer who entrusted Gower with his power of attorney in 1378, and again it was Chaucer who dedicated *Troilus* to Gower in the mid-eighties. When, later, Gower responded, the allusion at the end of the *Confessio Amantis* took the form of an admonition.

The relations between their writings fall into distinct periods. Before 1376, in the *Book of the Duchess* and *Cinkante Balades*, they began writing from different backgrounds of reading and experience: Gower from his acquaintance with groups like the merchant Pui, and Chaucer from his with the French court poets. What similar expressions and figures there are in these early pieces appear to be independent derivations from the courtly tradition.[9] The poems themselves show no evidence of dissatisfaction with the con-

ventions, although Chaucer was already revealing his genius for
transmuting anything he touched. The overtones of confession and
adaptation of the motif of "dying for love" to a real death give the
Book of the Duchess a poignancy not found in the *Cinkante
Balades*. After 1376, both Chaucer and Gower began to show dissatisfaction with "fols ditz d'amours." Gower turned directly to
moralistic social complaint in the *Mirour de l'omme* and *Vox
Clamantis*, while Chaucer wrestled more painfully in the *House of
Fame* and *Parliament of Fowls* with the relation between the style
and substance of courtly poetry and social satire. The conceptual
and verbal parallels between these two poems and the *Mirour* suggest that in seeking for ways to enlarge the compass of his poetry,
Chaucer was influenced by Gowerian moral philosophy. When,
after 1380, he succeeded magnificently in blending moral philosophy and courtly love in his two chivalric masterpieces, the Knight's
Tale and *Troilus,* he dedicated the moral dimension of the latter
to Gower. About 1385, in the *Confessio Amantis* and *Legend of
Good Women,* Gower and Chaucer returned to parallel love visions
used as frames for collections of stories. And after 1386, Chaucer
turned in the *Canterbury Tales* to social criticism closely paralleling
that in the *Mirour de l'omme* and *Vox Clamantis*. The fact that
he chose finally to assemble his pilgrims at the Tabard Inn, across
from St. Mary Overeys Priory in Southwark, could be interpreted
as an acknowledgment that in that piece he was finally taking
his departure directly from Gower's own *métier,* the vices and
virtues and criticism of the estates.

I

The order of Chaucer's works is not established, but it is generally
agreed that the *House of Fame* and *Parliament of Fowls* precede
Troilus. For our purpose, the chronology which places the *House
of Fame* between 1372 and 1380 and the *Parliament* about 1380 is
satisfactory, although the reverse order would do nearly as well.[10]
Among the more interesting interpretations of the *House of Fame*

is that of R. J. Allen [11] which focuses on the continual interest
throughout the poem in the nature of literary art and the material
with which the literary artist deals. Throughout the first two books,
nonliterary interpretation of experience is ridiculed, and in Book II
the eagle tries to educate "Geffrey" on the cosmology of Fame's
house, the physics of sound, and astronomy. At line 1000 he concludes, in effect, "If you knew the positions of all the stars, it might
help you read Ovid." To which Geffrey replies:

> "No fors," quod y, "hyt is no nede.
> I leve as wel, so God me spede,
> Hem that write of this matere,
> As though I knew her places here." (1011)

The contrast between the literary artist's approach to truth and
the scholar's could hardly be more dramatically stated than in this
contrast between Geffrey's and the eagle's attitudes towards astronomical lore, and Allen supposes that "to Chaucer's own friends of
court and town, it must have been more generally apparent than
to modern readers that the comic dialogue of Book II implied a
gay comment on the nature of poetry and expressed a delighted
belief in the world of human emotion in which the poet moves."

As a commentary on the material with which the literary artist
deals, Book I and the beginning of Book II have a significance not
noted in Allen's discussion. Book I is a pastiche of conventional
erotic emblems and allusions tied together by shreds of plot from
the *Aeneid*. Shaken by the reminders of love and war in the temple
of Venus, Geffrey feels that he must get out and compose himself:

> "A, Lord!" thoughte I, that madest us,
> Yet sawgh I never such noblesse
> Of ymages, ne such richesse,
> As I saugh graven in this chirche;
> But not wot I whoo did hem wirche,
> Ne where I am, ne in what contree.
> But now wol I goo out and see,
> Ryght at the wicket, yf y kan
> See owhere any stirying man,
> That may me telle where I am." (470)

He leaves the temple, only to find himself in a wasteland:

> Withouten toun, or hous, or tree,
> Or bush, or grass, or eryd lond;
> For al the feld nas but of sond
> As smal as man may se yet lye
> In the desert of Lybye;
> Ne no maner creature
> That ys yformed be Nature. (484)

One must be careful about attributing private significance to the imagery of pre-Renaissance art. Yet the interpretation of the *Parliament of Fowls* as a rejection of sterile courtly love and an advocacy of fertile natural love has been well received. The depiction of the temple of Venus in the *House of Fame* as merely a hallway leading to a sterile wasteland would appear to be an even more explicit judgment upon erotic love as the stuff of literature.

Dante had responded to the same artistic dissatisfaction with his early lyrics by spiritualizing courtly love in the *Vita Nuova* and *Divine Comedy*.[12] Chaucer acknowledged this solution by having Geffrey rescued from his wasteland in perhaps the noblest and most genuinely sympathetic echoes of Dante in all his poetry. "O Christ!" he prays, "Fro fantome and illusion/ Me save" (492). Suddenly above him appears the eagle that had carried Dante's body to the first terrace of Purgatory: "In dream I seemed to see an eagle with feathers of gold poised in the sky, with its wings spread, and intent to stoop. And I seemed to be there where his own people were abandoned by Ganymede, when he was rapt to the supreme consistory" (*Purgatorio*, ix.18).[13] This image is fused with that of Beatrice gazing at the sun: "I saw Beatrice turned to her left side and gazing upon the sun: never did an eagle so fix himself upon it. [Inspired by her example] I fixed my eyes upon the sun beyond our wont . . . Not long did I endure it, nor so little that I did not see it sparkle round about, like iron that issues boiling from the fire. And on a sudden, day seemed added to day, as if He who has the power had adorned the heaven with another sun" (*Paradiso*, 1.45). In this context, Chaucer's dreamer becomes aware:

That faste be the sonne, as hye
As kenne myghte I with my yë,
Me thoughte I sawgh an egle sore,
But that hit semed moche more
Then I had any egle seyn.
But this is sooth as deth, certeyn,
Hyt was of gold, and shon so bryghte
That never sawe men such a syghte,
But yf the heven had ywonne
Al newe of gold another sonne. (497)

Had Chaucer been able to sustain this note, he would have been a different poet. But we prefer to have him Chaucer, as he evidently preferred to be, for in the first ten lines of Book II, he rejected the mystical way out of the wasteland, employing the homely touches and incongruities of sound and situation of which he was already such a master to reduce Dante's divine bird to the slightly ridiculous, very human mentor who spoke "In mannes vois, and seyde, 'Awak!' " Even though the court may have seen the eagle as Philippa Chaucer, I am tempted to identify his "mannes voice" with John Gower's and read the rest of the poem as a reflection of the literary shoptalk of the first years of their association on what subjects and treatments are most appropriate to great poetry. Such an interpretation could be made to accord with the eagle's humorous references to Chaucer's personal life. But beneath the affectionate satire on the simple-minded old bird runs a more serious argument. Gower had rejected "fols ditz d'amour" when he turned to moralism in the *Mirour*. The eagle has picked Geffrey out of a wasteland into which he had been led by the poetry of eroticism and is carrying him at Jove's command to the house of Fame, where he will learn more about love than he has ever imagined possible (661–699). There follows the delightful exchange in which Geffrey the dreamer makes it clear that the eagle's schoolmasterish exposition is not his idea of poetry—we may imagine what Geoffrey the poet must have been saying about parts of the *Mirour!* Finally they come to the foot of the mountain of Fame, where the eagle sets him down with the command that he "Walke forth a pas,/

And tak thyn aventure or cas,/ That thou shalt fynde in Fames place" (1051).

The last book commences with Geffrey climbing laboriously up the steep slope, wondering what stuff the glistening rock is really made of, and observing the slippery impermanence of the names engraved on its surface (1119–47). "What may ever laste?" he asks, voicing the question that underlies the whole poem. As he looks through the window into the hall, he finds a partial answer. Fame's retainers are the entertainers of the world, and particularly the poets, whose songs well up about her throne (1200ff, esp. 1395). What lasts is what poets choose to sing of. The house of Fame is literally supported by the great poets of the past, each of whom forms a pillar holding up a section of the roof representing the fame of a nation or a hero. Josephus bears up the fame of Jewry; Statius of Thebes; Homer and others of Troy; Virgil of Aeneas; Ovid of Love; Claudian of Hell (1419ff). "What part of the house of Fame am I to bear up?" Chaucer would appear to be asking himself —a good deal more modestly than Dante when he placed himself among the great poets in Limbo. The answer manifests itself at once. No nation or hero appears. Instead a great din arises, and a rabble presses its way into the hall of Fame:

> A ryght gret companye withalle,
> And that of sondry regiouns,
> Of alleskynnes condiciouns
> That dwelle in erthe under the mone,
> Pore and ryche. (1528)

Chaucer was destined to be the poet who gave character to this rabble. His fame was to be immortalized by "Wel nyne and twenty in a compaignye,/ Of sondry folk, by aventure yfalle/ In felaweshipe," whose "condiciouns" he was so brilliantly to individualize. That is the ultimate development of a theme commencing here. Can it be coincidental that this initial allusion to satire on the estates contains Chaucer's first close parallel to Gower's *Mirour de l'omme*? The suitors in the throng all deserve good of Fame, Chaucer says, but they are variously served, "Ryght as her suster, dame

Fortune,/ Ys wont to serven in comune" (1547). They plead with
Fame for good report, but she denies them. It is not in man's power
to choose what kind of fame he will have. She then sends for her
messenger:

> And with that word she gan to calle
> Her messager, that was in halle,
> And bad that he shulde faste goon,
> Upon peyne to be blynd anon,
> For Eolus the god of wynde,—
> "In Trace, ther ye shal him fynde,
> And bid him bringe his clarioun,
> That is ful dyvers of his soun,
> And hyt is cleped Clere Laude,
> With which he wont is to heraude
> Hem that me list ypreised be.
> And also bid him how that he
> Brynge his other clarioun,
> That highte Sklaundre in every toun,
> With which he wont is to diffame
> Hem that me liste and do hem shame." (1567)

In the complaint on the estates in the *Mirour*, Gower used much
the same figure in an apostrophe to Fortune:

Fortune, tu as deux ancelles	*Fortune, you have two maid servants*
Pour toy servir, si volent celles	*to serve you, who fly*
Plus q'arondelle vole au vent,	*faster than swallows in the wind*
Si portont de ta court novelles;	*to carry news from your court.*
Mais s'au jour d'uy nous portent belles,	*But if today they bring us good news,*
Demein les changont laidement:	*tomorrow they change for the worse.*
L'une est que vole au noble gent,	*The one, who flies to noble people,*
C'est Renomée que bell et gent	*is Fame, which is pleasant and attractive;*
D'onour les conte les favelles,	*it tells tales of honor.*
Mais l'autre un poy plus asprement	*But the other, a bit more harsh,*
Se vole, et ad noun proprement	*flies under the name of*
Desfame, plaine de querelles.	*Dishonor, full of recriminations.*
Cist duy par tout u sont volant	*Each of these two, wherever she flies,*
Chascune entour son coll pendant	*bears hanging about her neck*
Porte un grant corn, dont ton message	*a great trumpet with which she trumpets*
Par les paiis s'en vont cornant.	*your message through all lands.*
Mais entrechange nepourqant	*Nevertheless, they often make an exchange*
Sovent faisont de leur cornage,	*in their trumpeting, for Fame,*
Car Renomé, q'ier vassellage	*which yesterday trumpeted prowess,*

Cornoit, huy change son langage,	today changes her language
Et d'autre corn s'en vait sufflant,	and trumpets from the other horn,
Q'est de misere et de hontage.	which is of misery and shame.

(MO, 22129)

There is no question here, or elsewhere, of *verbal* indebtedness. I am perfectly willing to accept H. R. Patch's view that Gower and Chaucer may have been drawing upon a common tradition which Gower treated first, although I see no reason whatever save Gower's critical reputation for Tatlock's belief that Gower borrowed from Chaucer.[14] What is really important is the evidence that Chaucer was beginning to turn away from love visions to the world of men, from erotic fantasies to the vices and virtues and satire on the estates, for the latter is the proper context for the consideration of the meaning of true fame in Book III of the *House of Fame*. The first seven companies that come before Lady Fame are not distinguished in any way, and their treatment reveals nothing other than man's helplessness in controlling his own reputation (1520ff), but in depicting the company of traitors and the individual sinners who have tried to secure fame by great crimes (1811, 1823), Chaucer was making a moral judgment. They deserve the ill fame of "Sklaundre" they receive (1865).

At this point, a friendly voice from behind asks Chaucer directly:

> . . . "Frend, what is thy name?
> Artow come hider to han fame?" (1871)

Having just observed the capriciousness and corrupting effects of fame, Geffrey replies, "Nay, for sothe . . ./ Sufficeth me, as I were ded,/ That no wight have my name in honde" (1873). He has come merely to learn some new tidings concerning love. The owner of the pleasant voice leads him out to the whirling house of Rumor, and who should he find perched beside it but "myn egle" (1990), who states even more explicitly than before his divine commission to see to Geffrey's enlightenment (2007). In another of those delightful fantasies that emphasize his superior size and strength, the eagle "Hente me up bytweene hys toon,/ And at a wyndowe yn me broghte" (2028). Inside, Geffrey sees another "congregacioun of folk," each peddling his own rumors and lies. These are the rumors upon first arrival, taking the shapes of their speakers on earth. True or false, but always exaggerated, they emerge from the house of Rumor and fly to the feet of Fame, where each receives his reputation and duration (2110).

I have no new suggestion as to the identity or message of the "man of gret auctorite" who is about to speak in the hall of Rumor when the poem breaks off, and I suggest identification of the eagle with Gower only because his personality and his role in the poem correspond so exactly to what I conceive Gower's personality and his relation to Chaucer to have been during the 1370's.[15] But no matter how deliberately ambiguous the contemporary allusions, one theme in the poem seems reasonably clear. In the *House of Fame* Chaucer was, like every serious artist, pondering what sort of poetry he should devote himself to. The erotic, the mystical, the expository, and the epic are one by one rejected, and the poem settles on "the common everyday experiences of men," "the world of human emotion," or "the intricacies of human character" [16] as the theme and substance of great poetry. Chaucer could have entered upon such self-evaluation and reached the same conclusion without direct external influence, so implicit is it in the Augustinian and Franciscan ethic of the Middle Ages. George Stewart and R. S. Loomis would attribute the deepening of his art to a genuine religious experience.[17] Certainly his Italian journeys brought a new light to his appreciation of art and life which illumines far more individual lines in the *House of Fame* than Gower ever could. But Chaucer's use at the crux of Book III of the figure of the two trumpets of fame, echoing Gower, who as the result of a similar self-evaluation had only recently rejected love poetry in favor of the *Mirour de l'omme*, strengthens the impression that Gower's moral earnestness and social conscience may have influenced Chaucer's artistic development in the 1370's.

II

The *Parliament of Fowls*, dating from nearly the same period as the *House of Fame*, shows the same movement from sterile eroticism toward social criticism. More obviously than the previous poem, the *Parliament* shows Chaucer's genius coming into its own, with a richness of allusion, depth of perception, and brilliance of wit and expression that Gower was never to match. Yet just as the *House of Fame* chooses at the climax of the third book to play upon a figure in Gower's *Mirour*, the *Parliament of Fowls* chooses to take its departure from one of Gower's favorite themes, the common profit. Chaucer began with the sort of references to his art, to love, and to bookishness that had by this time come to characterize his individual voice. The famous allusion to books:

> And out of olde bokes, in good feyth,
> Cometh al this newe science that men lere (24)

contrasts amusingly with Gower's parallel reference at the opening of the *Vox Clamantis*, which, as we have seen, must have been written about the same time:

> *Scripture veteris capiunt futuri,*
> *Nam dabit experta res magis esse fidem.* (VC, Prol.1)

> (Writings of the past contain fit examples for the future, for a thing previously experienced will produce greater faith.)

Again, the question is not who borrowed from whom. Rather, the delightfully different nuances of such parallels as these make it hard to believe that the two poets were not using phrases or ideas that they had discussed, with the deliberate intention of displaying their differing interpretations—all in good spirit, certainly, for why need such difference of literary opinion imply anything but the best of friendship? Chaucer was here giving the idea a brilliantly humanistic turn, reminiscent of his recent trip to Italy, whereas Gower was, characteristically, insisting on a pious interpretation. However, Chaucer's subsequent example of an old book, the moralistic

Somnium Scipionis of Cicero as transmitted by Macrobius, fits Gower's interpretation of the idea almost better than his own.

In his summary of the dream, Chaucer described how Africanus came to the younger Scipio, showed him Carthage, and told him that every man "lered other lewed/ That lovede commune profyt" (46) would go to heaven. Then Africanus took his adopted grandson up into the sky where he could look down and compare the torments of the world with the harmony of the spheres. Scipio asked how he might be sure of attaining immortal bliss. Africanus replied:

> . . . Know thyself first immortal,
> And loke ay besyly thow werche and wysse
> To commune profit, and thow shalt not mysse
> To comen swiftly to that place deere
> That ful of blysse is and of soules cleere.
> But brekers of the lawe, soth to seyne,
> And likerous folk, after that they ben dede,
> Shul whirle aboute th'erthe alwey in peyne. (73)

Now this is the theme of universal harmony based upon individual virtue and social law and order to the exemplification of which Gower fashioned his entire trilogy. Only his emphasis on the role of the ruler is here lacking, and Chaucer was to take that up shortly in "Palamon and Arcite," later to be refashioned as the Knight's Tale. Chaucer introduced "common profit" in both lines 46 and 75 to translate more general terms in Macrobius.[18] As observed in the last chapter, the term was a commonplace, but it must be remarked that one of Gower's favorite terms is here introduced to support his favorite theme. It may have been Chaucer who first gave shape to the larger concept. His insight and superior gift for expression could have helped develop the grand plan into which the *Mirour* and *Vox* eventually fitted. But this takes us into realms which we cannot penetrate, the oral exchange of ideas that must have preceded and accompanied the writing of both the *Mirour* and *Parliament*. We must allow at least that the theme of the common good founded upon law and Empedoclean love was an obsession with Gower, and that his obsession is more likely to have influenced Chaucer's expression of the idea than that such a glancing allusion as that in the *Parliament* triggered Gower's entire trilogy.

Having established a cosmic context and asserted a connection between waking experience and the dream (lines 99–105), the author-dreamer falls asleep to be wakened by Africanus in a sequence reminiscent of Virgil's coming to guide Dante in the *Inferno* (120).[19] He guides the dreamer to a gate over which are inscriptions in gold and black representing the courtly traditions of *amor* and *amar*. So in the *Roman de la rose*, Douz Regarz bears two sets of bows and arrows, one gold and the other black,[20] and Jupiter has two tuns of good and bad fortune [21] which Gower later transforms into *amor* and *amar* (CA, VI.333, VIII.2253). The black inscription, characterized by "Disdayn" and "Daunger," represents the sufferings of love. The golden inscription, characterized by "grene and lusty May," represents its joys. As conceived in the courtly tradition, the joys and sufferings of love have little to do with legitimacy or illegitimacy, nature or convention, fecundity or sterility. Such interpretations are later refinements upon the realization of the poets of Provençe that in love the moments of ecstasy are brief and the interims of separation long and desolate; and their more profound observation that for poetry the periods of desolation offer greater esthetic possibilities than the moments of ecstasy. In the *Troilus* Chaucer was to develop the pristine conception more sensitively perhaps than any poet since the troubadour Jaufré Rudel, but in the *Parliament of Fowls* he was toying with the philosophical refinements. He had already established that "brekers of the lawe and likerous folk" would not go directly to heaven. At least two scholars [22] have argued that the black sign over the gate and the temple of love in the garden—brazen, with Patience sitting on her hill of sand before it and Venus disporting herself with Richesse in a privy place within (231–287)—represent the sterility of courtly love; and that the golden sign, the verdant garden surrounding the temple, Dame Nature on her hill of flowers, and the mating birds represent fertile natural love.

This reading appears to me essentially sound. As with the *House of Fame,* one strand of the *Parliament of Fowls* is rejection of the purely erotic. But the opposition is by no means simple. We have already seen how Gower ended up perverting Chartrian naturalism by having Genius and Venus in the *Confessio* preach reason and self-discipline. As Lovejoy pointed out, Chartrian naturalism presented a dilemma. Nature might be divine and Eros a sacred power,[23] yet passion was still a disrupting force and sex a sin. Chaucer himself did some perverting of the Chartrian tradition of a sort that would have delighted Gower's heart. For his Nature, "vicaire of the almyghty Lord" (379), is the priestess of marriage, the instrument of human law by which the unruly life force is regulated. His one example of breakers of the law had been lecherous folk (72). The lovers listed at the end of the description of the temple (288) all came to grief through their illicit passion. Nature announces that the purpose of Valentine's day is for the birds to choose their mates (389), and the cuckoo claims to be speaking for the "comune spede" (507) in his criticism of the chivalric courtship. In this context, it appears that the royal birds are likewise contending for the formel eagle's hand in marriage, only using the elaborate ceremony of courtly love rather than a direct approach.

Gower knew Alan de Lille's *De Planctu Naturae,* Chaucer's acknowledged source for the naturalism in his poem. But, like most readers both medieval and modern, Gower was impressed mainly by its opening treatment of perversion:

Du Foldelit auci se pleint	*Nature also laments foolish joy*
Nature, au quelle meinte et meint	*in which many women and men*
Se sont forsfait de leur folie,	*have transgressed through their folly,*
Quant leur luxures ont enpeint	*when they have indulged their lusts.*
Comme jadys firont ly nounseint	*as did the sinners*
En la Cité de Sodomie.	*in the city of Sodom.*
(MO, 9505)	

It took Chaucer to see what R. H. Green has pointed out, that Alan's theme is "the human wretchedness which results from man's willful abuse of his nature, that is of the consequences of irrational and therefore unnatural behavior,"[24] and to transmute this truly

Gowerian theme into the robust and witty conflict between gallantry and married love that his whole poem appears to imply. Yet there is more to the conclusion of the *Parliament* than this. For again, as in the *House of Fame*, the dialogue between the dreamer and his guide and solitary roaming through the temple of love finally give way to observing human—or ornithoid—beings in a group, the reactions of different types to the same stimulus. There the stimulus had been fame; here it is sex. But in both poems, the dreamer's final vision is of a field of individualized folk.

By the time he had finished the *House of Fame* and *Parliament of Fowls* Chaucer was hardly more a poet of courtly love in the French tradition than was Gower after he put aside the *Cinkante Balades*. He was, instead, a poet of human nature. For Gower, to become a poet of human nature meant formally donning the spectacles of the Seven Deadly Sins and complaint against the failings of the estates. For Chaucer, it was to mean a more profound examination of genuine human motivation. He was to find until the end that love provided the most powerful of all searchlights under which to examine character and behavior, and so he continued to adapt the marvelous material of the courtly tradition to his more serious purpose. But aside from their consummate artistry, the solid core which gives shape and substance to the great poems he was next to write is the moral world view they share with John Gower.

III

This world view received its first development in *Troilus and Criseyde* and the Knight's Tale. Again, it is of no consequence to my argument which of these two was written first.[25] In them Chaucer was exploring two different facets of the moral philosophy being developed in Gower's works, in *Troilus* the eventual insufficiency of temporal human love, and in the Knight's Tale the relationship between natural passion, human law, and the ruler. Of the two, the Knight's Tale gains more by being examined from the vantage point of Gower's philosophy, even though it was *Troilus* that Chaucer himself chose to dedicate to Gower.

The Knight's Tale was evidently composed under the title "Palamon and Arcite" before the commencement of the *Canterbury Tales*. It takes up the one element in Gower's moral philosophy not mentioned in the summary statement at the beginning of the *Parliament of Fowls*, that is, the function of the king in preserving social law and order. As observed in Chapters Three and Four, Gower's interest in kingship can be traced from his disillusionment with Edward III in the *Mirour*, through his concern for Richard II in the *Vox Clamantis*, to his deep involvement with Henry IV in his writings in the 1390's. Whether Chaucer's study of Duke Theseus bears any similar relation to the external events of his day it is impossible to say. If there were specific applications, they were, as always, deeply sublimated. In any event, as emphasized by recent criticism, the Knight's Tale is as much Theseus' story as it is Palamon's and Arcite's.[26] Theseus throughout exhibits the traditional virtues of kingship that Gower detailed in the Epistle to the King in the *Vox Clamantis*, which dates from the same period as the Knight's Tale (i.e., between 1382 and 1386). To begin with, by conquering Femenye [27] and marrying the queen of the Amazons, Theseus has neutralized the temptations of the flesh in lawful matrimony as Edward III had not (MO, 22807), and as Richard II was most emphatically advised to do in the Epistle.[28] Theseus' marriage is an important motif in the development of the romance since the nature and superiority of the institution of marriage is one of its final lessons, inherited indeed from Boccaccio's original version.[29] It is noteworthy that Ypolita appears as one of Theseus' accouterments of office, so to speak, whenever he rides in state: at his homecoming (CT, 1.971), on the hunt in the forest (CT, 1. 1685), as he comes to the lists (CT, 1.2571). Theseus exhibits compassion for the widows of Thebes, martial valor against the tyrant Creon, judicial severity in condemning the two young knights to perpetual imprisonment, politic leniency in pardoning them when he comes upon them fighting in the forest, magnificence in his preparations for the tournament, and willingness to act by sage counsel in his final disposition of Palamon and Emelye—every detail of which is discussed in the Epistle to Richard II in the *Vox*.

Since the *speculum regale* material is conventional, and much of it had appeared already in Boccaccio's version of the story, Chaucer's treatment of this need not have been related to Gower's. However, it is possible to discern also in Chaucer's retelling three stages of experience corresponding to the *lex naturali, lex gentium,* and *lex civili* of the *Corpus Juris Civilis,* which are central to Gower's moral and political philosophy and for which there was no authority in Boccaccio.[30] The stage of *lex naturali* would be the passionate animal love of the two young knights that transforms cultured aristocrats and sworn brothers into wild beasts contending over the female. Arcite makes this stage explicit in replying to Palamon's accusation that in loving his friend's lady he is betraying the laws of brotherhood and chivalry:

> Thyn is affeccioun of hoolynesse,
> And myn is love, as to a creature . . .
> Wostow nat wel the olde clerkes sawe,
> That "who shal yeve a lovere any lawe?"
> Love is gretter lawe, by my pan,
> Than may be yeve to any erthely man;
> And therfore postif lawe and swich decree
> Is broken al day for love in ech degree. (CT, 1.1158)

Positive law was *lex civili,* "that which each people or state has established as proper to itself," including its laws of marriage. Between the sexual urge of natural law and the marriage contract of civil law lies the "might makes right" of *lex gentium,* the "wars, captivities, and slaveries" of the law of peoples.

Still behaving like beasts, after their escapes from prison, the two lovers meet next in the grove outside Athens. Every device is employed to emphasize the lawlessness of their conflict there. The grove is "Out of the court, were it a myle or tweye" (CT, 1.1504), the court representing human conventions and the grove nature. In the fight:

> Ther nas no good day, ne no saluyng . . .
> Thou myghtest wene that this Palamon
> In his fightyng were a wood leon,
> And as a crueel tigre was Arcite;
> As wilde bores gonne they to smyte,
> That frothen whit as foom for ire wood. (CT, 1.1649)

The final irony, as Arcite has already pointed out (CT, 1.1177) and Theseus is to observe a little later (CT, 1.1806), is that while they strove as "houndes for the boon," the female was actually quite beyond their reach.

Into the midst of the lawless, futile conflict spurs "The destinee, ministre general,/ That executeth in the world over al/ The purveiaunce that God hath seyn biforn" (CT, 1.1663), the figure of the king, who is responsible for the implementation of the law which distinguishes human from bestial existence. (Was Chaucer's decision to call Theseus Duke of Athens simply another evidence of the ingrained caution of a courtier?) The ensuing scene (CT, 1.1697–1818) illustrates the qualities of decisiveness, sternness, compassion, and magnanimity befitting the great prince. By substituting for the lawless fight a tournament for the lady's hand, the judicious ruler diverts futile, disruptive natural passion into a fruitful, lawful course. *Lex naturali* gives way to *lex gentium*. Theseus decrees for the ordered competition of the tournament round lists suggesting a microcosm of the universe, with three temples representing the belligerent, sexual, and spiritual proclivities of mankind.[31] However, over all Theseus' wisdom and foresight hangs the baleful shadow of "pale Saturnus the colde" (CT, 1.2443), natural calamity which can upset the most prudent plans of a human ruler. On the morning of the tournament, Theseus appears at his window, a veritable icon of kingliness (CT, 1.2528), and announces the laws by which the tournament is to avoid actual killing (CT, 1.2541); as a model for royalty he rides to the lists (CT, 1.2569). The gates are closed and there commences a melee (with time out between rounds, CT, 1.2621) in which the still essentially animal passions of the protagonists (CT, 1.2626, 2630) are carefully circumscribed, just as the natural passions are circumscribed by law in human society. But Saturn demonstrates that the king cannot finally decide human destiny. In the moment of his triumph Arcite is overcome by catastrophe, and his broken body passes beyond the jurisdiction of either society or nature to man's inevitable end, as elucidated by Egeus (CT, 1.2837). The ruler must still be concerned about the mortal remains and the survivors, however. Theseus prepares a great funeral for Arcite, and after a proper interval acts with the advice of a parliament (CT, 1.3076) to effect the union of Palamon and Emelye.

In contrast to the selfish, disruptive effects of the animal passions of Arcite and Palamon, the arranged marriage of Emelye and Palamon is associated by Theseus with the primal force which binds the universe together (CT, 1.2991). Only incidentally does it—or could it after what has gone before—gratify the personal emotions of the participants. Its real importance is as a social contract, presided over by the supreme judiciary of the state:

> Bitwixen hem was maad anon the bond
> That highte matrimoigne or mariage,
> By al the conseil and the baronage. (1.3095)

The Knight's Tale is, in the apt summation of Charles Muscatine, "a poetic pageant whose materials are organized and contributory to a complex design expressing the nature of a noble life." [32] It could be coincidental that the legal foundation for this noble life and the importance of the ruler in administering its laws and maintaining its serenity, that Chaucer added in his version, show such affinity with the views John Gower was just then addressing to young King Richard II in the Vox Clamantis. But as the thematic congruities pile up poem after poem, one can discern the shadow of his moral mentor looking over Chaucer's shoulder and at least nodding vigorous approval at the direction his art was taking.

IV

Either just before or just after he finished the Knight's Tale, with its symmetrical pattern and philosophical coloring, Chaucer completed *Troilus and Criseyde* in which symmetry and philosophy are even more marked. This piece he dedicated to "moral" Gower and "philosophical" Strode (v.1856). These epithets correspond to the conventional distinctions made first by Aristotle in the *Nicomachean Ethics*: "Now, on this division of the faculties is based the division of excellence; for we speak of intellectual excellences and of moral excellences; wisdom and understanding and prudence we call intellectual, liberality and temperance we call moral virtues or excellences." [33] In Quaestio LVIII of the *Summa Theologica*, "Of the Distinction of Moral Virtues from Intellectual," St. Thomas repeats the distinction: "If virtue perfects man's speculative or practical intellect in order that his action may be good, it will be intellectual virtue: if it perfects his appetitive part, it will be moral virtue." [34]

To Chaucer "philosophical" denoted speculative and intellectual excellence. Of the forty-four uses of the various forms listed in the concordance,[35] nineteen refer specifically to natural science. Five refer to classical philosophers, and six others to technical knowledge. The remaining thirteen are anonymous authorities for pithy dicta, "as saith the philosopher . . ." Judging by these meanings, Strode would have been expected to be interested in the astronomical and astrological lore [36] which in *Troilus* and the Knight's Tale was beginning to assume the significance in characterization and motivation that it has in the *Canterbury Tales*. He would have noted the many quotations from the classics and the fifty-seven or more proverbs. Most especially, he would have appreciated the Boethian treatments of necessity and free will, false felicity, fortune, and destiny. In reference to these last Thomas Usk called Chaucer himself "the noble philosophical poete in Englissh," and remarked that *Troilus* answered the question how, if God foresaw all, he could avoid being the author of evil.[37] But this extends the meaning into the realm of moral philosophy.

From the time Cicero coined *mos, moris* to render Aristotle's ἠθικός or moral excellence, *philosophia moralis* had designated the branch of philosophy dealing with the principles of human conduct, in contrast to *philosophia naturalis* which designated the natural sciences.[38] *Virtus moralis* was a rendering of Aristotle's ἀρετὴ ἠθική, excellence of character as distinguished from excellence of intellect. Gower clearly thought of his own writings as falling in the moral rather than the intellectual sphere when at the end of the *Confessio Amantis* he had Venus command "John Gower":

> And tarie thou mi Court nomore,
> Bot go ther vertu moral duelleth,
> Wher ben thi bokes, as men telleth,
> Whiche of long time thou hast write. (CA, VIII.2924)

Seven of Chaucer's fourteen uses of "moral" link it with "virtue" in just this way, and elsewhere he uses "moral" and "morality" to mean excellence of conduct. For example, in the Miller's headlink the reader who does not like fabliaux is advised to "Turne over the leef and chese another tale" of "gentilesse,/ And eek moralitee and hoolynesse" (CT, 1.3177)—romance, morality, and religion, as Tatlock put it, the sum total of medieval literature.[39] The notion of morality as not merely good conduct but the *principle* of good conduct is to be found in the familiar reference at the end of the Nun's Priest's Tale (CT, VII.3440). But the passage that casts most light on Chaucer's dedication to the moral Gower is that in the Monk's Tale describing Nero's tutor, Seneca:

> In yowthe a maister hadde this emperour
> To teche hym letterure and curteisye,
> For of *moralitee* he was the flour . . .
> He maked hym so konnyng and so sowple
> That longe tyme it was er tirannye
> Or any vice dorste on him uncowple. (CT, VII.2495)

Like Seneca, Gower was master of morality, that is, of the principles of human conduct. The most important evidence the double dedication provides is that Chaucer was as conscious of the moral dimension of the *Troilus* as he was of its learning, and that he submitted its moral philosophy to the correction of John Gower. This is acknowledgment of the line of influence that I have been arguing: that it was John Gower's ideas and ideals of human conduct that fostered Chaucer's own bent toward social criticism and character analysis. I have no intention of taking sides in the argument over whether Boethian determinism or Christian tragedy offers the best explanation for the philosophy of *Troilus*.[40] The cyclical movement set out in the fourth line of the poem, "Fro wo to wele, and after out of joie," capped by the Christian epilogue contrasting the vanity of temporal joy with "pleyn felecite" are par for medieval moral philosophy and offer no difficulties of interpretation. Chaucer's most important addition to Boccaccio's story is the *idea* of using it to symbolize the brevity of temporal bliss and the inevitability of human tragedy.[41] This contrast between temporal and spiritual love had been drawn very clearly at the beginning of the *Mirour de l'omme*. The fact that both the *Mirour* and *Troilus* begin with addresses to lovers does little more than emphasize their difference, for Gower immediately denounces temporal love as degrading, whereas Chaucer proceeds to refine it in every possible way to make the tragedy of its eventual insufficiency all the more dramatic. Yet the philosophy of Chaucer's entire poem is but a development of the first thirty-six lines of the *Mirour*, its theme well summarized in the last seven:

Car s'un soul homme avoir porroit	For if a man could have
Quanq'en son coer souhaideroit	whatever his heart desired
Du siecle, pour soy deliter,	of the world, to delight him,
Trestout come songe passeroit	it would all pass away like a dream
En nient, et quant l'en meinz quidoit,	into nothing, just as he thought it in his
Par grant dolour doit terminer:	hands—it would end in great sorrow.
Et puisque l'amour seculer	And thus secular love
En nient au fin doit retorner.	must in the end return to nothingness.

(MO, 25)

However, if we can detect an affinity with Gower in the moral theme of *Troilus*, the way in which the theme is developed may have had an indirect influence upon Gower's own *chef d'oeuvre*, the *Confessio Amantis*. For the sophistication of Chaucer's treatment grows not out of a moralistic opposition between human and divine love, but rather out of recognition of the essential connection between them. This insight, formalized in the neoplatonic naturalism of Chartres, and reflected in the sensual imagery of such mystics as Richard Rolle and St. Catherine of Siena, very early affected the literary convention of courtly love, if not in the *trobar clus*, then certainly in the Franciscan lyrics, Jean de Meun, Dante, and the poets of the *dolce stil nuovo*. The subtlety and human interest of Chaucer's poem derives from its use of this spiritualized conception of courtly love as the vehicle for its moralization.

Gower's works which antedate *Troilus* show no awareness of the literary possibilities of spiritualizing the romantic conventions. These conventions are used straightforwardly throughout the *Cinkante Balades* and barely mentioned in the *Mirour*. They reappear as part of the discussion of knighthood in *Vox Clamantis* (v.19–468), replete with the sort of moral judgments that Chaucer was to make dramatically. "What honor shall a conqueror have if a woman's love can conquer him?" Gower begins (VC, v.20). "The end will bring nothing but inevitable folly upon the man whom Venus initially leads to arms." Then follow thirty-nine lines of oxymoron (40–78) on the contradictions of love:

> Est amor egra salus, vexata quies, pius error,
> Bellica pax, vulnus dulce, suaue malum,
> Anxia leticia, via deuia, lux tenebrosa. (VC, v.53)

> (Love is sickly health, troubled rest, pious error, warlike peace, a pleasant wound, a delightful calamity, an anxious joy, a devious path, a dark light.)

Sixty-six lines more catalog the pernicious beauties of women, ending in troubadour figures:

> Quod videt, hoc nescit, set quod videt, vritur illo;
> Sic furit a ceco cecus amore suo:
> Frigidior glacie, feruencior igne cremante,
> Sic et in igne gelat, vritur inque gelu. (VC, v.141)

(He does not know what he sees, but he is consumed with what he sees. So he goes blindly mad because of his blind love. Colder than ice and hotter than burning fire, he both freezes with fire and burns with cold.)

Then a passage on the overmastering power of love, including the pun "Non amore in penis est par pene Talionis" (VC, v.159), which Stockton renders "Love with its pains is not equal to the pains of retaliation." The hero's malady from which Troilus, Palamon, and Arcite suffer is graphically described:

> *Nobilitas sub amore iacet, que sepe resurgit,*
> *Sepius et nescit nobile quid sit iter.* (VC, v.171)

> (A noble man may lie prostrate under the effects of love and often recover, yet more often he does not know what the noble course of action should be.)

A lament follows on the nature of man in whom lust of the flesh frustrates feeble reason (147–224). Carnal love extinguishes all chivalrous virtue in a man (225–250). The section ends with a long passage (293–468) on the virtues of a good woman, quoting at length from Proverbs 31, and the vices of an evil woman, quoting at even greater length from Ovid and the *Vita Monachorum*. The vices here listed feebly foreshadow the prologue of the Wife of Bath, but they draw upon none of Chaucer's witty, scholastic sources.

In contrast to such moralistic treatment, the elevation of courtly love had been one of the themes of Chaucer's first important poem, the *Book of the Duchess*, whose pattern of consolation illuminates the conventional love complaint with gleams of solemnity, if not spirituality. In the *Parliament of Fowls*, Chaucer had acknowledged his acquaintance with Chartrian thought and indicated the affinity between courtly conventions and natural urges by putting all of the birds under Dame Nature's sway. By this time we can almost see Chaucer, influenced by Gower's moral earnestness and seeking to give depth and richness to the fabric of his own work, saying to his friend over ale at the Tabard: "You're right, John, in insisting

that great poetry must have a coherent moral theme and must deal
with society. But you're wrong in thinking that the Seven Deadly
Sins and complaint on the estates are the stuff of poetry. *People*
and *stories* are the stuff of poetry—people as they reflect the vices
and virtues and represent the estates, especially stories of people
in love. I'll write you a love story showing how maximum instruction can be combined with maximum delight."

The principal device Chaucer employed to refine and elevate
Boccaccio's story was to make the love of Troilus and Criseyde a
manifestation of the universal creative urge of natural law, thus
mingling once again Chartrian naturalism and the essentially legal
concept which underlay Gower's moral philosophy. Destiny in
Troilus is only partly a metaphysical Boethian concept. Partly it is
simply another manifestation of the primal sexual urge man shares
with all sensible creatures. Chaucer's first extended interpolation
(TC, 1.213–266) injects this idea into the poem. After scoffing at
love, Troilus has been caught. Like proud Bayard,[42] he must bear
the yoke:

> Forthy ensample taketh of this man,
> Ye wise, proude, and worthi folkes alle,
> To scornen Love, which that so soone kan
> The fredom of youre hertes to hym thralle;
> For evere it was, and evere it shal byfalle,
> That Love is he that alle thing may bynde,
> For may no man fordon the lawe of kynde. (TC, 1.232)

The same motif is interpolated into the expanded conversation with
Troilus by which Pandarus learns Criseyde's identity (TC, 1.631),
and Pandarus reasserts it at length in another interpolated passage
at the end of the conversation (TC, 1.911–945). Later it is employed to elevate the character of Criseyde. Where Boccaccio's
Pandaro assures Troilo that his suit will be successful because "she
is a widow and she desires; and were she to deny it, I would not believe her" (2.27), Chaucer's Pandarus universalizes the compulsion:

> Was nevere man or womman yet bigete
> That was unapt to suffren loves hete,

Celestial, or elles love of kynde;
Forthy som grace I hope in hire to fynde. (TC, 1.977)

By the time we reach the marvelous poetry of the proem to Book
II, the contrast between the universal impulse of love and its expression in any particular society (specifically the difference between *lex naturali* and *lex civili,* as it happens) has a special
meaning. The tale of Troilus is an exemplum, an individual manifestation of a universal force that has existed through "sondry ages,/
In sondry londes" (II.27). The connection between the divine creative urge and the individual sexual impulse becomes the major
theme of the proem to Book III:

> God loveth, and to love wol nought werne;
> And in this world no lyves creature
> Withouten love is worth, or may endure. (TC, III.12) [43]

Since this proem is nearly all from the hymn to love Troilo utters
at the end of the third canto of the *Filostrato* (3.74–81), we cannot
say that the idea of depicting the lovers as helpless pawns in the
grip of a cosmic force was entirely Chaucer's. But under the influence of Chartrian philosophy and—as the dedication would appear
to indicate—Gower's view of a world in which natural passion is at
odds with law and the common good, the cosmic aspect of the love
of Troilus and Criseyde is so emphasized that Chaucer's version
takes on a quite different atmosphere from its original. The great
rainstorm Chaucer introduced to effect the final consummation of
the love has the effect of merging their sexual passion with the
primal force of nature. The mingled desire and reluctance with
which the lovers launch themselves into the storm is handled as
deftly as any Freudian could ask. Pandarus, the Serpent, plays an
enigmatic but indispensable role. However, natural forces are not
static. Their law is mutability.[44] They join and then sunder the
atoms of the universe. As Criseyde succumbs finally to Pandarus'
insistence, she voices her recognition of the "brotel wele of mannes
joie unstable" (TC, III.820), and Pandarus "ful sobrely" reiterates
the warning to Troilus the next day (TC, III.1636).

By identifying the love so closely with the forces of nature, Chaucer has provided an explanation for its tragic conclusion. The Boethian concept of Fortune's sway over temporal things, introduced at the end of Book III and in the proem to Book IV, emphasizes the brevity of temporal bliss and the inevitability of change within the realm of natural experience. In the last two books, the figures of Fortune and Destiny are used artistically to give an almost Greek sense of inevitability to the tragedy,[45] and morally to characterize human experience as necessarily impermanent and incomplete. The turn that Chaucer gives to Boethian thought in the famous soliloquy on free will and predestination (TC, IV.958) is a logical conclusion to the view of human love as an offshoot of the life force. How can Troilus come to any understanding of free will or conditional necessity? He must conclude in favor of the invariable natural law in whose grip he suffers.

The inability of Troilus to act in Books IV and V makes explicit what is less acceptable to the modern reader than it is supposed to have been to Chaucer's audience; that is, that the love affair was no wild animal passion like that of Palamon and Arcite before Theseus took them in hand. The liaison of Troilus and Criseyde may have straddled the shadow-line between ecclesiastical morality and immorality, but as is shown by the proem to Book II, the concern for Criseyde's good name, the elaborate machinery required to bring about the meeting at Deiphebus' house, and the final consummation at Pandarus' house, the game was played according to strict and socially accepted rules, not unlike those of marriage itself. As a result, when Pandarus advises Troilus to carry Criseyde off to avoid having her handed over to the Greeks, "Forthi tak herte, and thynk right as a knyght,/ Thorugh love is broken al day every lawe" (IV. 617), Troilus replies, "it is nat myn entente,/ At shorte wordes, though I deyen sholde,/ To ravysshe hire, but if hireself it wolde" (IV.635). The tragedy is, then, partly the result of a naturalistic Fortune or Destiny, but partly also of human convention and self-control. The Knight's Tale may teach that the *lex civili* of marriage produces happiness and harmony; *Troilus and Criseyde* teaches that the *lex civili* of courtly love produces its own kind of misery.

In the final analysis, the moral theme cannot account for the sublimity of Chaucer's poem. It has an intensity and elevation of emotion which sets it apart from anything else Chaucer wrote and anything Gower achieved. This is because its problem is spiritual rather than moral, as is finally explicitly recognized in the epilogue. From this vantage point, there can be no moral condemnation of the love affair of Troilus and Criseyde, or even of the machinations of Pandarus. These are simply the exigencies of temporal existence. Since such existence is all that a human being *can* experience, its joys and sorrows must represent his supreme ecstasies and agonies. But it takes no theologian to recognize in Criseyde's uncondemned betrayal the "false worldes brotelnesse" (TC, v.1832), nor in Troilus's celestial laughter the orthodox Christian hope for a higher order of existence in which joy is everlasting.

Furthermore, analysis of the moral theme takes no account of the exquisite poetry and marvelous narrative. But the moral theme does give one the sense that the brilliant technical achievements do not exist merely for themselves; that they have a "point." As a result of the moral theme, the poem produces a catharsis characteristic of the greatest literature. Such a serious achievement must have been what Chaucer was pondering in the *House of Fame* and groping toward in the *Parliament of Fowls*. That he achieved it in both the Knight's Tale and *Troilus* through the employment of a moral perspective that he shared with John Gower should help us perceive the nature of his success rather differently than if we attributed it entirely to the influence of Dante and the Italian Renaissance.

With the completion of *Troilus*, the pupil had far outstripped the master, if Chaucer and Gower can ever be imagined in such a relationship. Whether Gower ever realized how far is hard to tell. Obviously he liked the story of Troilus and Criseyde, for he referred to it in each of his important works, seven times in all. But only the first, in Balade xx of the *Cinkante Balades*, betrays any awareness of the overtones. There it is taken as an example of the instability of fortune:

. . . auci Diomedes,	. . . also Diomede,
Par ceo qe Troilus estoit guerpi,	because Troilus was rejected
De ses amours la fortune ad saisi,	seized the fortune of his love
Du fille au Calcas mesna sa leesce.	and had his pleasure of the daughter of Calcas.
(CB, xx.19)	

We recall the proem to Book IV of Chaucer's poem:

> [Fortune] From Troilus she gan hire brighte face
> Awey to writhe, and tok of hym non heede,
> But caste hym clene out of his lady grace,
> And on hire whiel she sette up Diomede. (TC, IV.8)

The allusion in the *Mirour* led Tatlock to argue for a pre-1377 date for Chaucer's poem. Rather than staying awake for the matins service, Sompnolent lays his head on the bench:

Et dort, et songe en sa cervelle	And sleeps and dreams in his mind
Qu'il est au bout de la tonelle,	that he is at the bottom of a cask
U qu'il oït chanter la geste	where he hears sung the story
De Troÿlus et de la belle	of Troilus and the lovely
Creseide. (MO, 5251)	Criseyde.

Tatlock's insistence that Gower could have known the Italian story only through Chaucer has been vitiated by R. A. Pratt's discovery that Chaucer was probably working from the French *Roman de Troylus*.[46] Gower could well have known the French translation, too. The spelling *Creseide* in the *Mirour*, which Tatlock considered important evidence of Gower's knowledge of Chaucer's poem, can hardly be taken as such. The substitution of *C* and *G* for the initial letter of Brixeida is to be found in 14th-century manuscripts of both Boccaccio and Guido della Colonna, as well as some manuscripts of the French *Roman* (although in the earliest, the name appears again as *Brisaida*).[47] Chaucer ended the name with both *e* and *a*; Gower used final *e* four times and final *a* twice.[48] Curiously, at *Confessio*, II.2451, "Brexeïda" and "Criseïda" are both cited as examples of infidelity to Agamemnon and Troilus, and at *Confessio*, V.6444 the love of Agamemnon is called "Criseide." The allusion to *Troilus* in the *Mirour* is echoed in the *Confessio*, when the Lover denies that he has been guilty of Sompnolence. He has served his lady day and night, even when "hir list comaunde/ To rede and here of Troilus" (CA, IV.2795). Four times more in the *Vox* and *Confessio*, Troilus and Criseyde are referred to as examples of fidelity and infidelity respectively (VC, VI.1325, CA, II.2451, V.7597, VIII.2531). In each of these instances, as in the balade, Diomede is likewise named, so that we get the triptych-like glimpse of Criseyde flanked by her two lovers that we have at the end of Chaucer's poem (TC, V.799). The only reference that shows any more knowledge of the story than this is at *Confessio* V.7597, where we hear that Troilus fell in love in a temple. At *Vox* I.995, Troilus is included as one of the heroes of Troy. In sum, we may conclude that although Gower knew the story, none of his references betrays real appreciation of Chaucer's elevated treatment. The impulse for treating the conventions of courtly love in a religious context in *Confessio Amantis* would thus appear to be less directly related to the subtle achievement of the *Troilus* than to the more overt religious coloring of the *Legend of Good Women*.

v

Confessio Amantis and the *Legend of Good Woman* appear to stem from the same royal command. One would like to know more about the boating party on the river at which Gower was asked to undertake his poem:

> In Temse whan it was flowende
> As I be bote cam rowende,
> So as fortune hir tyme sette,
> My liege lord par chaunce I mette;
> And so befel, as I cam nyh,
> Out of my bot, whan he me syh,
> He bad me come in to his barge.
> And whan I was with him at large,
> Amonges othre thinges seid
> He hath this charge upon me leid,
> And bad me doo my besynesse
> That to his hihe worthinesse
> Som newe thing I scholde boke,

> That he himself it mihte loke
> After the forme of my writynge. (CA, Prol.39*)

Who was with the King on his barge? His wife, Ann of Bohemia? His mother, Joan of Kent? His retainer, Geoffrey Chaucer? Others of the court circle whom Margaret Galway has attempted to identify in the audience to whom Chaucer is reading his *Troilus* in the frontispiece of MS. Corpus Christi College, Cambridge, 61?[49] What were the "othre thinges seid"? Did they perhaps turn on the debate between the flower and the leaf, in which Chaucer refuses to take sides (LGW, F.72, 189) and in whose emblems the companies of lovers at the end of the *Confessio* are dressed (CA, VIII.2468)?[50] Did the young royal couple at this time conceive the idea of having the two premier poets of the kingdom write parallel poems in praise of love? Was the "religion" of love so clearly specified as the theme that Gower adopted for his work the fiction of a lover's *confession* and Chaucer the fiction of a *penance* for sins against love?[51] Was the idea of a collection of stories itself suggested? While Gower does not state the form of the "newe thing" he was commanded to undertake, in the *Legend* Alceste specifies:

> Now wol I seyn what penance thou shalt do
> For thy trespas, and understonde yt here:
> Thow shalt, while that thou lyvest, yer by yere,
> The moste partye of thy tyme spende
> In makyng of a glorious legende
> Of goode wymmen . . . (F. 479)

Chaucer was, as usual, so circumspect in his allusions that we can do little more than guess about the occasion for his poem.[52] But both the *Legend* and the *Confessio* are addressed rather specifically to both the King and the Queen. Gower's dedication of the *Confessio* to the King we have just noted, and we shall examine in a moment the probable allusion to Richard in the "tirauntz of Lumbardye" passage of the *Legend*.[53] The direct allusion to a patron in the *Legend* is Alceste's command in the F version (excised in G), "whan this book ys maad, yive it the quene,/ On my byhalf, at Eltham or at Sheene" (F.496).[54] Gower likewise acknowledged the Queen's influence by attributing the flower and leaf garlands on the lovers at the end of the *Confessio* to "the newe guise of Beawme [Bohemia]" (CA, viii.2470).

Furthermore, the two adaptations of the conventional vision of the court of love have some remarkable parallels. After opening remarks on experience versus authority Chaucer's Prologue enters upon the praise of the "marguerite" with references to the debate between the flower and the leaf. Before daybreak upon "the firste morwe of May," he rises from his bed and walks "in the mede/ To seen this flour ayein the sonne sprede" (F.47, 108). Kneeling upon "the smale, softe, swote gras" he worships the daisy (F.118). The birds sing to their mates, "Blessed be Seynt Valentyn,/ For on this day I chees yow to be myn" (F.145). All day he lies adoring the daisy and communing with sweet nature. In the evening he returns to the "litel herber" where the dream occurs (F.203). Gower comes to his dream through the moral and political commentary of his Prologue and acknowledgment of the all-embracing power of love at the beginning of the first book, with its echoes of the love philosophy of the Knight's Tale and *Troilus*. But finally he, too, arrives "in the Monthe of Maii/ Whan every brid hath chose his make" (CA, 1.100) upon "a swote grene pleine, the wode amiddes" (CA, 1.112). Overcome by the anguish of love, he sinks to sleep; awaking, he prays Cupid and Venus for relief:

> And with that word I sawh anon
> The kyng of love and qweene bothe;
> Bot he that kyng with yhen wrothe
> His chiere aweiward fro me caste,
> And forth he passede ate laste.
> Bot natheles er he forth wente
> A firy Dart me thoghte he hente
> And threw it thurgh myn herte rote. (CA, 1.138)

There is no suggestion here that the king of love is the *son* of the queen. They are treated as a couple, like the god of love and Alceste in Chaucer's more vivid description:

> Me mette how I lay in the medewe thoo,
> To seen this flour that I so love and drede;
> And from afer com walkyng in the mede

> The god of Love, and in his hand a quene,
> And she was clad in real habit grene.
> A fret of gold she hadde next her heer,
> And upon that a whit crowne she beer
> With flourouns smale, and I shal nat lye;
> For al the world ryght as a dayesye
> Ycrowned ys with white leves lyte,
> So were the flowrouns of hire coroune white.
> For of o perle fyn, oriental,
> Hire white coroune was ymaked al . . .
>   Yclothed was this myghty god of Love
> In silk . . .
> And in his hand me thoghte I saugh him holde
> Twoo firy dartes, as the gledes rede,
> And aungelyke hys wynges saugh I sprede.
> And al be that men seyn that blynd ys he,
> Algate me thoghte that he myghte se;
> For sternely on me he gan byholde. (LGW, F.210)

The green clothing and pearly crown help maintain the figure of the daisy which does not appear at all in Gower. It is therefore the more surprising that in describing the company of lovers at the end of his poem, he should refer specifically to crowns of pearl:

> I sih wher lusty Youthe tho,
> As he which was a Capitein,
> Tofore alle othre upon the plein
> Stod with his route wel begon,
> Here hevedes kempt, and therupon
> Garlandes noght of o colour,
> Some of the lef, some of the flour,
> And some of grete Perles were;
> The newe guise of Beawme there,
> With sondri thinges wel devised,
> I sih, wherof thei ben queintised. (CA, VIII.2462)

The progress of the two allegories is somewhat different. Love turns his face away from Gower because Gower is not to speed in love; he looks sternly at Chaucer because of Chaucer's heresy against love. After piercing John Gower's heart with his fiery dart, Love goes away, but the sympathetic queen remains behind to assuage his suffering. She commands that he confess to her priest, Genius, and so the poem is launched (CA, 1.202). At the end of Book VIII, Genius has Gower address a letter of supplication to Venus. When she reappears, he falls on his knee before her and tells her his name (2321). She promises him relief in a serener love (2361), since he is now too old for the delights of the flesh (2377). At the realization that he is past love he falls into a swoon in which he observes Cupid and a throng of young people. In their company are to be seen the great lovers of history. Twenty-one "good women" are named specifically. The principal four among them, cited as representing conjugal fidelity, are Penelope, Lucrece, Alceste, and Alcione. Elde then leads in a company of rulers and philosophers who have also been victims of passionate love (2666). The old men intercede with Venus on John Gower's behalf. Cupid reappears, this time represented as the son of Venus rather than as king of love. After consulting with his mother, the "blinde god" gropes about until he finds the fiery dart and pulls it out (2785). Genius absolves Gower. Finally Venus gives him a black rosary inscribed *Por reposer* and sends him "ther vertu moral duelleth."

In Chaucer's version, Alceste and the god of love are followed at once by nineteen women, presumably intended to be the women in the balade *Hyd, Absolon,* although the figures do not work out.[55] Twelve of the eighteen or nineteen ladies in the balade are among Gower's twenty-one, and the final one, Alceste, likewise represents conjugal fidelity, but the two lists are conventional and clearly independent. The lovers all kneel and call upon Alceste in terms reminiscent of prayers to the Virgin (F.296). The dreamer, too, kneels before her, and the god of love asks how he dares approach so near the daisy when he has kept folk from their devotion to her by writing such heresies against love as the *Romaunt of the Rose* and *Troilus.* Alceste intercedes for the poet, addressing to the god of love a discourse on the responsibilities of kingship (F.374). She then goes on to catalog all of Chaucer's works to that time which have been in praise of love. The god heeds her admonition and turns the poet over to her for judgment. The poet pleads his innocence, and she assigns him the penance of a collection of legends of the saints of love (F.455). This pleases the god, who tells him to end with Alceste and begin with Cleopatra.

The points of direct similarity between the two versions are 1) the appearance of the king and queen of love; 2) general details of setting and dress such as the "swote pleine," the fiery darts, the pearl crowns, the company of lovers; 3) the displeasure of the king of love with the poets; 4) the intercession of the queen of love; and 5) her assignment of a confession or penance which provides motivation for a collection of stories. All but the last of these similarities might be taken as coincidental if we had no evidence that the authors were acquainted and that the two pieces were written at about the same time for the same royal patrons. Since Kittredge and Lowes at the beginning of the century detailed the parallels between Deschamps' four flower and leaf lyrics and *Lai de franchise* and the daisy cult in the Prologue of the *Legend* (F.40–196), and the parallels between Froissart's *Paradys d'amours* and the vision of the court of love (F.210ff), the debate over the sources of the Prologue has become a quagmire in which happily we may tread lightly.[56] As in his balades, Gower shows no discernible indebtedness in the love allegory of the *Confessio* to the French court poets upon whom Chaucer drew so heavily, although it is interesting to see him still adopting the pose of the anguished lover (found in the *Paradys*) which Chaucer had dropped years before in favor of the role of the detached reporter on love (found in the *Lai*). Furthermore, although age as an impediment to love was conventional, none of the analogues to the *Legend* plays up the incongruity of age in love which is such an effective feature of Gower's conclusion. In his earlier version of the Prologue Chaucer bowed in the direction of the personal convention by asserting his devotion to the daisy (F.56, 86, 103). These remarks were excised in G and replaced by references to the poet's age and unaptness for love (G.262, 315, 400). Beginning with the *House of Fame*, Chaucer had always made a joke of the fact that he was not shaped for love, but references to his age are to be found only in the G version of the

Legend, Scogan, and the *Complaint to Venus,* all dating from the middle nineties. Lowes argued that the references in the *Legend* were autobiographical and evidence of a post-1394 date for the G version; D. D. Griffith thought that they were inserted into the revised version of the *Legend* because Chaucer liked the way that Gower had handled the conclusion of the *Confessio.*[57]

There is no hint of the daisy cult in Gower's poem, and the brief allusion at the end to the flower and the leaf would appear by its juxtaposition to "the new guise of Bohemia" to be in response to a court fashion inaugurated by the young queen.[58] It has been several times demonstrated at length that the vision of the court of love can be traced to no one source;[59] indeed, it is paralleled as closely by the meeting between Theseus and the two young knights in the Knight's Tale as by any of the French analogues.[60] But two points of similarity set the treatments of Chaucer and Gower apart. 1) In none of the other analogues does the poet's appearance before the court of love provide a starting point for a *collection* of stories; and 2) in none of the closest analogues is the religion of love played up so overtly as in these two. The analogue with the closest parallels is Machaut's *Jugement dou Roy de Navarre,* which has a good many details in common with the *Legend.*[61] In both the poet must vindicate himself before a judge for missaying women and love. In both appear some of the same stories—Dido, Ariadne, Thisbe—but in the *Jugement* they are part of the argument of the trial rather than a separate collection. In both the judge is lectured on how to render his decision (in the *Legend* by Alceste, in the *Jugement* by Avis). In both the poet is condemned to write something in favor of love as a penance. But here the parallels end. The interest in the *Jugement* is in the process of the trial, and the penance is three short lyrics.

There is no reason not to suppose that the *Paradys d'amours, Jugement dou Roy de Navarre,* and many other courtly love visions were well known in the English court and helped shape the design assigned for the *Legend* and the *Confessio.* It was to be expected that Gower would use the barest outline of the courtly allegory and fill out his plan with the moral and political ideas with which he was obsessed, whereas Chaucer would turn again to the French court poetry for his inspiration, especially as he may have had the immediate incentive of responding to Deschamps' complimentary balade.[62] But the love vision as the starting point for a collection of tales remains unique. So also does the religious framework for a collection of secular love stories. The religious character of the frame of the *Confessio* and of the organization of its contents under the Seven Deadly Sins of love is all too clear. Skeat, Tatlock, and others have observed that the conception of the *Legend of Good Women* is likewise ecclesiastical-liturgical rather than love-allegorical. This is emphasized not only by its title and the allusion to it in the Man of Law's headlink (CT, II.61), but also by the rubrics which begin and end each legend, and the adaptation of details in the stories to make them resemble the legends of Christian saints.[63] Like the dream vision, the religion of courtly love is a familiar motif, characteristic of the marguerite and some of the flower and leaf poems. However, it is not marked in any of the immediate analogues to the court of love. Furthermore, much of the religious phraseology in the Prologue was removed in the G version. Perhaps this was because it had been introduced in the first place to fulfill the royal command, and when the piece was revised after the Queen's death, Chaucer felt that he could tone down the extreme adulation, and particularly the depiction of himself as a votary of Cupid.[64] In any case the religious framework of the whole *Legend*, and particularly of the F version, draws it closer in conception to the *Confessio*.

Both the historical context and special resemblances support the inference that the *Confessio* and the *Legend* were designed for concurrent presentation, their "matière et sens" dictated by their royal patrons. Chaucer's Prologue is a unified production suitable for independent presentation. In its present form, the beginning and end of Gower's poem are so widely separated that they lose any sense of coherence. Yet read continuously they are perfectly coherent. It is therefore logical to suppose that the court of love portions of the

Confessio were composed together about 1385, especially in view of the reference in Book VIII to the new guise of Bohemia, which would hardly have been so new by 1390. Margaret Galway has proposed May 1, 1385, as the occasion for which the Prologue to the *Legend* was composed. This date has to be supported by a good deal of special pleading. In particular, it depends on the assumption that Chaucer did not know Deschamps' *Lai de franchise,* which was composed for May Day 1385 and, according to Lowes' theory, brought to Chaucer along with Deschamps' complimentary balade in the spring or summer of 1386 by Sir Lewis Clifford. I am inclined to agree with those who argue that Chaucer did not need to know the *Lai.* The verbal echoes, which, as usual, form the most impressive part of Lowes' evidence, have been shown to be part of a literary convention traceable all the way back to Machaut's *Dit de la Marguerite.*[65] However, Richard's political involvement either before or immediately after the Parliament of 1386 would have provided sufficient motivation for Chaucer's introducing into the Prologue of the *Legend* some very direct advice upon the conduct of a king.

The most extended political commentary in Chaucer's writings is the thirty-six lines (F.373–408; in G extended to forty-three, 353–396) which Alceste addresses to the god of love in the *Legend,* counseling him to show the poet mercy for having written treason against love.[66] Margaret Galway holds that this paraphrases the lecture Joan gave Richard after he quarrelled with John of Gaunt in January 1385.[67] The fact that Joan delivered a lecture is to be found in the chronicles, but the two references in the only sentence from it that has been preserved (to a mother's concern for her son's bad end, and to flatterers) are not in Alceste's speech. As was pointed out in Chapter Three, the first is in the revised introduction to the Epistle to the King in *Vox Clamantis,* Book VI, and the second is a main topic in the body of the Epistle. While the speech in the *Legend* would have been an appropriate one for Joan, we cannot tell that it was the one she made. Several scholars have pointed out the parallels between Alceste's speech and the complaints against the King made before and during the Parliament of 1386. And Margaret Schlauch has examined its echoes of the doctrine of kings and tyrants in medieval political theory.[68] None of these discussions points out the inspiration that Chaucer himself appears to acknowledge in his opening lines. Undoubtedly he had had an opportunity to observe the tyrants of Lombardy on his trips to Italy, but he must have communicated his first reactions to his friend Gower, for it is a passage in the *Mirour de l'omme* that provides the best background for the opening lines of Alceste's speech:

Ascuns diont q'en Lombardie	They say that in Lombardy
Sont les seignours de tirandie,	there are tyrannous lords
Qui vivont tout au volenté	who live without restraint,
Sanz loy tenir d'oneste vie,	without law to hold their lives in check;
Ainçois orguil et leccherie	instead pride and lechery
Et covoitise ont plus loé.	and covetousness are greatly admired.
D'orguil ont sainte eglise en hée,	In their pride they hate the church,
Qu'ils la sentence et le decré	since they prefer not to regard at all
Pour dieu n'en vuillont garder mie,	the teaching or decree of God;
Et de luxure acoustumé	and through lechery they habitually
Commune font la mariée	violate both wives
Et la virgine desflourie.	and virgins.
Et d'avarice, dont sont plein,	Through avarice, with which they are filled,
Ils font piler et mont et plein,	they pillage mountain and plain.
N'est uns qui leur puet eschaper	No one may escape them
Qui soit a leur poer prochein.	who is close to their power.
(MO, 23233)	

And so on through thirty lines more, with "ces Lombardz" cited again at 23257. The behavior of the Lombard tyrants is referred to again in the Prologue to the *Confessio* (line 787; see below). These allusions provide a context for the first six lines of Alceste's speech:

> This shoold a rightwis lord have in his thoght,
> And nat be lyk tirauntz of Lumbardye,
> That han no reward but at tyrannye.
> For he that kynge or lord ys naturel,
> Hym oghte nat be tiraunt ne crewel,
> As is a fermour, to doon the harm he kan. (F.373)

The next five lines can be read against the opening lines of the Epistle to the King in the *Vox Clamantis*:

He most thinke yt his lige man,
And is his tresour, and is his gold in cofre.
This is the sentence of the philosophre,
A kyng to kepe his liges in justice;
Withouten doute, that is his office. (F.379)

Since every liege (*legius*) is subject to the law of his king and
serves him with all his might, it is fitting that every liege should
love him with faithful heart in a willing spirit. And it is proper
for the king to guide the people entrusted to him and govern
them with just law. (VC, vi.581)

More directly than to Gower, Chaucer was here alluding to the
Secretum Secretorum in his citation of the "philosophre." The English translation runs:

Dere sone, the peple and thi sugetis is the hous of thi memorie,
and þi tresore by the whiche thi reme is conformyd, thi sugetis
are thi gardyne, in the whiche are many trees, beryng diuerse
frutes, on these trees are many braunchis, beryng frutis and
sedis, and multiplien in many maners, and diffence and durabille
tresoure of þi rewme. It nedith the than þat thi sugetis be welle
governyd, and thou to haue in hert alle that is profitable vnto
hem, and that no vylenye ne extorcion be done vnto hem, and
that they be gouernyd aftir þe maners and oold customes of her
cuntrees, and yofe hem such officers that entende not to ther dis-
truccioun, but good condiciones, wijs, lele, and pacient . . . On
that othir side loke that thi Iustices be wijs and Iuste men.[69]

The idea that the people are the soil and the king the tiller, who
must till well to achieve a good harvest, is expressed in Gower's
Epistle (vi.1001), and like the *Secretum* he emphasizes judges and
the courts.

The next seven lines in the *Legend* again find parallels in the
Epistle:

Al wol he kepe his lordes hire degree
As it ys ryght and skilful that they bee
Enhaunced and honoured, and most dere—
For they ben half-goddes in this world here—
Yit mot he doon bothe ryght, to poore and ryche

> Al be that hire estaat be nat yliche,
> And han of poore folk compassyoun. (F.384)

> When you resolve to attend the complaints of the pauper and
> the widow, you should carry out judgment upon the wretched
> with compassion. Sometimes it is better to remit the decrees of
> the laws, lest mercy vanish because of your severity. So let your
> honor deem it fitting to be lenient to your subjects, for I believe
> that God often wishes the condemned man to live. Also let
> noble and peasant bear an equal burden. (VC, vi.741)

The "gentil kynde of the lyoun," which will not hurt a fly, is not to
be found in the Vox, although "Musca nocet modica, modicis sis
prouidus ergo" (Even a small fly is harmful, therefore be circumspect in small matters, VC, vi.791), provides at least the fly. The
advice in the remaining twelve lines of the speech, that the king
should judge with equity and compassion, repeats motifs already
expressed:

> In noble corage ought ben arest,
> And weyen every thing by equitee.
> And ever have reward to his owen degree.
> For, syr, yt is no maistrye for a lord
> To dampne a man without answere of word,
> And, for a lord, that is ful foul to use.
> And if so be he may hym nat excuse,
> But asketh mercy with a sorweful hert,
> And profereth him, ryght in his bare sherte,
> To ben ryght at your owen jugement,
> Than oght a god, by short avysement,
> Consydre his owne honour and hys trespas. (F.397)

Lines 397–398 resemble Vox, vi.801: "Do not let an angry impulse
suddenly rush upon you, O king, but further the causes of justice
with self control" (and also CA, vii.3955). And the last line, perhaps VC, vi.736: "Your reputation should be placed above money,
your duty above your affairs."

None of this suggests that Chaucer was quoting Gower. At most,
Chaucer's lines are a distillation from, and commentary upon,
Gower's more diffuse generalizations; and both passages grow out

of traditional *speculum regale* material and the popular unrest surrounding the Parliament of 1386. Furthermore, there are differences in emphasis between Alceste's speech and the Epistle in the *Vox*. Gower's emphasis upon counsel, echoing the chronicles and satirical poems of the day, is not reflected by Chaucer, nor do Chaucer's brief pleas for justice (382) and equity (398) match Gower's concern for law, judges, and the courts. Gower's concluding chapter, which holds up to Richard the example of his father (vi.xiii), may have been indirectly paralleled by Chaucer. If we accept the identification of the god of love with the Black Prince, Alceste's remarks are directed *at* Richard *through* the ghost of his father.[70] On the other hand, Chaucer lays greater emphasis upon the king's responsibility to uphold the rights of the lords (384–387) than we find in Gower's Epistle, though no more than Gower expressed in *Confessio* vii (1681–2710), written three or four years after the Epistle.[71] Chaucer's emphasis upon hearing the people's "excuses" (403), about which he felt so keenly that he added lines in revision repeating the same word (G.362), may reflect his more intimate acquaintance with Richard's haughtiness and obduracy concerning which Gower and the chroniclers speak more generally. Chaucer's other addition in revision, after the assertion that "to kepe his liges in justice" is the king's "office," "And therto is a kyng ful depe ysworn/ Ful many an hundred wynter herebyforn" (G.368), has been explained as a reference to the fact that Richard was required by the Parliament of 1388 to renew his coronation oath.[72]

The balade *Lak of Stedfastnesse* is generally cited as paralleling Alceste's speech in the *Legend*.[73] Its expression of the conventional complaint against an upsidedown world [74] resembles that of the Prologue to the *Confessio Amantis*, as Alceste's speech does the Epistle in the *Vox*:

(Stanza 1) Somtyme the world was so stedfast and stable
      That mannes word was obligacioun;
      And now it is so fals and deceivable
      That word and deed, as in conclusioun,
      Ben nothing lyk, for turned up-so-doun

Is al this world for mede and wilfulnesse,
That al is lost for lak of stedfastnesse.

(CA, Prol.93)   If I schal drawe in to my mynde
The tyme passed, thanne I fynde
The world stod thanne in al his welthe:
Tho was the lif of man in helthe,
(Ibid.113)   The word was lich to the conceite
Withoute semblant of deceite:
Tho was ther unenvied love,
Tho was the vertu sett above
And vice was put under fote.
Now stant the crop under the rote,
The world is changed overal,
And therof most in special
That love is falle into discord.

(Stanza 2)   What maketh this world to be so variable
But lust that folk have in dissensioun?
For among us now a man is holde unable,
But if he can, by som collusioun,
Don his neighbour wrong or opressioun.
What causeth this but wilful wretchednesse,
That al is lost for lak of stedfastnesse?

(CA, Prol.127)   And sein the regnes ben divided,
In stede of love is hate guided,
The werre wol no pes purchace,
And lawe hath take hire double face,
So that justice out of the weie
With ryhtwisnesse is gon aweie.
(Ibid.140)   Wherof the certain noman knoweth:
The hevene wot what is to done,
Bot we that duelle under the mone
Stonde in this world upon a weer.

(Stanza 3)   Trouthe is put doun, resoun is holden fable;
Vertu hath now no dominacioun;
Pitee exyled, no man is merciable;
Through covetyse is blent discrecioun.
The world hath mad a permutacioun

> Fro right to wrong, fro trouthe to fikelnesse,
> That al is lost for lak of stedfastnesse.

(CA, Prol.787)   Men sein, ful selden is that welthe
Can soffre his oghne astat in helthe;
And that was on the Lombardz sene,
Such comun strif was hem betwene
Thurgh coveitise and thurgh Envie,
That every man drowh his partie,
Which myhte leden eny route,
Withinne Burgh and ek withoute:
The comun ryht hath no felawe,
So that governance of lawe
Was lost, and for necessite,
Of that thei stode in such degre
Al only thurgh divisioun,
Hem nedeth in conclusioun
Of strange londes help beside.

As a parallel to the envoy to King Richard we need not quote the lengthy exhortation to just war and police action following *Confessio*, VII.3600. The vigorous conclusion resembles far more closely epigrammatic lines in the Epistle in the *Vox*.

(envoy)   Shew forth thy swerd of castigacioun,
Dred God, do law, love trouthe and worthinesse,
And wed thy folk agein to stedfastnesse.

(VC, VI.709)   Preciptur gladius vibratus semper haberi,
Prompcius vt crimen judiciale ferat.
(Ibid.733)   Sperne malos, cole prudentes, compesce rebelles,
Da miseris, sontes respue, parce reis.
(The sword should always be brandished that judicial punishment be carried out the more promptly. Spurn the wicked, cherish the wise, curb the rebellious, give to the unfortunate, cast aside the criminal, have mercy upon the condemned.)

That lines which can be read thus antiphonally are not the result of hours, indeed years, of mutual reading and conversation would appear to me incredible. The period about 1385–86 marked the

high point of Chaucer's and Gower's personal and literary relationship. By this time they were both intimate with the court and concerned about the direction of political affairs. Chaucer had progressed from the *House of Fame* to the moral philosophy of the
Troilus. Gower, perhaps influenced partly by the effectiveness of
Chaucer's philosophical treatment of love, had determined to take
the occasion of the royal command to round out his trilogy and
restate his moral philosophy in terms of Empedoclean love. It is
characteristic that Gower, having accepted his commission, should
set himself doggedly to fulfill it and should eventually emerge triumphant with the "testament of love" promised by his allegorical
frame. It is equally characteristic that Chaucer, having written a
brilliant introduction and adapted or composed about half the tales,
should tire, and his critical sense should rebel, at the thought of
plodding through all the monotonously similar series he had been
assigned.[75] Nevertheless, we can appreciate the note of complacency
in the message from Venus which Gower penned about 1390 as he
finished his task. What is most important about these lines, however, is that they imply that Chaucer was still supposed to get on
with his task. Alceste had assigned it in the first place; and now
Venus instructs Gower:

> Thow schalt him telle this message,
> That he upon his latere age,
> To sette an ende of alle his werk,
> As he which is myn owne clerk,
> Do make his testament of love,
> As thou hast do thi schrifte above,
> So that mi Court it mai recorde. (CA, vɪɪɪ.2951*)

Although Chaucer may still have planned to complete the *Legend*
when he revised its prologue after the Queen's death in 1394,[76] it is
more likely that he made another kind of reply to Gower's message.
For in the meantime, his interest had turned to a collection of
stories whose plan offered a greater range of possibilities than the
stereotypes of the *Legend*.

VI

The General Prologue to the *Canterbury Tales* is dated about 1387. It may be considered the same sort of ultimate tribute to the influence of Gower upon the mind and art of Chaucer that the determination to make a love allegory in English his *magnum opus* is to the influence of Chaucer upon Gower. For in the General Prologue Chaucer was avowedly turning from courtly to clerical literature for his inspiration. Before we begin tracing Gower's themes and expressions through the *Canterbury Tales*, however, the warning against confusing artistry with ideas must be repeated. By 1387 Chaucer was at the height of his powers, with a virtuosity far beyond anything Gower could ever command. His wider reading, his mastery of language, his wit, his characterization, his dramatic and narrative skill—surely none of these is brought into question by the assertion of an obvious but overlooked truth. No matter how much more technique and material Chaucer brought to his treatment, it remains a fact that Gower had been there first. Both priority and the many foreshadowings in the *Mirour de l'omme* and *Vox Clamantis* of the subject matter and point of view of the General Prologue entitle us to conclude that the social conscience of the moral Gower continued to exert its influence upon Chaucer's final great experiment.

For many years after Frederick Tupper's suggestion that the Seven Deadly Sins provide a conceptual frame for the *Canterbury Tales* had been pulverized by J. L. Lowes, and J. M. Manly had produced historical prototypes for many of the pilgrims, it was hazardous to suggest that the pilgrims had any universal qualities or that the poem might have thematic unity or present a unified social philosophy.[77] Fortunately, we are now beginning to concede that medieval authors could be as metaphorical in expression and universal in intention as any other writers, classical or modern. Tupper's mistake was that—like Lowes himself, when dealing in parallel passages—he schematized and delimited the moral pattern of the *Canterbury Tales* too sharply. The social interpretation of this poem, like the whole interrelationship between Chaucer and Gower, must be conceived more broadly. Religion has been called a type of Kantian category in terms of which medieval man perceived the social world.[78] The traditional ecclesiastical classifications of the vices and virtues, personified in the various classes of society, were the spectacles through which man's social and spiritual obligations were viewed in all medieval art and literature. There was no secular tradition of social criticism upon which an author could draw, as there was for—say—Voltaire or Sinclair Lewis. And, as observed previously, the literary mode of satire was practically nonexistent in the Middle Ages. The Seven Deadly Sins and the Three Estates were in a sense the *genera* and *species* of which individuals were the *exempla*. This was the Platonic, deductive world view of medieval complaint of which Gower's *Mirour de l'omme* is one of the most perfect embodiments. To varying degrees, *Piers Plowman*, the morality plays, and later allegorical and didactic works by such writers as Spenser, Jonson, Milton, and Bunyan carried on the tradition. But already by Gower's time the opposing, Aristotelian, world view was being reasserted. Roscelin's dictum of nearly three centuries earlier, *universalia post rem*, had flowered into the self-revelatory monologues of Jean de Meun's Falsemblent and La Vielle, the acid portraits of the *Inferno*, the narrative genius of the *Decameron*, and finally the brilliant satiric sketches of Chaucer's General Prologue. The tradition of medieval complaint provided the theme and substance for the Canterbury pilgrimage. Chaucer's adaptation of the tradition reflects not only his greater literary genius but also the new world view that makes him a man of the Renaissance rather than of the Middle Ages.

Chaucer's principal innovation was from as venerable an ecclesiastical tradition as the complaint on the estates.[79] The adoption of the pilgrimage as a frame, instead of the penitential of the *Legend* and *Confessio*, or the allegory of the marriage of the daughters of the devil and the war between the vices and virtues of the *Mirour de l'omme*, must be regarded as evidence of Chaucer's literary sensitivity. Its artistic advantages need hardly be labored again: the holiday spirit, the variety of the participants, yet withal the unity of purpose and sense of destination. All of these advantages are made manifest in the first twenty-nine lines of Chaucer's Prologue, which set the tone for the whole poem. With the Canterbury pilgrims we may compare the procession that winds to a May wedding in the *Mirour*:

Et c'estoit en le temps joly	It was in the beautiful time
Du Maii, quant la deesce Nature	of May, when the goddess Nature
Bois, champs, et prées de sa verdure	reclothes wood, field, and meadow with
Reveste, e l'oisel font leur cry,	verdure, and the birds make their cry,
Chantant deinz ce buisson flori,	singing in the flowery bushes,
Que pont l'amie ove son amy:	as the lover pricks his love.
Lors cils que vous nomay desseure	Then those whom I named above
Les noces font, comme je vous dy.	made their marriage, as I told you.

(MO, 939)

The recurrence of the *point-pricketh* figure here and again in the *Confessio* (vii.1048) in connection with the birds is itself worth noting. In this setting in the *Mirour*, a grotesque procession of personified vices rides to a symbolic wedding with the world, to the ultimate iniquitation of mankind.[80] In Chaucer's Prologue, a procession more realistic although very nearly as grotesque rides toward Canterbury to worship the saint "That hem hath holpen whan that they were seeke." Nothing could better set off the difference between the abstraction of complaint and the concreteness of satire than the conceptions of these two processions, and the fact that Gower chose to bury his nearly a thousand lines along in his poem and *follow* it by the lovely May setting, rather than to exploit the dramatic possibilities. Here, as always, Gower's mode is to underplay his material as if deliberately seeking to avoid the flamboyant.

Although the pilgrimage itself has no connection with the *Mirour*, the characterization of the pilgrims is related to it in both principle and detail. In the previous chapter, we discussed the relationship betwen the *Mirour* and confessional manuals, and the connection between confessional manuals and the criticism of the estates growing out of the directive that the priest was to adapt the penance to "the circumstance both of the sinner and the sin." [81] Though confession is relegated to the background in the *Mirour*, what is said about it crystalizes its connection with the estates in words reminiscent of those Chaucer used to introduce his character sketches:

Primer de qui s'om voet descrire,	First concerning the one to be described:
Ly confess son estat doit dire.	the confessor ought to tell his estate,
Queux homme il est, malade ou seins,	what man he is, ill or well,
Ou riche ou povre, ou serf ou sire,	or rich or poor, or serf or lord,
Ou clercs ou lais, n'el doit desdire,	or clerk or layman—he should not refuse—
S'il est champestre ou citezeins,	whether he is rural or urban,
Ensi dirra les pointz tous pleins:	he should tell these details fully.
Et lors falt que ly chapelleins	Then it is necessary that the chaplain
Son age et son estat remire,	examine his age and his estate,
Car en l'estat qu'il est atteins	for depending upon the estate he has attained
Le pecché poise plus ou meinz,	the sin weighs heavy or light,
Soit de mesfaire ou de mesdire.	be it of misdoing or missaying.
(MO, 14845)	

Me thynketh it accordaunt to resoun
To telle you al the condicioun
Of ech of hem, so as it semed me,
And whiche they weren, and of what degree,
And eek in what array that they were inne. (CT, 1.36)

Gower attributed his passage to a confessional manual by "un clercs Boëce" whereas Chaucer's has been attributed to the rhetoricians. Yet given the similarity in language and the subsequent catalog of individualized types, the a priori likelihood that Chaucer was looking at human character through the moralistic spectacles of his time is strengthened.

The basic misunderstanding of the Tupper-Lowes exchange over Chaucer and the Seven Deadly Sins was its failure to make clear the distinction between literature of the Sins and literature of the Estates. What bothered Lowes was that subheads such as hypocrisy, blasphemy, disobedience, grumbling, and the like, by which Tupper had identified individual pilgrims or stories as "formally" illustrating one or another of the Seven Sins, were to be found under several of the capital sins, and furthermore that several of the capital sins might be mentioned in connection with a given pilgrim or story.

Gower's *Mirour* reveals the reason for this overlapping. Its first 19056 lines are an elaborate analysis of the vices and virtues. In bare outline, this treatment is not unlike that in the Parson's Tale; indeed, out of thirty-eight items in Gower's treatment of the first two sins, pride and envy, only seven are not to be found in both the *Mirour* and the Tale.[82] But the Parson's Tale is a true confessional manual, terse and sparing in citation of authority. When the analysis was filled out to form a treatise of moral instruction, illustrations were introduced from contemporary society, and narratives ranging from historical anecdotes to folk, biblical, and classical stories. In this first part of the *Mirour*, then, we have a systematic presentation of sins and a haphazard presentation of estates. On the other hand, lines 19057–27360 of the *Mirour* are devoted to criticizing "les états du monde." Theoretically, in the second part the manifestations of every major sin and every subhead should be treated for every class in society.[83] But this was clearly impossible, even in a piece so limitless as the *Mirour*. Furthermore, each class was more liable to some sins than to others. Hence, the treatment of the sins in connection with any particular class is incomplete and disproportionate. In this part of the *Mirour*, and throughout the *Vox*, we have a systematic presentation of estates and a haphazard presentation of sins.

To the extent that he was working in a literary tradition and not drawing upon his own observation, Chaucer was working more in the tradition of the Estates than of the Seven Deadly Sins. Hence both Tupper's attempt to make the pilgrims and tales illustrate particular sins and Lowes elaborate rebuttal miss the point. Chaucer's pilgrims are types, but types of the Estates rather than types of the Seven Deadly Sins. Chaucer had a better eye than Gower for the representative features of the individuals he saw about him. He had by this time mastered the satiric mode in all its variations. Furthermore, he could draw upon a rich literary tradition of complaint upon the estates.[84] The claim is not, therefore, that either the details or the language of Chaucer's brilliant miniatures in the General Prologue and connecting links were drawn from the moralizations in the *Mirour de l'omme* and *Vox Clamantis*.[85] It is rather that the extensive parallels support the more significant argument that has been developed throughout this chapter—that without the influence and example of the moral Gower, there might never have been a *Canterbury Tales* at all. Once the stimulus had been provided, Chaucer could be expected to develop his poem according to his own genius.[86]

Ruth Mohl may be accurate in judging that in "the strict sense of the term," Chaucer's Prologue is not quite a piece of the literature of the Estates in that his superior artistry did not permit him to be satisfied with the customary exhaustive classification of the estates and their defections.[87] But she confuses technique with substance when she explains that "He was more interested in character than in denunciation, and for Gower's more or less morbid preachment Chaucer gives us a company of living personalities. Where Gower attempted an exhaustive catalogue, Chaucer the artist was brief." This is to equate literature of the Estates "in the strict sense" with exhaustiveness, dullness, denunciation, prolixity. Granted that Chaucer was more selective and more brilliant in his handling than Gower and his other contemporaries, the fact remains that he was molding the same material and producing a similar criticism of various classes of society. It is interesting, first of all, to compare the pilgrims Chaucer chose to include with the classes in the *Mirour* and the *Vox*: [88]

Canterbury Tales (those in italics have no parallels in Gower's poems): Knight, Squire, *Yeoman*, Prioress, Monk, Friar, Merchant, Clerk, Lawyer, Franklin, Artisans, Cook, *Shipman*, Physician, Wife of Bath, Parson, Plowman, Reeve, *Miller*, Summoner, *Pardoner*, *Manciple*, *Chaucer*, Host, Canon, *Canon's Yeoman*.

Mirour de l'omme (those in italics have no parallels in the *Canterbury Tales*): la Court de Rome (18421), *cardinals* (18841), *evesqes* (19057), archdeacones (20089), curetz (20209), *des autres prestres annuelers qui sont sans cure* (20497), clergeons (20785), religious possessioners (20833), freres mendiantz (21181), *emperours* (21781), *roys* (22225), *grans seignours* (23209), chivalers

(23593), gens du loy (24181), *jugges* (24625), *baillifs* (24817), marchans (25177), ceux qui vivent du mestier et d'artifice (25501), physicians (25633), vitaillers, citezein, labourier (25981).

Vox *Clamantis* (the one in italics is not in the *Mirour* but is in the *Canterbury Tales*): prelati (iii.i–xiii), in curia Romana (iii. xiv), curati (iii.xvi–xxviii), scholares (iii.xxix), monachi (iv.i–xii), *de mulieribus in habitu moniali* (iv.xiii–xv), ordines fratrum (iv. xvi–xxiv), de his qui in statu militari temporalia defendere et sup-portare tenetur (v.i–viii), de istis qui ad cibos et potus . . . per-quirendos agriculturae labores subire tenetur (v.ix), diversi vulgi laboraii (v.x), mercatores (v.xi–xiv), cives (v.xv–xvi), de illis qui juris ministri dicuntur, causidici et advocati (vi.i–v), ballivi (vi.vi), rex (vi.vii).

It may be noted that Chaucer included only representatives of those classes appropriate to his band of pilgrims. The higher ranks of both the clerical and lay hierarchies are omitted. Also, he chose to begin his catalogs of pilgrims and tales with the highest mem-ber of the secular hierarchy and to intermingle the secular and reli-gious throughout. His consciousness that he was not observing tra-ditional order helps account for the drawing of straws for the first tale (CT, 1.835), the Host's request that the Monk tell the second tale (CT, 1.3118), and the brilliant device of the quarrels to dra-matically motivate the subsequent order. In some respects the Canterbury group is closer to the estates in the Vox than to those in the *Mirour*. In the Vox, the secular estates begin with knight-hood, the higher orders of the nobility are not specified (the king appears as part of the *legal* heirarchy), and room is made for the Prioress. The additions Chaucer made to Gower's lists were sanctioned by the wide variations in the tradition. As Miss Mohl's study indicates, there was no canon of the estates beyond "clerus, milites, agricultores," named by Gower in the Vox (iii.i, headnote). Chaucer does not mention these three estates by name, but he re-affirms their historic significance by idealizing them in the persons of the Knight, Parson, and Plowman. Neither he nor Gower was bound by these estates, however. Some of the pilgrims not found

among Gower's estates increase the verisimilitude of Chaucer's
group (the two yeomen); some may have been suggested by internal
or external association (the Shipman, Miller, and Manciple), or by
a particular aversion (the Pardoner). Although various elements in
the characterization of the Wife of Bath, as well as her tale, are
paralleled in Gower's works, she is not provided for by his classifications. For her, Chaucer again drew independently upon a feature of
the tradition that Gower ignored, that of including a special estate
of Women or Matrimony.[89]

The *Mirour* introduces the medieval ideal of knighthood directly:

Car chivaler, u qu'il devient,	The knight, wherever he is,
De son devoir le droit sustient	must as his duty sustain the right
Dont sainte eglise est enfranchie;	by which holy church is enfranchised;
Ou si tirant le droit detient	or if a tyrant endangers the right
Du vierge ou vieve, lors covient	of virgin or widow, it is necessary
Que chivaler leur face aïe.	that the knight come to their assistance.
(MO, 23599)	

A few lines later the theory of the estates is clearly stated:

Chascum estat, le quel qu'il soit,	Each estate, whatever it may be,
Est ordiné par son endroit	is ordained by its position
De faire au siecle ascun labour.	to perform in the world a specific task.
(MO, 23617)	

The two shortcomings featured most prominently in the *Mirour*
and in the *Vox* (v.1ff), are not mentioned at all in connection with
Chaucer's Knight. The *Mirour* complains that the chivalric aristocracy is being replaced by a financial aristocracy: knights have become greedy for money, now fight only for ransom (MO, 23695),
and engage in trade rather than seeking military prowess (MO,
23713).[90] The *Vox* accuses them of having become more interested
in lovemaking than in fighting (VC, v.37–468, practically the
whole of the discussion of knighthood). Nevertheless, the parallels
between Chaucer's treatment and Gower's are marked. The debili-
tating effects of love in the *Vox* put into vivid context the shortcomings of the Squire who fought not for Christendom, but "In
hope to stonden in his lady grace" (CT, 1.88). The contrast be-

tween the motive for the Knight's "viage" and the Squire's is made categorical in the *Mirour:*

O chivaler, je t'en dirray,	*O knight, I speak to you,*
Tu qui travailles a l'essay	*you who labor in errantry*
Devers Espruce et Tartarie.	*in Russia or Tartary.*
La cause dont tu vas ne say,	*The reason for your going I do not know.*
Trois causes t'en diviseray,	*Three causes I discern,*
Les deux ne valont une alie:	*two of which aren't worth an alder-berry:*
La primere est, si j'ensi die,	*The first is, if I may say so,*
De ma prouesce enorguillie,	*because of my prowess and pride,*
'Pour loos avoir je passeray';	*'To have praise, I will adventure';*
Ou autrement, 'C'est pour m'amye,	*or else, 'It is for my lady,*
Dont puiss avoir sa druerie.' . . .	*that I may have her love.' . . .*
La tierce cause n'est ensi,	*The third reason, for which a prudent man*
Pour quelle ly prodhons travaille;	*strives, is not like these.*
Ainz est par cause de celluy	*But it is for the sake of Him*
Par qui tous bons sont remery	*by whom all good is rewarded*
Solonc l'estat que chascun vaille.	*according to what each one deserves.*
Ton dieu, q'a toy prouesce baille,	*It is right that you should*
Drois est q'au primer commençaille	*from the first, before all others,*
Devant tous autres soit servi.	*serve the God who gives you valor.*

(MO, 23893, 954)

Flügel pointed out that knights' fighting in Prussia and Tartary, as well as in many of the other areas specified for Chaucer's Knight, is to be found in poems by Machaut and Deschamps,[91] which Chaucer knew. But while the details are there, the context is not. The French poets are ironic or humorous. It is the moralistic tenor of Gower's criticism that provides the best background for Chaucer's idealization. The emphasis upon humility as one of the principal virtues of chivalry here (MO, 23872, 23900) and earlier in the discussion of "Vergoigne" (Modesty, MO, 12073), culminate in a catalog of virtues which may be set alongside the Knight's "chivalrie,/ Trouthe and honour, fredom and curteisie" (CT, 1.45):

Qant cils en qui toute prouesce,	*When those in whom all prowess,*
Honour, valour, bonte, largesce	*honor, valor, goodness, generosity,*
Et loyalté duissent remeindre,	*and loyalty ought to remain*
Se pervertont de leur noblesce	*are perverted from their nobility*
Par covoitise ou par haltesce,	*by covetousness or pride,*
De l'onour seculer atteindre,	*to strive for worldly honor,*
Ne say a qui me doy compleindre.	*I don't know to whom I ought to complain.*

(MO, 24085)

Gower's moralizations do not match the phrasal nuances nor individualizing details which immortalize Chaucer's Knight. But they do show how Chaucer's characterization parallels the traditional complaint upon the estate. Chaucer's description of the Squire depends even more heavily than the Knight's on sheer delight in detail, and its universal quality is less criticism of the estate than a distillation of carefree, fortunate Youth as he appears in the love visions. Yet, as already indicated, Chaucer managed to imply in this apparently guileless description some of the criticisms that he had avoided in describing the Knight. One was of the motive for chivalry. Set against the diatribe in the Vox, in particular, there can be no doubt that the Squire's motive represents a lesser ideal than that of his father. Another indirect criticism would appear to be of the Squire's "chyvachie" in France. Gower's emphasis upon the fact that true chivalry must be in behalf of Christendom has already been noted. At Vox, III.651, Christian chivalry is castigated for its failure to retake Jerusalem from the pagans: "Instead we are fighting open battles over worldly possessions with our brothers, whom the water of baptism indicates as reborn."

The portrait of the Prioress is again a measure of the skill with which Chaucer could handle the tools of satire. The "imperfect submergence of the woman in the nun" (to repeat Lowes' fine phrase) [92] and the overtones of institutional criticism reveal Chaucer at his subtlest and most sensitive. The Prioress emerges as virtuous and good-hearted enough; ironically it is her institution which keeps her out of touch with the realities of life and betrays her into sentimentalism and petty vanities. In an England impoverished by war and ravaged by the Black Death, she weeps over dead mice and feeds her dogs cake. Unerringly Chaucer fixed upon the very word by which Marie Antoinette would be immortalized four centuries later—*gâteau* being merely the French form of *wastel* bread. Concerning the negligent curate, Gower had written:

His dog, which barks with faithful voice on the hunt, will certainly get whatever it wants to have. But as for the poor wretch who cries at the door and needs food—alas! Not a crumb or a drop is given to him. (VC, III.1499)

In comparison with the rapier delicacy of Chaucer's criticism, the description of nuns in the *Vox* is as blunt and tactless as the whole tradition of *Hali Meidenhad*. Women cannot possibly be strong enough to withstand the urge of the flesh.[93] "Crescere nature sunt iura que multiplicare/ . . . Hecque dei scripta seruare volunt" (To be fruitful and multiply are the laws of nature, and these are the scriptures of God they wish to obey, VC, IV.571). Food is likewise central to Gower's discussion, but it is again a conventional accusation of gluttony rather than the subtle indirection by which Chaucer reveals the Prioress' superficial values through devoting thirty out of the forty lines of her characterization to her concern for dress and table manners.

The corpulent monk and avaricious friar were such stock figures in 14th-century literature that hardly any descriptive detail can be considered unique. Nevertheless, the parallels between Chaucer's and Gower's treatment of these two are the most striking of the series. Gower's criticism of this estate begins with the observation that monks have become great landowners, concerned only with their temporal wealth:

Cil moigne n'est pas bon claustral	*That monk is not a good cloisterer*
Q'est fait gardein ou seneschal	*who is made a guardian or seneschal*
D'ascun office q'est forein;	*of any outside office;*
Car lors luy falt selle et chival	*for then he needs saddle and horse*
Pour courre les paiis aval,	*to ride around the country,*
Si fait despense au large mein;	*and he spends largely.*
Il prent vers soy le meulx de grein,	*He takes the best of the grain for himself*
Et laist as autres comme vilein	*and leaves others, as to churls,*
La paille, et ensi seignoral	*the straw. Thus lordly*
Devient le moigne nyce et vein.	*becomes the monk, foolish and vain.*
(MO, 20953)	

Besides Gower's "seignoral" monk who must have horse and saddle we may set Chaucer's manly "outridere" with his "dainty" mounts and jingling bridle.[94] The monk out of his cloister is again likened to a fish out of water:

Saint Augustin en sa leçoun	*St. Augustine in his writing*
Dist, tout ensi comme le piscoun	*says that just as the fish*
En l'eaue vit tantsoulement,	*lives only in water,*
Tout autrecy Religioun	*in like manner religion*
Prendra sa conversacioun	*will flourish only*
Solonc la reule du covent	*according to the rule of the convent,*
El cloistre tout obedient.	*wholly obedient in the cloister.*

(MO, 20845)

And Gower's monk, too, knows a better rule than St. Augustine's:

Ne croi point de saint Augustin,	*He doesn't believe in St. Augustine,*
Ainz est la reule du Robyn,	*but rather in the rule of Robin,*
Qui meyne vie de corbyn,	*who lives the life of a raven,*
Qui quiert primer ce q'il engouste	*seeking first what he may eat*
Pour soi emplir, mais au voisin	*to fill himself, and giving no*
Ne donne part.	*part to his neighbor.*

(MO, 20885)

In the Vox there is not only the fish-out-of-water figure (iv.280), but also the complaint of the "modern" monk:

> *Nil modo Bernardi sancti vel regula Mauri*
> *Confert commonachis, displicet immo, nouis:*
> *Obstat avarus eis que superbus et invidus alter,*
> *Ordinis exemplum qui modo ferre negant.*
> *Expulit a claustris maledictus six Benedictum,*
> *Sic gula temperiem, sic dolus atque fidem.* (VC, iv.337)

(The rule of St. Bernard or St. Maure is of no use to our modern fellow monks. On the contrary, it displeases them. A greedy fellow sets himself against them as does another, proud and envious. They refuse to carry out the precepts of their order. Thus malediction has driven Benedict out of the cloister, thus gluttony has driven out temperance, and guile faith.)

Concerning the monk's gluttony and self-indulgence, Chaucer was, as usual, indirect:

> His heed was balled, that shoon as any glas,
> And eek his face, as it hadde been enoynt.
> He was a lord ful fat and in good poynt;
> His eyen stepe, and rollynge in his heed,
> That stemed as a forneys of a leed. (CT, 1.198)

In Gower's complaint gluttony becomes a major theme. "Tout scievont bien que gloutenie/ Serra du nostre compaignie" (MO,

20893), the monks assert in the *Mirour*, and go on to elaborate in detail (MO, 20857ff). "Fit modo curtata monachorum regula prima,/ Est nam re dempta, sic manet ipsa gula" (The original rule [*regula*] for monks is now curtailed; *re* has been subtracted so that only *gula* remains, VC, IV.128), begins the complaint in the *Vox*. Its long diatribe casts light on some of the details in Chaucer's description of the monk: it is practical for him to be shaved bald lest long flowing hair get in his way when he guzzles (VC, IV.135); when he drinks, he must sit down first lest his foot fail beneath the weight of his belly (IV.133); when envy makes him wrathful "his face swells with anger, his veins grow black with blood, and his rolling eyes flash brighter than fire" (IV.175).

More than he does for the other estates, Gower dwells upon the rich dress of the monks, and his discussion helps to explain the relationship between the "condiciouns" of Chaucer's pilgrims and the "array that they were inne":

Jerom nous dist que celle ordure	Jerome tells us that the filth
Que moigne porte en sa vesture	which a monk wears on his habit
Est un signal exteriour	is an exterior sign
Qu'il sanz orguil et demesure,	that his heart inside is
Du netteté q'est blanche et pure,	of pure, white cleanness,
Ad le corage interiour:	without pride or arrogance.
Mais nostre moigne au present jour	But our present-day monk
Quiert en sa guise bell atour	seeks to wear gay attire
Au corps, et l'alme desfigure:	on his body and to disfigure the soul.
Combien q'il porte de dolour	Although he wears the habit
La frocque, il ad du vein honour	of grief, he has [over it] the vain honor
La cote fourré de pellure.	of a furred coat.
(MO, 20989)	

All of which is summed up in the Nun's Priest's quiet observation on the poor widow: "Her diete was accordant to her cote" (CT, VII.2836). Again in the *Mirour*:

Ne quiert la haire ainz quiert le say	He does not seek a hair shirt
Tout le plus fin a son essay,	but rather the finest wool,
Ove la fourrure vair et gris,	furred with ermine and squirrel,
Car il desdeigne le berbis;	for he despises fleece.
L'aimal d'argent n'ert pas oubliz,	The enamelled silver is not forgotten,
Ainz fait le moustre et pent tout gay	but makes a gay show hanging
Au chaperon devant le pis.	from his hood upon his chest.
(MO, 21016)	

The same warm furred cloaks make their appearance at Vox iv.26, and the comparison between clothes and spiritual condition in connection with canons at Vox iv.360.[95]

Chaucer's identification of the enamelled brooch by which Gower's monk fastened his hood as a love knot is an oblique thrust at the immorality of the religious. On the face of it, Chaucer's monk would seem to have had no need of women:

> . . . he was a prikasour aright:
> Grehoundes he hadde as swift as fowel in flight;
> Of prikyng and of huntyng for the hare
> Was al his lust, for no cost wolde he spare. (CT, 1.189)

There is no way of telling whether Chaucer intended "venerie" earlier, and "prikyng," "huntyng," and "lust" here to have any double entendre. But it is certain that they would have had for Gower. Like Chaucer's, his monk appeared to have no need for women:

> Et pour delit tient plus avant
> A la rivere oiseals volant,
> La faulcon et l'ostour mué,
> Les leverers auci courant
> Et les grantz chivals sojournant,
> Ne falt que femme mariée.
> (MO, 21043)

> And for pleasure he esteems especially
> flying birds by the river,
> the falcon and moulted hawk,
> greyhounds coursing also,
> and great horses standing ready—
> he lacks only a wife.

But Gower goes on immediately:

> Du femme ne say consailler,
> Mais je me puiss esmervailler,
> Car j'ay de les enfantz oÿ
> Dont nostre moigne pourchacier
> Se fist, quant il aloit chacer
> Un jour et autre la et cy;
> Mais ils ne poent apres luy
> Enheriter; pour ce vous dy,
> Les grandes soummes falt donner
> Dont ils serront puis enrichy.
> (MO, 21049)

> Concerning the wife, I can't say,
> but I find myself wondering,
> for I have heard of children
> whom our monk acquired
> when he went hunting
> one day and another, here and there.
> But they cannot inherit after him;
> therefore, I tell you,
> great sums must be given
> that they may be then enriched.

Again in the Vox monks are forced to provide for their "nephews" out of the church's wealth (VC, iv.257). In the Vox, Gower joined the accusation of immorality to that of excessive drinking: "I do not know how a wine bibber may remain properly chaste, for Venus rages as hotly with wine as fire does with flame" (VC, IV.165)— recall the Wife of Bath's "A likerous mouth moste han a likerous tayl" (CT, III.466).

The parallels between Chaucer's portrait of the Friar and Gower's criticism of the mendicants are likewise commonplace but illuminating. The "lymytour's" familiarity with his district, appearance when husbands were away at work, and special privileges of visitation gave him the reputation the iceman has sometimes had in modern society. Chaucer suggested the Friar's immorality throughout his portrait, by calling him at the outset "wantowne"; by speaking of the marriages he had made "Of yonge wommen at his owene cost"; by stressing his familiarity with worthy women of the town and "tappesteres"; by describing his trinkets for "faire [or yonge] wyves"; and by referring to his "daliaunce," "fair langage," and lisping "To make his Englissh sweete upon his tonge." The ubiquity and immorality of "lymytours and others hooly freres" is stated even more directly by the Wife of Bath (CT, III.866).[96] Gower spoke repeatedly of their superfluous numbers (MO, 21529, VC, IV.711, 951). He used *limitantz* several times, twice in two almost identical passages, the first in discussion of the sin of "incest," the second in the criticism of the friars:

D'Incest del ordre as mendiantz   From the incest of the mendicant orders
Je loo que tous jalous amantz   I advise that all jealous lovers
Pensent leur femmes a defendre: take care to protect their women.
Ly confessour, ly limitantz,   The confessor, the limitor,
Chascun de s'aquointance ad tant   by his acquaintance has so many
Pour confesser, et pour aprendre,   to confess and to learn about
Que ce leur fait eslire et prendre   that he need choose and take
Tout la plus belle et la plus tendre,   only the prettiest and most tender,
Car d'autre ne sont desirantz.   for the others he does not desire.
Itiel Incest maint fils engendre   This incest engenders many children
Dessur la femeline gendre,   upon the female sex
Dont autre est piere a les enfantz.   when another is the father of the children.
(MO, 9145)

D'incest des freres mendiantz   From the incest of the mendicant friars
Je loo as tous jalous amantz   I advise all jealous lovers
Q'il vuillent bonne garde prendre;   that they take good care.
Car tant y ad des limitantz   For there are so many limitors

Par les hostealx et visitantz,	*in homes as visitors*
Q'au paine nuls s'en poet defendre.	*that one can hardly protect himself.*
Mais je vous fais tresbien entendre,	*But I assure you*
Q'ils nulle femme forsque tendre	*that they seek no woman except*
Et belle et jofne vont querantz;	*the tender and pretty and young.*
Siq'en la femeline gendre	*Thus it is that women*
Sovent avient que frere engendre,	*often have babies that a friar begets*
Dont autre est piere a les enfantz.	*when another is the father of the children.*

(MO, 21325)

The *Vox Clamantis* is equally direct in its accusation of immorality:

> While the man is gone, the audacious, adulterous friar enters and takes over the role of another for himself. Thus does he approach the master bedroom with its smooth bed—a bedroom he has enjoyed again and again; yet quite often it will be for the first takings . . . The friar's devotion makes up for the husband's failures, and his growing progeny fill the paternal halls.
> (VC, IV.837)

Here, in brief, is one motif of the Shipman's Tale. Gower is likewise specific about the friar's reason for arranging marriages: "The man who takes a bride because urged on by a cleric will contribute heavily to Venus, since the cleric may be adulterous in the matter" (VC, VII.170). In the *Vox* he adapts to his own purpose the figure of the bees and flowers:

> I feel that nature decreed something to be observed among bees so that a friar might take note: for if a bee stings, its mischief retaliates against it, so that it does not possess its sting any more. And afterwards it keeps to the hidden recesses of its dwelling place and flies forth no more to take honey from the flowers of the field. O God, if the adulterous friar would only lose his swollen pricker in the same way when he has stung, so that he would not pluck women's flowers nor go wandering about the world away from his home. (VC, IV.877)

The friar's "daliaunce and fair langage" appear in the *Mirour*:

Ils ont la langue liberal,	*They have a generous tongue*
Dont la mençonge serra peinte,	*with which to paint lies.*
Ils ont parole belle et queinte	*They have pretty and quaint speech*
Dont font deceipte a lour aqueinte.	*with which they deceive their acquaintances.*

(MO, 21233)

This theme is developed in fifty lines in the Vox (IV.1041–90), including

> They sway the minds of the naive by speaking sweetly. But the temple of the Lord shuts out such men, abhors the trappings of such speeches, and shuns their smooth talk. Poet's writings, which painted language gilds over, are rendered with a golden tongue, but beware of them. The simple word is good.
>
> (VC, IV.1068)

Gower goes into much greater detail than Chaucer about the competition between the friars and the secular clergy. Like the friars at the beginning of the Summoner's Tale, Gower's travel in a pair:

> L'un ad noun frere Ypocresie,   The one is named Brother Hypocrisy
> Qui doit ma dame confesser,   who confesses milady,
> Mais l'autre la doit relesser,   but the other who absolves her
> Si ad noun frere Flaterie.   is named Brother Flattery.
> (MO, 21249)

Hypocrisy goes ahead because of his simple, saintly appearance, and Flattery comes behind bearing the sack (MO, 21361):

> Ipocresie tielement   Hypocrisy thus
> Du dame et seignour ensement   seeks to hear confession
> Quiert avoir la confessioun;   from both lady and lord.
> Mais Flaterie nequedent   But Flattery, nevertheless,
> Par l'ordinance du covent   by the ordinance of his convent
> En dorra l'absolucioun,   gives them absolution.
> Car il ad despensacioun,   For he has a dispensation,
> Solonc recompensacioun   in return for recompense
> Que vient du bource au riche gent,   that comes from the purses of rich people,
> Qu'il puet donner remissioun   so that he can grant remission
> Sanz paine et sanz punicioun,   without pain or punishment
> Pour plus gaigner de leur argent.   to get more of their money.
> (MO, 21277)

This comes close indeed to:

> Ful wel biloved and famulier was he
> With frankeleyns over al in his contree,
> And eek with worthy wommen of the toun;
> For he had power of confessioun,
> As seyde hymself, moore than a curat,
> For of his order he was licenciat.
> Ful swetely herde he confessioun

And pleasaunt was his absolucioun:
He was an esy man to yeve penaunce,
Ther as he wiste to have a good pitaunce. (CT, 1.215)

"Therfore in stede of wepynge and preyeres/ Men moote yeve silver
to the povre freres" (CT, 1.231) is explained by the extensive criticism of friars' confessing and burying for money in the Vox (IV.
xvii). At Vox IV.690 Gower asserts that he does not wish to blame
the whole mendicant body for the corruption of the few, but Caps.
xix–xx question seriously whether there is any justification for the
existence of the friars. All of the work of the church was well in
hand before they were created:

> Does there seem, then, any reason or cause for the friar's ap-
> propriating the special role of another for himself? It is forbid-
> den for the raven, which every flock recognizes as unwelcome, to
> take its place among white birds, and all justice forbids the friar
> who shirks his responsibility to take his place among the mem-
> bers of the church.[97] (VC, IV.901)

Like Chaucer's (CT, 1.240), Gower's friars seek out the wealthy
and refuse to minister to the poor (MO, 21340, 21470, and VC,
IV.735). The description of the begging friar in the Mirour reminds
us of Chaucer's:

O comme le frere se contient,	O, how the friar behaves
Qant il au povre maison vient!	when he comes to a poor home!
O comme le sciet bien sermonner!	How well he knows how to preach!
Maisque la dame ait poy ou nient,	Although the woman has little or nothing,
Ja meinz pour ce ne s'en abstient	for that he does not abstain
Clamer, prier et conjurer;	from clamoring, praying, conjuring.
La maile prent s'il n'ait denier,	He will take a mite, if not a penny,
Voir un soul oef pour le soupier,	even a single egg to eat,
Ascune chose avoir covient.	anything suits him to have.
"Way," ce dist dieus, "au pautonier,"	"Woe," says God, "upon such a vagabond
"Qui vient ensi pour visiter	who comes thus to visit
Maison que povre femme tient!"	the home of a poor woman."
(MO, 21373)	

He was the beste beggere in his hous;
For thogh a wydwe hadde noght a sho,
So plesaunt was his "In principio,"
Yet wolde he have a ferthyng, er he wente. (CT, 1.252)

The friars' skill in *brocage* (business intrigue, MO, 21386), and his busyness as an advisor and go-between are discussed in the *Vox*, IV. xviii: "Nunce medicus, nunc confessor, nunc est mediator" (833). "Lovedays" are discussed later in connection with the estate of chivalry (MO, 23683).

In his observation that the Friar was not dressed like a cloisterer or poor scholar, but like a master or a pope, Chaucer hinted at another criticism to which Gower devoted many lines: the friars' overweening pride in their status as masters of arts and schoolmen (MO, 21493, VC, IV.xviii), and their luring young boys into joining their orders before they had reached the age of discretion (MO, 21541; VC, IV.xxi). Their proclivity for rich habits (CT, 1.263) and fine buildings (CT, III.2099, in the Summoner's Tale) is also treated at length by Gower (MO, 21397, VC, IV.xxiii). Another accusation implied by Chaucer runs throughout Gower's discussions, echoing the opprobrium of the Wycliffite "Tractatus de Pseudo Fréris." [98] The friars are said to resemble a false prophet named "Pseudo" who once appeared to mankind (MO, 21627). The accusation of hypocrisy was perhaps the most universal and devastating of the many leveled at the mendicants. In general, Gower complained that their conduct belied their preachments:

Tout ensi vein verras faillir	*You will see if you search their lives*
Sermon des clercs sanz parfournir	*that the sermons of clerks are*
Si tu leur vie sercheras.	*vain and useless without performance.*
(MO, 21706)	

This Wycliffite contrast between pretensions and practice is exactly that which Chaucer emphasized between the Parson on the one hand and the Monk, Friar, and Pardoner on the other. The parallels in Gower's and Chaucer's treatments of the Parson are largely by way of antithesis in that Gower's treatment is essentially critical, whereas Chaucer chose the Parson as one of the three characters in the General Prologue to idealize. In the Canterbury group, the Parson and Summoner, and possibly the Nun's Priest and Pardoner, stand as the representatives of the secular clergy, and the Prioress, Monk, and Friar as representatives of the regulars. As we shall see, the Summoner personifies the corruption of archdeacons and officials of the ecclesiastical courts, and the Pardoner bears a vague resemblance to the corruption Gower subsumed under "la court de Rome." Their portraits caution us against concluding that by a sympathetic description of the Parson, Chaucer was entering any general defense of the secular clergy against the regular. Yet the obvious contrast between the sincere, useful Parson and the other hypocritical, useless—or worse—representatives of the clergy clearly implies that the proper function of the clergy was to minister to the spiritual and, where necessary, the temporal needs of its lay parishioners rather than to exist for its own ends. This corresponds to the view Wyclif advances in his treatise "Of Feigned Contemplative Life," [99] and elsewhere. Many of Wyclif's criticisms of other bodies in the church, whom Chaucer does not mention, are paralleled in Gower's works. Undoubtedly both he and Chaucer were familiar with the Wycliffite criticisms, sympathized with some, and rejected others. But whereas Gower's temperament and literary method led him to continue the tradition of wholesale denunciation and condemnation, which almost buries the slight references to "les bons curetz du temps jadis" (MO, 20437), Chaucer saw the artistic advantage of opposing the tradition by creating an ideal character.

The introduction of the Parson as "povre" but "riche of hooly thoght and werk" (CT, 1.479) takes on added meaning against the background of the criticisms in the *Mirour* and the *Vox*. Both condemn the wealth of the curates and their employment in business and secular affairs:

Des fols curetz auci y a,	*There are also foolish curates*
Qui sur sa cure demourra	*who live off their cures,*
Non pour curer, mais q'il la vie	*not to care for them but so that*
Endroit le corps plus easera;	*they can live lives of bodily ease;*
Car lors ou il bargaignera	*they do business there*
Du seculiere marchandie,	*in secular merchandise*
Dont sa richesce multeplie.	*whereby their riches multiply.*
(MO, 20305)	

And *Vox* III.xix is devoted to rectors who amass worldly wealth by "buying and selling all kinds of temporal goòds from day to day,

just like lay merchants." In connection with their worldliness and
luxury, Gower denounces harshly the immorality of parish priests,
which Chaucer's portrait does not even hint at by indirection. Absolon in the Miller's Tale is foreshadowed:

O prestre, q'est ce courte cote?	O priest, what is this short coat?
L'as tu vestu pour Katelote,	Are you dressed for Katelote,
Pour estre le plus bien de luy?	to be even gayer than she?
Ta coronne autrement te note.	Your tonsure denotes you another sort,
Et d'autre part qant tu la note	and of another kind when you sing
Au lettron chanteras auci,	the service at the lectern.
U est, en bonne foy me di,	Upon my faith, I ask whether
Sur dieu ton penser, ou sur qui?	your thought is upon God or upon whom?
(MO, 20677)	

And if the remarks about friars provide an analogue for the monk's
supplying the husband's failings in the Shipman's Tale, those about
the curates provide an analogue for the wife's failings:

Les foles femmes mariez,	Foolish married women,
Qant n'ont du quoy estre acemez	when they have not the wherewithal to be adorned
Du queinterie et beal atir,	with quaintery and fancy clothes,
Lors s'aqueintont des fols curetz	make the acquaintance of foolish curates
Qui richement sont avancez,	who have been prosperously advanced.
Et par bargaign se font chevir,	And through their bargain each acquires
Dont l'un et l'autre ad son desir;	from the other what he wants:
La dame avera de quoy vestir,	The woman will have the wherewithal to dress,
Et l'autre avera ses volentés.	And the other his desire.
(MO, 20365)	

Vox III.xviii makes an even more direct connection between hunting and lechery than that cited above for the monk:

His mass is short, but long are his devotions in the fields, where
he appoints his dogs as cantors. The hare and the fox are what
he wants most; as he speaks of God his mind is still on the
hare. Thus one fox chases another and hunts something just like
itself, when all the while it is ravaging the young flock. For when
wandering about he investigates where the pretty women of
tender age are, so that he can glut his passion. Indeed, such a
rector lies in ambush for women like a wolf circling about the
sheep in the fold. When he sees an old groom and a young bride,
he pays a call upon people like this in his charge. There the
rector takes full control of the groom and properly explains the
bride's bounden duties. Thus the rector takes the good-looking

bodies under his care and leaves the souls to wander about corrupted. (VC, III.1509)

Gower takes up overhasty cursing and excommunications in connection with bishops rather than curates. He uses again the figure
of the bee; this time its sting resembles the episcopal curse:

Cil fol prelat, q'a dieu se joynt,	This foolish prelate who is joined
Del aguillon trop se desjoynt,	to God from his sting is dis-
Qant il l'autry du point adesce;	joined when he uses it upon others.
(MO, 19372)	

Mais saint Gregoire la sentence	But St. Gregory compares
De ton orguil vait resemblant	the effect of your pride
A l'oisel de son ny volant.	to a bird flying from its nest.
(MO, 19407)	

Even more than the statement in the Prologue, "Ful looth were
hym to cursen for his tithes" (CT, 1.486), these lines resemble
those in the Parson's Tale:

> Swich cursynge bireveth man fro the regne of God, as seith Seint
> Paul./ And ofte tyme swich cursynge wrongfully retorneth
> agayn to hym that curseth, as a bryd that retorneth agayne to his
> owene nest./ (CT, x.618) [1]

The Parson's almsgiving is explicated by the *Mirour*'s one positive
observation:

Les bons curetz du temps jadis,	The good curates of former times
Qui benefice avoient pris	who received benefices
Du sainte eglise, deviseront	from holy church divided their goods
En trois parties, come je lis,	into three parts, as I read.
Leur biens, siq'au primer divis	The first part they
A leur altier part en donneront,	gave to the altar;
Et de la part seconde aideront,	with the second they aided,
Vestiront et sauf herbergeront	and clothed, and gave shelter
De leur paroche les mendis;	to the poor in their parish;
La tierce part pour soy garderont:	with the third they cared for themselves.
D'oneste vie ils essampleront	They gave example of honest life
Et leur voisins et leur soubgitz.	to their neighbors and underlings.
(MO, 20437)	

Less formally, these ideas appear in Chaucer's portrait as:

> Bot rather wolde he yeven, out of doute,
> Unto his povre parisshens aboute

Of his offryng and eek of his substaunce.
He koude in litel have suffisaunce. (CT, 1.487)

The Parson's teaching his flock by example is again paralleled in Gower's discussion of bishops. Rather than leading, the present-day bishop commands.

Julius Cesar en bataille	*Julius Caesar in battle*
Jammais as gens de son menaille	*never said to his men*
Ne dist "Aletz!" ainz dist "Suietz!"	*"You go!" but he said "Follow me!"*
Car au devant toutdiz sanz faille	*For before all others without fail*
Se tint et fist le commensaille,	*he held the van,*
Dont tous furont encoragez:	*by which all were encouraged.*
Mais no prelat nous dist "Aletz!"	*But our prelates say "You go!*
"Veilletz! junetz! prietz! ploretz!"	*You wake! You fast! You pray! You weep!"*
C'est la parole qu'il nous baille;	*This is the word they give us,*
Mais il arere s'est tournez:	*but they themselves turn back.*
Nuls est de son fait essamplez,	*Their behavior is no example;*
C'est un regent qui petit vaille.	*this is a rule worth very little.*[2]
(MO, 19333)	

Instead of the figure of the gold and iron (CT, 1.500), Gower uses the figure of the blind leading the blind (MO, 20401), but in the Vox, he joins it to that of the tainted shepherd (CT, 1.504): "Sic ouis ex maculis pastoris fit maculosa,/ Et cadit in foueam cecus vterque simul" (Thus the sheep becomes tainted with the shepherd's stains, and each falls into the ditch like a blind man, VC, III.1063). The figure of the bishop as a good shepherd is nicely elaborated in Vox III.xiii.

The Parson's modest speech but courage to "snybben sharply" anyone who deserves it (CT, 1.523), Gower likewise treated in connection with bishops, whom he criticizes for censuring poor folk for their sins, but remaining quiet about the sins of the great:

Evesque, om dist, et je le croy,	*Bishop, it is said—and I believe it—*
Comment les poverez gens pour poy	*that you vilify the poor*
De leur errour tu fais despire,	*for their small errors*
Et les grantz mals et le desroy	*and remain silent about the*
De ces seignours tu laisses coy,	*great evils and misrule of the nobles,*
Qe tu n'en oses faire ou dire:	*to whom you dare not do or say a thing.*
Tu es paisible vers le sire,	*You are peaceable toward the lord*
Et vers le serf tu es plain d'ire,	*and full of wrath toward the serf.*
L'un est exempt de toute loy,	*The one is exempt from all law*
Et l'autre souffre le martire.[3]	*and the other suffers torment.*
(MO, 19093)	

The fact that the portrait of the Parson in the Canterbury Prologue draws so heavily upon matters that Gower treats in connection with bishops suggests that he was intended to represent a category broader than himself—indeed, that he represents the clergy in all of its justifiable occupation with the cure of souls, in whatever office, from the bishop on down.

Gower's discussion of curates impinges upon Chaucer's portrait of the Clerk of Oxenford, although the problem of keeping the clergy at their ordained task of ministering to their parishioners is noted in Chaucer's portrait of the Parson (CT, 1.507.) The complaints in both the *Mirour* and *Vox* are first against those who leave their cures to advance themselves in civil or episcopal offices, or to lead lives of indolence and corruption at the university (MO, 20221, VC, III.xvi):

Par autre cause auci l'en voit,	For another reason also one sees
Des fols curetz ascuns forsvoit,	that foolish curates go astray,
Qant laist sa cure a nonchaloir,	when they leave their cures in disregard,
Et pour le siecle se pourvoit	and strive for worldly
Service au court par tiel endroit	service in court, by which it may be seen
Q'il puist au siecle plus valoir,	that they place greater value on the temporal
Et ensi guaste son avoir.	and thus waste their goods.
Mais le dieu gré n'en puet avoir,	But God can have no pleasure in that,
Car nuls as deux servir porroit	for one cannot serve two masters
Sanz l'un ou l'autre decevoir;	without deceiving one or the other.
Car cil qui fra le dieu voloir,	For one who will serve God
Servir au siecle point ne doit.	ought not to serve the world at all.
* Cil q'est servant de la dieu court*	He who is a servant in God's court
Et pour servir au siecle court,	and runs to serve in the world
Fait trop mal cours a mon avis.	takes a very bad course, in my view.
(MO, 20245)	

Earlier, in discussing the virtues, Gower had explained that Saint Purpose, as opposed to Simonie, would never

Par doun, priere, ou par service,	By gift, prayer, or by service
Dont elle acate benefice,	buy a benefice,
Q'ensi ne voet en nulle office	for he does not want thus to enter any office
Du sainte eglise entrer l'ovile:	in the fold of holy church.
N'est pas si sote ne si nyce,	He is not so stupid or foolish
Q'offendre voet la dieu justice	as to want to offend God's justice in either
Ou par Canoun ou par Civile.	canon or civil law.
(MO, 16086)	

At least the rhymes resemble those of him who "hadde geten hym yet no benefice,/ Ne was so worldly for to have office" (CT, 1.291).

The discussion of students in the Vox (III.xvii) begins with an elaboration of the accusation that curates leave their parishes to live in lechery at the university. The chapter is colored by the play upon words like *ars*, *natura*, and *scola*. The student seeks "natural" knowledge with his *socia* (female fellow); his art consists of fulfilling God's command to be fruitful and multiply; his seed is plentiful; and so forth. Finally, at the end of the book on the secular clergy (VC, III.xxviii–xxix), Gower takes up the tension between the university as a preparation for the ministry and for worldly advancement. "A cleric used to go to school with a patient spirit, but now worldly glory is his master" (2067):

> There used to be saints who disdained worldly pomp and longed for the highest good. And since becoming acquainted with schools incited their spirits to be holy, they gave themselves over to pious study of the Scriptures. Ambition and love of possessions did not move them, but they rightly went out of eagerness for virtue. In contemplating heaven, they shunned the earth, and no lascivious purpose drew them aside. Nor did they wish to be in the service of a king, nor have the name of rabbi among the people. Nor did vain, sumptuous adornment, nor indulgence in wine, nor women's love overcome them. Well versed in good morals, they furnished good examples for those to come which the student ought to adopt for his own instruction.
>
> (VC, III.2121)

"Sownynge in moral vertu was his speche,/ And gladly wolde he lerne and gladly teche" (1.308). Chaucer's Clerk is clearly one of these scholar saints, even though described by the wry pen of one who knew how much it costs the hewers of wood and drawers of water to maintain such saints in their ivory towers.

As the Parson and Clerk exemplify the true vocation of the church, the Summoner and Pardoner represent Chaucer's severest comment upon its institutions. There are no close parallels for either figure in Gower's poems. Hayselmayer, Kellogg, Work, and others have shown how directly they are paralleled in episcopal decrees, court writs, and records.[4] As always, the individualizing details are Chaucer's own. There is nothing in any of the documents to suggest the Summoner's leprous visage nor the Pardoner's unnatural hair and eyes. Furthermore, rather than being, as often, merely emblematic, these details appear to be symbolic. The evidence of corruption in the appearance of the Summoner and of sterility in that of the Pardoner corroborate the predominant criticisms of the ecclesiastical courts and of the whole system of papal indulgences. Hence these two personifications are Chaucer's way of criticizing the institutions themselves.

Chaucer's most direct criticism of the ecclesiastical courts is put, ironically, in the mouth of the Friar (CT, III.1301), who accuses the "erchedeken" of his north country (?Richard Ravensere, who took Gower's fine for acquiring William de Septvauns' manor of Aldington[5]) of being particularly hard on lechery and "small tything." This archdeacon had a summoner "redy to his hond," who in turn:

> Hadde alwey bawdes redy to his hond,
> As any hauk to lure in Engelond. (CT, III.1339)

The opening lines of the Friar's Tale provide the context for the portrait of the Summoner in the General Prologue, and for the apothegm by which he sums up the corruption of the ecclesiastical courts: "Purs is the ercedekenes helle" (CT, I.658). Gower developed the criticism of the ecclesiastical courts in much greater detail, as we observed in the last chapter in connection with the "positive law" of the church. He accused deans and archdeacons themselves of the misdeeds of which Chaucer accused the Summoner—blackmail and trafficking in vice: "Lessont au ferm le putage" (MO, 20155).[6] He, too, finds avarice their chief sin—"ainz ta penance/ Serra del orr (MO, 20179)—and plays upon "purse" as the symbol of this corruption:

Le dean, qui son proufit avente,	*The dean who follows after profit*
Par tout met les pecchés au vente.	*puts sins on sale everywhere.*
(MO, 20101)	

Maisque la bource soit benoit,	Provided the purse is blessed,
Le corps ert quit de celle extente.	the body is forgiven to that extent.
(MO, 20108)	
Qant dieus m'ad fait pardonnement,	After God has pardoned me,
Ma bource estuet secondement	my purse must then make accord
Faire acorder le dean et moy.	between the dean and me.
Ne sai ce que la loy requiert,	I don't know what the law requires,
Mais merveille est de ce q'il quiert	but the marvel is that he seeks
Dedeinz ma bource m'alme avoir.	in my purse for my soul.
(MO, 20194)	

The same play upon *bursa* appears at *Vox* III.223, although the *Vox* does not take up any of the officers of the ecclesiastical courts directly.

The portraits of the Man of Law and the Summoner in the General Prologue of the *Canterbury Tales* imply the judgment upon the superior merit of the civil courts that we have seen Gower expressing directly and repeatedly. In the Prologue, the ecclesiastical courts are represented by only the vile Summoner. But Chaucer has nothing to say about the equally vile "questours" and bailiffs of the civil courts. Instead, the latter are represented only by the Man of Law, a perfectly respectable character even though he may be guilty of a certain venality. On the contrary, having accused the major officials themselves of being extortioners and purveyors of vice, Gower had nothing to say about the minor officials of the ecclesiastical courts. But he had a great deal to say about the misdeeds of the minor officials of the civil courts. The bailiff is as merciless in his extortion as the Summoner in the Friar's Tale, or as the Friar himself:

Car qant baillif visitera,	For when the bailiff visits, there is no
N'est maison q'il pour dieu respite;	house that he will respite for God's sake.
Comme plus la voit povere et despite,	The more poor and despised he sees it,
Tant plus d'assetz l'oppressera,	the more he will oppress it,
Q'ascune chose enportera;	that he may carry something off.
La qu'il l'esterling ne porra	There where he cannot have sterling,
Avoir, il prent la soule myte.	he will take a single mite.
(MO, 24999)	

Gower has no comment upon either the Pardoner or the system of indulgences. In both the *Mirour* (18481) and the *Vox* (III.iv), he condemns the fact that papal dispensations can be readily bought for a price. But this is a different matter from the downright

fraud of the Pardoner. In this instance alone, Chaucer goes beyond
Gower in his social criticism.

Gower's respect for merchants and for the wool trade was discussed in the third chapter. He is the only author Ruth Mohl cited
as finding merchants divinely ordained (VC, v.xi), along with the
traditional Three Estates of nobility, clergy, and peasants.[7] Most of
his discussion of the economics of trade has no place in the Canterbury Prologue, although Chaucer can, as usual, find a way to touch
upon the key issues. The Merchant was skillful in both the wool
trade and money market:

> Wel koude he in eschaunge sheeldes selle.
> This worthy man ful wel his wit bisette:
> Ther wiste no wight that he was in dette,
> So estatly was he of his governaunce
> With his bargaynes and with his chevyssaunce. (CT, 1.278) [8]

Gower laments:

Eschange, usure et chevisance,	*Exchange, Interest, and Profit,*
O laine, soubz ta governance	*O Wool, under your governance*
Vont en ta noble Court servir;	*come to serve in your noble court.*
Et Triche y fait lour pourvoiance,	*Trickery makes provision for them,*
Qui d'Avarice l'aquointance	*who attracts his acquaintance*
Attrait, et pour le gaign tenir	*Avarice, and to hold his gain*
Il fait les brocours retenir.	*brokers must be employed.*
(MO, 25417)	

In a brilliant passage following *Mirour* 25237 Gower plays upon the
word *triche* in all the trading centers of Europe. Earlier he had discussed *chevisance* as a form of usury, accusing merchants of charg-
ing from 66 percent to 100 percent profit for their grain and other
goods (MO, 7236, 7321). Chaucer's Merchant spoke "Sownynge
alwey th'encrees of his wynnyng." Formerly merchants talked in
twenties and hundreds, said Gower, but what they had was their
own:

Mais ils font ore lour parlance	*But they now speak*
De mainte Mill; et sanz doubtance	*of many thousands; yet without doubt*
Des tieus y ad que s'il paioiont	*there are some who, if they paid*
Leur debtes, lors sanz chevisance	*their debts, then they wouldn't possess*

Ils n'ont quoy propre a la montance	the value of one florin
D'un florin, dont paier porroiont.	which they could spend without bargaining.
En leur hostealx qui vient entrer	Whoever enters their homes
Leur sales verra tapicer	will see their rooms carpeted
Et pour l'ivern et pour l'estée,	both winter and summer,
Et leur chambres encourtiner,	and their bedchambers curtained,
Et sur leur tables veseller,	and vessels on their tables
Comme fuissent Duc de la Cité.	as if they were dukes of the city.
Mais en la fin qant sont alé	But when they are departed
De ceste vie et avalé	from this world and lowered
Bass en la terre, lors crier	deep in the earth, then one can hear
Om puet oïr la niceté	the foolishness of their pride
De leur orguil, que povreté	cry out, for poverty is obliged
Leur debtes covient excuser.	to excuse their debts.

(MO, 25819)

The pilgrimage becomes a refuge for those merchants who have cheated their neighbors (MO, 25852).

"Gule," Gluttony, is Jupiter's cousin rather than "Epicurus owne sone," but otherwise her description might stand for the Franklin:

> His breed, his ale, was alweys after oon;
> A bettre envyned man was nowher noon.
> Withoute bake mete was nevere his hous
> Of fissh and flessh, . . .
> After the sondry sesons of the yeer,
> So chaunged he his mete and his soper.
> Full many a fat partrich hadde he in muwe,
> And many a breem and many a luce in tuwe. (CT, 1.341)

The *Mirour* on Gule:

Celle est a Jupiter cousine,	He is Jupiter's cousin,
Q'estoit jadys dieus de delice,	who was originally god of delicacy,
Car n'est domeste ne ferine	for there is no domestic or wild
Du bestial ne d'oiseline	beast or fowl
Qe n'est tout prest deinz cel office:	which is not present to do its office;
La sont perdis, la sont perdice,	there are cock and hen partridges,
La sont lamprey, la sont crevice,	there are lampreys, there are crabs,
Pour mettre gule en la saisine	to put gluttony in possession
De governer tout autre vice.	and thus submerge all other vices.

(MO, 7826)

Her fine breads and wines had been mentioned at *Mirour* 7801.

"Triche," Fraud, summarizes Gower's judgment upon all the artisans and victualers. His own interests and possibly those of the audience he was addressing in the *Mirour* are betrayed by the fact that in contrast to the commonplace, useful trades exemplified by Chaucer's five burghers, Gower's all represent the luxury trades: goldsmiths, jewelers, spicers (apothecaries), furriers, tailors, and saddlers (MO, 25513ff). All are accused of debasing their products or of violating the sumptuary laws. There is no suggestion of the religious fraternities to which Chaucer's artisans belong nor of their civil and financial pretensions. However, the pretensions of their wives and of the Wife of Bath had been characterized earlier by Gower, under "vaine gloire":

C'est une dame trop mondeine:	She is a very worldly lady,
Car pour la vanité du monde	because for worldly vanity
Son corps ove tout dont elle abonde	her body and all she owns
Despent et gaste en gloire veine:	she spent and wasted upon vain glory;
Tout se travaille et tout se peine	everyone toils and labors
Pour estre appellé cheventeine,	to be called mistress,
Du quoy son vein honour rebonde.	from which her vain honor redounds.

(MO, 1203)

The artisans' wives in the Prologue found:

> It is ful fair to been ycleped "madame,"
> And goon to vigilies al bifore,
> And have a mantel roilliche ybore. (CT, 1.376)

The Physician is treated by Gower in connection with the spicer-apothecary. Chaucer slyly observed:

> Ful redy hadde he his apothecaries
> To sende hym drogges and his letuaries,
> For ech of hem made oother for to wynne—
> Hir frendshipe nas nat newe to bigynne. (CT, 1.425)

This is the theme of Gower's complaint:

Phisicien de son affaire	The physician in his business
En les Cités u q'il repaire	in the cities where he goes
Toutdis se trait a l'acquointance	always makes the acquaintance
De l'espiecer ipotecaire.	of the spicer-apothecary.

(MO, 25633)

Phisique et Triche l' Espiecer	Physic and the cheating spicer
Bien se scievont entracorder;	know well how to make accord;

Car l'un ton ventre vuidera	for the one empties your stomach
Asses plus que ne fuist mestier,	more than is needful,
Et l'autre savra bien vuider	and the other knows just as well how
Ta bource, qu'il dissolvera.	to empty your purse, until it dissolves.
(MO, 25645)	

Heavy-handed, perhaps, but a try for a joke. In Gower's lines there is no astrological medical lore, no allusion to the famous physicians of the past, no physical description. Only the accusation of avarice and collusion. Both what Chaucer took from the complaint on the estates and what he added to it stand out here in bold relief.

The Cook and the Host fall into the category of victualers (MO, 25981ff), who call forth some of Gower's most vivid sketches of London life, but whom Chaucer for reasons personal or political passed over very lightly.[9] The remarks of the Host to the Cook in the Prologue to his tale (CT, 1.4344) resemble Gower's criticism more than does the portrait in the General Prologue, and if the Cook had ever finished the tale of the "hostileer" as he promised (CT, 1.4360), we might have still more parallels with the *Mirour*. The taverner is the first victualer to be treated by Gower, and his hospitality is very different from the "vitaille at the beste" and "strong wyn" (CT, 1.749) at the Tabard Inn:

Du Taverner fai mon appell,	Concerning the Taverner I make my
Qant il le vin del an novell	accusation,
Ove l'autre viel del an devant,	that he falsely mixes the fresh wine
Qui gist corrupt deinz son tonell	with the old wine of the previous year
Et n'est ne sein ne bon ne bell,	which lies spoiled in its cask
De sa falsine vait mellant,	and is neither wholesome nor good;
Et ensi le vait tavernant.	this is the way with tavernkeeping.
(MO, 25993)	

All the wines of Europe come out of a single tun (MO, 26052). The taverner causes the city dames to tipple at his tavern (MO, 26082). Beer sellers, bakers, butchers, and sellers of fowl are likewise accused of fraud. Peddlers are the worst of the lot. Gower's overall complaint is that by fraud and overcharging, the victualers as a class fail to fulfill their divinely ordained mission of providing the community with food and drink (MO, 26209).

The parallel to the Reeve appears, like that to the Franklin, in

Gower's treatment of a vice rather than in his treatment of an estate. Concerning "Larcine" he had written:

Larcine auci par autre guise,	Larceny also in another way,
Quant doit servir, son fait desguise	as he serves, disguises his behavior
Au sire du qui la maisoun	from the lord whose house he governs;
Governera; car lors sa prise	for the gain from
Diversement est de reprise,	his thieving is varied,
Puis qu'il ad tout a sa bandon:	since he has all in his power.
Des toutes partz prent environ	From every part he takes a bit,
Et au garite et au dongon,	from attic to cellar;
Ne laist braiel ne laist chemise,	he misses not a girdle nor a shirt,
Neis la value d'un tison,	nor the value of a piece of kindling,
Dont il ne prent sa partison,	from which to take his part
Puisqu'il la main ait a ce mise.	because it is all in his hands.
Office soutz la main du liere	An office under the hand of a robber,
Sicomme chandelle en la maniere	like a candle, drips and
Du poy en poy gaste et degoute;	wastes away little by little,
Car il sa main viscouse emblere	for he cannot pull back
Ja ne la poet tenir arere,	his sticky, thievish hand
Ainçois par tout u q'il la boute	without stealing a grain or piece
Luy fault piler ou grain ou goute	of everything that it has touched—
Tout en celée, que point ne doute	all in secret, for no one can doubt his
D'acompte, si nuls le surquiere,	account or know that he has broken faith,
Ne de ce qu'il sa foy ad route:	if no one follows him.
Qui tieux servans tient de sa route:	One who keeps such a servant
Poverte n'est pas loign derere.	has poverty following close behind.
Soubtilement de son mestier	Subtly can Larceny excuse
Larcine se sciet excuser;	his behavior to his master,
Car si n'en soit atteint au fait,	for if he is not detected in the act
Ja nuls le savra tant culper.	none will know him guilty.

(MO, 7045)

Vivid details such as the mortal fear of the tenants, the Reeve's handsome house, the presents given him by his grateful lord, and his age and appearance are not found in Gower's description. These are the concrete peculiarities of real life by which Chaucer transformed the abstract complaint into vivid satire. But his description and Gower's are two sides of the same coin.

The Plowman in the General Prologue has the same idealized role as the Knight and the Parson.[10] His resemblance to symbolic Piers the Plowman has been previously remarked. In designating him the Parson's brother and stressing his Christian virtues, Chaucer may really have intended some figurative representation. But as previously observed, the fact that the Knight, Parson, and Plowman are the only pilgrims described without any evidence of satiric intent indicates that whatever their other functions, they represent idealizations of the traditional Three Estates. Each tends to resemble Gower's description of the "good" prototype of yesteryear. But whereas Chaucer concentrated on the charitable and devout service of the Plowman, Gower stressed the peasant's former simplicity in contrast to his present demands:

Les labourers d'antiquité	*The laborers of olden times*
Ne furont pas acoustummé	*were not accustomed*
A manger le pain du frument,	*to eat wheat bread,*
Ainçois du feve et d'autre blé	*but of beans or other grain*
Leur pain estoit, et abevré	*was their bread, and their drink*
De l'eaue furont ensement, . . .	*was water. . . .*
Lors fuist le monde au tiele gent	*Then was the earth well provided*
En son estat bien ordiné.	*for these folk in their ordained estate.*

(MO, 26449)

The discussion in the *Vox* begins a bit more nearly in Chaucer's vein, although with an aristocratic bias:

> They are the men who seek food for us by the sweat of their heavy toil, as God himself has decreed. The guiding principle of our father Adam, which he received from the mouth of God on high, is rightly theirs. For God said to him, when he fell from the glories of Paradise, "O sinner, the sweat and toil of the world be thine; in them shalt thou eat thy bread." So if God's peasant pays attention to the plowshare as it goes along, and if he thus carries on the work of cultivation with his hand, then the fruit which in due course the fertile field will bear, and the grape, will stand abundant in their due seasons. Now, however, scarcely a farmer seeks to get such work. Instead he loafs everywhere in vices. (VC, v.561)

VII

The Man of Law and the Wife of Bath are best considered in relation to their tales. It must be borne in mind that the parallels we have been citing from the *Mirour* and *Vox* date from about 1377, or nearly ten years before the General Prologue to the *Canterbury Tales* was begun. Chaucer could have read and discussed these

pieces with Gower as they were being written; their moral philosophy seems to have helped shape the philosophical romances he
wrote during the first years of the 1380's; finally, parallels to their
depiction of the estates appeared in both the conception and treatment of the General Prologue. All of this came about during the
years that Chaucer occupied the apartment over Aldgate and
worked at the Custom House, both so conveniently near to Gower's
residence in St. Mary's Priory. This period came to an end when
Chaucer surrendered the customs post in the autumn of 1386. Presumably he then moved out to Kent.[11] At the time he left London,
he was at work on the stories to fill out the frame of the *Legend of
Good Women*, and presumably he was already writing, or was on
the point of beginning to write, the General Prologue. There is
evidence that he left with a plan or draft of a Prologue and continuation that would have been more pleasing to his moral friend
than the version of the *Canterbury Tales* with which he returned
to the city in 1389.

At line 542 of the General Prologue, Chaucer pauses in his enu-
meration of the pilgrims to reassure us that we are nearing the end:

> Ther was also a Reve, and a Millere,
> A Somnour, and a Pardoner also,
> A Maunciple, and myself—ther were namo.

As Paull F. Baum has observed,[12] these final descriptions contain
the only signs in the Prologue that point ahead. The Miller is
described as leading the procession out of town and the Reeve as
bringing up the rear, and they introduce the first quarrel. The
Miller is described as talking "moost of synne and harlotries" (CT,
I.561); in his headlink we are warned that both the Miller and
the Reeve tell "harlotrie" (CT, I.3184); and their tales are the first
fabliaux. It would therefore appear that these characters were added
after Chaucer conceived of introducing both the quarrels and the
fabliaux to enliven his collection. Miss Hammond earlier pointed
out that each of these five pilgrims tells a tale, which several of

the others do not, and their tales come separately or at the end of fragments where they could have been added without disturbing existing composition.[13]

Now, it is worth observing that of the five pilgrims who have no parallels in Gower's poems (Yeoman, Shipman, Miller, Pardoner, Manciple), three come in this final group (Miller, Pardoner, Manciple). Furthermore, as we have seen, Gower has no direct treatment of the Summoner, and the parallel to the Reeve comes from the section on the vices rather than from that on the estates. Finally, the one pilgrim before the last five in the General Prologue who has no parallel in Gower's poems is the Shipman, who turns out like the Miller, Reeve, and Summoner to tell a tale of conspicuously fabliaux type. All of this leads us to conclude that the five rascals and the fabliaux may have been added to the scheme of the *Canterbury Tales* after Chaucer moved away from Gower's influence.

These additions represent the final, consummate stage in Chaucer's artistic development. Here his genius and gusto find their ultimate expression. But what are we to suppose that John Gower thought of the new turn the Canterbury pilgrimage was taking when he got to see it again, in 1389 or thereabouts? In 1386, he and Chaucer had parted with instructions to get on with collections of more or less the same sort. For a while their paths appear to have followed somewhat the same course. At least, between 1386 and 1390 they both translated and adapted the stories of Pyramus, Dido, Medea, Lucrece, Ariadne, Philomela, Phyllis, and Phoebus and Cornida (these from Ovid), and Virginia (from Livy and the *Roman de la rose*). All of these are to be found in the *Confessio Amantis,* and the first seven in the *Legend of Good Women.* Phoebus ended up as the Manciple's Tale and Virginia as the Physician's in the Canterbury collection. There is no reason to pore over the possible relationships. Bech (1882) and all who have compared them since have concluded that Gower and Chaucer were translating independently,[14] which accords with the biographical fact that they were not living near one another during the three years (1386–89) in which the *Confessio* was being completed and Chaucer was at work on the tales in the *Legend*.

But in 1389 Chaucer returned to London as Clerk of the King's Works bringing with him the completed Prologue of the *Canterbury Tales*, with the Knight's Tale reworked as its first member and the Miller's and Reeve's as its second and third, and launched into the Cook's Tale as its fourth. We can do no more than guess at Gower's reaction to this perversion—for so it must have seemed to him—not only of the royal command to do a collection of love legends but also of the moralistic literature of the estates. Why, after the first, Chaucer's lusty tales seemed actually to revel in sins both of the flesh and of the spirit! Did Gower remonstrate? Is the 1390 allusion to Chaucer at the end of the *Confessio* a plea that he drop the bawdry toward which his new collection appeared to be rapidly tending and get on with the refined collection he had been commissioned by the Queen to make? Was Chaucer sufficiently mindful still of his friend's moral and esthetic standards to stop short and reconsider his course? At any rate, we know that the Cook's Tale, which bade fair to be even more indecent than the Miller's and Reeve's, *was* abruptly abandoned after fifty-seven lines, and the next fragment (II) contains in both its headlink and tale the most universally accepted allusions in all the *Canterbury Tales* to Gower and to the literary milieu of 1386 when Chaucer and he had been last together.

As Carleton Brown pointed out,[15] the Man of Law's headlink represents a fresh start for the Canterbury collection, recalling the beginning of the General Prologue in its restatement of the date (CT, II.5) and the end in its restatement of the conditions of the storytelling (CT, II.35). Only Brown would have this introduction come about 1387 as a transition added to I.826, followed by *Melibee*, the Wife of Bath telling the Shipman's Tale, and the rest of Fragment VII. However, if Gower's reference to Chaucer at the end of the *Confessio* was a reaction to learning that Chaucer had abandoned the "Seintes Legende of Cupide" for the indecorous fabliaux, the Man of Law's headlink could well be Chaucer's reply to Gower.

In view of Gower's legal interest and connections, there may be some temptation to identify the Man of Law with Gower himself. At least one detail of the portrait in the General Prologue would fit well: both Gower and the Man of Law were extensive and skillful "purchasours." But the identification of the pilgrim specifically as a Sergeant of the Law and the stress on his employment in assizes and his command of the "caas and doomes alle" conjure up the image of a professional career for which we have found no evidence in connection with Gower. Furthermore, in the headlink, the Man of Law speaks as Chaucer's surrogate, not Gower's. Yet the fact that Chaucer chose, out of all the different possibilities, to put this allusion to his own and Gower's work in the mouth of the Man of Law offers support for the Leland tradition that the two met in the Inns of Court and for the evidence of the 1378 power of attorney that their relationship persisted in a legal context.

If the Man of Law is speaking for Chaucer, and in reply to Venus' reminder that he has yet "To sette an ende to alle his werk,/ As he which is myn owne clerk" by making "his testament of love" (CA, viii.2953*), the opening lines of his reply to the Host take on a double meaning:

> "Hooste," quod he, "*depardieux*, ich assente;
> To breke forward is nat myn entente.
> Biheste is dette, and I wole holde fayn
> Al my biheste, I can no bettre sayn.
> For swich lawe as a man yeveth another wight,
> He sholde hymselven usen it, by right;
> Thus wole oure text." (CT, ii.39)

Biheste means "promise" or "command"; it is appropriate to the pilgrims' agreement to accept the Host's jurisdiction over their game, but even more appropriate to describe the royal command in which both the *Confessio* and the *Legend* originated. And how Gowerian are the last three lines! "I know I promised to write a collection," says Chaucer, "and you have a right to reproach me since you've finished yours. But—" and then a twinkle comes into his eye:

> But nathelees certeyn,
> I kan right now no thrifty tale seyn
> That Chaucer, thogh he kan but lewedly
> On metres and on rymyng craftily,
> Hath seyd hem in swich Englissh as he kan
> Of olde tyme, as knoweth many a man;
> And if he have noght seyd hem, leve brother,
> In o book, he hath seyd hem in another.
> For he hath toold of loveris up and doun
> Mo than Ovide made of mencioun
> In his Episteles, that ben ful olde.
> What sholde I tellen hem, syn they been tolde? (CT, II.45)

This is irrelevant as a reply to the Host, but it is exactly to the point as a humorous defense for not having got on with the *Legend*. Tatlock speaks of the "weariness" and "sense of monotony" progressively evident through the legends that were written.[16] By this time, Chaucer *felt*, at least, as though he had "toold of loveris up and doun/ Mo than Ovide made of mencioun." He had done enough in that vein!

The Man of Law continues with a studiedly inaccurate reference to the lovers Chaucer had treated before undertaking the *Legend*: Ceix, but no Dido (in the *House of Fame*) or Criseyde. Then he refers to "his large volume . . ./ Cleped the Seintes Legende of Cupide," and gives a very inaccurate, somewhat ironic description of its contents. The inaccuracy can hardly be accounted for chronologically, since one of the two *Legend* heroines omitted (Cleopatra) is mentioned at the end of the Prologue of the *Legend* and is the subject of its first story. Chaucer may possibly have contemplated some day telling the stories about the eight lovers in this list not mentioned in the balade "Hyd, Absalon." But if so, that was to be another chapter, for the "large volume" is here treated as complete. Whatever obligation he may have incurred in undertaking it, he firmly announces, has been discharged. No one need expect any more in that connection.

Next the Man of Law asserts unctuously (II.77) that "he" [Chaucer] would never have written such tales of incest as those of Canace and Apollonius of Tyre. Tyrwhitt's interpretation of this remark as a thrust at the *Confessio Amantis* has been almost universally accepted.[17] The jibe appears gratuitous and it gave rise to the tradition of a quarrel between the two poets whose history was traced in the first chapter. But in the context now established, its meaning becomes clear. Gower reproached Chaucer for abandoning the love legends for fabliaux. In reply Chaucer expressed boredom with classical love tragedies and asserted that he *had* finished the *Legend of Good Women*. "Furthermore," he now concludes, "your own hands aren't so clean, leve brother, for if I've told fornication, you've told incest." Again, Chaucer's allusion appears to be deliberately vague. Antiochus's added indignity of throwing his daughter "upon the pavement" (CT, II.85) does not appear in Gower's version and has not been found in any of the other versions. Chaucer may possibly have been misremembering the suicide of Canace in the *Confessio* (III.307), or more likely, as suggested by the use of the word "pavement," the assault of Antiochus upon his daughter in the Latin version.[18] The ensuing assertion that "he" "Nolde nevere write in none of his *sermons*/ Of swiche unkynde abhomynacions" (II.87) could be taken as a direct reference to the didacticism of the *Confessio*. The idea that Chaucer was nettled by Gower's suggestion that he get on with the *Legend* as Gower had with the *Confessio*, or by professional jealousy of Gower's poetic achievement, might be supported by interpreting the Man of Law's final disclaimer as ironic: "Me were looth be likned, doutelees,/ To muses that men clepe Pierides" (CT, II.91). The Pierides were the nine daughters of Pierus who were transformed into magpies for presuming to compete with the muses.[19] The Man of Law (*vice* Chaucer) might thus be taken as saying, "I don't want to be compared to that pretentious poet who writes of 'swiche unkynde abhomynacions.'" However, since I can find no other evidence of acerbity on the part of either poet towards the other, I prefer to read the allusion to the Pierides, and to the Man of Law's speaking in prose, dramatically, as an introduction dating from a stage in the composition of the *Canterbury Tales* when the headlink was followed by a prose tale such as *Melibee.*

The decision to follow the Man of Law's headlink by a prose tale must have been very soon altered. If Chaucer had been influenced by Gower to desist in his cultivation of naturalism and return to more "moral" literature, and if he were even slightly annoyed at the implication that, by finishing the *Confessio,* Gower had somehow surpassed him in poetic achievement, what would have been more natural than that he demonstrate both his return to the strait and narrow and his poetic superiority by outdoing Gower at one of his own stories? The several detailed comparisons of Gower's and Chaucer's versions of the tale of Constance with one another and with Trivet amply vindicate the poetic superiority of Chaucer's version. Nevertheless, all scholars except Skeat (and, interestingly, Macaulay) [20] grant verbal borrowing by Chaucer from Gower's version. In the most recent and most detailed comparison, E. A. Block restricts this to no more than forty words in nine passages. Nevertheless, Block concludes, "Actually, it is as if Chaucer carefully combed Gower for the kind of deviation [from Trivet's version] in which he himself was so interested, and having found a few proceeded to appropriate them. For when we analyze Chaucer's borrowings from Gower, it will be found that they are intelligibly motivated by one or another of the controlling purposes so persistently revealed elsewhere in the *Man of Law's Tale* when he deviated from Trivet without borrowing from Gower." [21] And what are these controlling purposes? Aside from the achievement of economy, emphasis, and unity, Block judges that they were to make the story more dignified, more exalted, more poetic than Trivet's— and, one might add, than Gower's. "He also made a series of additions which emphasize the religious element and heighten the general piety of tone. Most of these additions center upon Constance, their general effect being to make her even more religious and pious than she is in Trivet. Other less numerous additions stress the Christian piety of Alla, the constable, and Maurice, while the

biblical allusions and the moral indignation expressed in many of
the apostrophes contribute further edifying touches." [22] Whether
or not Gower inspired such treatment, it is safe to say that he would
not have been displeased by it.

But about Chaucer one can never be sure. He was working from
Trivet. Could he have known that Trivet's inartistic repetition of
the mother-in-law motif as the cause for Constance's two voyages
was in order to avoid the initial incident in his sources—the flight
of the heroine to avoid an incestuous union with her father? [23]
Having just castigated Gower for telling the story of Apollonius
of Tyre, in which incest is a very brief and perfunctory initial incident, he took the same sort of picaresque Greek tale from which
the same sort of initial incident had been crudely expunged as the
basis for his new legend of a good woman. Then there are the two
references to Maurice's behavior at the end of the tale, which
Tyrwhitt also interpreted as jibes at Gower. Concerning the feast
of Alla, Gower had written:

> And thanne he [King Allee] thoghte in reverence
> Of his astat, er that he wente,
> To make a feste, and thus he sente
> Unto the Senatour to come
> Upon the morwe and othre some,
> To sitte with him at the mete.
> This tale hath Couste noght foryete,
> Bot to Moris hire Sone tolde
> That he upon the morwe scholde
> In al that evere he cowthe and mihte
> Be present in the kinges sihte. (CA, ii.1358)

This Chaucer had rendered:

> And so bifel that in a day or two
> This senatour is to kyng Alla go
> To feste, and shortly, if I shal nat lye,
> Custances sone wente in his compaignye.
>
> Som men wolde seyn at requeste of Custance
> This senatour hath lad this child to feeste;

> I may nat tellen every circumstance,—
> Be as be may, ther was he at the leeste.
> But sooth is this, that at his moodres heeste,
> Biforn Alla, durynge the metes space,
> The child stood, lookyng in the kynges face. (CT, II.1005)

Later, with reference to the invitation to the Emperor:

> The king Allee forth with thassent
> Of Couste his wif hath thider sent
> Moris his Sone, as he was taght,
> To themperour and he goth straght,
> And in his fader half besoghte, . . .
> That he wolde ones with him ete. (CA, II.1479)

To this Chaucer takes even more specific exception:

> Som men wolde seyn how that the child Maurice
> Dooth this message unto this Emperour;
> But, as I guesse, Alla was nat so nyce
> To hym that was of so sovereyn honour
> As he that is of Cristen folk the flour,
> Sente any child, but it is bet to deeme
> He wente hymself, and so it may wel seeme. (CT, II.1086)

In both instances, Gower was following Trivet; nevertheless, again
with the exception of Skeat, most scholars have accepted "som
men" as referring to Gower, who (as Tyrwhitt said) Chaucer "insinuates had treated the subject before him with less propriety." In
other words, while Chaucer may have turned from broad fabliaux
to a lay saint's legend partly out of deference to Gower's opinion,
and while the choice and shaping of the legend itself may have
been indebted to Gower, there was probably more than a glint of
humor in his decision to outdo his old friend at his sanctimonious
best. "If we're going to be proper, leve brother, let's be *really*
proper." The glint must have grown to a grin when he conceived
the notion of expanding the Wife of Bath's prologue and assigning
to her yet another tale from the *Confessio Amantis*.

VIII

When Chaucer first decided to include among his pilgrims a representative of the estate of women, he drew upon the general moralistic tradition represented by Gower's works and the Parson's Tale. Gower had no estate of women, and Chaucer did not in the General Prologue draw upon the discussion of matrimony and lechery in the *Mirour* nor the vices of women in the *Vox*. But his criticisms, as contrasted with his brilliant individualizing strokes (*juxta Bathon*, deafness, weaving, spurs), are commonplaces of the complaint against all of the estates: *pride* (insistence at being first at the offering, pride in dress), *concupiscence* (physical appearance, many marriages, company in youth, knowledge of the art of love), and *waywardness* (predilection for pilgrimages). Owst has shown that these are staples of the homiletic tradition.[24] Parallels to the Wife's insistence at being first at offering and the dangers of pilgrimages have been cited in the *Lamentia* of Matheolus.[25] In the Parson's Tale (x.405–410) insistence on going to offering first and "outrageous array of clothyng" are cited as sins of pride. And so on. There is in the portrait of the Wife in the General Prologue no hint of the sophisticated antifeminist tradition which was to provide the material for her own prologue and the marriage group.[26] The Shipman's Tale, incorporating motifs that we have found in Gower's criticisms of foolish women who allow themselves to be seduced by friars and curates, is appropriate to this stage, when the Wife of Bath was considered merely an aspect of the satire on the estates.

But Chaucer evidently decided after 1390 to treat the problems of sex and marriage in the *Canterbury Tales* more deeply than they had been treated in the General Prologue and the initial fabliaux. This must be regarded as an artistic decision rather than as a new development in Chaucer's interest or insight. In his pre-1386 pieces, culminating in the Knight's Tale and *Troilus*, he had exploited fully the possibilities of courtly love. Between 1386 and 1390 he had experimented with the possibilities of the fabliaux, in the Knight's, Miller's, and Reeve's Tales setting in direct contrast decorous and ribald characters and situations. The final step, logically, was to combine these romantic and satiric themes. This he undertook to do in the Wife of Bath's prologue and tale and the other tales of the marriage group. It is of no small interest to observe the evidences of Gower's influence upon this final stage of Chaucer's artistic development.

We have seen already that Gower's criticism may have been a factor in bringing to an end Chaucer's initial experiments with the fabliaux. As he cast about for a middle way between the Reeve's Tale and the Man of Law's Tale, Chaucer's mind lighted upon the artistic possibilities of the clerical antifeminist materials, the tradition of Theophrastus, St. Jerome, Walter Map, and Eustace Deschamps. This he molded into the brilliant prologue of the Wife of Bath and into the Merchant's Tale much as Gower had previously molded penitential material into moral philosophy—that is, by adapting the traditional arguments and examples to express a unified, positive conception of human relations. It must be observed that the theme upon which the Wife of Bath launches the argument—sovereignty in marriage—is transformed by Chaucer into a much more humane conception than that of her antifeminist sources. The clerical tradition assumed as a matter of course that since God had created Eve from Adam's rib, woman was intended to be subservient to man.[27] A cardinal precept of medieval antifeminist complaint, so masterfully personified in the Wife's own prologue, was that women violated this God-given order. The clerical point of view is criticized in the characterizations of the marquis in the Clerk's Tale and the old knight in the Merchant's Tale, and a new and more equal order is enunciated at the beginning of the Franklin's Tale:

> Heere may men seen an humble, wys accord;
> Thus hath she take hir servant and hir lord,—
> Servant in love, and lord in mariage.
> Thenne was he both in lordshipe and servage.
> Servage? nay, but in lordshipe above
> Sith he hath bothe his lady and his love;

His lady, certes, and his wyf also,
The which the lawe of love acordeth to. (CT, v.791)

We have seen that the "law of love" as an amoral life force played
an important part in Gower's moral philosophy and in the philoso-
phies of *Troilus* and the Knight's Tale. Marriage as a device for
controlling and directing this force has universal implications which
undoubtedly give richness to Chaucer's marriage argument. But the
philosophizing so evident in *Troilus* and the Knight's Tale is in
the marriage group artfully sublimated in dramatic action and
personal emotions. Even in the Clerk's Tale, the relation of man
to God, or to the king, or to society and law in the abstract disap-
pears almost entirely. Instead, Chaucer concentrates with preter-
natural intensity upon the relation of man to woman and man to
man in the most intimate of domestic situations. As literature has
moved in the direction of Joyce and Proust, this has become the
most significant segment of Chaucer's art.

Although its very existence has been sometimes discounted or
argued away,[28] the marriage group has been recognized as the core of
this profound human comedy, ever since it was first pointed out by
Kittredge. "Maistrye" is the negative force, the irritant, in this
comedy, and "gentilesse" the positive bond.[29] "Gentilesse" may be
taken as the unifying theme of the whole group, beginning with the
formal discourse in the Wife's Tale; going on to contrast hereditary
gentilesse with God-given gentilesse in the Clerk's Tale; to various
examples of un-gentilesse in the Merchant's Tale; and to a final
assertion of its virtues in the Franklin's Tale. If *gentilesse* mirrored
in *marriage* thus emerges as the central topic of Chaucer's most
mature artistic achievement, it becomes important to observe that
these themes were first joined the way Chaucer joins them in
Gower's Tale of Florent and *Mirour de l'omme*.

Let us suppose that out of deference to Gower's opinions, Chaucer had laid aside the Cook's Tale and written the Man of Law's
headlink and tale, superbly retelling one of Gower's stories. With
Gower still on his mind, and seeking for a way to get back to some-

thing saltier than the tale of Constance, he decided to recast the Wife of Bath as a shrewish wife, making use of material from Jankyn's book of wicked wives. No motive need be sought for this. The problem of sovereignty and fidelity in marriage had already been touched upon in the headlink to the Miller's Tale; in *Melibee*, which had just been replaced as the Man of Law's story; in the Shipman's Tale; and in the Nun's Priest's Tale, if that was written by this time.[30] Either to tease Gower (by this time using one of his tales in so questionable a context), or simply because he found the story an extremely appropriate vehicle for the amalgamation of the satiric and romantic, Chaucer decided to assign to the Wife of Bath the tale of the Loathly Lady. Comparisons have led to the conclusion that Chaucer's version is independent of Gower's Tale of Florent.[31] But if he knew Gower's Tale of Constance from Book II of the *Confessio*, it is hard to imagine that Chaucer did not know Florent from Book I. Furthermore, the differences in his version are best explained as conscious alterations designed to improve the pace and structure of the story and to adapt it to the new conception of the Wife of Bath. None of the differences can be explained by reference to different sources, and Chaucer's and Gower's versions are, in spite of their variation, far more similar than any of the ballad and romance analogues. Chaucer's first alteration is in the motive for posing the riddle: the rape episode and the intercession of the queen and ladies of the court have been remarked as Chaucerian irony at its most exquisite. But note what Chaucer was changing *from* in Gower: Florent "was Nevoeu to themperour/ And of his Court a Courteour/." When captured by his enemies, he was not summarily executed because of "remembrance/ That thei toke of his worthinesse/ Of knyghthod and of gentilesse" (CA, 1.1410, 34). As he altered the introduction to make it more titillating and more appropriate to the Wife of Bath, the notion of the gentilesse of the young knight must have sunk into the well of Chaucer's unconscious.

Although the contexts are different, the question is put in nearly the same words in both versions:

What alle wommen most desire
This wole I axe. (CA, 1.1481)

I grante thee lyf, if thou kanst tellen me
What thyng is it that wommen moost desiren. (CT, iii.904)

After the question has been posed, both knights search in vain for
an answer. Here Chaucer's vivid verbal embroidery and genius for
synthesizing materials from widely different sources shows itself to
best advantage. Near the end of their period of grace, both knights
are riding through the forest. Chaucer introduces the dance of the
twenty-four (and more) ladies; Gower has Florent simply spy the
Loathly Lady under a tree. Gower has the hag at once demand that
Florent promise to marry her and in return tell him the answer with
which he rides off to court alone. Chaucer maintains suspense by
having the knight merely promise to grant the hag's next request,
having her whisper the answer in his ear (still keeping it from the
audience), and having them ride off to court together. Again, the
handling of the answering scene is all to Chaucer's advantage, but
the answers are phrased similarly:

That thou schalt seie, upon this Molde
That alle wommen lievest wolde
Be soverein of mannes love. (CA, 1.1607)

"My lige lady, generally," quod he,
Wommen desiren to have sovereynetee
As wel over hir housbond as hir love." (CT, iii.1037)

In Chaucer's version, the hag starts up immediately after the answer has been accepted and demands her boon, while the knight
falls back crying "Taak al my good, and lat my body go" (CT, iii.
1061). This is a more dramatic parallel to Florent's earlier attempt
to bargain:

Florent behihte hire good ynowh
Of lond, of rente, of park, of plowh,
Bot al that compteth sche at noght. (CA, 1.1565)

After his answer has been accepted, Florent returns to the old hag. The one passage in which Gower is more vivid than Chaucer is in his description of the "vecke" proffering herself "lich unto the wollesak" (CA, III.1675ff), which asks comparison with some of the ghastly details of the marriage bed in the Merchant's Tale (CT, IV.1824ff). However,

> Thogh sche be the fouleste of alle
> Yet to thonour of wommanhiede
> Him thoghte he scholde taken hiede;
> So that for pure *gentilesse*,
> As he hire couthe best adresce,
> In ragges, as sche was totore,
> He set hire on his hors tofore
> And forth he takth his weie softe. (CA, 1.1719)

The honorable behavior of Florent at the end and the lady's explanation of her transformation bring together the ideas of gentilesse and sovereignty:

> That my Stepmoder from an hate,
> Which toward me sche hath begonne,
> Forschop me, till I hadde wonne
> The love and *sovereinete*
> Of what knyght that in his degree
> Alle other passeth *of good name*. (CA, 1.1844)

These passages would, in turn, have recalled the more specific discussion of gentilesse as the catalyst in marriage in the *Mirour de l'omme*.

At the end of his treatment of the virtues in the *Mirour*, just before turning to the criticism of the estates, Gower took up "Matrimoine." This follows an extended praise of virginity (MO, 16824–17136, quoting St. Jerome at 16864) of the sort to which the Wife of Bath was objecting at the beginning of her prologue. In the ensuing section, matrimony receives the approval of civil and canon law (MO, 17140), sexual intercourse for the begetting of children is regarded as natural (MO, 17190), and marriage for money and position is condemned (MO, 17245). This last leads to the admonition that one should marry for virtue, not for wealth, and conversely that women should not seek to marry aristocratic husbands:

Et nepourqant j'ay bien oï	Nevertheless I have heard
Sovent les dames dire ensi,	women often say thus
Q'avoir vuillont par lour haltesce	that for their pride they wish to have
Un gentil homme a leur mari:	a gentleman as their husband.
Mais certes endroit moy le di,	But certainly about that I say
Ne say q'est celle gentilesce;	that I don't know what this gentility is.
Mais d'une rien je me confesse,	But one thing I maintain:
Qant Eve estoit la prioresse	when Eve was the originator
Du no lignage en terre yci,	of our lineage on this earth
N'y fuist alors q'ot de noblesce	there was then no one who had more
Un plus que l'autre; ou de richesce	nobility than another; nor do I know
Ne sai comment gentil nasqui.	how gentility can be born of riches.
Tous nous faisoit nature nestre,	Nature brought us all to birth,
Ensi le servant comme le mestre,	both the servant and the master,
Dont par nature ce n'avient;	so the difference did not come from nature.
Ne du parage ce puet estre,	Nor can it be from rank
Car tous avoions un ancestre,	for we all have one ancestor,
Par celle voie pas ne vient;	so it cannot have come from that.
Et d'autre part bien me sovient	On the other hand, it seems
Qe par resoun ce n'appartient	reasonable to me that it should not pertain
A la richesce q'est terrestre,	to temporal riches
Q'est une chose vile et nient:	which are vile and valueless.
A sercher plus avant covient	It is necessary to search higher
La gentilesce q'est celestre.	for celestial gentility.
Nature en soy n'ad quoy dont fere	Nature of itself has nothing with which
Un gentil homme ne desfere,	to make or unmake a gentleman.
Ainz dieus qui les vertus envoit	But God, who dispenses virtues,
Cil puet bien de sa grace attrere	He can by His grace well invest
Un homme de si bon affere,	a man with such good qualities,
Si vertuous, tanq'il en soit	so virtuous, that he thereby becomes
Verrai gentil et a bon droit:	truly gentle in his own right.
Mais qant a ce, sovent l'en voit,	And as to this, it is often seen,
Des bonnes mours qui voet enquere,	if one wants to look for good manners,
Q'un homme povre les reçoit	that a poor man receives them
Plus largement en son endroit	even more largely
Qe cil q'est seignour de la terre.	than one who is ruler of the land.
(MO, 17329)	

Dante's *Convivio* may well have been a source for some of the phrasing in the passage on gentilesse in the Wife of Bath's Tale, although Chaucer was no doubt also acquainted with similar discussions in Boethius, the *Roman de la rose*, and elsewhere. Again, once he had the idea, Chaucer had better sources than Gower to turn to for material. But the inspiration for linking happy marriage with true nobility could have come from none of the other analogues to the passage on gentilesse in the Wife of Bath's Tale. This may well have been Gower's contribution to the marriage argument. The association of ideas which led Chaucer to put the discourse on gentilesse into the mouth of the Loathly Lady—if any is needed aside from that in the Tale of Florent—can be found a few lines later in the *Mirour*:

Car de nature ed de sa loy	*For by Nature and her law*
Chascune femme endroit de soy,	*every woman who is good*
Q'est bonne, est able et digne au Roy;	*is in her own right worthy of a king;*
Et chascun homme veritable,	*and any real man,*
Combien q'il ait ou ninet ou poy,	*however much he has, even little or nothing,*
Au quelque dame en droite foy	*to any woman is marriageable,*
Par ses vertus est mariable.	*in good faith, because of his virtue.*

(MO, 17394)

Any good woman, by the laws of nature, is worthy to marry a king —an admirable epitome of the old wife's argument and an even better introduction to the Clerk's Tale. The discussion in the *Mirour* next takes up the question of sovereignty, deciding that "la droiture/ Du mariage est en balance" (MO, 17410). Eve was formed neither of the head to be sovereign to man, nor of the foot to be subject, but of his rib to be his companion; but as she caused the original sin, she must be subject to man "en loy judicial." An ensuing passage of 150 lines beginning

Roy Salomon, q'estoit bien sage,	*King Solomon, who was very wise,*
Dist que la femme en mariage	*said that a woman should not have*
Ne doit avoir le seignourie	*sovereignty in marriage*

(MO, 17593)

deals with sovereignty, with the burden that woman should be obedient to man. The authority of Aristotle, Cato, Seneca, and the Bible—but significantly not of Jankyn's scholastic authorities—is called in to illustrate women's indiscretion. And finally, good marriage is described in terms not too different from the beginning of the Franklin's Tale:

L'omme ert loyal en governance,	The man shall be loyal in governance;
Et femme auci de sa souffrance	the woman also in her sufferance
Ert vergoignouse et debonnaire	shall be modest and good spirited,
En fait, en dit, en contienance,	in deed and word and countenance,
Sanz faire ascune displaisance	not doing any displeasure
A son mary.	to her husband.
(MO, 17689)	

From gentilesse and sovereignty in the *Confessio* and *Mirour* to the marriage group in the *Canterbury Tales*—this is Chaucer's final and most stunning transformation of Gower's themes and moralizations. This became the "testament of love" Gower begged him to get on with in 1390. The other verbal and figurative echoes of Gower in the Wife of Bath's prologue and the tales of the marriage group may be confined to the notes.[32] They would serve only to confuse the argument. That must rest, as stated at the outset of this chapter, upon the notion of "stimulus diffusion." If the larger themes first enunciated by Gower and then masterfully converted into poetry by Chaucer—the moral basis for literature, the philosophical universality of love, the political interest in kingship, the criticism of the estates, and finally the fusion of marriage and gentilesse—if there is no relationship between the treatment of these major themes by the two poets, then their personal association, allusions to one another in their works, and similar turns of phrase and figure are of little significance. The argument may be summed up finally in a sentence from J. L. Lowes, with some of whose specific points we may differ, but who remains one of the wisest and most sensitive of all interpreters of the poet: "Sources other than the books that Chaucer read—sources that lie in his intercourse with men and in his reaction upon the interests, the happenings, the familiar matter of his day—entered likewise into 'that large compass' of his, and must be taken into account in estimating his work." [33]

A final disclaimer. There is always danger in exploring an author or a group of writings from one point of view only. Of course there were many motives and influences in the work of Geoffrey Chaucer besides those he shared with John Gower. As the last decade of the

14th century drew to a close, their literary interests grew further and further apart. Gower grew more and more absorbed in political pamphleteering for the Lancastrian cause while Chaucer continued to rearrange and add to the poetic masterpiece that he could never bring himself to complete. The justification for the concentration of this chapter is that the other influences on Chaucer's thought and art—French, Italian, and classical literature and the day-to-day realities of his London life—have all been explored at great length many times. Only the parallels between his work and Gower's have not hitherto received full consideration. If they prove as significant as this examination would appear to indicate, the other influences will need to be reevaluated in their light. But that is the subject for another book.

The Gower Manuscripts

The following list is intended to codify and supplement the information about those features of the manuscripts of Gower's works which are important to an understanding of his literary career. I have not undertaken a full collation of the manuscripts. Macaulay's collations throughout his edition, and his descriptions of the French manuscripts (1.lxviii and lxxix), English manuscripts (2.cxxxviii), and Latin manuscripts (4.lx) are remarkably accurate. Of the manuscripts unknown to him (16, 27, 28, 29, 30, 31, 32, 49), I have been able to examine and classify 16, 28, and 32. I have checked the details listed below in both French manuscripts and 49 of the 61 English and Latin manuscripts, supplementing the information found in Macaulay's edition. Information on MSS. 4, 11, 22, 24, 25, 39, and 43 is from Macaulay's descriptions; on 27, 29, 30, 31, 49, from catalogue descriptions.

The manuscripts of the *Confessio Amantis* and *Vox Clamantis* are referred to by numbers since Macaulay's abbreviations are overlapping and hard to locate in a long list. In the following list, Macaulay's abbreviations are included in parentheses after each number, and his identifications for those which have changed hands since his time in parentheses after each manuscript identification. For the Bodleian and a few other manuscripts, summary catalogue numbers are included after the more familiar identifications. The dates given are those of Macaulay and the manuscript catalogues. The abbreviations of features important to this study are:

P^1 Original Prologue, dedicated to Richard (CA, Prol. 24–92*)
P^2 Revised Prologue, dedicated to Henry (CA, Prol. 24–92)
M^1 Miniature of Nebuchadnezzar at Prol.585
M^2 Miniature of the confession at CA, 1.204
C^1 Original conclusion, dedicated to Richard (CA, VIII.2491–3114*)
C^2 Revised conclusion on the state of England (CA, VIII.2491–3172)
E^1 Original 4-line explicit, not mentioning Henry (Macaulay 3.478)
E^2 Six-line explicit, dedicated to Henry (Macaulay 3.478)
K^1 1390 colophon of MS. Bodley 902 (1), in Appendix B
K^2 1400 colophon of MS. Fairfax (40), in Appendix B
K^3 1394–1408 colophon of MS. Bodley 294 (37), in Appendix B
S^1 Elegant execution and sumptuous illumination, as of MSS. 33, 40, 51 from Gower's scriptorium and MSS resembling them.

S² Good execution, but simpler, as of Trentham, *Mirour*, and 50, 52, 53 from Gower's scriptorium and MSS resembling them.

X MSS clearly later or in another style

$ Examined personally

FRENCH MANUSCRIPTS

Trentham (Duke of Sutherland, Dunrobin Castle). *In Praise of Peace, Cinkante Balades, Traitié, Rex celi deus.* ca. 1400 S² $

Mirour Camb. Univ., Add.3035. MO only. Before 1400 S² $

ENGLISH MANUSCRIPTS
Confessio Amantis

First version revised

1 (A)   Bodley 902 (27573, Arch D.33). P lacking, M² C¹ E¹ K¹. Early 15c S¹ CA only $

2 (J)   St. John's Coll., Camb., 34 (B12). P¹ C¹ E¹ K¹. Early 15c S² CA only $

3 (M)   Camb. Univ. Lib., Mm 2.21. P¹ M¹ M² C¹. 15c S¹ CA only $

4 (P₁)   Garrett 136 (Phillipps 2298). P¹ C¹. ca. 1400 CA only

5 (Ch)   Chetham's Lib., Manchester, 6696 (A 6.11). P lacking, C¹ E¹. Late 15c X CA only $

6 (N₂)   New Coll., Oxf., 326. P² C¹. 1478 X CA only $

7 (E₂)   BM Egerton 913. P¹ C lacking. Mid 15c X $

First version intermediate

8 (H₁)   BM Harleian 3490. P¹ C¹. Mid 15c X CA after St. Edmund's *Speculum Vitae* $

9 (Y)   Marquess of Bute. P and C lacking. Early 15c S¹ $

10 (X)   Society of Antiquaries, London, 134. P¹ C¹ E² K¹. Early 15c S¹ CA between Lydgate's *Lyf of Our Lady* and Hoccleve's *Regement of Princes* $

11 (G)   Advocates' Library, Glasgow, Hunterian S.1.7. P¹ C lacking. Early 15c

12 (O)   BM Stowe 950. P and C lacking. Early 15c S² $

13 (Ad₂) BM Add 22139. P lacking, C¹ E² K¹. 1432 S¹ CA followed by Chaucer's lyrics $

14 (Cath) St. Catharine's Coll., Camb., 7. P¹ M¹ M² C lacking, E² K¹. Mid 15c S¹ CA only $

15 (Q)   Morgan Lib. 125 (Quaritch-Hastings). P lacking, M² C¹ E² K¹. Early 15c S² CA only $

16   Morgan Lib. 126 (Narford-Fontaine). P¹ M¹ M² C¹ E² K¹. Late 15c X CA only $

First version unrevised

17 (E)   BM Egerton 1991. P lacking, M² C¹ E² K¹. Early 15c S¹ CA only $

18 (C)   Corpus Christi Coll., Oxf., 67. P¹ M¹ M² C¹ E¹ K¹. Early 15c S¹ CA only $

19 (R)   BM Royal 18 c.22. P¹ M¹ C¹ E² K¹. Early 15c S¹ CA only $

20 (L)   Bodley, Laud 609 (754). P¹ M¹ M² C¹ E¹ K¹. Early 15c S¹ CA only $

21 (B₂) Bodley 693 (2875). P¹ M¹ M² C¹ E² K¹. Early 15c S¹ CA only $
22 (Sn) Bodley, Selden B.11 (3357). P¹ C¹ E¹ K¹. Mid 15c CA only
23 (D) Camb. Univ. Lib., Dd. 8.19. P¹ M¹ (space left), C lacking. 15c S² CA only $
24 (Ar) College of Arms, London, Arundel 45 (65). P¹ C lacking. Mid 15c
25 (Hd) Louis H. Silver, Chicago (Earl of Carlisle, Castle Howard). P lacking, C¹ E¹ K¹. Late 15c CA only
26 (Ash) Bodley, Ashmole 35 (6916). P lacking, C¹. Early 15c X CA only $
27 Pembroke Coll., Camb., 307. Early 15c S¹ $
28 Morgan Lib. 690 (Ravensworth). P and C lacking, M¹. Early 15c X CA only $
29 Rosenbach 368 (Earl of Aberdeen). ca. 1450
30 Plimpton 265 (Verney). ca. 1400
31 Maggs Catalogue 456 (1924), Item 184. ca. 1420
32 Shrewsbury School, fragment of one leaf, Prol. 189–195, 226–244, 274–294, 324–343. ca. 1400 S² $

Second version

33 (S) Huntington El. 26 A.17 (Stafford). P² M¹ C² E². Late 14c S¹ CA only $
34 (Δ) Sidney Sussex Coll., Camb., 63 (Δ.4.1). P lacking, C². Mid 15c X CA followed by Cato's *Disticha* $
35 (Ad) BM Add 12043. P and C lacking. Early 15c S² CA only $
36 (T) Trinity Coll., Camb., 581 (R 3.2). P lacking, C² E² K³. Early 15c X CA, *Traitié, Carmen viciorum* $
37 (B) Bodley 294 (2449). P¹ M¹ M² C² E² K³. Early 15c S¹ CA, *Traitié, Carmen viciorum* $
38 (Λ) Wollaton Hall (Lord Middleton-Nottingham). P² C² (with Chaucer allusion), K³. Early 15c S² CA, *Traitié, Carmen viciorum* $
39 (P₂) Rosenbach 369 (Phillipps 8192). P² M¹ C² K³. Early 15c CA, *Traitié, Carmen viciorum*

Third version

40 (F) Bodley, Fairfax 3 (3883). P² M¹ M² C² K². Late 14c S¹ CA, *Traitié, Carmen viciorum, Eneidos* $
41 (H₂) BM Harleian 3869. P² M¹ M² C² K². Early 15c S² CA, *Traitié, Carmen viciorum, Eneidos*. Copied from 40 $
42 (N) New Coll., Oxf., 266. P² C². Early 15c S¹ CA only $
43 (K) Gurney 121 (Keswick Hall). P² C² K². CA, *Traitié, Carmen viciorum, Eneidos*. Probably copied from 40
44 (H₃) BM Harleian 7184. P² C lacking. Mid 15c X CA only. Copied from same source as 43 $
45 (Magd) Magdalen Coll., Oxf., 213. P² C² E². Mid 15c S¹ CA only. Likewise from same source as 43 $
46 (W) Wadham Coll., Oxf., 13. P² C² E². 1470 X CA, *Traitié* $
47 (P₃) Folger Lib. Sm.1 (Phillipps 8942). P² C². Mid 15c X CA only $
48 (Hn) Bodley, Hatton 51 (4099). P¹ C lacking. 16c Copied from Caxton $
49 Clumber (Newcastle-Bedford). 15c Listed as 3d version in Maggs Catalogue 691 (1940), Item 242

Latin Manuscripts

50 (S)   All Souls Coll., Oxf., 98. ca. 1400 K² S¹. Revised version of Vox *Cla-mantis* and *Cronica Tripertita*, Laureate poems, etc. $

51 (G)   Advocates' Library, Glasgow, Hunterian T.2.17. ca. 1400 K² S¹. Revised version of Vox and *Cronica*, Laureate poems, coat of arms $

52 (C)   BM Cotton, Tiberius A.iv. ca. 1408 K²&³ S². Revised version of Vox and *Cronica*, Laureate poems, etc. $

53 (H)   BM Harleian 6291. ca. 1408 K²&³ S². Revised version of Vox and *Cronica*, Laureate poems, etc. $

54 (E)   Huntington Lib. Hm. 150 (Ecton-Sothby). ca. 1400 S¹. Revised text of Vox, pre-1399 Latin poems $

55 (D)   Bodley, Digby 138 (1739). Early 15c S². Mixed text of Vox only $

56 (L)   Bodley, Laud 719 (1061). Early 15c S². Mixed text of Vox, pre-1399 Latin poems, and *H. aquile* $

57 (L₂)   Lincoln Cathedral Lib. A.72. 16c X. Copied from 56 $

58 (T)   Trinity Coll., Dublin, D.4.6. Early 15c K¹ S². Unrevised text of Vox only $

59 (H₂)   Hatfield Hall. Early 15c S¹. Unrevised text of Vox only $

60 (C₂)   BM Cotton, Titus, A.xiii. 16c X. Copied from 55 $

61 (H₃)   Bodley, Hatton 92 (4073). Early 15c X. *Cronica* and Laureate poems along with non-Gowerian matter $

Selections (not considered in Chapter Three)

62   Bodley, Rawlinson D. 82 (12908). Mid 16c. ff 25–33, CA, VIII.2377–2970, Venus' conclusion (second version)

63   Balliol Coll., Oxf., 354. ca. 1520. f 55, CA, VIII.271–2028, Apollonius; f 70ᵛ, II.587–1865, Constance and Perseus; f 81ᵛ, v.4937–5162, Adrian and Bardus; f 83ᵛ, VI.485–595, Pirithous, Galba; f 84ᵛ, VI.975–1238, Dives; f 86ᵛ, II.3187–3507, Constantine; f 89ᵛ, I.2785–3066, Nebuchadnezzar; f 91ᵛ, III.1201–1502, 1655–1672, Pyramus, Diogenes; f 94ᵛ, v.141–312, Midas; f 171ᵛ, I.3067–3402, Three Questions (second or third version, cf. E. Flügel, *Anglia*, XII [1889], 631)

64   Trinity Coll., Oxf., 29. 15c. f 190, CA, Nebuchadnezzar

65   Camb. Univ. Lib., Ee 2.15. End 15c. f 38, CA, I.3124–3315, Three Questions; f 54, I.2083, Trump of Death (Manly and Rickert, ed., *Chaucer's Canterbury Tales* [1940], I.126)

66   Camb. Univ. Lib., Ff. 1.6. 15c f 3, CA, v.5920–6052, Tereus; f 5, IV.1114–1466, Rosiphelee; f 46ᵛ, I.3067–3425, Three Questions; f 81, IV.2746–2926, Somnolence; f 84ᵛ, VIII.271–846, Apollonius (second version)

67   BM Harleian 7333. Last half 15c. f 120, CA, v.5551, Tereus; f 122, II.587, Constance; f 126, I.3067, Three Questions; f 127ᵛ, II.291, Travellers and Angel; f 127ᵛ, v.2031–2498, Coveitise (Manly and Rickert, *Chaucer*, I.207)

68   Penrose 10 (Delamere). ca. 1455. f 3, CA, I.3067–3402, Three Questions; f 5ᵛ, v.5551–6048, Tereus; f 8ᵛ, VI.1789–2358, Nectanabus (transcript from BM Add 38181, Brown-Robbins, *Index*); f 11ᵛ, II.1613–

1864, Philip of Macedoyne (transcript id.); f 13, v.4937–5162, Adrian;
f 158, Prol. 585–1088, 1.2785–3042, Nebuchadnezzar (R. H. Robbins,
PMLA, LIV [1939], 935; Manly and Rickert, *Chaucer*, 1.108)

69   Phillipps 22914. 4 leaves, CA, v.775–1542, Religions of the World

An outline of the relationships between the versions and manuscripts of the *Vox Clamantis,* based upon the discussion in Chap. Three, pp. 99–106, would be as follows:

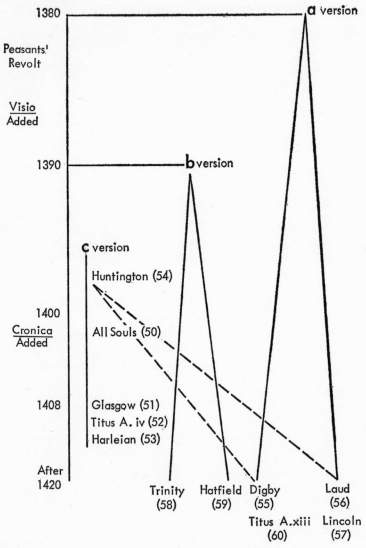

An outline of the relationships between the versions and manuscripts of the *Confessio Amantis*, based upon the discussion in Chap. Three, pp. 116–127, would be as follows:

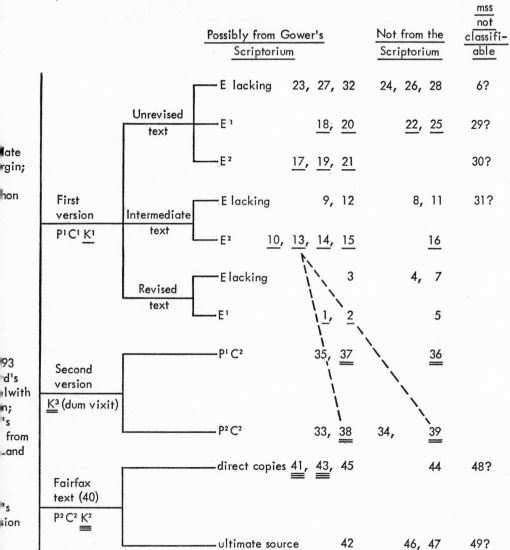

	Possibly from Gower's Scriptorium	Not from the Scriptorium	mss not classifiable
E lacking	23, 27, 32	24, 26, 28	6?
E¹	18, 20	22, 25	29?
E²	17, 19, 21		30?
E lacking	9, 12	8, 11	31?
E²	10, 13, 14, 15	16	
E lacking	3	4, 7	
E¹	1, 2	5	
P¹C²	35, 37	36	
P²C²	33, 38	34, 39	
direct copies	41, 43, 45	44	48?
ultimate source	42	46, 47	49?

Left-side labels:
- First version P¹C¹K¹ — Unrevised text, Intermediate text, Revised text
- Second version K³ (dum vixit) — P¹C², P²C²
- Fairfax text (40) P²C²K² — direct copies, ultimate source

The Colophons

[Paragraph 1]

[Bodley 902] Quia unusquisque prout a deo accepit alijs impartiri tenetur Johanes Gower super hijs que deus sibi intellectualiter donauit, uillicacionis sue racionem, dum tempus instat, secundum aliquid alleuiare cupiens, inter labores et ocia ad alior[um] noticiam tres libros doctrine causa forma subsequenti propterea composuit.

[Fairfax] Quia vnusquisque prout a deo accepit alijs impartiri tenetur Johanes Gower super hijs que deus sibi sensualiter donauit villicacionis sue racionem, dum tempus instat, secundum aliquid alleuiare cupiens, inter labores et ocia ad aliorum noticiam tres libros doctrine causa forma subsequenti propterea composuit.

[Bodley 294] Quia vnusquisque prout a deo accepit alijs impartiri tenetur Johanes Gower super hijs que deus sibi sensualitere donauit villicacinis sue racionem, secundum aliquid alleuiare cupiens, tres precipue libros per ipsum, dum vixit, doctrine causa compositos ad aliorum noticiam in lucem seriose produxit.

[Paragraph 2]

[Bodley 902] Primus liber Gallico sermone editus in decem diuiditur partes, & tractans de uicijs et uirtutibus, nec non et de uarijs huius seculi gradibus, uiam qua peccator transgressus ad sui creatoris agnicionem redire debet, recto tramite docere conatur. Titulus libelli istius Speculum hominis nuncupatus est.

[Fairfax] Primus liber Gallico sermone editus in decem diuiditur partes, et tractans de viciis et virtutibus, necnon et de variis huius seculi gradibus, viam qua peccator transgressus ad sui creatoris agnicionem redire debet, recto tramite docere conatur. Titulusque libelli istius Speculum Meditantis nuncupatus est.

[Bodley 294] Primus liber gallico sermone editus in decem diuiditur partes, et tractans de vicijs et virtutibus viam precipue qua peccator in penitendo Cristi misericordam assequi poterit, tota mentis deuocione finaliter contemplatur. Titulusque libelli istius Speculum meditantis nuncupatus est.

[Paragraph 3]

[Bodley 902] Secundus enim liber, sermone latino uersibus exametri & pentametri compositus, tractat super illo mirabili euentu qui in Anglia tempore

311

domini Regis Ricardi secundi anno regni sui contigit, quando seruiles rustici impetuose contra nobiles et ingenuos regni insurrexerunt. Innocenciam tamen dicti domini Regis tunc minoris etatis causa inde excusabilem pronuncians, culpas aliunde, ex quibus et non a fortuna talia inter homines contingunt enormia, euidencius declarat. Titulusque voluminis huius cuius ordo Septem continet paginas, Vox Clamantis nominatur.

[Fairfax] Secundus enim liber sermone latino metrice compositus tractat de variis infortuniis tempore Regis Ricardi Secundi in Anglia contingentibus. Vnde non solum regni proceres et communes tormenta passi sunt, set et ipse crudelissimus rex suis ex demeritis ab alto corruens in foueam quam fecit finaliter proiectus est. Nomenque voluminus huius Vox Clamantis intitulatur.

[Bodley 294] Secundus liber versibus exametri et pentametre sermone latino componitur, tractat de varijs infortunijs tempore regis Ricardi secundi in anglia multiplicitur contingentibus, vbi pro statu regni compositor deuocius exorat. Nomenque volumina huius, quod in septem diuiditur partes Vox clamantis intitulat.

[Paragraph 4]

[Bodley 902 with inserts from St. John's, Camb., B.12] Tercius iste Anglico sermone in octo partes diuisus, qui ad instanciam serenissimi Principis dicti domini Regis Anglie Ricardi secundi conficitur, secundum Danielis propheciam super huius mundi regnorum mutacione a tempore Regis Nabugodonosor usque nunc tempora distinguit. Tractat eciam secundum Nectanabum & Aristotilem super hijs quibus Rex Alexander tam in sui regimen quam aliter [eius disciplina edoctus fuit. Principalis tamen huius libri materia] super amorem & amantum condiciones fundamentum habet. Vbi uariarum cronicarum historiarumque [finem] necnon poetarum Philosophorumque scripture ad exemplum distinccius inseruntur. Nomenque presentis opusculi Confessio Amantis specialiter intitulatur.

[Fairfax] Tercius iste liber qui ob reuerenciam strenuissimi domini sui domini Henrici de Lancastria, tunc Derbeie comitis, Anglico sermone conficitur, secundum Danielis propheciam super huius mundi regnorum mutacione a tempore regis Nabugodonosor vsque nunc tempora distinguit. Tractat eciam secundum Aristotilem super hiis quibus rex Alexander tam in sui regimen quam aliter eius disciplina edoctus fuit. Principalis tamen huius operis materia super amorem et infatuatas amantum passiones fundamentum habet. Nomenque sibi appropriatum Confessio Amantis specialiter sortitus est.

[Bodley 294] Tercius iste liber qui in Octo partes ob reuerencia serenissimi domini sui domini Henrici de lancastria tunc Derbie Comitis Anglico sermone conficitur secundum danielis propheciam super huius mundi regnorum mutacione a tempore regis Nabugodonosor usque nunc tempora distingui[t]. Tractat eciam secundum Aristotilem super hijs quibus rex alexander tam in sui regimen quam aliter eius disciplina edoctus fuit, principalis tamen huius operis materia super amorem et infatuatas amantum passiones fundamentum habet. Nomenque sibi appropriatum Confessio Amantis specialiter sortitus est.

Septvauns Inquisitions De Etate Probando

Calendar of Inquisitions Post Mortem, Edward III, Vol. xi (1935), p. 468.
[Inquisition of 1364]
611. William son and heir of William Sepvans.
Writ to the escheator to take proof of the age of the said William, the lands
of whose inheritance are in the custody of Alice de Staunton by the king's
commitment. 16 July, 38 Edward III.

Kent. *Proof of age* made at Canterbury, 18 September, 38 Edward III.

Thomas atte Gate, aged 50 years, says that the said William was born at
Melton by Canterbury on Monday the feast of St. Augustine, 17 Edward III
[28 May 1344 [1]], and baptized in the church of St. Margaret there, and
was 21 years of age on Wednesday the feast of St. Augustine the Doctor last.
William late abbot of St. Augustine's, Canterbury, and Thomas Daldon,
knight, together with Juliana countess of Huntington, lifted him from the
sacred font. This he knows because on the eve of St. Augustine the Doctor,
17 Edward III, he acquired some tenements at Westgate, Canterbury, from
Richard Lovel, vicar of the church of Westgate by his charter of that date.

John Ropere, aged 40 years, agrees and says that he had a son, by name
John, who died on the morrow of St. Augustine last, his death being enrolled
in a certain psalter of the same John the father.

Thomas Austyn, aged 43, agrees and says that on Sunday after the birth
of the said William he married his wife Joan, and that was 21 years ago on
Wednesday after St. Augustine last.

John Bounde, aged 34 years, agrees and says that he had a daughter Joan
born on the feast of St. Augustine, 17 Edward III, and she was 21 years of
age on the feast of St. Augustine last.

Henry Bolle, aged 40 years, and Michael Seymakere, aged 50 years, agree
and say that they started on a journey to Santiago for the amendment of
their lives on the morrow of St. Augustine, 17 Edward III.

Richard Smelt, aged 40 years, and Alexander Raven, aged 46 years, agree
and say that on the day of the birth there was a great quarrel between them,
and peace was restored on St. Augustine's day, 17 Edward III.

John Pykeryngg, aged 36 years, Thomas Ropere, aged 43 years, Peter atte
Welle, aged 31 years, and John Arnald, aged 30 years, agree and say that

[1] August 28, if the feast of St. Augustine, Bishop of Hippo. May 26 or 28, if the
feast of St. Augustine of Canterbury, as seems more probable.

they were summoned to the gaol delivery of the city of Canterbury on the morrow of St. Augustine, 17 Edward III.

The escheator, John de Tye, warned Alice de Stonton at Melton, who had no reason to offer why the lands &c. should not be restored to the said William as being of full age.

Calendar of Inquisitions Post Mortem, Edward III, Vol. xii (1938), no. 96. [Inquisition of 1366]
96. William son and heir of William de Septvans, knight.
Commission to John de Cobeham of Kent, Thomas de Lodelowe and William Waure to enquire as to the age of the said heir, the proof of his age made before the escheator being erroneous; and, if it be found that he is still a minor, to ascertain by whom the previous proof was made and by whose procurement, imagination and information, who has been in possession of his lands since the said proof, in whose company the heir has been and by whom he has been counselled and led, what waste and destruction has been done in the said lands, and what profit the king has lost by reason of the incorrect proof of age. Russhyndon in the isle of Shepeye, 13 *April, 40 Edward III.* By letter of the seal called 'le signet.'
Writ of venire facias to the sheriff of Kent to provide a jury of knights and others for the said commissioners. Russhyndon in the isle of Shepeye, 13 *April, 40 Edward III.*
Precept of John de Cobham, Thomas de Lodelowe and their fellows, justices, to the sheriff of Kent to provide a jury of twenty-four knights and others on Tuesday before St. George at Canterbury. London, 15 *April.*
Panel of twenty-one (twelve of whom are noted as jurors), and their pledges.
Inq. taken at Canterbury, Tuesday before St. George, 40 Edward III.
Jurors, John de Northwode, knight, Thomas Apuldrefeld, knight, Thomas Chicche, knight, Richard atte Lese, knight, John de Brokhull, knight, John Barry, William Apuldrefeld, Thomas Colpepir, Henry Apuldrefeld, the elder, Henry Anger, Fulk Payforer and Geoffrey Colpepir.

The said heir will be 20 years of age and no more on the feast of St. Augustine the Doctor next. Twelve men whose names are attached to this inquisition were summoned before the escheator, John de Tye, at Canterbury on a certain day now past, to prove the age of the heir, and three of them, Alexander Raven, John Pykeryng and Thomas Ropere, were not sworn, so that the proof of age was not duly or lawfully made as the jurors understand.

William de Chirchehull, clerk, was the first to procure and suggest to the said heir at Canterbury that he should sue to have his lands &c. out of the king's hand and prove his age; and after the return of the inquisition *de etate probando* the said William de Chirchehull and Luke Whetyndon sued to have the said lands &c. out of the king's hand, the said Luke being retained as counsel of the said heir.

The said heir had a moiety of the manor of Aldyngton [worth 10£. per year [2]], and also certain marshes called 'Lokelyng' and 'Herlyng' in Ywade [worth 40s.—*quadrajaunt solidos*], of which he was in possession from the

2 Matter in brackets added from the *Rotuli Parliamentorum*, see below.

time when the king removed his hand until Christmas, 38 Edward III, when he enfeoffed thereof John Gower and his heirs in return for 80 marks. The latter has had possession since then and received the issues. The manor contains wood worth 100£. to sell.

William de Chirchehull was the first to procure &c. the suing out of the king's hand of the manor of Melton [worth 20£.] and a messuage in Canterbury [worth 20s.], and after the inquisition &c. he and Luke de Whetyndon sued this manor and messuage, as well as 10£. rent in Litelebourne and Welle, out of the king's hand. Afterwards, on Michaelmas day, 39 Edward III, at the order of Sir Nicholas de Loveyne, the said heir, by virtue of a covenant made between him and the same Nicholas, enfeoffed Walter de Multon and Richard de Sugworth, chaplains, and Richard Maufe, all servants of Nicholas, of the said manor and rent to the use of Nicholas, by virtue of which feoffment the said Walter, Richard and Richard have had possession of the manor until now and have received the issues &c. to the use of Nicholas, and the heir has continuously remained in possession of the rent of 10£. The said heir also had the manor of Promhill by gift and feoffment of Richard de Alesle, rector of the church of Hariettesham worth 35£. It is charged with a yearly rent of 10£. to John Septvans for his life, and is held of the archbishop of Canterbury. This manor the heir alienated to the aforesaid Walter, Richard and Richard for the use of said Nicholas.

After the aforesaid feoffment made to John Gower, the heir continually dwelt in the company of Richard de Hurst and the said John Gower, at Canterbury and elsewhere, until Michaelmas last, and during the whole time he was led and counselled by them to alienate his land &c. From Michaelmas last until the feast of St. Gregory last he dwelt with the aforesaid Nicholas Loveyne at Penesherst and elsewhere, and during that time was led and counselled by the said Nicholas, and by the aforesaid Walter, Richard and Richard Maufe, to alienate his lands &c. There is no waste.

Simon de Burgh, at his own suit, caused himself to be retained with the said heir as of his counsel, and made the heir grant a yearly rent of 10£. to him and his heirs out of the manor of Melton by a writing. The writing was delivered to Richard de Hurst to keep at the wish of the said heir, and was afterwards delivered by Richard to the said Simon against the wish of the heir.

Evidences (in French) by which the jurors know that the child is under age.

Many of the knights and esquires of the jury were with the earl of Huntyngton when the king was at Came and the earl with him, at the time where the count of Ew and the chamberlain Tankervyle were taken and sent into England. And at that time the earl of Huntyngdon returned to England to be cured of a sickness, and Sir William de Septvauns, the child's father, who was of the earl's company, returned with him. They found Sir William's wife, the child's mother, great with child. The earl went away to Popeler to stay there and have his medicines near London, and made the countess remain at Preston to be godmother to the child when it should be born. The child was born on the day of St. Augustine the Doctor next following, and the abbot of St. Augustine's, predecessor of the present abbot, and Sir Thomas de Aldon, the elder, were his godfathers, the countess being his godmother. Soon afterwards the earl was cured and returned beyond sea to the siege of Calais, and Sir William with him; and Sir William told his companions, knights and esquires on this jury, how that since he left them he had had a son.

Moreover, William abbot of St. Augustine's, the child's godfather, died within a month after the baptism, and the licence to elect a successor to him was applied for at once and is dated in the king's twentieth year.

Moreover, there is a certain Sir John Frebodi, parson of the church of Bocton, who was treasurer to Sir Thomas de Aldon, the child's second godfather; and in his account it appears that he delivered to his lord and master a cup and ewer of silver to be given to the child, and that the gift was made on the morrow of St. Augustine, 20 Edward III.[3]

List of the jurors of the original proof of age of the said heir.

Memorandum that, upon this inquisition &c. being read and examined in the Parliament held on the morrow of the Invention of the Holy Cross, 40 Edward III, the heir himself being present, it appeared to the prelates, magnates and commonality that he was not of full age. It was therefore resolved that the proof of his age should be of none effect, that his lands should be taken back into the king's hands, that all bonds &c. made by him should be annulled, and that process should be made by writs of *scire facias* against all persons to whom he had alienated any lands &c. of his inheritance since the proof of his age.

Writ of certiorari to Fulk Horewod, mayor of the staple of Westminster, touching the tenor of all recognisances and bonds of the staple made before him by the said heir. 10 May, 40 Edward III.

Return. The said heir came before John Pyel, mayor of the said staple, on 22 June, 39 Edward III, and acknowledged himself bound to John Gouwer in 60£. to be paid at All Saints then next following.

He also came before Fulk de Horwood, the present mayor, on 27 September in the same year, and acknowledged himself bound to Nicholas de Lovaygne, knight, in 1000£., to be paid at Easter then next following. *Writ of scire facias* to the sheriff of Sussex, ordering him to warn Richard Herst and Joan his wife, to whom the said heir, after proof of his age, granted the manor of Morhalle with lands &c. in Nemnefeld, Wertelyngge, and Hoo, to be in Chancery on the octave of Trinity next to shew cause why the said grant should not be annulled in accordance with the above decision in Parliament. 12 May, 40 Edward III.

Endorsed. Certificate by the sheriff that he gave notice to Richard and Joan by Thomas Hunte and Richard Clerk.

Second endorsement. They, being called, did not appear, so that it was awarded that the grant should be annulled and the mesne profits answered for to the king.

Similar writ to the sheriff of Essex with regard to William de Boudon, chaplain, to whom the said heir granted the manor of Wyghebergh and a yearly rent of 10£. from all his lands in Essex. 12 May, 40 Edward III.

Endorsements. Certificates of notice given by Thomas Whitheved and Stephen Bampton, and of judgement of court as above.

---

[3] *Rotuli Parliamentorum* follows to this point fairly closely. Its version of the decision is quoted below.

Similar writ to the sheriff of Essex with regard to Robert de Denton, chaplain, to whom the said heir granted a yearly rent of 10£. from all his lands in Essex. 12 May, 40 Edward III.

Endorsements. Certificates of notice given by John Everard and Stephen Brampton, and of judgement of court as above.

Similar writ to the sheriff of Kent with regard to John Gower, to whom the said heir granted the manor of Aldyngton, with rents of 14s. 6d., a cock, 13 hens, and 140 eggs in Maplescomp and the homages and services of the tenants from whom the same are due, and a yearly rent of 10£. from the manor of Wygebergh and all his lands in Essex. 12 May, 40 Edward III.

Endorsements. Certificates of notice given by John Northbourne and Robert Sare, and of judgement of court as above.

Similar writ to the sheriff of Kent with regard to John Gower, to whom the said heir, on 22 June, 39 Edward III, before John Pyel, then mayor of the staple of Westminster, bound himself in 60£. 15 July, 40 Edward III.

Endorsements. Certificates of notice given by Richard Smyth and Thomas Stafford, and of judgement of court that the recognisance be annulled.

Similar writ to the sheriff of Kent with regard to Nicholas de Lovayne, knight, to whom the said heir, on 26 September last, before Fulk Horewod, mayor of the staple of Westminster, bound himself in 1000£. 15 July, 40 Edward III.

Endorsements. Certificates of notice given by Walter de Wy and William Benge, and of judgement of court that the recognisance be annulled.

Two copies of the commission to John de Cobeham and others, their inquisition, the evidences as to the age of the heir, and the decision in Parliament.

The Parliamentary decision appears in the *Rotuli Parliamentorum*, II.292–293, as follows:

Prout per Recordum & Processum inde habit' & in Cancellar' Dñi Regis retorn' plenius poterit apparere. Et quia Dñus Rex informatus, quod predčus Wilłus postquam terre & tenem' que sunt de hereditate sua, & rãcoe minoris etatis sue in manũ Regis extiterunt, eidem Wilło pretextu probationis predče extra manus Regis, liberata fuerunt, magnam partem terrar' & tenem' eořdem diversis personis alienavit, & se in diversis pecuniar sumis & annuis redditibus, tam per Literas de Statuo Mercatorio quam per alia facta diversa in Rotulis Cancellar' Regis irrotulata, pluribus personis obligabit; Recordum & Processum predča, tam pro Indempnitate ipsius Regis ne custodiam terrarũ & tenem' predčor' per hujusmodi decepcõem amitteret, quam predči Wilłi ne durante minori etate sua exheredaretur, in Parliamento suo apud Westm' die Lune in crastino Inventitionis Sancte Crucis, anno Regni dči Dñi Regis quadragesimo tento, venire fecit. Quibis Recordo & Processu ac Inquisicõe & Evidentiis predčis corã ipso Dño Rege, Prelatis, Magnatibus, & Cõitate Regni Angel' in eod' Parliamento ostensis, lectis, & examinatis, dčo Wilło filio Wilłi Septvans ibidem personaliter existente, visum est toti Parliamento, quod idem Wilłus fil' Wilłi non erat plene etatis, sicut in probatione predicta continetur. Perquod consideratum est in dčo Parliamento quod probatio illa nullius sit valoris vel effectus; & qv omnia terr' & tenem' cum petin' que fuerunt predči Wilłi de Septvans, patris predči Wilłi fil' Wilłi, & que ratione minoris etatis ipsius Wilłi fil' Wilłi heredis dicti Wilłi de Septvans in manū Regis copta, & eidem heredi ut plene etatis p̄textu probacõis predc̄e sic minus sufficienter facte extra manus Regis liberata, in manum Regis ad quorumcumq; manus devenerint, una cum exitibus inde a tempore probacõis predc̄e facte perceptis, reseisiantur, & in manū Regis remaneant usq; ad legitimam etatem heredis predc̄i. Et quod omnia Carte, Scripta, & Obligacões tam Statutis Mercatoriis & de Stapulis quam alia quecumq̄, ac etiam Recognicões per ipsum quibuscumq; personis ante hec tempora facta revocentur, cassent', & omnio adnullent': Et quod Processus fiant per Br̄e de Scire fac' versus omnes illos quib' aliqua terre seu ten' de hereditate predc̄i Willi fil' Willi, post probacõem etatis predc̄e & liberacõem terrar' & tenem' de hereditate sua extra manus ñras factos, per ipsum Willm fil' Willi sunt aleinta; & etiam versus illos quibus idem Willus fil' Willi aliquos redditus annuos concessit; necnon versus omnes illos quibus idem Willus fil' Willi in aliquibus debitis per Statua Mercatoria vel de Stapula, vel per Recognicões seu Cartas, Scripta, aut alia Facta obligatur, ad venire faciend' eos in Cancellar' Regis, ad ostendend' si quid pro se habeant vel dicere sciant quare terre, tenem', & redditus predc̄a sic alienta in manū Regis reseisiri, & Carte, Scripta, Statuta, Recognicões, Obligacões, & alia Facta que per dc̄m Willm fil' Willi fiebant, tanquam irrita & erronea cassari & adnullari non debeant; & ad faciend' & recipiend' quod justum fuerit in hac parte.

This was something of a *cause célèbre*. It was produced in the Exchequer in 46 Edward III by William son of William de Septvans to prove that he was a minor when summoned to take up knighthood, and a translation from the Patent Rolls (which missed the *Rotuli* continuation) was printed in *Archaeologia Cantiana*, 1 (1858), 126–133, as an example of how the king could be defrauded. The presentation is naïve and there is no particular comment on Gower, but the transcript does say that he paid *fourscore* (misread by Macaulay as 24?) marks for Aldington.

Abbreviations

Note Abbreviations

BM	British Museum
CHEL	*Cambridge History of English Literature*
DNB	*Dictionary of National Biography*
EETS	Early English Text Society
	OS Original Series
	ES Extra Series
ELH	*Journal of English Literary History*
JEGP	*Journal of English and Germanic Philology*
LR	Chaucer Life Records (Chaucer Society)
Med. Stud.	*Mediaeval Studies* (Toronto)
MED	*Middle English Dictionary* (University of Michigan)
MLR	*Modern Language Review*
MLN	*Modern Language Notes*
MP	*Modern Philology*
N&Q	*Notes and Queries*
OED	*Oxford English Dictionary*
PL	*Patrologiae cursus completus, Series Latina*
PMLA	*Publications of the Modern Language Association of America*
PRO	Public Record Office (London)
RES	*Review of English Studies*
RR	*Romanic Review*
SATF	Société des anciens textes français
SP	*Studies in Philology*
TLS	*London Times Literary Supplement*
VCH, YNR	*Victoria County History, Yorkshire North Riding*
YRS	Yorkshire Record Society

Notes

CHAPTER 1

1. *History of English Poetry* (1871 ed.), III.15.
2. *Histoire de la littérature Anglaise* (Paris, 1877), 1.228.
3. *My Study Windows* (1887), p. 258.
4. *A Literary History of the English People* (1895), 1.364, 368.
5. John Peter, *Complaint and Satire in Early English Literature* (1956), Chaps. 2 and 3.
6. Gower allusions have been collected by G. C. Macaulay, *The Works of John Gower*, 4v (1899–1902), 2.viii; and by Heinrich Spies, *Englische Studien*, XXVIII (1900), 161; XXXIV (1906), 169; XXXV (1907), 105. Many of the 15th- and 16th-century allusions in Caroline Spurgeon's *Five Hundred Years of Chaucer Criticism and Allusion*, 3v (1925 ed.) relate to Gower as well.
7. *Curia Sapiencie*, Spurgeon, 1.16. H. N. MacCracken judged that this piece was not by Lydgate.
8. *The Kingis Quair*, Spurgeon, 1.34.
9. *Active Policy of a Prince*, Spurgeon, 1.54.
10. *The Regement of Princes* (1412), Spurgeon, 1.22.
11. *Fall of Princes*, Prologue (1430), Spurgeon, 1.41. Leland repeated that Chaucer might justly be compared with Homer, Virgil, Dante, and Petrarch, *Commentarii de scriptoribus Britannicis* (ca. 1540), Spurgeon, III.15. In John Bale's appendix to his Life of Chaucer, *Catalogus scriptorum illustrium maioris Britannię* (Basle, 1557), p. 527, the comparison is restricted to medieval writers in the vernacular: "Adde huc, quod Italos & Gallos, qui plurima suis linguis terse ac nitide scripserunt in partĕ operis euocauerit. Dante & Petrarcha Italicam linguam, Alanus Gallicam, Ionnes Mena Hispanicam, atq; alij alias, infinitis modis tunc expolierãt: hi Chaucero calcar addiderunt."
12. Erasmus (ca. 1490), Spurgeon, 1.73, III.8. (J. H. Lupton in his edition of *The Lives of Vitrier and Colet* by Erasmus, from which Spurgeon took the passage, identified the *gens* as Gower and Chaucer.) Sidney, ed. Lord Thurlow (1810), p. 5; part of the passage is in Spurgeon, 1.121.
13. *Leuys of Seyntys* (1443–47?), Spurgeon, 1.46.
14. *Praise of the Mass* (1500), Spurgeon, 1.65.

15. *The Palis of Honoure* (1501), Spurgeon, 1.65.

16. *Pastime of Plesure* (1506), Spurgeon, 1.67.

17. William Dunbar, *The Goldyn Targe* (1503), Spurgeon, 1.66; John Rastell, *Terens in englysh*, Spurgeon, 1.73; John Skelton, *Chapelet of Laurell* (1523), Spurgeon, 1.74; David Lindsay, *Testament of a Popiniay* (1530), Spurgeon, 1.77; William Forrest, *History of Joseph* (1545), Spurgeon, 1.86; John Coke, *Debate betwene Englande and Fraunce* (1550), Spurgeon, 1.90; William Turner, Letter to Mr. Fox (1550), Spurgeon, 1.90.

18. As late as 1810, H. J. Todd, *Illustrations of the Lives and Writings of Gower and Chaucer*, p. xxvi, could still write: "In giving Gower precedence, as well in what relates to the manuscripts of his poetry as to the extracts which are made from his works, no one will suppose me influenced by any other motive than that of chronological propriety. He was born before Chaucer. Authors, both historical and poetical, in the century after the decease of these poets, usually coupling their names and describing their accomplishments, place Gower before Chaucer; not intending (for I cannot think so badly of their taste as to suppose that they preferred Gower to Chaucer) any precedence in respect to *talents*, but merely the accustomed tributes due to seniority."

19. Edition of 1773, n. p. A further comment by Johnson in the *Idler*, LXIII (June 30, 1759), deserves quotation: The rudeness of "our language may be said to have continued to the time of Gower, whom Chaucer calls his master, and who, however obscured by his scholar's popularity, seems justly to claim the honour which has been hitherto denied him, of showing his countrymen that something more was to be desired, and that English verse might be exalted into poetry."

20. Macaulay, *Works* (1900), 2.xii; TLS, August 18, 1932.

21. Spurgeon, 1.x.

22. *Ecclesiasticall history* (1570), Spurgeon, 1.xx and 106. The Urry Life of Chaucer (see below) observes that the works of Chaucer were excepted from the 1546 Act of Parliament "for the advancement of True Religion"—see Eleanor P. Hammond, *Chaucer: A Bibliographical Manual* (1908), p. 37. In both instances, Chaucer is approved for his supposed criticism of Roman Catholicism. The Urry Life refers to Gower as "Bigot to the Church of Rome." MSS. Stow 950 (12) and Royal 18 (18) of the *Confessio Amantis* have sporadic erasures of words like *pope*, *papacy*, and *purgatory*.

23. *Mirrour of Good Maners* (1570), Spies, *Englische Studien*, XXXIV (1906), 172.

24. Ed. F. J. Furnivall, EETS, ES, 3 (1868), p. 32 (Oriel text).

25. *Pastime of Plesure* (1506), Spurgeon, 1.67.

26. See the list of manuscripts in Appendix A.

27. See the discussion of the editions by Macaulay, 2.clxviii.

28. Printed by Spurgeon, 1.77.

29. Tyrwhitt (Aldine ed., 1830) observed that Leland's biographies must have been finished before 1540. In the *Itinerary*, Pt. i, Leland speaks of them as complete. On January 1, 1546, he presented his New Year's gift to Henry VIII and said that he had spent the last six years traveling about the kingdom. In 1533 he had been granted a commission to search the libraries

of monasteries, colleges, etc. The biographies were the fruit of the earlier search, not the one from 1540 to 1546.

30. Jo. Leland, *Commentarii Scriptoribus Britannicis* (Oxford, 1709), p. 414.

31. Leland, op. cit., p. 421; translated in T. R. Lounsbury, *Studies in Chaucer*, 3v (1892), 1.134; Latin text in Hammond, pp. 1–7.

32. Lounsbury, 1.146ff, has an extensive discussion of the Berthelette-Thynne problem. He does not, however, mention that Henry Bradshaw's letter detailing the connections between Berthelette and Godfray was printed by Furnivall in his edition of Thynne's *Animadversions*, Chaucer Society (1875), p.xxvi, and that Tyrwhitt in the introduction of his edition (Aldine ed., p. xiv, note e) surmised that Leland's and Berthelette's references were to the Thynne-Godfray edition. Lounsbury is violent in his criticism of commentators from Leland through Warton and Johnson who stated that Gower was Chaucer's mentor.

33. See the list from Bale and discussion in Macaulay 4.lviii.

34. Todd, *Illustrations*, p. xiii, notes the date established by Gower's will and calls attention to the error in Ritson, Ellis, and Godwin.

35. Thomas Speght, *Works of Chaucer* (1598), fol. bii–iii.

36. Francis Thynne, *Animadversions* (ed. cit.), p. 18.

37. Buckley's testimony is recorded in Speght. For the identity of Buckley and reliability of his testimony, see Edith Rickert, "Was Chaucer a Student at the Inner Temple?" *Manly Anniversary Studies* (1923), p. 20.

38. *Relationum historicarum de rebus Anglicus: De illustribus scriptoribus Britanniae* (Paris, 1619), p. 575.

39. *History of the Worthies of England*, ed. John Freeman (1952), p. 648.

40. *Equitem auratum & poetam laureatum* is evidently Fuller's own inference from Bale's adaptation of Leland's statement: "Habet ibidem statum duplici nota insignem, nempe aurea torque, & hederacea corona rosis interserta: illud militis, hoc poetae ornamentum," *Catalogus*, p. 525.

41. Lydgate, *Life of Our Lady* (1409), Spurgeon, 1.19. *Kingis Quair* (1423), Spurgeon, 1.34.

42. Lounsbury, 1.174.

43. *Theatrum poetarum* (1675), p. 109.

44. *Lives of the English Poets* (1687), p. 18.

45. Lounsbury, 1.185.

46. *The English Historical Library* (1696), p. 215. In the edition of 1714, p. 81, the last clause ("which . . . Chronicle") is omitted.

47. *The Chronicles of England* (1631), p. 325.

48. *Dictionary of National Biography* (DNB).

49. DNB.

50. Thomas Hearne, *Remarks and Collections*, ed. C. E. Doble et al., 11v (1886–1921), 11.201.

51. *Collections*, III.264. And see "A Letter to Mr. Bagford, containing some remarks upon Geffrey Chaucer and his Writings," in *Robert of Gloucester's Chronicle*, ed. Thomas Hearne (1724), Appendix IV, p. 596. The letter, dated 1709, points out the defects in existing editions of Chaucer and urges that a completely new edition is necessary. This letter was the

impulse for the Urry edition, as W. Thomas observes in the interleaved copy of the edition in the British Museum, and as Hearne himself implies in the preface (p. lvi). It repeats Speght's remarks on Chaucer's political career found in the Diary entry of 1709, quoted above. See DNB for a short life of Urry, which describes his text of Chaucer as "probably the worst ever prepared on account of Urry's unpardonable habit of lengthening and shortening Chaucer's words, and even introducing words of his own to suit his views of the metre."

52. *Collections*, IV.232.

53. *Historia vitae et regni Ricardi II* (1729), p. xv: "Ricardo Regi inimicus acerbissimus . . . At veroquum e principis eximii hostibus esset nequissimis cujus tamen afflictse fortunae facile multorum opes & auxilia allexerint ad misericordiam, maximeque eorum, qui (sicuti profecto fuit Gowerus) principi fuerint subditi . . . Adde quod gravis atque vehemens opinio per animos clericorum aliquot pervaserit, haud pauca contra clericum in operibus Goweri historicis contineri, quae non tantum consulto debent praeteriri, sed & penitus deler atque eradi."

54. *Collections*, V.33.

55. John Dart, *Westmonasterium* (1723), p. 87. The evolution of the Urry edition offers a field for further investigation that I have not pursued. William Thomas presented an annotated, interleaved copy in two volumes to the British Museum in 1764. It contains the contract for the book. Urry had the Queen's license to print Chaucer for fourteen years from July 25, 1714. His part of the profit was to go toward completing Peckwater Triangle of Christ Church College, Oxford. A MS note at the beginning of the Life observes, "This life was very uncorrectly drawn up by Mr. Dart, & corrected and enlarged by W. T. especially in that part which gives an accot. of the author's Works [?the remarks on the *Testament of Love*]." The glossary is signed "Timothy Thomas" by William Thomas.

56. Life of Chaucer in the Aldine edition of the *Works of Chaucer* (1845), reprinted in the Morris edition (1866), 1.31.

57. Skeat, *Oxford Chaucer*, VII.xix; *The Chaucer Canon* (1900), p. 98.

58. John Urry, ed., *The Works of Geoffrey Chaucer* (1721), fol. [c].

59. Ibid., fol. [d].

60. Ibid., fol. [e].

61. Ibid., fol. [e].

62. *Register of the Garter* (1724), II.116.

63. *Biographia Britannica* (1757), IV.2244. This was not Anstis' suggestion, as implied by the *Biographia* and stated by William Godwin, *Life of Chaucer* (1803), p. 344. For Life of Chaucer in *Biographia Britannica*, see II.1293.

64. *John Gower's Beziehungen zu Chaucer und König Richard II* (Bonn, 1889), p. 45, where the Gloucester theory is attributed to Godwin.

65. "John Gower, the Poet," *Retrospective Review*, II (1828), 117.

66. Aldine edition (1830), p. clxxxvi.

67. A brief summary is to be found in Hammond, p. 278.

68. *Archaeologia Cantiana*, VI (1866), 83.

69. *The Lives of the Poets of Great Britain and Ireland* (1753), 1.20.

70. *Bibliographia Poetica* (1802), p. 24.

71. *Riches of Chaucer* (1835), p. 39.
72. *Chaucer* (1879), p. 17.
73. *The English Poets*, ed. T. H. Ward (1881), 1.102.
74. *Age of Chaucer* (1901), p. 102.
75. *Life of Chaucer*, 1.340, 346.
76. *Illustrations*, p. xxxiii.
77. Morris edition (1891), 1.27. On the publication of Nicolas's Life of Chaucer, see Hammond, p. 40.
78. *Confessio Amantis*, 3v (1857), 1.xiii.
79. "John Gower and His Works," *British Quarterly Review*, xxvii (1858), as reprinted in *Littell's Living Age*, lvii (1858), 167.
80. "The Book of the Poets," *Athenaeum*, June 4, 1842, p. 499, as reprinted in *Poetical Works*, 6v (1890), v.211.
81. Ward, *Chaucer* (1879), p. 82; Meyer, op. cit., p. 13. Morley, *English Writers* (1897), iv.233, and Courthope, *History of English Poetry* (1895), 1.306, follow Mrs. Browning's suggestion of professional jealousy.
82. *Selections* (1903), p. viii; CHEL, ii.135.
83. Spies, *Englische Studien*, xxxv (1907), 105; J. S. P. Tatlock, *Development and Chronology of Chaucer's Works*, Chaucer Society (1907), p. 173.
84. Pauli, 1.xxxi; J. W. Hales, *Athenaeum*, December 24, 1881, p. 851, as reprinted in *Folia Literaria* (1893), p. 115.
85. E. Lücke, *Anglia*, xiv (1892), 77.
86. Tatlock, *Development and Chronology*, p. 173.
87. Tatlock, MP, 1 (1903), 317.
88. Margaret Galway, MLR, xxxvi (1941), 30.
89. *The Chaucer Tradition* (1925), p. 431.
90. Galway, N&Q, cxciii (1948), 3.
91. Pauli, 1.lxx; *British Quarterly Review*, loc. cit., p. 164; Wright, *Political Songs and Poems*, Rolls Series (1859), 1.lxxxiv.
92. "John Gower in His Most Significant Role," *Elizabethan Studies in Honor of George F. Reynolds*, University of Colorado Studies (1945), p. 52.
93. "John Gower, Mentor for Royalty," PMLA, lxix (1954), 953.
94. Maria Wickert, *Studien zu John Gower* (Cologne, 1953).
95. Spurgeon, 1.34.
96. Peter, *Complaint and Satire*, Chap. 1 et passim.

CHAPTER 2

1. Macaulay, 4.viii. For a calendar of most of the documents mentioned in this chapter see JEGP, lviii (1959), 1–23.
2. On the history of the church see Canon Thompson, *The History and Antiquities of the Collegiate Church of St. Saviour* (1898). The tomb was moved to the south transept in 1832 at the expense of the Marquis of Stafford, George Granville Leveson-Gower. At this time, or earlier, Gower's bones disappeared. In 1894, the empty tomb was moved to its present position on the north aisle, this being the supposed site of St. John's Chapel. The restoration of the painting and lettering was by Miss Rosamund Borradaile. The completion of her work was announced in the London *Times*, September 24, 1958, among the "Personals."

3. I quote from Stow's *Survey of London*, 1603 edition, ed. W. J. Thomas (1876), p. 152. The description of Gower's tomb in Speght's *Chaucer* (ed. of 1598, biij) is drawn directly from Stow as are many of the details about Chaucer. The wording is nearly identical, and see also pp. 171–172 in the *Survey*. Macaulay prints various descriptions of the tomb, 4.xx.

4. Macaulay 4.xxii. From *Annales*, ed. of 1615, p. 326.

5. Gower's popish reputation: see above, Chap. One, note 22.

6. Thynne's statement of 1599 is likewise taken from Stow: "Bale hath muche mistaken yt, as he hath donne infynyte thinges in that Booke 'de scriptoribus Anglie,' beinge for the most parte the collections of Lelande, for in truth the armes of Sir Johne Gower, beinge argent, on a cheuerone azure, three leopardes heddes or, do prove that he came of a contrarye howse to the Gowers of Stytenham in York-Shyre, who bare barruly of argent and gules, a crosse patye florye sable," *Animadversions* (1599), Chaucer Society ed. (1875), p. 19.

7. John Weever, *Ancient Funerall Monuments* (London, 1631), p. 270.

8. On the Stittenham Gowers, see *Victoria County History, Yorkshire North Riding*, II.183.

9. Harris Nicolas, *The Retrospective Review*, II (1828), 103.

10. Robert Glover, *Visitation of Yorkshire, 1584–85*. Joseph Foster, ed. (1875), p. 267.

11. W. Brown, ed., *Yorkshire Deeds*, Yorkshire Record Society [hereafter YRS], XXXIX (1909), 135 and references.

12. Wm. Berry, *Encyclopaedia Heraldica*, II (1828), s.v. Gower: "Gower of Durham: azure a chevron, between three hounds argent; Gower of York-shire: argent a fesse [a horizontal band], between three talbots passant sable; Gower of Woodhall, Worcestershire: azure a chevron, between three wolves' heads erased [torn off jaggedly], or; Gower: azure on a chevron or, three leopards' heads gules; the Rev. Thos. Foote Gower of Essex (1824): argent a chevron, between three wolves' heads, erased, or." *An Elizabethan Roll of Arms*, Surtees Society, XLI (1863), Appendix II, xxviii: "Roger Gower, Gillinge Weste Wapentake, Yorkshire, N. R.: argent, a fesse between three talbot dogs passant sable."

13. J. W. Papworth, *Alphabetical Dictionary of Arms* (1874), p. 114: arms of Heneage ,"or a greyhound courant betw. three leopard's heads az." and "arg. a greyhound courant betw. wolf's heads erased gu."

14. C. T. Clay, "Some Yorkshire Armorial Seals," *Yorkshire Archaeological Journal*, XXXVI (1944–47), 54; and see YRS, CII (1940), 19. Three dogs on a bend appear in IInd quarter of the arms of William Veyle, m. daughter of John Gower of Wotton, Surrey, evidently related to the Gowers of Clapham, Surrey (note 37 below), *Miscellanea Genealogica et Heraldica*, 4 ser, V (1912–13), 205.

15. The brass of Sir Robert Gower was formerly placed over the present tomb of Sir John Scott on the north side of the choir: see James Renat Scott, *Scott of Scott's Hall* (1876), p. 58. The sketch is in Philipot's "Church Noates of Kent," MS. BM Harleian 3917, f 77. Papworth observes under the heading "leopards" (p. 61), "some of these are probably lions."

16. 3 *Feb* 1329, *Inquisitions Miscellaneous Chancery*, II (1916), 275. References are to the printed calendars of the Public Record Office unless

MS designations are stated. The spellings of the names of persons and places have been regularized in the text, but in the notes they follow the sources. Dates are those of the printed calendars or similar interpretations, always given in new style.

17. *16 December 1332, Patent Rolls Edward III, 1330–34* (1893), p. 385. This grant was for life. *28 Feb 1335*: order to the sheriff of Suffolk to restore to Robert Gower the manor of Kentewell, seized under a general order to confiscate all of the Earl of Athol's lands because he had joined the Scots, *Close Rolls Edward III, 1333–37* (1898), p. 381. *4 March 1339*: royal confirmation of a quitclaim by David de Strabolgi, late earl of Athol, to Robert Gower, his heirs and assigns, of Kentewell. Witnessed among others by John de Denton (see note 22 below) and Geoffrey le Say (see note 70), *Patent Rolls Edward III, 1338–40* (1898), p. 213. This secured Kentwell permanently to Robert Gower. On the history of Kentwell Manor, see S. Tymms, *Suffolk Archaeology,* II (1895), 59.

18. *6 March 1335, Close Rolls Edward III, 1333–37* (1898), p. 379. The record is a plaint for the restoration of a manor seized, like Kentwell, when Strabolgi joined the Scots. One of the plaintiffs, William de Patesle, was evidently of a Brabourn family (see note 37). Like other Strabolgi holdings, Westlexham was originally held by the earl of Pembroke, see MS. Chancery Miscellaneous, Bundle 88, File 7, no. 150.

19. *4 April 1335, Close Rolls Edward III, 1333–37,* (1898), p. 385.

20. For an account of the Strabolgi earls of Athol, see Cokayne-Gibbs, *Complete Peerage* (1910), I. s.v. Atholl. J. R. Scott, op. cit., p. 15, has a somewhat different account of the relations between the Strabolgis and Baliols. An ancient altar stone in Brabourn Chapel called the Heart Shrine is reputed to have once contained the heart of John Baliol-Scott, founder of Baliol College and father of John Baliol, king of Scotland, and Alexander Baliol, husband of Isabel of Chilham Castle. Members of the Baliol-Scott family were the chief patrons of the chapel in the 15th and 16th centuries.

21. The evidence of Robert Gower's patron's place of birth (*Documents Relating to Scotland,* III [1887], no. 1001, p. 182), the fact that no Kentish manors are listed in the first order for the release of his holdings (*9 Feb 1329,* ibid., no. 975, p. 176), that he had to sue for his rights to Chilham (*27 May 1328,* ibid., no. 128, p. 25; no. 872, p. 159), and that his wife had trouble securing possession of Brabourn (see note 24), are all important as circumstantial evidence that Robert Gower himself came from the north of England rather than from Kent.

22. *23 Oct 1334*: John de Greye of Rotherfield, Yorks, and Reginald de Cobham (see note 56) and William de Eynsford of Kent mainperned before the king at York to have Robert Gower, knight, before the king whenever he should please at three weeks' notice, and that Robert has betaken himself to the March of Scotland in the company of Edward de Bohun, the king's kinsman and keeper of said March, *Close Rolls Edward III, 1333–37* (1898), p. 347. Here we have the sort of Yorkshire and Kentish associations which suggest that Robert is the link between the Langbargh Gowers and the poet. For whatever it may be worth, a Reginald Cobham and a Johan de Eynsford are listed along with Chaucer in 1368 as members of the king's household (Reginald's name is struck through), *Chaucer Life Records*

(hereafter LR), Chaucer Society (1900), no. 53. *25 Nov 1335:* John de Denton (see note 17)gives up Ponteland to David de Strabolgi because "among other conditions for the surrender of the earl to the king's peace, it is contained that he shall have again all his lands in England which had escheated," *Patent Rolls Edward III, 1334–38* (1895), p. 146, and see also *Documents Relating to Scotland,* III [1887], no. 1141, p. 206.

23. Petition to Parliament no. 23, 1347, *Rotuli Parliamentorum,* II.181. The Countess complained that her whole wardrobe, valued at more than 16,000 marks sterling, was lost at Lochindorb. This must have comprised most of the Strabolgi household effects. On behalf of her son, born ca. 1334, she petitioned for arrearage in income from manors settled on him in 1337, including property in Yorkshire but none in Langbargh. On Katherine's genealogy, see *Documents Relating to Scotland,* III (1887), p. lxvii, nos. 47, 201, 886, 897; *Inquisitions post mortem,* File 653 (10), p. 97, in Public Record Office (PRO).

24. *11 March 1337:* order to escheator south of Trent to deliver to Katherine, late the wife of David de Strabolgi, Earl of Athol, the manor of Brabourn, Kent, which the king has assigned to her in dower, together with a list of other manors from which she is to derive income, *Close Rolls Edward III, 1337–39* (1900), p. 27. *30 May 1337:* order to the sheriff of Kent to go in person, taking with him the *posse comitatus* if necessary, and deliver to Katherine the manor of Brabourn being held by force by William Foxhunte and John le Bedel, deputed by Robert de Athol, p. 74. *12 June 1337:* same order repeated, with a fine of 100s. to be levied if it is not carried out, p. 133. *26 Aug 1337:* account of rents assigned to the Countess, including Westlexham (see note 18), p. 166. *31 Aug 1337:* the English king granted Robert de Athol 10£. 10s. in a list of royal grants to Scottish retainers, *Documents Relating to Scotland,* III (1887), no. 1280, p. 234. *15 Feb 1338:* Robert de Athol was permitted to ship wool without customs from Hartlepool in Durham (cf. the poet Gower's connection with the Staple), no. 1303, p. 237. For a history of Brabourn Manor, see J. R. Scott, op. cit., pp. 63–81.

25. *Documents Relating to Scotland,* III (1887), no. 1253, p. 229; no. 1455, p. 265.

26. See below, note 42. Macaulay 4.xi to the contrary notwithstanding, the Gowers were never widely established in Kent. For example, the *Probate Registry at Canterbury, 1396–1558, 1640–50,* ed. H. R. Plomer, Kent Archaeological Society (1920) lists not one *Gower. Gore* appears many times from 1328 on, both there and in the Kent Visitation Rolls, *Archaeologia Cantiana,* XXXIII (1918), 36, etc.

27. On the Scottish Moubrays see R. R. Stodart, *Scottish Arms* (Edinburgh, 1881), II.185, and Alexander Nisbet, *A System of Heraldry* (Edinburgh, 1722), I.287. Philip de Moubray, founder of the Scottish family, sat in *curia regis* in 1208. On the offices of Philip, father of Margaret Gower, see *Documents Relating to Scotland,* III (1887), nos. 121, 242, 244, 424, and 433. In 1335–36 his brother Alexander sued for his barony of Kirkmichael against his three daughters, married to Anselm de Guyse, Robert Gower, and David Mareschal, *Documents Relating to Scotland,* III (1887), p. 318. In 1320, David, Earl of Athol, received Alexander and others when

they came over to the English side, ibid., no. 729. In 1334, Alexander acted for Edward Baliol in Scotland, ibid., no. 1111. In 1335, upon the death of the earl of Athol, Alexander was granted the Strabolgi manor of Dalswynton, ibid., p. 318.

28. *12 Feb 1336, Patent Rolls Edward III, 1334–38* (1895), p. 222. Aymer de Valence, Earl of Pembroke, married as his third wife Marie daughter of Guy de Chastillon, Count of St. Pol. Marie is asserted to have lived at Brabourn (J. R. Scott, op. cit., p. 68), and in 1377, Ralph Strode acted for the City in taking possession of her London residence (see note 84).

29. *17 June 1335*: attestation, at the request of Anselm de Guyse and Philippa de Moubray, his wife, of a writing acknowledged before the king reciting that said Philippa, when she was unmarried, of full age with power of disposal, granted to Mary de Sancto Paulo her right in the third part, etc., *Patent Rolls Edward III, 1334–38* (1895), p. 120. *12 May 1334*: to Anselm de Guyse, who left David de Strabolgi when the latter joined the Scots, and came with his wife, a Scotswoman, to England, where he remains at the king's allegiance, by his own hands by way of a gift from the king in aid of his support, 20£., *Documents Relating to Scotland*, III (1887), no. 1156, p. 209.

30. *27 Jan 1333*: grant by David de Strabolgi, Earl of Athles, son and heir of David, late Earl of Athles, and Joan his wife, kinswoman and coheir to Aymar de Valence, late Earl of Pembroke, of all his French holdings in Mounteignak, Belak, Rancon, and Champeignak, which came to him at the death of the said Aymar, to Mary de St. Pol, wife of the said Aymar, *Close Rolls Edward III, 1333–37* (1898), p. 81.

31. "The Moubray fief, the greatest baronial estate in Yorkshire, owed its origin to the grant by Henry I of England of the English fief of Robert de Stutevill, called Fronteboef, to Nigel de Aubignay, younger brother of William de Aubignay, ancestor of the earls of Arundel, in reward for his services in the battle of Tinchbray in 1106." So begins Farrer's uncompleted history of the Moubray family, MS. 869, Yorkshire Archaeological Society Library, Leeds. Birdforth in Birdforth Wapentake, just south of Langbargh, was the seat of the family. Its history from 1106, including the Honor of Gower in Wales, lordship of the island of Axholm, and dukedom of Norfolk, is traced in VCH, YNR, II.3ff. The lordship of Gower in Wales is of interest in view of the fact that Caxton traced the poet's ancestry to that region. *Vox Clamantis* was presented to Thomas of Arundel, Archbishop of Canterbury, and the Arundels were *in capite* lords of Gower's manors of Feltwell and Multon (see note 92). The Moubrays were early benefactors to St. Mary Overeys. In the 13th century Nigel de Mowbray bequeathed to it the advowson of the Church of St. Margaret, and Mabel his wife a virgate of land in Surrey, Dugdale, VI.170.

32. A small group of citations will suffice to suggest the sort of evidence: Stokesley is the central town of Langbargh Wapentake. In the 13th century, William de Mowbray had a mill there (VCH, YNR, II.302). *No date*: deed witnessed by William Moubri and John Gower of Sexhow (YRS, CII [1940], p. 24). *6 June 1316*: deed witnessed by John Gower of Faiceby, Thomas de Moubray, John Gower of Sexhow (YRS, L [1914], p. 93). *Easter, 1334*: Alexander de Percy, knight, and Nicholas Gower, his attorney,

versus William de Dalehus, Agnes wife of William de Moubray, and others, for abduction of William son and heir of Roger Terry whose marriage belonged to Alexander (De Banco Rolls, Yorkshire, Harrison Extracts, IV.539, PRO). *Octave of Michaelmas, 1353*: Thomas de Swynford (probably the father of Hugh de Swynford, first husband of Katherine, Duchess of Lancaster) and John de Chartreye buy Whereleton Castle from John Darcy of Knayth and his wife, with homage and service of many tenants including Agnes Gower, Joan Gower, William Gower of Ingelby, Nicholas de Moubray (YRS, LII [1915], p. 221).

33. Cokayne-Doubleday, *Complete Peerage*, IX (1936), s.v. Mowbray.

34. 1327, *Close Rolls Edward III, 1327–30* (1896), p. 154. *3 Feb 1333*: order to the Abbot of St. Mary's, York, to pay money of the king's gift to several, including David de Strabolgi, 200£.; John de Moubray, 200 marks, *Close Rolls Edward III, 1333–37* (1898), p. 7.

35. *21 Aug 1307*: David, son of John, late earl of Athol, Aymer de Valencia, John de Moubray, of Scotland, and Alexander de Abernaythy acknowledge that they owe Ralph de Monte Hermerii 5,000 marks, *Close Rolls Edward II, 1307–13* (1892), p. 43. *20 Jan 1320*: acknowledgment of John de Moubray and others that they owe Aymer de Valencia and others 6,000 marks, *Close Rolls Edward II, 1318–23* (1895), p. 220.

36. Cokayne-Doubleday, IX.381. The Gower documents come later. *3 March 1356*: commission of *oyer* and *terminer* to John de Moubray, William de Notton, and others on complaint of John Darcy of Knayth that John Lely of Carleton, William Gower of Cold Ingelby, John Gower of Seggeshowe, John Gower of Cold Ingelby, and others broke his park at Templehurst, Yorks, hunted therein, took and carried away deer, and assaulted his servants, *Patent Rolls Edward III, 1354–58* (1909), p. 395. *26 Oct 1359*: commission of *oyer* and *terminer* to John Moubray, John de Fencotes, and others on complaint of Richard de Thorpe that John Gower of Elton and others broke his close at Great Lemyng, Yorks, etc., *Patent Rolls Edward III, 1358–61* (1911), p. 321. *2 March 1361*: commission of *oyer* and *terminer* to John Moubray and others on complaint of Peter de Malo Lacu the sixth, that John Gowere of Sexhowe, John Gowere of Fayceby, Laurence Gowere of Fayceby, and others broke his parks, etc., *Patent Rolls Edward III, 1358–61* (1911), p. 581. At least we know that the Langbargh Gowers were avid huntsmen. Other kinds of excitement are suggested by a transcript of proceedings against Nicholas de Meinil for endeavoring (ca. 1300) to marry his ward Robert Gower to the illegitimate daughter of his uncle, John de Stouteville (YRS, Extra Series VII [1952], p. 40). Episodes of this sort might help explain the "obscurity" in the pedigree of the Langbargh family.

37. VCH, YNR, II.313–14. See ibid., p. 286, for the Gowers of Sexhow, who were also fond of the names John and Robert. Alexander de Cave and Robert Gower were collectors of lay subsidies in 1301. W. Brown gives biographies of the collectors, but concerning Robert he reports, "I am unable to find anything about his person" (YRS, XXI [1897], p. 1). There is no evidence that Alexander de Clapham of Faceby was related to the 15th-century Gowers of Clapham in Surrey, but there was clearly some relation between the Kentish and Surrey branches. Nicolas, *Retrospective Review*, p. 113, and J. R. Scott, op. cit., p. 60, considered the Gowers of Clapham,

Surrey, relations of the poet. The godmother of Joan, second daughter of Robert Gower of Brabourn, was Joan de Passhelee, and Sir Edmund de Passhelee is mentioned in the proof of her age (p. 48). The widow of the elder John Moubray of Yorkshire (d. 1321) married "Sir Richard Pashale." The Passeles-Pashleys are interred in Brabourn Chapel. In 1458 Thomas Gower of Clapham, Surrey, died leaving his wife Joan and his sons his property, but he willed that if his sons died without issue, the property was to go to William and Isabel Passele (J. R. Scott, op. cit., p. 63). In the *Chartulary of the Hospital of St. Thomas, Southwark*, no. 480, p. 101, is an indenture made November 22, 1506, between John Scott of Sussex (of the Baliol-Scotts) and Anne his wife, daughter and heir of Reynold Pympe and Elizabeth his wife, daughter and heir of John Passhelye, cousin and heir of John Gower deceased, etc., selling to John Reed of London, notary, all their property in St. Mary Magdalene, Southwark, late Reynold Pympe's. J. R. Scott, loc. cit., makes an effort to trace the Pashley-Clapham connection by assuming that the poet Gower had a brother Thomas, but for this there is no documentary evidence whatsoever.

There may have been a relationship between the Langbargh and Stittenham Gowers at a much earlier date. In 1166–67, "William son of Guhier" was tenant at Stittenham (VCH, YNR, II.183). First mention of the Langbargh family is when "Willelmus filius Goheri" witnessed a bequest to Guisborough Priory ca. 1170 (see Surtees Society, LXXXIX [1894], p. 284; W. Brown, *Yorkshire Archaeological Journal*, XVI [1900–01], p. 121). Robert de Bruce, ancestor of another of the claimants for the Scottish crown, founded Guisborough Priory, ca. 1120 (VCH, YNR, II.336) and Bruces-Bruses were buried there until 1295. Perhaps coincidentally, 8 *Feb 1312*: the king commanded the sheriff of Northumberland to deliver Mary de Brus, a Scottish prisoner, in Newcastle-on-Tyne to Philip de Moubray, Margaret Gower's father, to exchange for his brother Richard or get what ransom he could for her, *Documents Relating to Scotland*, III (1887), no. 244, p. 49. For a biography of Nicholas Gower, son of John Gower of Sexhow, owner of the armorial seal resembling the poet's arms (p. 37) and Parliamentary representative for Yorkshire in June 1344, January 1348, and March 1348, see YRS, XLI (1935), p. 90.

38. The letter was sent in duplicate by different bearers, see *Ancient Correspondence*, XLIX.52. Abstract quoted from *Documents Relating to Scotland*, III (1887), no. 790, p. 147. The next entry reads "Total harness lost at Ryvaux by a sudden attack of the Scots there on the 14th of October, 11£. 7s. 11d."

39. The number of Gowers in important ecclesiastical positions in Yorkshire is interesting in view of the poet's own preoccupations. 3 *April 1333*: Robert de Colvyll of Ernclif grants lands to Sir John Gower of Ingelby, Chaplain (Calendar of ZFL MSS. in the Brown Collection, North Riding Record Society, Northallerton). In 1349 Archbishop Zouche confirmed the election of Alice Gower as prioress of St. Stephen's Nunnery in Cleveland (W. Brown, *Yorkshire Archaeological Journal*, IX [1886], p. 337). Between 1369 and 1383 William Gower was abbot of Fountains Abbey (Dugdale, v.288).

40. *19 Nov 1343, Close Rolls Edward III, 1343–46* (1904), p. 250. John

de Pultney, draper, was alderman of London 1327–35, 1336–38. He was knighted in 1337. His widow married the Nicholas de Lovaigne associated with Gower in the Septvauns affair (see p. 54). For a sketch of his career see Sylvia Thrupp, *The Merchant Class of Medieval London* (1948), p. 361. He and Richard Chaucer were assessed together for a tax in 1340 (LR, 15).

41. PRO, Chancery Miscellanea, Bundle 88, File 8, Divers Counties, no. 177.

42. *6 Aug 1349*: order to William de Middleton, escheator in the county of Suffolk, to take into the king's hands the lands late of Robert Gouer [sic] to make inquisition thereon, *Fine Rolls Edward III, 1347–56* (1921), p. 123, and see records cited by Macaulay 4.xii. *10 Nov 1349*: commitment to Katherine, Countess of Athol, of the wardship of the manor of Kentewell, Suffolk, late of Robert Gower, tenant in chief, to hold until the lawful age of the heirs, rendering 20 marks a year to the Exchequer, *Fine Rolls*, id., p. 178.

43. *8 May 1355, Close Rolls Edward III, 1354–60* (1908), p. 130.

44. *22 Dec 1359, Close Rolls Edward III, 1354–60* (1908), p. 604.

45. [1363] Document in the form of an indenture, without date, purporting to be proposals at a conference between the Privy Councils of the kings of England and Scotland. If the present king of Scotland dies without issue, one of the sons of the king of England is to be king, and restitutions are to be worked out for the exiled nobility. Among those mentioned are Strabolgi, Beaumont (Katherine's family), Ferrers (the family of Elizabeth, wife of the last Strabolgi earl of Athol), and Sir Roger Moubray (family of Margaret Gower), *Documents Relating to Scotland*, IV (1888), no. 92, p. 21. "La Contesse de Atheles" is mentioned as one of the Queen's damoiselles along with Philippa Chaucer in December 1368 (LR, 53), and like Philippa received black cloth for mourning at the Queen's funeral in September 1369 (LR, 58). The second reference must be to Elizabeth since Katherine died in 1368.

46. Proof quoted from *Inquisitions post mortem Edward III*, x (1921), no. 395. *15 May 1357*: order to the escheator of Suffolk to seise Katherine and Joan with their father's lands, *Close Rolls Edward III, 1354–60* (1908), p. 358.

47. *23 May 1366*: order to the escheator in Suffolk to deliver to William Neve and Joan, Joan's portion of the manor of Kentewell which they have recovered by action at St. Edmund against David de Strabolgi, *Close Rolls Edward III, 1364–68* (1910), p. 224. *25 June 1366*: inquiry showing that Katherine died about Christmas 32 Edward III [1358]. *Radwintir*, a moiety of 4£. yearly rent, held as belonging to the manor of Kentewellehalle, Suffolk. Immediately after Katherine's death, Joan her sister and heir entered and took possession of said moiety, and received the profit for 15 days. Then David de Strabolgi, Earl of Athol, entered and took the profits until 6 June 38 Edward III [1364] by what title the jurors know not. Since then the escheator, Roger de Wolferston, has been in possession and has accounted to the Exchequer. *Kentewell*, date of death, heir, and possession since death, as above, *Inquisitions post mortem*, XII (1935), no. 62. *25 June 1366*: order to the escheator in Suffolk to deliver Katherine's portion of Kentewell to William and Joan, Joan having proved that she is the lawful heir. Order

vacated because it was not fulfilled, *Fine Rolls Edward III, 1356–68* (1923), p. 336. *3 Dec 1366*: record of a fine of 100s. paid by William and Joan for entering upon possession of Kentewell without license of the king, *Patent Rolls Edward III, 1364–67* (1912), p. 343. *14 Dec 1366*: same order in the *Fine Rolls Edward III, 1356–68* (1923), p. 343. *22 Feb 1367*: further suit by William and Joan for their property. Repeats the statement about the license and fine, and adds that the property was "never in seisin of the said earl of Athole, the said earl of Stafford, or of others," *Close Rolls Edward III, 1364–68* (1910), p. 317.

48. *28 June 1368*: Thomas Syward and Joanna his wife, daughter of Robert Gower, grant Kentewell to John Gower, *Harleian Charters* 56. G. 41 (cited by Macaulay 4.xii). *22 July 1368*: pardon for 16 marks paid to the king by John Gower for his trespass in acquiring in fee the manor of Kentewell from Thomas Syward, late citizen and peutrer of London, *Patent Rolls Edward III, 1367–70* (1913), p. 146.

49. *1369*: fine between John Gower on the one hand and John Spenythorn and Joan his wife on the other by which they give up the right to Kentewell, except 10£. rent, John Gower paying 200 marks. Confirmed in the king's court 1380, *Harleian Charters* 50. 1.13 (cited by Macaulay 4.xii). *1380*: John Gower versus John Spenythorn and Johanna his wife of the manor of Kentewell, *A Calendar of the Feet of Fines for Suffolk*, ed. W. Rye, Suffolk Institute of Archaeology and Natural History (1900), p. 252. *21 April 1385*: John Spenythorn, citizen and tailor of London, to John Gower, esquire of Kent. General release of all actions, real and personal, all plaints and demands. Dated 15 March 1385. *Memorandum* that acknowledgment was taken by John Burton, clerk (see p. 67; a "John Burton" is listed in 1368 along with Chaucer as an esquire of the king's household, LR, 53), *Close Rolls Richard II, 1381–85* (1920), p. 619. The Maydenwater entry is garbled: "The manor of Maydewater was the only manor within the banlieu of St. Edmund which did not form part of the Abbey lands. It formed part of the lands of David de Strabolgi, Seneschal of Scotland, who gave it to Sir Roger [sic] Gower, knight. Upon the death of Sir Roger Gower it passed to his daughter Joan, wife of John Spenythorn," *Registrum Sacristae*, fol. 89 (a register of Bury St. Edmund's Abbey rentals, among the Bury corporation records), cited by V. B. Redstone, *Suffolk Archaeology*, XIII (1909), p. 207.

50. "The Book of St. Mary Overes" (see Chap. Three, p. 93), MS. BM Cotton Faustina A. VIII, f. 165ᵇ, lists John Syward among the mid-14th-century tenants of St. Mary Overeys' property. *1349*: John Syward, "peauterer," on a jury to investigate the death of John Sence who died seised of 12d. quitrent of "the prior of Suthwerk at Ebbegate" (i.e., St. Mary Overeys) London, Guildhall, Calendar of Rolls of Assizes, Fresh Force, etc., (m.18), p. 24. Further possible association is suggested by a record of *2 Jan 1380* in which Dame Mary Syward [relation to Thomas and John not established], Prioress of St. Leonard of Stratford, offered herself by Richard Forester her attorney [evidently the same who shared with Gower Chaucer's power of attorney in 1378] against William Bartilmeu, goldsmith [Thomas and John were pewterers], *Guildhall Plea and Memoranda Rolls, 1364–81* (1929), p. 267.

51. Edward Hasted, *History of Kent* (1798 ed.), v.468, 526.

52. For the transcript of the proceedings see Appendix C.

53. *1365*: inquiry whether it will be to the prejudice of the king to put John Gower in possession of half of the manor of Aldyngton, acquired by him without license from William de Septvans, etc., *Inquisitions post mortem* 39 *Edward III* (cited by Macaulay 4.xi, but not located in the printed calendars). *15 Feb 1365*: reported that Gower's acquisition of Aldyngton would not be to the prejudice of the king, and accordingly on March 9, Gower pays 53s. which appears to be the annual value of the property, and is pardoned for the offense of entering without license, *Rot. Orig.*, 39 *Edward III* (cited by Macaulay 4.xii, but not located in the printed calendars). *18 Feb 1365*: inquisition at Maidstone taken *virtute officii*: William de Septem Vannis three days ago alienated a moiety of the manor of Aldyngton to John Gower and his heirs, *Inquisitions Miscellaneous Chancery*, III (1937), no. 596. *9 March 1365*: pardon for acquiring and restitution to John Gower of the manor of Aldyngton, upon his paying 53s. to the king, *Patent Rolls Edward III, 1364–67* (1912), p. 99. *23 June 1365*: charter of William Sepvauns giving John Gower and his heirs a yearly rent of 10£. issuing from the manor Wygebergh and from all the grantor's lands in Essex. Writing of William Septvauns being a quitclaim with warranty to John Gower and his heirs of the whole manor of Aldyngton with 14s.6d. of rent and a rent of one cock, 13 hens, and 140 eggs in Maplescompe, and the homages and all the services of the tenants who ought to render the same. Witnesses named. Memorandums acknowledged, *Close Rolls Edward III, 1364–68* (1910), p. 185. Aldington has further literary association in that in 1205–06 it was acquired by William of Cheriton, father of Odo of Cheriton, author of sermons and an attractive collection of fables. William was heir to Robert of Sevanz (Septvauns). His property passed to Odo, but Aldington had evidently returned to the Septvauns family by Gower's time, see A. C. Friend, "Master Odo of Cheriton," *Speculum*, XXIII (1948), 643.

54. See Appendix C for the transcript from *Inquisitions post mortem Edward III*, XII (1938), no. 96, p. 75, and *Rotuli Parliamentorum*, II. 292.

55. *6 Feb 1368*, *Patent Rolls Edward III, 1367–70* (1913), pp. 83, 96. *23 July 1368*: John Gower pays Richard Ravensere, clerk, 20£. *Close Rolls Edward III, 1364–68*, (1910), p. 482. Macaulay 4.xv suggests that the payment was in connection with Gower's re-acquiring Aldington. Richard de Ravenser was in 1357 clerk of the hanaper and from 1362 until he died in 1386 a master in Chancery. From 1368 until his death he was also archdeacon of Lincoln, and Manly, *Some New Light On Chaucer* (1926), p. 108, proposed him as one of two possible originals for the archdeacon described at the beginning of the Friar's Tale (CT, III.1301). See Chap. Five, p. 276.

56. *29 Sept 1373*: John Gower grants to John de Kobham, knight, William de Weston, Roger Asshebournhame, Thomas Brokhull, and Master Thomas de Preston, rector of the church at Tunstall, all of his manor of Kent Well in Suffolk, *Harleian Charters*, 50. 1.14. Latin quoted in full by Nicolas, p. 106, with an engraving of the seal in Fig. 6, above. *8 April 1374*: pardon for 12 marks paid to the king by the same five of their trespass in acquiring in fee the manor of Kentwell and a moiety of Aldyngton, held in chief from

John Gower, and a grant that they may retain the same, *Patent Rolls Edward III, 1370–74* (1914), p. 425. *24 June 1382*: receipt by John Gower to Monsr John de Cobham for 106s.6d. in full payment for all debts. Sealed with the seal in Fig. 7 above. From the Surrenden MSS, printed in *Archaeologia Cantiana*, VI (1866), 87. It is interesting to find Cobham's associate Roger Asshbournham later buying land with Thomas Pyncebeck, the Sergeant-of-the-Law Manly identified as the model for Chaucer's Man of Law (*New Light*, p. 149), London, Guildhall, Calendar of Hustings Rolls, Roll 112 (75) [1383].

57. In 1377 Chaucer was evidently with Cobham on peace negotiations with France (LR, 102 [p. 204 note 1]); in 1385 and 1386 Cobham, Chaucer, and Brockhill (see next note) were associated as justices of the peace for Kent (LR, 183, 188).

58. *1377*: deed of Thomas Brockhull releasing lands in Kent to Sir John Frebody, rector of Bocton Aluph, and John Gower, Halstead, *Kent* (1790 ed.), III.425. This is one of the records dismissed by Macaulay, 4.xiv, but in view of the reappearance of familiar names, it seems likely that it refers to the poet. "Thomas Brockhill" is twice associated with Chaucer as Justice of Peace for Kent (1385, 1386; LR, 183, 188).

59. Sir William de Chirchehull, chaplain, London, Guildhall, Calendar of Hustings Rolls, Roll 112 (5) [1383]; in 1367 guardian of the temporalities of the bishopric of Chichester, with London business associations, *Close Rolls Edward III, 1364–68* (1910), p. 31. In June 1366 he was imprisoned in the Flete prison "for an alleged deceit committed against the King touching proof of the age of William de Sepvauns" (ibid., p. 279).

60. In LR, 53 (1368), a Simon de Burgh is listed along with Chaucer as an esquire of the king's household; in LR, 57 and 58 (1369), 73 (1373), and 109 (1377) he receives robes or cloth with other members of the household.

61. *16 July 1364*: the king orders Nicholas de Lovayne, Seneschal of Ponthieu, to try the action for debt brought by Simon, Abbot of Clugny, Rymer's *Foedera* (1830) III, pt. II, 743.

62. See Reginald Tower, "The Family of Septvans," *Archaeologia Cantiana*, XL (1928), 111. The Septvans were related to the Cobhams by marriage, Cocayne-Gibbs, *Complete Peerage*, s.v. Cobham.

63. To appear in the Staple court, an individual had to be either himself a Staple merchant or of the household of a Staple merchant, A. H. Thomas, ed., *Calendar of the Plea and Memoranda Rolls of the City of London, 1381–1412* (1932), pp. xvi–xvii. Macaulay, 4.xxvii, considered it likely that Gower was a merchant because of his sympathetic treatment of this group and his patriotic eulogy on wool as the foundation of the national wealth (MO, 25360). Sylvia Thrupp, *The Merchant Class of Medieval London*, Chaps. I and III, has shown that members of all classes and guilds engaged in trade.

64. G. R. Corner, "Observations on Four Illuminations from a Manuscript of the Time of King Henry VI," *Archaeologia*, XXXIX (1862–63), 358, with fine color reproductions; cited by Edith Rickert, "Was Chaucer a Student in the Inner Temple?" *Manly Anniversary Studies* (1923), p. 31 note.

65. Stow continues: "To follow precedent of former time, the clerks of companies were to inquire for them of their companies that would have the mayor's livery, their money as a benevolence given, which must be twenty shillings at the least put in a purse, with their names that gave it, and the wardens to deliver it to the mayor by the first of December; for the which every man had then sent him four yards of broad cloth, rowed or striped athwart, with a different colour to make him a gown, and these were called ray gowns, which was then the livery of the mayor and also of the sheriffs, but each differing from others in the colours. . . . More, in the 16th of Henry VIII, Sir William Bayly, then being mayor, made a request, for that clothes of ray (as he alleged) were evil wrought, his officers might be permitted (contrary to custom) for that year to wear gowns of one colour," p. 196.

66. *Pourchace* at MO, 24540, 24555, 24579, 24581, 24585, 24812, 24899, etc.

67. Macaulay 4.ix. At 4.xxvi, Macaulay is "disposed to attach some weight" to the reference to rayed sleeves in MO, and allows "the possibility that Gower was bred to the law, though he may not have practised it for a living."

68. W. H. Gunner, N&Q, 1st Ser, IX (1854), 487: "Willelmus permissione divinia Wyntoniensis Episcopus, dilecto in Christo filio, domino Willelmo, capellano parochiali ecclesiae S. Mariae Magdalenae in Suthwerk, nostrae diocesis, salutem, gratiam, et benedictionem. Ut matrimonium inter Joannem Gower et Agnetem Groundolf dictae ecclesiae parochianos sine ulteriore bannorum editione, dum tamen aliud canonicum non obsistat, extra ecclesiam parochialem, in Oratorio ipsius Joannis Gower infra hospicium suum in prioratu B. Mariae de Overee in Suthwerk praedicta situatum, solempnizare valeas licenciam tibi tenor praesentium, quatenus ad nos attinet, concedimus specialem. In cujus rei testimonium signillum nostrum fecimus his apponi. Dat. in manerio nostro de alta clera vicesimo quinto die mensis Januarii, A.D. 1397, et nostrae consecrationis 31mo." Macaulay (4.xvii) translates *infra* "within," and corrects "hospicium cum" to "hospicium suum."

69. See Chap. One, p. 15, above.

70. *18 July 1378*: to the sheriff of Bedford. Writ by mainprise to Edmund Clay of Nott., John de Kirkeby of Yorks., John Cauntelo of Wilts., and William de Huntyngdon of London in favor of William Bromesford of London and Isabel his wife at suit of Agnes who was the wife of Henry Huntyngfeld, for alleged trespass by them and John Gower, *Close Rolls Richard II, 1377–81* (1914), p. 206. *18 March 1381*: Isabel, daughter of Walter de Huntyngfeld, to John Gower and John Bowland, clerk. Quitclaim of all lands of her father in the parish of Thrwleye and Stalesfeld, Kent, *Close Rolls Richard II, 1377–91* (1914), p. 505. *20 Feb 1382*: Isabel, late the daughter of Walter de Huntyngfeld of Kent, to John Gower of Kent. General release of all actions real and personal, *Close Rolls Richard II, 1381–85* (1920), p. 111. *12 April 1385*: the same to the same. Release of all actions, dated in London, 10 June 1385, *Close Rolls Richard II, 1381–85* (1920), p. 635. *28 May 1390*: William Brounesforde the elder to John Gower. General release of all actions, *Close Rolls Richard II, 1389–92*

(1922), p. 181. *11 Nov 1348:* John de Pulteneye (see p. 47) versus John de Huntyngfeld, knight, to be acquited of the service which Geoffrey de Say exacted for a free tenement in Speldhurst, Kent, PRO Assiz Rolls, Justices Itinerary 1/393 (m.10). For Geoffrey de (or le) Say as witness of Strabolgi quitclaim to Robert Gower, see above, note 17. Robert Chaucer, the poet's grandfather, was in 1308 attorney for a Henry de Say, the king's butler (LR, 2). *1355:* Say versus Huntyngfeld as to custody of Isabel, daughter and heiress of Walter de Huntyngfeld. Decision that Geoffrey de Say should have custody of Isabel who is unmarried and 14 years old, MSS. Chancery Miscellanea, Bundle 64, File 2, no. 32, Placita de Banco 27 Edward III. *ca. 1396:* Sir Walter Huntyngfeld disposes of property on London Bridge to Thomas Squiry, London, Guildhall, Calendar of Bridgemasters' Account Rolls, Roll 15 (m.1), p. 187.

71. *26 May 1367:* writing by John Gravesende citizen and draper of London, giving with warranty to John Gower, his heirs and assigns, 10£. free quitrent to be taken every year at Michaelmas of all the lands of the grantor as well in Kent as in the city of London, with power to distrain for arrears. Witnesses, John de Stodeye, John Tornegold, William de Essex, citizens of London. John Page, William Galoun of Kent, *Close Rolls Edward III, 1364–68* (1910), p. 379. There is no evidence that this is the poet save for the London and Kentish associations. John de Stodeye, alderman and mayor in the 1360's, was the John of Gaunt of the guilds. Four of his daughters made good marriages: Idonia to Nicholas Brembre, Margaret to John Phillipot, Margery to Henry Varmer, Johanna to Thomas Goodlak. On Torngold and Stodeye, see Thrupp, *The Merchant Class of Medieval London*, pp. 367, 370. There are many references to these two and John Gravesend or Graveshende in the London, Guildhall, Calendars of Hustings and Assize Rolls, in the last quarter of the 14th century. A John Stodeye, vintner, had frequent business association with John Chaucer, the poet's father, and others of Chaucer's relatives, see LR, 17 (1342), 21 (1346), 30 (1352), 36 (1363), 40 (1365), 54 (1369), Addition 4 (ca. 1348).

72. See note 91.

73. This is translated from the colophon of MS. Bodley 902 (1). See below, p. 89, and Appendix B.

74. Macaulay 4.xxv was likewise of the opinion that "it is probable that he passed a considerable part of his literary life in those lodgings within the Priory of St. Mary Overey which are mentioned in his marriage license and his will."

75. For a history of Southwark, see W. Rendle, *Old Southwark and Its People* (1878), including a map of ca. 1542; see also Canon Thompson, *History and Antiquities of St. Saviour* (above).

76. Reproduced by Gordon Home, *Old London Bridge* (1931), p. 109.

77. Home, p. 123.

78. LR, 80; translated by H. T. Riley, *Memorials of London* (1868), p. 377.

79. *20 May 1378:* "Galfridus Chauser, qui de licencia Regis versus partes transmarinas profecturus est, habet literas Regis de generali attornato, sub nominibus Johannis Gower, et Ricardi Forester, sub alternacione, ad lucrandum, &c. in quibuscumque curiis Anglie, per vnum annum duraturas, &c.

Teste Rege, apud Westmonasterium xxi° die Maii. Willelmus de Burst' clericus Regis attornauit. Rot. Franc. I Richard II, part ii, m.6." LR, 120. Transcribed with differences in Nicolas, Life of Chaucer, Morris ed. (1891), 1.99. On Forester and Aldgate, see J. M. Manly, ed., *Chaucer's Canterbury Tales* (1928), p. 19. Manly, op. cit., p. 515, and Edith Rickert MP, xxiv (1926), 118, report one other record linking Chaucer and Gower: both borrowed money from Gilbert Maghfeld. Forester appears at least 11 times as an attorney between 1378 and 1405 in the Calendars of Rolls of Assizes, Fresh Force, etc., London, Guildhall. For Forester's lease on Aldgate, see LR, 192.

80. A. B. Emden, A *Biographical Register of the University of Oxford* (1959), iii.1807, caps a series of articles in the journals citing new records of business associations between Ralph Strode of London and members of Merton College, including John Wyclif. H. B. Workman, *John Wyclif* (1926), ii.125, discusses intellectual and political relations between Strode and Wyclif.

81. Strode was dead (d. 1387) by the time selected for the basis of the calculation in the two works (1391). See A. C. Crombie, in *Medieval England*, ed. A. L. Poole (1958 ed.), ii.593, on the Merton school. P. Pintelon, ed., *Chaucer's Treatise on the Astrolabe* (1940), and D. J. Price, ed., *The Equatorie of the Planetis* (1955), present full discussions of authorship and mathematical tradition.

82. Discussion in Emden. On Strode's writings and international reputation as a logician see Workman, loc. cit. and Appendix Q (ii.412); G. Sarton, *Introduction to the History of Science* (1927), iii. Pt. ii. 1412; and G. E. Mohan, *Franciscan Studies*, xii (1952), 349. For Gollancz's suggestion, see his edition of *The Pearl* (1921), xlvi, and TLS, October 25, 1928, p. 783.

83. T. F. Tout, *Speculum*, iv (1929), 365, denies the possibility of identity between the Oxford and London Strodes. Tout's lecture provides a point of departure for the needed study of London literary life at the end of the 14th century.

84. The record granting Strode the apartment over Aldersgate is translated by Riley, *Memorials of London*, p. 388. In view of Gower's comment on his own rayed sleeves, a 1377 petition by Strode to the Corporation is of some interest: "Pray the simple servants, the serjeants of your chamber, that they have now greater duties and labours than they or their predecessors, serjeants, have ever had heretofore, whereas their salaries and their fees are so small that they will not suffice to find their shoes [note: each of them would of course follow his own trade, the duties of serjeant being occasional] and that besides this, your serjeants at great assemblies ought to be dressed alike to be known as officers of the City: may it therefore please your very wise Lordships, for the honor of the City, to add to their salaries and to grant that they be arrayed in like suit to that of the serjeants of the Mayor, the Chamber paying for their vestments," Riley, op. cit., p. 414. Records of Strode's legal activities are in Riley, p. 376ff, and Thomas, ed., *Calendar of Plea and Memoranda Rolls of the City of London*, 1364–81 (1929), pp. 189, 228, and index s.v. Strode.

85. The DNB account for Usk is the most complete. *The Calendar of*

Plea and Memoranda Rolls (ed. cit.) includes three entries relating to his affairs: *13 Sept. 1375* (p. 204), Usk called "clerk"; *11 July 1376* (p. 221), Usk attorney to John Bere; and *21 Nov. 1379* (p. 257).

86. Skeat, *Oxford Chaucer*, vii.xxv.

87. "Quod Love, 'I shal telle thee, this lesson to lerne. Myne owne trewe servaunt, the noble philosophical poete in Englissh, whiche evermore him besieth and travayleth right sore my name to encrese (wherefore al that willen me good owe to do him worship and reverence bothe; trewly, his better ne his pere in scole of my rules coude I never fynde) . . .'" *The Testament of Love*, iii.iv (Skeat, *Oxford Chaucer*, vii.123). Compare Venus's message in CA, viii.2940*, above, Chap. One, p. 6.

88. F. J. Furnivall's biographies in the DNB and in his edition of Hoccleve's *Minor Poems*, EETS, es, 61 (1892), do not include the record of his dealings with Rouclif: *16 June 1392*: to the sheriff of York. Writ of *supersedeas* by mainprise of Thomas Fairfax, Richard Giffoun of Yorkshire, and John Wyles and Thomas Hoccleve clerks, in favour of Guy de Rouclif clerk at suit of John Sayville knight for detinue of 249£., *Close Rolls Richard II, 1389–92* (1922), p. 564. *Close Rolls Richard II, 1392–96* (1925), p. 249, records the maintenance at Hayling Island. See below note 93 for the Furnivall-Kirk reference to Rouclif as clerk in Privy Seal.

89. Hoccleve, *Regement of Princes*, ed., F. J. Furnivall, EETS, os, 72 (1897), pp. 71–72.

90. On Chaucer, Strode, and Hende, see Edith Rickert, TLS, October 4, 1928, p. 707; Manly ed., *Canterbury Tales* (1928), p. 43. On Hende: Thrupp, *Merchant Class*, p. 349.

91. *1 Aug 1382*: Guy de Rouclif clerk, to John Gower esquire of Kent. Charter of the manors of Feltwelle, Norfolk, and Multon, Suffolk, which the grantor had by feoffment of Thomas de Catherton. Witnesses: John Tydde, John Northfolk, Thomas Noreys, John Trace, Walter Clider, John Overton. Memorandum of acknowledgment August 28, *Close Rolls Richard II, 1381–85* (1920), p. 211. A Thomas Noreys, haberdasher (Roll 101 [63] [1373]), and two John Norfolks, a tailor (Roll 117 [145–146] [1389]) and a chaplain (Roll 121 [205–207] [1393]) in the Calendar of Hustings Rolls in London Guildhall suggest that this was a London transaction. Another John de Northfolk is recorded as receiving money from the king's wardrobe in 1369, along with Chaucer, LR, 61. *3 Aug 1382*: John Gower, esquire of Kent, to Guy de Rouclif, clerk, and to his heirs. Release of the warranty contained in the above charter, *Close Rolls Richard II, 1381–85* (1920), p. 214. *4 Aug 1382*: Elizabeth Dame Lutterall of Devon to John Gower, esquire. Quitclaim of the manors of Feltwell, Norfolk, and Multon, Suffolk, *Close Rolls Richard II, 1381–85* (1920), p. 220. The Lutteralls had earlier connections with the Yorkshire Gowers. *Inquisitions and Assessments Relating to Feudal Aids, 1284–1431*, vi (1920), York, p. 155: [1302–03] Wapentachium de Buck[rose]. De foedo de Lutrell [tenants include] Johannes Gower xiij bov.

92. *Inquisitions and Assessments Relating to Feudal Aids, 1284–1431*, iii (1904) Kent-Norfolk, p. 654: Hundreda de Waylond, Grymeshowe [Norfolk], Johannes Gower tenet in Feltwelle, j.f.m. de comite Arundellie, et idem de rege [1401–02]. The historical connection between the two man-

ors is indicated by two earlier entries. *15 March 1325:* order to escheator in Norfolk, Suffolk, etc., to deliver to Mary, late wife of Aymer de Valencia, Earl of Pembroke, the following of his knight's fees, which the king has assigned to her in dower . . . a fee in Feltwell, Suffolk, which William de Bello Campo [Beauchamp] holds, *Close Rolls Edward II, 1323–27* (1898), p. 266. *22 April 1331:* William de Bello Campo acknowledges that he owes money to Richard de Tye, parson of Multon, near Kenteford, and to Richard de Rokele, *Close Rolls Edward III, 1330–33* (1898), p. 306. This William de Beauchamp could be the father of Sir William de Beauchamp for whom Chaucer mainperned when he was granted custody of the Pembroke estates in Wales; Manly, *New Light,* p. 89.

93. Guy appears in various Yorkshire transactions. *1364:* Margery widow of John de Rouclif, William Fairfax, and Guy de Rouclif, son of the same Margery, quer., Brian de Rouclif, knight, and Katherine his wife, def., various lands in Yorkshire, *Feet of Fines for Yorkshire, 1347–77,* YRS, LII (1915), p. 102. *1375:* Guy de Rouclif, clerk, and Thomas de Midelton, quer., Thomas son of Stephen de Grillyngton and Margaret his wife, def., lands and rents in York, ibid., p. 187. *11 Feb 1382:* John de Roma of Monkesfreton to Guy de Rouclyf, clerk, and to his heirs. Release of a warranty whereby the said Guy and others gave the said John the manor of Cattebeeston by Ledes, *Close Rolls Richard II, 1381–85* (1920), p. 110. Presumably Guy was related to John de Rawcliffe who in 1373 founded the hospital of Jesus Christ and the Blessed Virgin Mary in Fossgate, York (YRS, L [1940], p. 206 note), and who was in 1380 appointed one of the deputy *ulnagers* (cloth inspectors) of York: *The Early Yorkshire Woolen Trade,* YRS, LXIV (1924), p. 115. The appearance of Guy de Rouclif with William Fairfax is worth noting. In 1345, a John de Rouscliff appeared in a transaction with John Mauleverer (YRS, LII [1915], p. 23). The Fairfax MS. (40) of the CA is one of the most important, and MS. Morgan 126 (16) was once owned by the Mauleverers. In Chaucer LR, 61 (1369) a Guidone de Rouclyf is advanced 100s. for military expenses as a member of the King's household, but this is hardly the same person as the *clerk* of the Gower and Yorkshire records. In a roll for Easter, 10 Richard II (1387), there is record of a payment of 6£. 13s. 4d. to Guy de Roclyffe, one of the clerks in the office of the Privy Seal, sent by an order of the Lords of the Council to the King "for certain matters touching the state of the King and Kingdom," R. G. Kirk's record, Furnivall's Life in *Hoccleve's Minor Poems,* EETS, ES 61 (1892), p. x.

94. *6 Aug 1382:* John Gower of the one part, Thomas Blakelake parson of St. Nicholas, Feltewelle, John Sybile, Edmund Lakynghethe and John Wermyngton of the other part. Indenture of demise to the said Thomas and others, their heirs and assigns, of the manors of Feltewelle, co. Norffolk, and Multon, co. Suffolk, rendering yearly 40£. in the abbey church of the monks at Westminster during John Gower's life, power being reserved to distrain for arrears, and to enter and hold those manors all of his life and seven days longer if the rent shall be six weeks in arrears; and if John Gower, his executors or assigns shall so enter, they shall not be bound to repair any houses thereto pertaining. *Memorandum* of acknowledgment by said John Sybile and Edmund Lakynghethe, 24 October, *Close Rolls, Richard II, 1381–85*

(1920), p. 218. Repeated with acknowledgment by John Gower and John Wermyngton, 29 Feb 1384, ibid., p. 426. "Lakynghethe" is such a distinctive name that it is worth noting that in 1390 a monk named John Lakynghith delivered Chaucer 20£. on account of repairs to St. George's Chapel at Windsor (LR, 290).

95. *24 Oct 1396:* pardon to John Cook of Feltewell for not appearing to answer John Gower, esquire, touching a debt of 10 marks, *Patent Rolls Richard II, 1396–99* (1909), p. 128. For the *Feudal Aids*, see note 92.

96. Henry Morley, *English Writers*, iv (i) (1889), p. 156; Macaulay 4.xxv. On the presentation and vacating of this living see *Patent Rolls Richard II, 1388–92* (1902), p. 367; ibid., *1396–99* (1909), p. 70. The same or another John Gower was in 1391 presented to the parish church at Tyntenhull in the diocese of Bath and Wells, ibid., *1388–91* (1902), p. 477.

97. Macaulay ed., vol. 4. page 1, headnote and line 29.

98. The epitaph, printed by Macaulay 4.lix, is among John Bale's unpublished papers, evidently taken from Agnes Gower's tomb in St. Mary Overeys Church, mentioned by Leland but not by Stow.

99. Latin text of the will is in Nicolas, *Retrospective Review*, p. 104; translation in Macaulay 4.xvii. *Martilogium*, which Macaulay appears to take as the title of a book, is a generic term; see Baxter and Johnson, *Medieval Latin Word List* (1934).

1. London, Guildhall, Calendar of Bridgemasters' Account Rolls, Roll 11 (m.1,ij), p. 76, gives a list of increases in rent, including: "and for 14s. 8d., received of increase of rent of a certain new inn in the parish of St. Olave's, Southwark, outside the gate of the bridge-house, which Sir Arnold Savage now holds." Calendar of Bridgemasters' Account Rolls, Roll 17 (m.3,xxv), p. 244, lists purchases on July 4 [1405]: "also thirty-two feet of glass for the chapel of Sir Arnold Savage, knight, at 13d. a foot, 34s. 8d.; of which the aforesaid Arnold paid half, and the aforesaid masters the other half." If this was not the Chapel of St. Thomas, it is hard to see why the bridgemasters would help glaze it. On the rebuilding of the Chapel of St. Thomas, see Gordon Home, *Old London Bridge* (1931), p. 100.

2. Sir Arnold Savage Senior was of the Chaucer-Gower circle and his political views and activities coincided with Gower's. In 1386 he witnessed a document returning Chaucer to Parliament (LR, p. 261). In 1392 he went surety to secure the release of John Hende, imprisoned in the quarrel between Richard II and the London citizens (*Close Rolls Richard II, 1392–96* [1925], p. 78). His mother, Eleanor, had been Richard's nurse in his infancy (*Patent Rolls Richard II, 1377–81* [1915], p. 450), and he himself was speaker of the House of Commons and extremely important in the formulation of policy in the new government of Henry IV (DNB, s.v. Savage, Sir Arnold).

3. See note 49.

4. *16 Feb 1410:* Hugh Lutterall, knight, to Agnes Gower, late the wife of John Gower, esquire, gift for her life of a yearly rent of 20£. to be taken of his manor of Feltwelle, Norffolk, with power to distrain for arrears there and in his manor of Multon, Suffolk, *Close Rolls Henry IV, 1409–13* (1932), p. 80.

5. The entry is curiously phrased: "Livrez a Richard Dancaster pour

un Coler a luy doné par monseigneur le Conte de Derby par cause d'une autre Coler doné par monditseigneur a un Esquier John Gower, vynt et sys soldz oyt deniers," Duchy of Lancaster Miscellanea, Bundle X, No. 43, undated but in the company of documents dated October and November 1393. Henry was evidently in the habit of impetuously giving his own or his retainers' collars away and then having to have duplicates made: see Macaulay 4.xvi.

6. John Anstis, *The Register of the Garter* (1724), II, 116. Edward Foss, *Archaeologia Cantiana*, 1 (1855), 73, speaks of the collar of S's as an insigne of the Lancastrian livery at the end of the 14th century. The collar may have had some connection with Gower's being called "the King's esquire" in 1399 (see next note). Elias Ashmole, *The Institution, Laws, and Ceremonies of the Most Noble Order of the Garter* (1672), p. 225, "In the ancient creation of an Esquire in England, part of the ceremony was, that the King put about his neck a silver collar of SS, as an Ensign of that dignity." Ashmole goes on to point out that the collar of S's eventually became an insigne of civil or judicial distinction.

7. *21 Nov 1399:* grant for life to the King's esquire John Gower of two pipes of wine of Gascony yearly in the port of London. By p.s., *Patent Rolls Henry IV, 1399–1401* (1903), p. 128. *5 April 1400:* to the chief butler for the time being, or his representatives in the port of London. Order to deliver to John Gower, the King's esquire, two pipes of wine of Gascony a year for life, to him granted in that port by the King 21 November last. By K. *Et erat patens, Close Rolls Henry IV, 1399–1402* (1927), p. 78.

8. Text in Macaulay 4.345. The five lines dealing with the wine (17–21) appear in their original version in MSS. 53 and 61: "While he drinks your pious respects, your fame cannot dry up, but will be exhibited bountifully with praise. Not so will fare he who dies a tyrant. He who does [not] undertake great things will suffer the lesser. But he who seeks merit will achieve his destiny." They are rewritten over erasure in MSS. 50–52, on the whole less effectively, save that the reference to drinking comes as the climax: "Who comports himself well will suffer no evil, but he will reveal himself pious who reveals the piety of God. Who behaves thus will be accompanied by piety. God will see to it that he will not perish by enmity. And thus will he conclude, who drinks your pious respects."

9. *11 Dec 1397: memorandum* of mainprise under pain of 40£. made in Chancery 6 December this year by John Frenche, Peter Blake, Thomas Gandre, all of London, and Robert Markle, serjeant at arms for Thomas Caudre, canon of the priory of St. Mary Overey in Southwerke, that he shall do or procure no harm to John Gower, *Close Rolls Richard II, 1396–99* (1927), p. 238. This must surely refer to the poet; but what of these other two records? *22 Nov 1398:* to the sheriff of Kent. Writ of *supersedeas omnio,* and order by mainprise of Thomas Kempe, John Cranewelle of Kent, William Canynges, and John Sandeforde of Surrey to set free John Stoffolde of Crundale [about four miles from Brabourn] if taken at suit of John Gower of Crundale averring threats, *Close Rolls Richard II, 1396–99* (1927), p. 417. *11 Jan 1405: memorandum* of a mainprise under pain of 100£. made in Chancery 12 January this year by James Norwode of Kent, esquire, and John Mokkynge, John Sandyforde, and William Kirton of Surrey, for John

Solas, and of an undertaking by him under the same pain, that he will do and procure no hurt or harm to John Gower and William Weston his servant, *Close Rolls Henry IV, 1402–05* (1929), p. 484. These last two are linked by the name John Sandeforde. A Thomas Gandre is listed as "pouchmaker" as late as 1397 in the London, Guildhall, Calendar of the Hustings Rolls, Roll 126 (88) [1397]. A John Mokkyngge held a shop on London Bridge ca. 1393, London, Guildhall, Calendar of Bridgemasters' Account Rolls, Roll 12 (m.2,xx), p. 120.

John Gour, steward of the Earl of March, is the Gower most likely to be confused with the poet in the records. For example, *20 Aug 1359*: license for Roger de Mortuo Mari, earl of March, to grant to William, Bishop of Winchester, Ralph Spigurnell, knight, John de Bisshopeston, clerk, John Laundel, and John Goure manors in Kent, Sussex, etc., *Patent Rolls Edward III, 1356–61* (1911), p. 266. *16 October 1366*: commission to John Gower and others to make diligent scrutiny in the town and port of Melcombe for jewels, gold, and silver, taken from the realm without license. By testimony of Ralph Spigurnell, the King's admiral, *Patent Rolls Edward III, 1364–67* (1912), p. 362. This John Gour is found in the public records of the 1360's and 1370's as steward, attorney, and eventually executor of the Earl of March. He bore the Langbargh arms (see Nicolas, p. 108, Pauli ed., i.viii), and so must have been a distant relative of the poet. His name is frequently spelled Gour, and when associated with Spigurnell, Bisshopeston, and others is fairly easy to distinguish. He may be the John Gower who in 1386 and 1387 was ordered to receive and distribute victuals at Dover Castle, *Patent Rolls Richard II, 1385–89* (1900), pp. 208, 266; and see Macaulay 4.xi.

CHAPTER 3

1. Unless otherwise specified, the texts are those in Macaulay: *Balades*, 1.335ff.

2. See description of the Trentham MS. in Macaulay 1.lxxix. Macaulay's manuscript descriptions, on the whole extremely full and accurate, have been verified and supplemented by a personal examination of fifty-one of the sixty-three recorded manuscripts of Gower's works, microfilms of which are deposited in the Duke University Library. See Appendix A for a classified list.

3. Macaulay 1.lxxxi; Warton in a letter kept with the Trentham MS., and in his *History* (1871 ed.) III.33.

4. As indicated by notations in the MS; see Macaulay's description.

5. Macaulay 3.481. This piece was first printed in Thynne's edition of Chaucer from another MS.

6. Macaulay 1.336. The Latin is a combination of the first eight lines of *O recolende*, the poem acknowledging Henry's grant of wine to Gower in 1399 found in five MSS (above, Chap. Two, note 8 at the end; Macaulay 4.345), and four lines of the epigram *H. aquile pullus*, also found in five MSS (Macaulay 4.344), defending Henry as a legitimate ruler. Only the concluding lines of prose appear to be unique to the Trentham text.

7. Macaulay 4.365, found in three forms in five MSS.

8. Macaulay 4.343, found in six MSS. The corresponding passage in the Vox is at VI.1159*.

9. Warton, *History of English Poetry* (1871 ed.), III.33.

10. G. L. Kittredge, *The Date of Chaucer's Troilus* (Chaucer Society, 1909), p. 76.

11. Macaulay 1.lxxii.

12. *Oeuvres de Guillaume de Machaut*, Ernest Hoepffner, ed., 3v (Paris, 1908–21).

13. *Oeuvres de Froissart, Poésies*, A. Scheler, ed., 2v (Brussels, 1871).

14. For general discussion of the balade, see H. L. Cohen, *The Ballade* (1915), p. 33, etc.

15. Quixley (below) called Gower's *Cinkante Balades* "balades ryale."

16. CB, III.12; IX.33. Guillaume de Machaut, *Poésies lyriques*, ed. V. Chichmaref (Paris, 1909): XX (35); XXII (37); LXIII (77); CLXI (133). And see J. L. Lowes, *Anglia*, XXXIII (1910), 440.

17. CB, VIII.23; XVII.11; XXIII.3; XXVIII.16; etc. *Oeuvres Complètes de Eutasche Deschamps*, ed. G. Raynaud, 11v (1878–1903): DXXVIII (III. 363); DXXX (III.366); DXXXII (III.368); DCCLXV (IV.259), one of the flower and leaf balades; etc. Grandson, Recueil de Paris, IV.5; V.9; XI.11; XXII.49–50. Reference to A. Piaget, *Oton de Grandson* (1949). It is interesting to note that an "Otto de Grandisson" died in 1364 seised of land upon which he paid quitrent to St. Mary Overeys: London, Guildhall, Calendar of Escheat Rolls (m.48), p. 77.

18. See F. N. Robinson's note on PF, line 680.

19. Deschamps CCCCXVII (III.220).

20. Machaut XXXIV (48).

21. Grandson, Recueil de Neuchatel, XXVII; and Robinson's note to LGW, F 249.

22. I leave to those expert in prosody judgment as to the merit of Gower's technical proficiency in French verse. Macaulay 1.lxxiv observed that he combined English stress and French syllabic verse, varying the caesura more freely than was customary with French poets. Macaulay's examples in the chapter on Gower in the CHEL (II.142) are clearer than those in the edition. Chaucer idolatry is evident in the more recent generalization by Albert Friedman: "Gower's two *balade* sequences in French . . . are dilute in thought and strained in execution—the work of a foreigner, or perhaps better, provincial, attempting a complicated verse pattern in a language whose resources are not readily at hand. He reaches for rimes with notice-able effort; the dynamics of the French balade, particularly the graceful pivoting on the central couplet in the seven-line (ababbcC) and eight-line (ababbcbC) stanzas, elude him. His balades show, however, that the French fashion was at least appreciated in England, if only indifferently practised. It remained for Chaucer to introduce the *genre* into English with his 'sov-eryn ballades' modelled on those of his admirer Deschamps," *Medium Aevum*, XXVIII (1958), 98. Gower's rhymes seem to me very easy, and Macaulay's punctuation, usually a heavier stop either in the middle or at the end of the central couplet, is evidence that he knew about "pivoting on the central couplet."

23. CB, VII.1; XXI.5; XXIIII.6; XXXI.5 (fine force amer); XXXVII.2; XLVII.2, 15; and MO, 28968.

24. In CB the terms appear, but they are not personified, cf. *danger* in CB, XII.8 and XXIII.10. Deschamps DXIII (III.344); DXV (III.347), DXVII (III.349). Grandson, Recueil de Paris, x, XVII; Recueil de Neuchatel, XIII, XIV.

25. Jean Audiau, *Les Troubadours et l'Angleterre* (1927), p. 103.

26. H. T. Riley, ed., *Monumenta Gildhallae Londoniensis: Liber Custumarum*, Rolls Series (1860), Vol. II, Pt. i, p. 216; trans. II, Pt. ii, p. 579.

27. Ibid., Pt. ii, trans., pp. 589, 590.

28. On the history of the Pui see H. T. Riley, *Liber Custumarum*, II, Pt. i, Int. xlviii; *Memorials of London Life* (1868), p. 42. The more general discussions of the Pui contain nothing beyond what they could get from Riley: Cohen, *The Ballade*, pp. 43–44; J. M. Lambert, *Two Thousand Years of Guild Life* (1891), Chap. XI; George Unwin, *The Guilds and Companies of London* (1909), p. 98; J. J. Jusserand, *A Literary History of the English People* (1895), 1.355.

29. See Dugdale, *Monasticon Anglicanum*, 6v (1846 ed.), VI. Pt. i, 169, for a list of the priors of St. Mary Overeys. On Henry le Waleys' grant to the Pui, R. R. Sharpe, ed., *Calendar of Letter-Books of the City of London, Book E* (1903), p. 1; and on his continental holdings, Charles Bemont, ed., *Rôles Gascons* (1900), II.225.

30. St. Mary Guildhall, H. A. Herben, *A Dictionary of London* (1918), p. 395.

31. P. E. Jones, ed., *Calendar of Plea and Memoranda Rolls, City of London*, VI (1959), ix–xi, etc.

32. On John Cheshunt see Riley, *Liber Custumarum*, II.1, p. 219. Thomas Chesthunte is noted in London, Guildhall, Calendar of Hustings Rolls, Roll 98 (88) [1370]. On Gravesende and Gower, above, Chap. Two, note 71.

33. Cohen, p. 33.

34. Ibid., p. 44.

35. For discussion of the MSS of the *Traitié*, see Macaulay 1.lxxxv. The balades follow the *Confessio* in MSS. 36–38, 40–41, 43, 46. They follow the Vox in MSS. 50–51. They follow the *Cinkante Balades* in Trentham. The heading in the MSS in which they do not follow the *Confessio* (51; 50 and Trentham are imperfect at the beginning) is: "Cest vn traitie quel Johan Gower ad fait selonc les auctours touchant lestat de matrimoine dont les amantz marietz se pourront essampler a tenir la foi de lour seintes espousailes."

36. G. L. Hamilton suggested that this and other passages in the balades came directly from a version of Benoit, PMLA, XX (1905), 179.

37. See the linguistic analysis in the edition of the translations by H. N. MacCracken, "Quixley's Ballades Royal (?1402)," *Yorkshire Archaeological Journal*, XX (1909), 33–51.

38. The Whixley (i.e., Quixley) Chartulary, MS abstract by Francis Collins in the Yorkshire Archaeological Society Library in Leeds, is filled with names of families found in the Gower life records: the Thwengs and Fencotes who owned land in Faceby; the Thwaytes who once owned the Fairfax

MS; most interesting of all, on 16 Oct 1382, John Forester de Quyxley gave the prior of the Dominican convent of York a certain annual rent for the personal use of Frater John de Quyxley, son of the said John Forester. Witnesses include John Mauleverer, etc. (p. 72). It is too much to suppose that this John Forester is related to the London lawyer who shared with Gower Chaucer's power of attorney, but the contents of the Stow MS. would have been a most appropriate exercise for a Dominican friar.

39. MS. B.M. Stow 951 (ca. 1440), contains folio 1, History of the Three Magi, an abridged English translation of the *Historia Trium Regum* of John of Hildesheim (d. 1375). The text is imperfect, but agrees with the second printed by C. Horstman, *The Three Kings of Cologne*, EETS (1886). Folio 32, *The Speculum Vitae*, a version of Frère Laurent's *Somme le roi*. The author, William of Nassyngton, may have been an advocate in the ecclesiastical court at York: see H. E. Allen, "Authorship of the Prick of Conscience" (Radcliffe Monographs, no. 15, 1910), p. 168. Folio 313 *Exhortacio contra vicium adulterii*, Quixley's translation.

40. 13 *May* 1328: John de Mauleverer's purchase of Quixley, YRS, XLII (1910), p. 2. For the Mauleverer arms, see *Yorkshire County Magazine*, I (1891), 112. Nicholas Gower was the ancestor of the Gowers of Stainsby, whose arms represented the Langbargh Gowers (p. 39 above); for his biography see YRS, XLI (1935), p. 90. For Roucliff connections, see Chap. Two, p. 64 above. For the Mauleverers and Gowers and Ingelby-Arncliffe, see W. Brown, *Yorkshire Archaeological Journal*, XVI (1900–01), 121.

41. See above, Chap. Two, note 36.

42. The three versions are paralleled in Appendix B from Bodl. 902 (1), first version; Bodl. 294 (37), second version; and Fairfax (40), third version. The last is printed by Macaulay 3.479, with the variants from the other two, but the complications of the variants make it difficult to reconstruct the other versions from the notes. At 4.360 Macaulay prints the colophon from All Souls (50), again the Fairfax version.

43. Macaulay 2.cxxix, note 2, includes MS. 39, and at 3.479 in the list of MSS collated he omits it. I have not had access to 39. MSS. 52–53 of the Vox have the interim version in the first paragraph and the Fairfax version in the other paragraphs.

44. Macaulay, CHEL, II.158, feels that Gower himself was responsible for the "dum vixit" in the third version of the colophon: that in this version he was addressing posterity. Significantly, however, this phrase occurs in only two of the MSS which Macaulay himself regarded as produced under Gower's direct supervision (note 8 at the end of this chapter), and the variation in these two (52–53) points strongly to a change in wording after his death (p. 101).

45. Bale gave incipits of the pieces he had seen, but merely identified the *Speculum Meditantis* from the description in the colophon, *Catalogus*, p. 525. Stow wrote, "Confessio Amantis . . . is printed. *Vox Clamantis*, with his *Cronica Tripartita*, and other, both in Latin and French, never printed, I have and do possess, but *Speculum Meditantis* I never saw, though heard thereof to be in Kent," *Survey of London*, p. 152; cf. *Annales* (1631), p. 326. In a letter kept with the Trentham MS., and in his *History*, Warton identified the *Traitié* as "Gower's *Vox Meditantis*, a French poem, with

two short epilogues in Latin verse"; Ellis noted the slip, T. Warton, *History of English Poetry* (1871 ed.), III.16 and note 2.

46. Macaulay announced the discovery and gave preliminary proof of the authorship in threee notes in *The Academy*, April 13, 1895 (p. 315); July 27, 1895 (p. 71); and August 3, 1895 (p. 91). Most of this and other evidence is to be found in the preface to the first volume of his edition, 1.xxxiv.

47. See Macaulay 1.lxix. Some accounts for work done by "Richard Eldridge" dated 1740 and 1745 have been partly cut away by the binder, and there is a reference to "Margat . . . leved at James . . . in the year of our Lord 1745 and was the dayre maid that year . . . and her swithart name was Joshep Cockhad Joshep Cockhad carpenter . . . glosterr."

48. Macaulay 1.lxix.

49. G. L. Kittredge, Review of Macaulay's edition of the *Mirour*, *Nation*, LXXI (1900), 254.

50. Dugdale, VI.170 lists MSS. B.M. Cotton, Faustina, A.viii; Cotton, Nero, c.iii; and B.M. Add. 6040; and a MS in the Stow Library, Press III, as containing records of St. Mary Overeys. The last I have not identified. Nero, c.iii is composed of 12th- and 13th-century deeds, charters, and indulgences. Add. 6040 is made up of a series of deeds and bequests, evidently from the same book as the more extensive records in Faustina, A.viii, f. 49ᵛ–119, 145ᵛ–152ᵛ, et passim. These fragments were rescued by Thomas Martin of Palsgrave from the heads of children's drums, which had been made in Exeter. The four leaves are cut roughly round and the marks of the drumhead are still to be seen. For fuller discussion of the historical materials in Faustina, see M. Tyson, *Surrey Archaeological Collections*, XXXVI (1925), p. 26.

51. See Macaulay 1.xlii. Wickert, p. 26, suggests that the reference to the Schism was inserted in revision.

52. Gardiner Stillwell, SP, XLV (1948), 454. Macaulay 1.xlii; Tatlock, *Development and Chronology of Chaucer's Works* (Chaucer Society, 1907), p. 220; Kittredge, *Date of Troilus*, p. 79, all accept these lines as referring to Alice and Edward III. B. F. Huppé, PMLA, LIV (1939), 37, cites two instances of what appears to him to be punning on the name of Alice Perrers in MO, 25575–84. After speaking of the dishonesty of goldsmiths, Gower goes on:

Je ne say dire tout pour quoy	*I cannot say*
Que j'ay oÿ sovent en coy	*why I have often heard the people*
Les gens compleindre et murmurer,	*quietly complaining,*
N'en say la cause ne ne voi,	*nor have I seen or heard the cause,*
Mais que l'en dist avoy, avoi!	*save that they say shame, shame!*
Qe sur tous autres le mestier	*That above all others,*
Des perriers est a blamer.	*the guild of jewelers is to blame.*
N'est Duc ne Conte ne Princer,	*There is no duke or count or prince,*
Voir ne le propre corps du Roy,	*not even the king himself,*
Qui s'en porront bien excuser;	*who can excuse them;*
Trestous les ad fait enginer	*They have all been trapped*
Ly perriers ove son desroy.	*by the dishonesty of the jewelers.*

(MO, 25573)

Although the behavior of jewelers is here credited with more far-reaching effects than we would consider possible, the context in which it appears and its 300-line separation from the discussion of kingship lead me to feel that Gower would be surprised to see it taken as a reference to Alice.

53. Dorothea Siegmund-Schultze, *Zeitsch. f. Anglistik und Amerikanistik*, III (1955), 6, offers a keen, persuasive discussion of the mixture of aristocratic and bourgeoisie sentiments in Gower's poems, and their consistent apology for feudalism. This tells us a good deal more about the age, however, than about the man and his art. For the evolution of the Seven Deadly Sins from monastery to market place, see Morton Bloomfield, *The Seven Deadly Sins* (1952), passim.

54. On the divine origin of the estate of merchants (almost unique in its time according to Ruth Mohl, *The Three Estates in Medieval and Renaissance Literature*, [1933], p. 278):

Dieus establist, et au bon droit,	God established rightly
Qe l'une terre en son endroit	that one country should
Del autry bien busoignera:	have need of another.
Sur quoy marchant dieus ordina,	Therefore God ordained merchants
Qui ce q'en l'une ne serra	who should search in other
En l'autre terre querre doit;	lands for what one doesn't have.
Pour ce qui bien se gardera,	Therefore one who looks to himself
Et loyalment marchandera,	and trades honestly
De dieu et homme il est benoit.	is blessed by God and man.
(MO, 25192)	

On the principle of capitalism:

La loy le voet et c'est droiture,	The law ordains and it is right
Qe qui se met en aventure	that one who puts himself in
De perdre doit auci gaigner,	danger of loss should also win
Qant sa fortune le procure:	when his good fortune procures it.
Pour ce vous dy, cil qui sa cure	Therefore, I say to you, that
Mettre voldra pour marchander,	he who ventures to trade
Et son argent aventurer,	and risk his silver
S'il gaigne, en ce n'est a blamer,	is not to be blamed if he gains,
Maisq'il le face par mesure	if he does so in measure,
Sanz fraude.	without fraud.
(MO, 25201)	

And see below, under the discussion of the Merchant in Chap. Five, p. 278.

55. D. Siegmund-S, p. 29, discusses Gower's failure to understand the principles of banking in his criticism of the Lombards. A glance through the quotations under "chevisaunce" in the *Middle English Dictionary* (University of Michigan, 1952—) shows that Gower's phrases and sentiments were shared by many of his contemporaries.

56. At MO 3337 the poor are excepted from the sin of "supplantacioun" as having nothing that envy could desire; MO, 15817, praise of poverty in connection with almsgiving; MO, 17329, natural equality in connection with marriage; MO, 23338, defense of both poverty and natural equality of the poor after condemnation of tyrants of Lombardy.

57. For Bishop Brunton of Rochester's complaints, see W. A. Pantin,

The English Church in the 14th Century (1955), p. 183. Compare *Piers Plowman* and the *Mirour*:

> Laboreres that haue no lande to lyue on but her handes,
> Deyned nou3t to dyne a-day ny3t-olde wortes.
> May no peny-ale hem paye ne no pece of bakoun,
> But if it be fresch flesch other fische fryed other bake,
> And that *chaude* or *plus chaude* for chillyng of her mawe.
>
> (Skeat ed., B.vi.309)

Les labourers d'antiquité	*The laborers in olden times*
Ne furont pas acoustummé	*were not accustomed*
A manger le pain du frument,	*to eat wheat bread,*
Ainçois du feve et d'autre blé	*but of beans or other grain*
Leur pain estoit, et abevré	*was their bread, and their*
De l'eaue furont ensement,	*drink was water,*
Et lors fuist leur festoiement	*and their festival food was*
Formage et lait, mais rerement	*cheese and milk; but only*
Si d'autre furent festoié.	*rarely did they feast.*
(MO, 26449)	

Compare Trevelyan and the *Mirour*:

> The free labourers attempted to ignore the statutes fixing their wages, and conducted strikes that were frequently but not always successful. Those who had no land of their own often emigrated to towns or manors where their illegal demands were accepted. . . . But the Justices entrusted with the enforcement of the Statute of Labourers often succeeded in keeping wages from rising as high as they would have gone in an open market. (*History of England* [1926], p. 239)

Poy font labour, mais grant soldée,	*Little was their labor but great the wages,*
Trois tant plus q'ils n'ont labouré,	*three times more than their work,*
Vuillont avoir sanz leur merit.	*that they wanted without deserving.*
Trop vait le mond du mal en pis,	*So goes the world from bad to worse*
Qant cil qui garde les berbis	*when they who guard the sheep,*
Ou ly boviers en son endroit	*or the herdsmen in their places,*
Demande a estre remeriz	*demand to be rewarded*
Pour son labour plus que jadys	*more for their labor than*
Le mestre baillif ne soloit:	*the master bailiff used to be.*
Et d' autre part par tout l'en voit,	*And on the other hand it may be seen*
Quiconque labour que ce soit,	*that whatever the work may be*
Ly labourier sont de tieu pris,	*the laborer is so expensive*
Qe qui sa chose faire en doit,	*that whoever wants anything done*
La q'om jadys deux souldz mettoit,	*must pay five or six shillings*
Ore il falt mettre cink ou sis.	*for what formerly cost two.*
(MO, 26434)	

58. See Appendix A for the list of MSS and key to Macaulay's abbreviations.

59. Macaulay 4.420. Macaulay's suggestion that this was likewise addressed to Archbishop Thomas is logical in view of "ouile regis" (sheepfold of the king), but it is odd that MS. 50, containing the dedicatory epistle to Thomas, is the only one of the four presentation MSS that does not contain this piece.

60. Macaulay 4.lxix does not note this version of the colophon, which led Maria Wickert, p. 16, to the mistaken conclusion that the early version of the colophon is not found in any of the Latin MSS.

61. See Macaulay 4.xxxi and Wickert, Chap. 1, to both of which this part of the discussion is indebted.

62. See Macaulay 4.105 and 200 for the revised passages. MS. 50 does not contain the second.

63. See below, Chap. Four, note 44.

64. See also VC, III. Prol.79; III.1269; IV.710; VI.545*; VI.577; VI.1179. Wickert, p. 72ff, discusses the *vox populi* motif as additional evidence of the relation of VC to the homiletic tradition. In MSS. 50–53, 55, beside III.375 there is a sidenote applying the criticism of the clergy's using weapons to the Bishop of Norwich's crusade of 1383. Tatlock, *Development and Chronology*, p. 187, took this as evidence that the poem was not finished before that time, but Macaulay felt (4.383) that the crusade "probably took place soon after the completion of our author's book" and the note was added to 50–53, 55, in an identical hand, "possibly that of the author himself."

65. *Historia Anglicana*, ed. H. T. Riley, Rolls Series (1863), 1.186.

66. On the part played in civil affairs by these and other clerics, see, for example, Anthony Steel, *Richard II* (1941), p. 34.

67. On Thomas of Arundel see DNB and Steel, p. 272.

68. Steel, p. 16. Steel sees the political conflict through Richard's reign as a struggle for power between the "Caesarian" civil service and "a court party of laymen looking for their shadow government to the only other educated class, the common lawyers," p. 13. Concerning the languages, Owst, *Literature and the Pulpit*, p. 4: "Until the second half of the fourteenth century, French remained the invariable tongue of the gay 'chanson de geste,' the tongue of the English law courts and of polite society in general, with Latin, of course, as the official language of the clergy." For Thomas Usk's comment on the use of these languages, see Skeat, *Oxford Chaucer*, VII.2.

69. May McKisack, *The Fourteenth Century, 1307–1399* (1959), pp. 429–437. Subservience to flatterers is a traditional failing of tyrants. John of Salisbury, *Polycraticus*, III.15, introduces tyranny first in connection with the moral dangers implicit in flattery. See Margaret Schlauch, *Speculum*, xx (1945), 133, for much background material. While the word tyrant is not mentioned in the Epistle, the failings Richard is being warned against are those commonly associated with tyrants, and are, as we shall see below (Chap. Five, p. 243), paralleled by Chaucer's own admonitions to Richard in the Prologue to the *Legend of Good Women*.

70. Steel, p. 41.

71. On Richard and counsel see below, Chap. Four, p. 183. Knighton's *Chronicon*, Rolls Series (1895), II.219, may be cited as another chronicle reference to Richard's bad counsel.

72. Schlauch, *Speculum*, xx (1945), 133. Gower repeated this convention in connection with his description of tyrants of Lombardy, MO, 23233.

73. There are three references to the King's youth and helplessness in Book I of the Vox: at 1.1075 and 1155 he is unable to prevent the murder of the Archbishop of Canterbury; at 1.1757 he is led away from the frenzied

mob by Wat Tyler. Coffman remarks in PMLA, LXIX (1954), p. 954, "There is nowhere in Book 1 the least intimation of Froissart's boy hero."

74. Thomas Wright, ed., *Political Poems and Songs*, Rolls Series (1861), 1.363–366. In the lampoon, Warwick is a "bereward"; Henry Duke of Lancaster is figured as an "eron"; the foolish populace are "gees" and "pecokes." Some of the same recognizances appear in "On the Deposition of Richard II," ibid., p. 368.

75. *Cron.* 1.63; McKisack, p. 447.

76. *Cron.* 1.77; McKisack, p. 453.

77. *Cron.* 1.121; McKisack, p. 453.

78. *Cron.* 1.131ff; McKisack, p. 454.

79. *Cron.* 1.217.

80. *Cron.* 11.22 sidenote.

81. *Cron.* 11.53; McKisack, p. 478.

82. *Cron.* 11.31; McKisack, p. 479.

83. *Cron.* 11.77; McKisack, p. 479.

84. *Cron.* 11.86; McKisack, p. 482.

85. *Cron.* 11.141; McKisack, p. 481.

86. *Cron.* 11.170, 217, 239; McKisack, p. 482; Steel, p. 234.

87. *Cron.* 11.320; Steel, p. 261.

88. *Cron.* 111.27; Steel, p. 246.

89. *Cron.* 111.73, 131; Steel, pp. 252, 263.

90. *Cron.* 111.160; Steel, p. 260.

91. *Cron.* 111.170ff; Steel, p. 265.

92. *Cron.* 111.244; Steel, p. 268.

93. *Cron.* 111.268ff; Steel, p. 279.

94. Steel, p. 273. It is worth adding, as evidence of how close Gower was to the center of things, that the Sir Arnold Savage who witnessed Gower's will was the "incomparable" speaker of the House of Commons in the crucial Parliament of 1401, DNB, s.v. Savage, Sir Arnold.

95. *Cron.* 111.268, 284, 300, 338 sidenote.

96. *Cron.* 111.400; Steel, p. 287. Gower's technical familiarity with the administrative organization of the kingdom is evidenced by his calling London the "king's chamber," i.e., private treasury: "Regis enim camera fuit urbs hoc tempore vera" *Cron.* 111.426, and see Tout, *Chapters in Administrative History* (1928), IV.319 and note 2.

97. Steel, p. 44.

98. See citations in Wickert, p. 19.

99. Usk's *Cronicon*, ed. and trans. E. M. Thompson (1904), pp. 143–144. Whether Joan actually said these words is questionable since Usk dates them 1387 and she died in 1385. But while this raises problems with regard to Miss Galway's dating of the *Legend of Good Women* (see Chap. Five, note 65), the fact that his mother's prediction of his bad end was circulating after 1387 casts light on the change in popular regard for the King. W. E. Weese, MLN, LXIII (1948), 474, deals with the various reports of Joan's speech.

1. Macaulay 4.lvii. The continuity of the two pieces is demonstrated at some length by Wickert, Chap. 1.

2. T. F. Tout, *Speculum*, IV (1929), 380, speaks of the civil servant

writers of the 14th century as the Crown's or the opposition's "publicity departments."

3. MSS of the first version of CA containing both the preliminary and final dedications and the Chaucer allusion: 2–4, 8, 10, 16, 18–22.

4. MSS of the first version of CA *lacking* initial dedication (P), final dedication (C), or both (PC): 1P, 5P, 7C, 9PC, 11C, 12PC, 13P, 14C, 15P, 17P, 23C, 24C, 25P, 26P, 27?, 28PC, 29–31?, 32PC. The question marks indicate that the MSS have been assigned to the first version but that the descriptions are not sufficiently detailed to make any judgment upon their completeness and I have not had access to them.

5. MSS of the first version of CA ending with the first version of the colophon: 1–2, 10, 13–22.

6. MSS of the first version *lacking* the final folios, which may once have ended with a colophon: 7, 9, 11, 12, 14, 23, 24, 28, 32.

7. Complete MSS of the first version of CA lacking the colophon: 3–6, 8, 26.

8. Macaulay lists all of the MSS he feels were written under Gower's own direction together in CHEL, II.512. Any scribe copying manuscripts for Gower in 1400 could easily have been writing with nearly the same script in 1425, and vice versa. Therefore any MS dated solely by execution as "early" or "first quarter" 15th century could be moved back to the last decade of the 14th. The MSS appear to me to be grouped as follows: *very fine*, usually with heavily floreated borders on pages beginning books, 33, 40, 51 (these three identified by Macaulay as from Gower's scriptorium), and 1, 3, 9, 10, 13 (dated 1432), 14, 17–21, 37, 42, 45; *fine*, but with simpler initials and illumination, Trentham, *Mirour*, 50, 52, 53 (all five identified by Macaulay as from Gower's scriptorium), and 2, 12, 15, 23, 32, 35, 41; in clearly later and/or more cursive hands, 5–8, 16, 26, 28 (commercial), 34 (commercial), 36 (good but in a different style), 44, 46, 47 (commercial).

9. MS. New College, Oxford, 326 (6) has the revised Prologue and unrevised conclusion. Its text is of the first version. Hence, although it is included in the total for the first version, it cannot be included among MSS with the original Prologue. This accounts for the difference between the thirty-one MSS discussed above, and the thirty-two mentioned here.

10. Macaulay 2.cxxxi lists MSS. 1–7 as first version textually revised; 8–15 intermediate; 17–26 unrevised. MS. 16 may be added to the intermediate category: it agrees with the unrevised readings in Book 1 and with the revised readings from there on. MS. 28 may be added to the unrevised category. MSS. 27, 29, 30, and 31 are the others not known to Macaulay. In the notices they are described as having the original introduction and conclusion, but I have been unable to ascertain their stages of revision.

11. The *anno quarto-decimo* (or *xiiij*) note is found in MSS. 33–34 of the second version and 40–41, 43, of the third.

12. Tout, *Chapters in Administrative History*, III.456.

13. Tout, III.479–482, has a circumstantial account of the quarrel. McKisack, p. 467, and Steel, p. 198, add other details.

14. See above, Chap. Two, note 90. Thrupp, *The Merchant Class of Medieval London*, p. 349, has a thumbnail sketch of Hende's career.

15. A poem by Richard de Maidstone (Wright, *Political Poems*, 1.282)

describes the elaborate pageantry of the reconciliation, in Southwark and in the city. This is summarized by Gordon Home, *Old London Bridge*, p. 96.

16. Tout, III.457.

17. Manly ed., pp. 31–32.

18. See Macaulay's notes to CA, Prol.331 and VIII.2973.

19. Macaulay 2.cxxviii. I have not seen MS. Rosenbach 369 (39), but from Macaulay's description it is difficult to see why it should be included among those of the second version. It does not contain additions 1–3, and Macaulay does not list its readings for 4 and 5. Lines 3149–81* of addition 3 are not found in MSS. 33–34, and 35 is here defective. The lines omitted in 4 are found in MS. 38.

20. In MSS. 36–38, the tale of the Jew and the Pagan is preceded by thirty-one lines (3149–80*) on the importance of pity in a ruler, another evidence of the unstable state of the intermediate version.

21. On Henry's movements see the summary in the DNB.

22. E¹ is found in MSS. 1–2, 5, 18, 20, 22, 25 of the first version. E² is found in MSS. 10, 13–17, 19, 21 of the first version, and 33, 36, 37, 45–46 of the second and third versions.

23. K. Holzknecht, *Literary Patronage in the Middle Ages* (1923), p. 147. Macaulay 2.xxiii.

24. Macaulay 2.clii has a detailed description of the MS. On Gloucester's use of the swan, see John Anstis, *The Register of the Garter* (1724), II.116.

25. See immediately above, note 19.

26. MSS. 36–39 contain the Bodley 294 version of the colophon in Appendix B.

27. Macaulay 2.cxxx and clvii.

28. Macaulay 4.346.

29. G. R. Coffman, "John Gower, Mentor for Royalty: Richard II," PMLA, LXIX (1954), 953–964. The article discusses the *Visio* in VC, the *Carmen*, and *O deus immense*. I am pleased to acknowledge again the seminal influence of this and Professor Coffman's earlier study on my understanding of the proper approach to Gower's writings.

30. Coffman, pp. 955–958 and references.

31. For comment on his reputation as a bigot, see above. The *Carmen super multiplici viciorum* is found in MSS. 36–41, 43, 50–54, 56–57.

32. G. R. Owst, *Literature and the Pulpit in Medieval England* (1933); W. A. Pantin, *The English Church in the 14th Century* (1955), on Wyclif and the doctrine of dominion, pp. 129–130.

33. Macaulay 4.355; MSS. 50, 52–54, 56.

34. Macaulay 4.358.

35. Macaulay 4.362; MSS. 50, 52–54.

36. McKisack, p. 498.

37. Horace, *Epistles* I.ii.14, but proverbial: G. Walz, *Das Sprichwort bei Gower* (1907), no. 242b. It appears again as a marginal note in CA, VII.3928.

38. Coffman, p. 962. Discussion of the charges against Richard are found in McKisack, p. 494, and Steel, p. 283.

39. Macaulay 3.481; on the text in Thynne, Macaulay 3.551.

40. For accounts of the parliamentary proceedings leading to Henry's accession, McKisack, p. 495, Steel, p. 283.

CHAPTER 4

1. See above, p. 91.

2. The reference in the last paragraph of the colophon is in Appendix B. The miniatures of the dream of Nebuchadnezzar (M^1, CA, Prol.596) and of the Lover making his confession (M^2, CA, 1.204) appear to be features of Gower's original MS. They appear as follows in the MSS: $1M^2$, $3M^{1\&2}$, $14M^{1\&2}$, $15M^2$, $16M^{1\&2}$, $18M^{1\&2}$, $19M^1$, $20M^{1\&2}$, $23M^1$ (space), $28M^1$, $33M^1$, $37M^{1\&2}$, $39M^1$, $40M^{1\&2}$, $41M^{1\&2}$. MSS. 1 and 15 have P lacking. Obviously M^1 was considered more important than M^2 in that it appeared in 19, 23, 28, 33, and 39 alone. Of this whole group, only 18 and 28 are not likely to have come from Gower's own scriptorium.

3. E. J. F. Arnould, *Manuel des péchés* (1940); C. R. Cheney, *English Synodalia of the 13th Century* (1941); and W. A. Pantin, *The English Church in the 14th Century* (1955) provide sufficient background for both the ecclesiastical and literary influences emanating from the Fourth Lateran Council.

4. John T. McNeil and Helena Gamer, *Medieval Handbooks of Penance* (1938), p. 414. Cf. the opening lines of the Penitential of Cummean (ca. 650), p. 99, and especially the selections from the Bigotian Penitential (ca. 700), p. 148. St. Jerome likewise defended his diatribes in terms of cautery and the surgeon's knife: PL, 22.473 and 954; and John Peter, *Complaint and Satire in Early English Literature* (1956), p. 20.

5. The best published discussion of this development is by D. W. Robertson, Jr., *Speculum*, XXII (1947), 162, which is based upon the fuller discussion in his unpublished dissertation, "A Study of Certain Aspects of the Cultural Tradition of *Handlyng Synne*," Univ. of North Carolina, 1945. There is also a useful distinction between the contemplative instructional treatise and the confessional manual in Father J. B. Dwyer's unpublished dissertation, "The Tradition of Medieval Manuals of Religious Instruction in the Poems of John Gower," Univ. of North Carolina, 1950, p. 130.

6. Quoted from W. F. Bryan and Germaine Dempster, eds., *Sources and Analogues of Chaucer's Canterbury Tales* (1941), p. 735.

7. Ernst Curtius lists references to the mirror metaphor in ancient and medieval literature, *Literature of the Latin Middle Ages*, trans. W. R. Trask (1953), p. 336. Sister Bradley associates the metaphor with contemplative, devotional material, JEGP, LV (1956), 624. See also Georgiana L. Morrill, *Speculum Guidonis de Warwyk*, EETS, ES, 75 (1898), p. xxii; Dwyer, p. 88; Wickert, *Studien zu John Gower*, p. 81. VC is called a *speculum*, Dedicatory Epistle, line 15; likewise *Cronica* at III.283 and 480. CA is never so designated.

8. Guilelmus Peraldus, *Summa de virtutibus* (Basle, ca. 1475), "De virginitate: Tercio commendatur" (unpaged).

9. English translations of the *Somme le roi* are discussed by W. Nelson Francis, *The Book of Vices and Virtues*, EETS, os, 217 (1942), Introduction.

10. Preface to Roxburgh Club ed. (1862), p. iv.

11. In the nearly 30,000 lines of MO, J. A. Mosher, *The Exemplum in the Early Religious and Didactic Literature of England* (1911), pp. 124–126, identified only nineteen exempla, and in VC none. While one might quibble about some of his inclusions and omissions, it is clear that these two pieces are radically different in this respect from CA.

12. Macaulay 1.xlvii.

13. R. Elfreda Fowler, *Une source française des poèmes de Gower* (1905).

14. J. B. Dwyer, SP, XLVIII (1951), p. 482.

15. Arnould, p. 7.

16. Pantin, p. 235.

17. Wickert, p. 68, in reference to Alain de Lille's *Summa de arte praedicatoria* (PL, 210), and Lecoy de la Marche, *La chaire française au Moyen Age* (1886), p. 276.

18. Quoted by T. F. Crane, *The Exempla of Jacques de Vitry* (1890), p. xxxix. A list of seventy-four *sermones vulgares* is printed pp. xlii–xlvi. G. L. Hamilton, MLN, XIX (1904), p. 51, points out two parallels between Gower and Jacques de Vitry, MO, 23449 and CA, v.6498.

19. G. R. Owst, *Literature and the Pulpit in Medieval England* (1933), p. 230; G. C. Macaulay, CHEL, II.143.

20. Owst, *Literature and the Pulpit*, pp. 292, 564.

21. Owst, *Literature and the Pulpit*, pp. 558, 564.

22. Ewart Lewis, *Medieval Political Ideas*, 2v (1954), 1.319.

23. "Et ideo joh. respondit de seipso: Ego vox clamantis in deserto. Non solum joh. sed quilibet predicator ydoneus vox Christi per ipsum clamantis dicitur," John Waldeby's Sermons, MS. Bodl. 687, f 84; quoted from Wickert, p. 66, note 3. Wickert has a full discussion of the liturgical and homiletic parallels, pp. 65–86.

24. "Praedicatio Joannis commendatur primo quo ad exigentiam populi tripliciter.—Quantum ad primum notandum, quod secundum triplicem differentiam personarum audientium diversas instructiones administrat: primo, ad turbas, quae gerunt personam subditorum; secundo, ad publicanos, qui gerunt personam ministrorum; tertio, ad milites, qui gerunt personam rectorum sive praepositorum," St. Bonaventura, *Commentarium in Evangelium Lucae, Opera* (1895), VII.75.

25. The miniature and four lines of commentary may have been inserted in the revision of VC. They do not occur in MSS. 58 and 59, the unrevised versions; they are found just after the contents in 51, 52, and 54 (reproduced from 54 as a frontispiece in Macaulay, vol. 4). The pages on which they would occur are missing from the revised MSS. 50 and 53. In the problem MS. 56, the miniature and verses come at the beginning of VC, III. See p. 101 above, and Wickert, p. 79.

26. Wickert, pp. 83–86.

27. Wickert, p. 90.

28. *Ex Ponto* and *Tristia*, ed. A. L. Wheeler (Loeb, 1924); *Fasti*, ed. J. G. Frazer (Loeb, 1931); *Heroides* and *Amores*, ed. G. Showerman (Loeb, 1914).

29. These statistics are based on the notes in Eric Stockton's translation

of VC in which many more borrowed lines are identified than in Macaulay's edition. For statistics and further discussion see Stockton, p. 27.

30. Paul E. Beichner, *Speculum*, xxx (1955), 582.

31. Beichner, p. 592.

32. Robert Raymo, MLN, LXX (1955), p. 315, and J. H. Mozley and Robert Raymo, eds. *Nigel de Longchamps' Speculum Stultorum* (1960), text and notes.

33. Parallels are indicated in Macaulay's notes, and the text is in T. Wright, *The Anglo-Latin Satirical Poets* (1872), II.175.

34. Macaulay's references are to the 1584 and 1726 editions of the *Pantheon*. Gower's allusions are to the earlier portions listed in the "Particulae" which are omitted from the historical portions printed in the *Monumenta Germaniae historica: Scriptorum*, XXII (1872), p. 107. On Godfrey himself see F. J. E. Raby, *A History of Christian Latin Poetry*, (1927), p. 291.

35. CA, VIII.271 and Macaulay's note.

36. See the new parallel uncovered by Robert Raymo, MLN, LXXI (1956), p. 82.

37. John Peter, *Complaint and Satire in Early English Literature* (1956), traces the development of complaint in medieval English literature. Although he recognizes that "From the thirteenth century until Nashe's time the whole genre virtually stands still and the same themes come up again and again" (p. 58), he does not relate this to the influence of the Fourth Lateran Council. His failure to include the Seven Deadly Sins in the analysis of the moral themes of complaint (Chap. 4) makes his classification more miscellaneous than it need be.

38. The term *civil law* is found in MO at 4731, 9093, 14138, 15193, 15217, 16092, 17140, 19114, 22266, 23748, 26365; in VC at III.2105; in CA at II.83.

39. "To do right to poor and rich" is a common formula in legal writs, see Chap. Five, note 71.

40. *The Digest*, Book XXII, Title vi, #7 and #9 (Scott v.239). References to the *Corpus juris civilis* are to S. P. Scott, ed. and trans., *The Civil Law*, 17v (1932). On the doctrine of laches, including this sentence and others like it, see *Bouvier's Law Dictionary*, s.v. "laches."

41. *Justinian Code*, Book IV, Title lxiii (Scott XIII.125); Book x, Title xxxi, #34 (Scott XV.118): Book XI, Title ix, #4 (Scott, XV.175); Book XII, Title xxxvi, #13–16 (Scott XV.281).

42. Macaulay, note to CA, II.83.

43. For discussion of the convention see John A. Yunck, *American Bar Association Journal*, XLVI (1960), 267.

44. Similar disclaimers are found at MO, 18448 (Pope); 19059 (Prelates); 21183 (Friars).

45. The tradition of commentary on the law's being compiled under the pretext of an attack upon false judges is found in both the 14th-century *Mirour of Justices* and late 13th-century *Fleta seu commentarius juris Anglicani*, which purport to have been written by authors falsely imprisoned. F. W. Maitland discusses the tradition, *Mirror of Justices*, Selden Society (1895), p. xxii.

46. *Summa theologica*. Latin from *Opera omnia impensaque Leonis XIII*, 16v (Rome 1882–1948); English trans. Anton C. Pegis (1945), ɪa, ɪɪae, 91, 1–3; ɪa, ɪɪae, 95, 1–3 (Lewis, 1.48, 56).

47. References for the devil as fowler are cited by D. W. Robertson, MLN, ʟxɪx (1954), 470.

48. *Institutions*, Book ɪ, Title ii (Scott, ɪɪ.5); Gratian, *Concordantium Discordantium Canonum*, Distinction vɪɪɪ, Canon ɪɪ (Lewis, 1.35).

49. A. O. Lovejoy, *The Great Chain of Being* (1936), Chaps. ɪɪ and ɪɪɪ.

50. The conflict between eros and morality, and the influence of the school of Chartres are discussed by Curtius, pp. 106, 112, 122, etc. E. C. Knowlton, MLN, xxxɪx (1924), 89, discusses the inconsistency of Gower's personification of Genius.

51. *Roman de la rose*, ed. Ernest Langlois, 5v (SATF, 1914–24), line 19505. *The Romance of the Rose*, trans. Harry W. Robbins (1962), p. 413.

52. Lovejoy's best quotations on this topic come from Robert Fludd in the 17th century (op. cit., p. 94), but the principle of sterility and vacuity opposing fecundity and plenitude was familiar: for example, the symbolism of Dante's frozen Judecca and the garden atop Purgatory.

53. Willard Farnham, *The Medieval Heritage of Elizabethan Tragedy* (1956 ed.), p. 15. Cf. Boethius, *Consolation of Philosophy*, ɪɪɪ, pr. 12. The first six chapters of Wyclif's *De civili dominio* begin the argument that the unrighteous have no right to lordship from the starting point of the negativity of evil. St. Augustine had, of course, regarded evil as a negation, *De civitate Dei*, xɪɪ.6–7.

54. At MO 2092 Adam's sin is the cause of serfdom (cf. Augustine, *De civitate Dei*, xɪx.15, which reflects the notions of *lex gentium* in the *Corpus*); at VC, vɪɪ.620, all sin is derived from Adam; at VC, vɪɪ.68 and frequently elsewhere, man's sin is the cause of all ill in the world; at CA, Prol.1005, division in society is the result of sin.

55. J. M. Steadman, MLN, ʟxxɪɪɪ (1958), p. 83; N&Q, vɪ (1959), 367. For similar parallels between Milton and Prudentius, see Ann Grossman, N&Q, ccɪɪ (1957), 439.

56. G. L. Kittredge, *Nation*, ʟxxɪ (1900), 254; J. S. P. Tatlock, MLN, xxɪ (1906), 239. Milton refers to CA twice: on the donation of Constantine (CA, ɪɪ.3475) in "An Apology Against A Pamphlet Call'd A Modest Confutation, etc.," *Columbia Milton*, ɪɪɪ, 1 (1931), p. 359; and on the lawfulness of crusades, evidently CA, ɪɪɪ.2488, although the allusion is not clear, in the "Commonplace Book," ed. cit., xvɪɪɪ (1938), p. 21.

57. For general history and references, Owst, *Literature and the Pulpit*, p. 93. The origin of the story was studied by Paul Myer, *Romania*, xxɪx (1900), 54, and is mentioned by Morton Bloomfield, *The Seven Deadly Sins* (1952), p. 397. Bloomfield (p. 423) denies the suggestion of J. L. Lowes, PMLA, xxɪx (1914), p. 388, that the marriage procession may have influenced Spenser's procession of the Seven Deadly Sins in Canto ɪv, Book ɪ, of the *Faerie Queen*.

58. Opusc. xxxv, *De duobus praeceptis charitatis et decem legis praeceptis*, opening lines; translated by Thomas Gilby, *St. Thomas Aquinas, Philosophical Texts* (1960), p. 325.

59. St. Thomas, "Conscience is the dictate of reason, the application of theory to practice," *Summa*, ia, iiae, 19, 5 (Gilby, p. 291).

60. Rufinius, *Summa decretorum*, ed. H. Singer (1902), p. 4 (Lewis, i. 37). On the association of *ratio* with *virtus* see Dorothea Siegmund-Schultze, *Wiss. Zeitsch. de Martin-Luther Univ.*, Halle-Wittenberg, viii, 4–5 (1959), 757.

61. See R. W. and A. J. Carlyle, *Mediaeval Political Theory*, 6v (1903), 1.8–9, with quotations from Cicero's *De Legibus*.

62. *Summa*, iia, iiae, 64, 2, ad 3. In Opusc. xi, *De Regimine Principum*, Cap. i, Aquinas sets man above animals on the basis of reason (Lewis, 1.7, 51, 175).

63. For Grosseteste, see Steadman, N&Q, vi (1959), 367. Bloomfield, *The Seven Deadly Sins*, Appendix 1, gives a list of the various animals associated with each sin.

64. On Gower and astrology see T. O. Wedel, *The Medieval Attitude Toward Astrology* (1920), p. 132. In the medieval apothegm "vir sapiens dominabitur astris," *vir sapiens* came to be taken as the man who could by reason control his lower nature which was under the influence of the stars. Although this concept would have supported Gower's treatment of reason, here and elsewhere he altered it to the religious man who can by prayers avert fate. It is interesting to note that at CA, vii.670, is to be found the first Isidorian distinction between astrology and astronomy in English.

65. From Gregory, *Hom. in Evang.* ii.39 (PL, 76.1214). Found at MO, 26869, VC, vii.639, CA, Prol.945. Aquinas has approximately the same scale of being in *Summa contra gentiles*, Cap. iv. (Gilby, p. 182). This was a favorite passage for analysis by the Chartrian scholastics, cf. J. M. Parent, *La doctrine de la création dans l' école de Chartres* (1938), p. 30. Boethius, *Consolation*, v, pr. iv–v, reflects the classical glorification of reason.

66. The pastiche of quotations from which the *Visio* is constructed has been suggested already. Wickert, p. 33, finds an Ovidian mood of despair which accords well with the lines borrowed, and she points out that dream visions of a pleasant sort generally occurred by day and nightmares by night.

67. Macaulay, VC, 1.941 note; T. F. Tout, *Chapters in Mediaeval Admistrative History*, 6v (1920–33), iv.46.

68. See above, p. 98.

69. Wickert, p. 47. The ship and castle figures were both favorites in the sermons, cf. Owst, *Literature and the Pulpit*, pp. 69, 72, 83. St. Thomas, *De Regimine Principum*, Cap. i and ii. Gower called the church "The schip which Peter hath to Stiere" (CA, v.1872); and "Petres schip" (*In Praise of Peace*, line 230); cf. VC, iii.1251.

70. Kenneth Sisam, *Fourteenth Century Verse and Prose* (1921), p. 158.

71. Wickert, p. 50.

72. Wickert, p. 62.

73. For discussion and references see Pantin, pp. 183–184; Lewis, 1.142; A. Dampf, *Ethik des Mittelalters* (1927), p. 68.

74. Owst, *Literature and the Pulpit*, p. 551.

75. Carlyle, 1.4.

76. Aristotle, *Politica*, iii, 13.1283^{b}, trans. Benjamin Jowett, vol. 10 (1921).

77. Lewis, s.v. "common good" in the index.

78. Hope Emily Allen, *Writings Ascribed to Richard Rolle* (1927), p. 176, note 1. On John Ball, G. G. Coulton, *Medieval Panorama* (1938), p. 80. On the responsible state, M. E. Temple, *Romanic Review*, IV (1915), 402.

79. Carlyle, 1.ii.22.

80. St. Augustine, *De civitate Dei*, XIX.17, finds a natural hierarchy, with soul, father, and king, respectively, at the apex.

81. Wickert, p. 122 and refs., for discussion of Gower's ethical basis for kingship. Owst, *Literature and the Pulpit*, p. 565, for discussion of this theme in the sermons. Pantin, pp. 129–130, shows that the concept of dominion by grace is both papal and Wycliffite.

82. *De Regimine*, III.ii.29 (Lewis, 1.291).

83. The significance of the parallels between Gower and Chaucer will be discussed in the next chapter. The distinction between the prince and the tyrant evidently stems in medieval thought from John of Salisbury, *Policraticus*; see Lewis, 1.276.

84. On the role of fortune, Carlyle, 1.ii, 22; Lester K. Born ed., *Erasmus' Education of a Prince* (1936), p. 84. On the role of virtue, St. Augustine, *Enarrationes in Psalmos*, IX.8 (*Corpos Christianorum*, Series Lat. vol. 38 [1956]) states that the king is not to be chosen from the oldest, or richest, or bravest of the citizens, but from the best. Lewis cites many medieval developments of this idea, s.v. "sacred character of kingship," in her index.

85. Cf. Tertullian, *Liber de Poenitentia*, XII–XIII (PL, 1.1248, 1269).

86. Bracton: *De legibus et consuetidunibus Angliae*, 4v, ed. G. E. Woodbine (1915–42), II.305 (Lewis, 1.282).

87. Gardiner Stillwell, SP, XLV (1948), 454, argues that "pastour" has political signifiance, see above, Chap. Three, p. 96.

88. The general subject of Richard II and counsel is treated by A. B. Ferguson, *Studies in the Renaissance*, II (1955), 67. Gardiner Stillwell lists references to Richard's bad counsel, *Speculum*, XIX (1944), 433.

89. On the medieval concept of the king's superiority to law, see Lewis, 1.246, 269.

90. *Commentorium in Apocalypsin*, Cap. vii (PL, 100.1129). Cf. Rupertus Abbatus, PL, 167.1505.

91. *De statu interioris hominis* (PL, 196.1266–73).

92. *Vivat rex* (1405), quoted by Temple, p. 420.

93. C. S. Lewis, *The Allegory of Love* (1936), p. 200, remarks that the Middle Ages knew Empedocles. But Gower, like Chaucer, no doubt found a more immediate source for this concept of universal love in Boethius, *Consolation*, Book II, met. viii.

94. J. A. W. Bennett, *The Parlement of Foules* (1957), p. 34.

95. The concepts of nature as "being" or "becoming" were central to the Chartrian interpretations of Plato's *Timaeus*. Discussions are to be found in Parent, passim, and Bennett, p. 195.

96. The English versions of the *Secreta Secretorum*, ed. R. Steele, EETS, ES, 74 (1898), pp. 97, 208.

97. Cf. Macaulay's notes to CA, VII, on p. 521. G. L. Hamilton, MP, IX (1911), 323, and A. H. Gilbert, *Speculum*, III (1928), 84, argue from

parallel passages that Gower knew the *Secretum* in a Latin version and perhaps also in the French translation of Jofroi de Waterford.

98. William Holdsworth, *A History of English Law*, 9v (1953 ed.), III. 457.

99. Wickert, p. 134.

1. See, for example, the discussion of the behavior of the Earl of Oxford and the Court party in Anthony Steel's *Richard II* (1941), p. 112.

2. Steele, ed. p. 129.

3. The tale of the Pagan and the Jew (CA, VII.3207*) in some of the second recension MSS is from the *Secretum* (see Macaulay's note, p. 532). And the English versions advocate mercy (Steele, ed., pp. 17, 18, 61, 142, 180). Wickert, p. 135, asserts that the *Secretum* advocates brutal methods of rule.

4. Wickert, p. 120, sees some influence by Cassiodorus upon Gower's view of kingship, a notion I should like to embrace for the support that it would give the legalistic interpretation of Gower's thought. However, the three quotations appear to be quite miscellaneous, as if they were picked from other contexts: "Pietas custodit imperium" from *Varia*, XII.13, here at CA, VII.3161, previously at MO, 13920 and 23059, and apparently adapted in "wher that pite reigneth, there is grace," PP. 331; "all other virtue dies if it is not guided by civility (*maniere*)," not located in Cassiodorus' works, but attributed to him at MO, 11770; similarly "he who opposes law intends to destroy all authority" at MO, 24592.

CHAPTER 5

1. W. W. Skeat, ed., *Oxford Chaucer*, 7v (2 ed., 1899), III.413.

2. R. K. Root, *The Poetry of Chaucer* (2 ed., 1922), p. 17. Similar views are expressed in his edition of *Troilus and Criseyde* (1926), p. xlv.

3. J. L. Lowes, *Geoffrey Chaucer and the Development of His Genius* (1934), p. 129.

4. M. W. MacCallum, *Chaucer's Debt to Italy* (1931), p. 25.

5. Chanoine Looten, *Revu de littérature comparée*, v (1925), 545. Mario Praz, *The Flaming Heart* (1958), pp. 23, 31, etc.

6. A recent elaborate treatment of the relation between Chaucer's poetry and religious thought is in D. W. Robertson, Jr., *A Preface to Chaucer* (1962), Chaps. iv–v.

7. John Peter, *Complaint and Satire in Early English Literature* (1956), pp. 9–10.

8. Peter remarks: "The Elizabethans failed to make the distinction between Complaint and Satire, lumping together the pagan ferocity of Juvenal at his most bitter with the Christian gravity and indignation of Langland," p. 109.

9. The futility of attempting to gauge indebtedness by the verbal commonplaces in these poems is revealed by the eleven parallels adduced by E. Koeppel, *Englische Studien*, xx (1895), 154. Actually many others, some closer than Koeppel's, could be cited, but they are still commonplaces.

10. See the chronology in F. N. Robinson ed., *The Works of Chaucer* (2 ed., 1957), p. xxix. All quotations from Chaucer are from this edition.

The scholars who argue that the *Parliament* celebrates Richard's betrothal to Marie of France in 1377 (e.g., H. Brady, in *Three Chaucer Studies* [1932], no. ii), and the *House of Fame* his betrothal to Ann of Bohemia in 1380 (e.g., A. Brusendorff, *The Chaucer Tradition* [1925], p. 161, and Margaret Galway, MLR, XLIV [1949], 171) would have them in the other order.

11. R. J. Allen, JEGP, LV (1956), 393. R. A. Pratt's discussion of Chaucer's poetic adaptation of Boccaccio's more scholarly attempts to recreate the past supports Allen's thesis, PMLA, LXII (1947), 621.

12. This view of Dante's artistic development is put forward by Umberto Cosmo, *A Handbook of Dante Studies*, trans. David Moore (1950), passim.

13. *The Divine Comedy of Dante Alighieri*, trans. Charles Eliot Norton, 3v (1902 ed.).

14. H. R. Patch in Robinson's note, p. 786. J. S. P. Tatlock, *Development and Chronology of Chaucer's Works*, Chaucer Society (1907), p. 38.

15. Margaret Galway, MLR, XLIV (1949), 171, identifies the eagle with Richard's tutor, Sir Simon Burley, but the relationship between Chaucer and the eagle is more personal and the theme of the poem more intellectual than she allows.

16. Allen and Root as above. R. C. Goffin suggested that the "newe tydynges" of line 1886 are "the common experiences of men," *Medium Aevum*, XII (1943), 44.

17. A. Dinaux, *Les trouvères de nord de la France*, 4v (1837–63), IV.51, on the creative cycle of medieval poets: "Poets in their youth begin by singing of love and its delights; later they choose to versify the anecdotes, histories, and animal fables of their country; finally, in old age and infirmity, they turn to sacred and philosophical themes," cited by G. R. Owst, *Literature and the Pulpit in Medieval England* (1933), p. 469. The sentiments of the Wife of Bath (CT, III.688) should be recalled at this point. George R. Stewart, Jr., in *University of California Publications in English*, 1 (1929), 106; R. S. Loomis, in *Studies in Medieval Literature in Honor of A. C. Baugh*, ed. MacEdward Leach (1961), p. 30.

18. The original for line 46 runs: "Omnibus qui patriam conservarint, adiuverint, auxerint, certum esse in caelo definitum locum, ubi beati aevo sempiterno fruantur." For line 73: "Hanc [naturam] tu exerce in optimis rebus; sunt autem optimae curae de salute patriae." Cited from Skeat's notes, pp. 506, 508.

19. Chaucer's lovely rendering of the opening lines of *Inferno* II, "The day gan faylen and the derke nyht,/ That reveth bestes from here besynesse . . ." (85), as well as the opening lines of *Purgatorio* IX introducing the eagle in the *House of Fame* may have been echoed when Gower added the *Visio* to the *Vox Clamantis*: "Tempus erat quo cuncta silent, quo mente sopita/ In vaga nonnulla sompnia corda ruunt" (VC, 1.151). There is no evidence that Gower himself read Italian, but he adds an anecdote about Dante in the intermediate version of CA (VII.2329*), and Tatlock felt that MO, 3931–34 quoted *Inferno*, XIII.64–66 (*Development and Chronology*, p. 221). He, Lowes (PMLA, XXIII [1908], 305), and Kittredge, (*The Date of Troilus and Criseyde*, Chaucer Society [1909], p. 76), all suggest that

knowledge of these passages and knowledge of the tyrants of Lombardy came to Gower through Chaucer.

20. In the Chaucerian translation, line 923. *Le Roman de la rose*, ed., E. Langlois, 5v (SATF, 1914–24), line 908; *The Romance of the Rose*, trans. H. W. Robbins (1962), 4.98.

21. Langlois, line 6813; Robbins, 34.129.

22. Charles O. McDonald, *Speculum*, xxx (1955), 444; J. A. W. Bennett, *The Parlement of Foules* (1957), p. 64.

23. The phrase is from Dorothy Bethurum, PMLA, LXXIV (1959), 551.

24. R. H. Green, *Speculum*, XXXI (1956), 649, comments on earlier scholarship and explicates Alan's poem.

25. See Robinson, pp. 669, 674, for a summary of the discussion about the date. He is inclined to place "Palamon" before *Troilus*. Tatlock, *Development and Chronology*, p. 70, and Pratt, PMLA, LXII (1947), 608, advance cogent reasons for placing it between *Troilus* and LGW.

26. In Boccaccio's version, Teseo is an epic hero whose personality and deeds are the core of the poem, and his chief function is managing the marriage of Emilia: Pratt, PMLA, LXII (1947), 601. The importance of Theseus in Chaucer's version has been stressed by William Frost, RES, xxv (1949), 289; and Charles Muscatine, PMLA, LXV (1950), 911.

27. Gower, who next used the term "Femenye" in English (CA, v.2548; cf. MED), picked it up either from Chaucer or directly from his French sources.

28. Here is a pastiche of admonitions in Gower's Epistle: (VC, VI.733) Spurn the wicked, cherish the wise, curb the rebellious, give to the unfortunate, cast aside the criminal, have mercy upon the condemned. Whatever you do, your integrity should never be plunged into vice. Your reputation should be placed above money, and your duty above your affairs. You should contrive nothing for the sake of this world, O King, whereby you would be reputed as just among nobles, but guilty before God. . . . (741) When you resolve to attend the complaints of the pauper and the widow, you should carry out judgment upon the wretched with compassion. Sometimes it is better to remit the decree of the laws lest mercy vanish because of your severity. So let your honor deem it fitting to be lenient with your subjects. . . . (755) When necessity calls upon you to transact the business of the realm, let one old man with another govern your counsel. . . . (853) Above all, O King, avoid letting blind lust of the flesh arouse you toward its allurements. Instead, you as a husband should enjoy your own wife according to law, and not deprive your holy marriage of honorable praise. . . . (917) It is also your concern, O King, to be your people's defender in arms. . . . (1158 headnote) Here he briefly brings the King's letter to an end. He says that just as a king shall strive to elevate himself through the prerogatives of his privileged status, and hence rule magnificently in the eyes of the people, so shall he present himself as humble and just in the eyes of God.

29. R. A. Pratt, PMLA, LXII (1947), 598–621, provides a full comparison between Boccaccio's and Chaucer's versions.

30. Pratt notes (loc. cit., p. 612) that the Knight's Tale is different in effect from the *Teseida*: "classical allusions are reduced to a minimum; the heroine is virtually uncharacterized; the amorous psychology is pretty much

subdued. These modifications of the *Teseida* were presumably warranted by Chaucer's conception of the story as a simple but colorful romance; yet one may ask why the poet decided upon a treatment so different from that of Boccaccio." The answer might be that he was intent upon bringing out the legal and regal implications of the plot.

31. The round lists were adapted from Boccaccio's marble colosseum, but Chaucer's conscious microcosmic adaptation is suggested by his attaching to the lists the three temples which in the *Teseida* were scattered about Athens: Pratt, PMLA, LXII (1947), 600, 617. Magoun, *Med. Stud.*, xv (1953), 111, compares the shape and structure of the lists to Roman circuses.

32. Muscatine, PMLA, LXV (1950), p. 929.

33. *Nicomachean Ethics*, end of Book 1; quoted from Benjamin Rand, *The Classical Moralists* (1909), p. 65. Root calls the dedicatees "a poet-moralist and a learned professor of philosophy," (*Troilus*, p. xlviii). Perhaps Chaucer's addition of the name of "Sophie" to that of "Prudence" in *Melibee* reflects the same tradition.

34. *Summa*, 1a, 11ae, 58, 3.

35. Tatlock and Kennedy, *Concordance to the Complete Works of Chaucer* (1927). In addition to the forty-four instances in Chaucer's poetry, "philosophical" appears nineteen times in *Boece* and one time in the *Romaunt of the Rose*.

36. On the learning in *Troilus* see Root ed., p. xli.

37. *Testament of Love*, Skeat, *Oxford Chaucer*, VII.123.

38. OED, s.v. "moral." Cicero first used the word in *De Fato*, 11.i; St. Thomas repeated the definition of *mos* in *Summa*, Quaestio LVIII, Article 1 (Rand, p. 196). By 1267 *moralis* already implied "moral philosopher": Baxter and Johnson, *Medieval Latin Word List* (1934), s.v. "moral." But the real flowering of moral philosophy came with the rationalism of the Enlightenment: Grotius, Hobbes, Kant, and the Scottish "common sense" philosophy. For a discussion of moral philosophy as the core of the arts curriculum in 19th-century Scottish universities, see G. E. Davis, *The Democratic Intellect* (1961): for the effect of Scottish moral philosophy on American education and the American novel, Terence Martin, *The Instructed Vision* (1961). The repudiation of this curriculum, as well as the supposed naïveté and hypocrisy of Victorian morality, have no doubt played their part in reducing the epithet "moral," which Gower himself and commentators in the succeeding three centuries thought complimentary, to a half contemptuous imputation of conventionality and obtuseness. Thus the very history of Western morals has forged another link in the chain of *ad hominem* criticism by which Gower's literary reputation has been weighed down.

39. J. S. P. Tatlock, SP, XVIII (1921), 424.

40. The case for determinism was best made by W. C. Curry, PMLA, XLV (1930), 129; that for Christian tragedy by D. W. Robertson, Jr., ELH, XIX (1952), 1.

41. See Root's discussion of the moral import of *Troilus*, op. cit., p. xlviii.

42. Blind Bayard as a type of the blind lover is referred to at CA, VI.1280.

43. Love's compulsion upon fish, fowl, beast, and man is referred to at CA, VI.1264.

44. The theme of mutability, frequent in both Chaucer and Gower, is well phrased later in the *Confessio:* "I se the world stonde evere upon eschange,/ Nou wyndes loude, and nou the weder softe . . ." (VIII.2259).

45. The mounting emphasis upon Fortune and Destiny can be demonstrated statistically. Fortune is referred to four times in Book I, twice in Book II, three times in III, *eleven* times in IV, and six times in V. Destiny is referred to once in I, II, III, V, and *twice* in IV.

46. J. S. P. Tatlock, MP, I (1903), 317. J. L. Lowes, PMLA, xx (1905), 823. Lowes, arguing for the 1383–85 date which has come to be generally accepted, discusses other sources for Gower's knowledge of the story. Tatlock reargued his case vigorously in *Development and Chronology*, p. 15. R. A. Pratt cites the evidence that Chaucer worked from the French, SP, LIII (1956), 509.

47. L. Moland and C. D. Héricault, *Nouvelles françoises en prose du XIVe siècle* (1858), Int., cxxxv.

48. Creseide: MO, 5255. Criseide: CA, v.6444, v.7597, VIII.2531. Crisaida: VC, VI.1325. Criseida: CA, II.2456.

49. Margaret Galway, MLR, XLIV (1949), 161.

50. Little is known about the cult of the flower and the leaf. G. L. Kittredge, MP, I (1903), 1, suggested without evidence that it reflected the existence in the court of two amorous orders introduced by the young queen. G. L. Marsh, MP, IV (1906), 121, 281, gathered many more literary allusions but no more historical evidence.

51. The underlying fiction of sins against love was, of course, a convention. Cf. Brusendorff, *The Chaucer Tradition*, p. 140, for examples in Machaut, Jean de Meun, etc.

52. On the literature seeking to identify the characters and occasion see Robinson's notes, pp. 839ff.

53. Chaucer's only other direct address to royalty is in the *Complaint to his Purse*, see Chap. Three, p. 132 above.

54. Lydgate spoke of both the religious coloring of the *Legend* and its connection with the Queen: "[Chaucer] wrot, at request off the queen,/ A legende off perfite hoolynesse,/ Off Goode women to fynde out nynteen," *Fall of Princes*, EETS, OS, 121 (1924), p. 10. Tyrwhitt first pointed out the connection with the Queen implied by the reference to Eltham and Sheene. On subsequent scholarship see Tatlock, *Development and Chronology*, p. 102. Lowes argued that the references to the residences did not connect the piece with Ann, PMLA, xix (1904), 593, and MP, VIII (1910), 331, 334 notes.

55. As with the twenty-nine pilgrims in the *Canterbury Prologue*, the total of nineteen takes special figuring. It simply cannot be arrived at in the F version which names the following (those also named by Gower are in italics): 1) Ester, 2) *Penalopee*, 3) Marcia Catoun, 4) *Ysoude*, 5) *Eleyne*, 6) Lavyne, 7) *Lucresse*, 8) *Polixene*, 9) *Cleopatre*, 10) *Tisbe*, 11) Herro, 12) *Dido*, 13) Laudomia, 14) *Phillis*, 15) *Canace*, 16) Ysiphile, 17) Ypermestre, 18) Adriane. Ester, included in this total, is not properly one of the "good women," but like Absolon and Jonathan a scriptural type for a special virtue. In the G version *Alceste's* name is added in the refrain, bringing the total in the balade to nineteen. But the problem has not yet been solved,

since the nineteen were supposed to be *following* Alceste and the god of love. Gower added to those he had in common with Chaucer: Gunnore (Guinevere), Creusa (Jason's love instead of Ysiphile), Phedra, Eseonen, Pantaselee, Criseide, Deyanire, Deÿdamie, and Alcione. It would be pleasant to support the date of 1385 and the number nineteen with Bilderbeck's observation (*Chaucer's Legend of Good Women* [1902], p. 90) that in 1385 Queen Ann was nineteen. But in that case what are we to do with Gower's twenty-one?

56. For a summary, see Robinson's notes, pp. 839–841. M. Bech, *Anglia*, v (1882), 365, made the first comparison arguing that Gower imitated Chaucer. Kittredge, MP, I (1903), 1, building upon suggestions by Tyrwhitt and Sandras, first discussed the relation between LGW and Deschamps' flower and leaf poems, nos. 764–767, and suggested without evidence the existence of a court fashion introduced by the young queen. G. L. Marsh, MP, IV (1906), 121, 281, printed Deschamps' balades as well as a good many more references to the cult postdating Chaucer and Gower; he is alone in his denial that CA, VIII.2453, referred to the flower and leaf convention (p. 134). J. L. Lowes, PMLA, XIX (1904), 593; XX (1905), 802, pointed out the parallels between LGW and *Lai de franchise* and *Paradys d'amour*. See notes below for some of the dissenting opinions.

57. Tatlock, *Development and Chronology*, p. 96; Lowes, PMLA, XX (1905), 782; Kittredge, PMLA, XXIV (1909), 343; Griffith, *Manly Anniversary Studies* (1923), p. 40.

58. So suggested by Tatlock, *Development and Chronology*, p. 110.

59. The most extended argument is by W. O. Sypherd, *Studies in Chaucer's House of Fame* (1907), p. 25. Marian Lossing, SP, XXXIX (1942), 15, continues the demonstration in her argument that Chaucer did not need to know the *Lai*, and R. M. Estrich, SP, XXXVI (1939), 20, in connection with his argument that Chaucer was influenced by the *Jugement dou Roy de Navarre*.

60. Tatlock, SP, XVIII (1921), 419.

61. See the full comparison by Estrich, loc. cit. The poet's vindicating himself against the displeasure of the god of love is conventional. In Froissart's *Tresor amoureux* (Scheler ed., II.52), Amour commands the poet to keep a record of his experiences. Of course, in VC a divine voice commands Gower to write down his *Visio* of the Peasants' Revolt (1.2147).

62. Lowes, PMLA, XX (1905), 749. For text and translation of Deschamps' balade see J. M. Manly, ed., *Chaucer's Canterbury Tales* (1928), p. 22.

63. Skeat, *Oxford Chaucer*, III.139; Tatlock, SP, XVIII (1921), 419; H. Lange, *Anglia*, XLIX (1925), 173. W. G. Dodd, *Courtly Love in Chaucer and Gower* (1913), p. 218, discusses the adaptation of the legends as saints' lives.

64. Griffith, loc. cit., analyzes in detail the tempering of the religious tone between F and G. Tatlock, *Development and Chronology*, p. 114, suggested that the cult of the daisy, having been introduced to honor Queen Ann [Joan of Kent would do as well], was toned down after her death.

65. Lossing, loc. cit., pretty well demolishes Lowes' verbal parallels. Carleton Brown, MLN, LVIII (1943), 274, supports Lossing's argument

that Chaucer need not have known the *Lai* and Galway's that Alceste was Joan of Kent. The Gower parallels fit neatly into this argument for a 1385 date for LGW, but they are by no means limited to this interpretation. There were probably several occasions between 1382 and 1386 when the two poets could have been together in court.

66. *Melibee* might be considered a more direct and longer political statement if it is actually a commentary on current events: see G. Stillwell, *Speculum*, XIX (1944), 433. The balade *Lak of Stedfastnesse* is just as direct as Alceste's speech, and perhaps related to it—see below.

67. See above, Chap. Three, note 99, Galway, MLR, XLIV (1949), 174. W. E. Weese, MLN, LXIII (1948), 474, comments on the chronicle accounts of Joan's speech.

68. Bilderbeck, op. cit., p. 93, was the first to suggest that Alceste's speech was linked to the political events of 1385, although his reading of the events has been completely superseded. Lowes, PMLA, XX (1905), 778, while maintaining that the speech was aesthetically rather than politically motivated, points out some interesting parallels in Knighton's *Chronicle*. Margaret Galway, MLR, XXXVI (1941), 1, and Florence Scott, *Speculum*, XVIII (1943), 80, treat Chaucer's involvement with the Parliament of 1386. Margaret Schlauch, *Speculum*, XX (1945), 133, makes a valuable collection of statements about kingship and tyranny from John of Salisbury on.

69. Robert Steele, ed., *Three Prose Versions of the Secreta Secretorum*, EETS, ES, 74 (1898), p. 36. In the articles of arraignment against Michael de la Pole in the Parliament of 1386, he is accused of having "prist a ferme la dit profite du roy pur xx. marc per an," J. R. Lumby, ed., *Chronicon Henrici Knighton*, Rolls Series (1895), II.222.

70. Galway, MLR, XLIV (1949), 174n.

71. Lowes, PMLA, XX (1905), 778n., points to Knighton, II.217 as a parallel to the "rich and poor" of line 388. The king is to call Parliament together each year and like the sun in the heavens dispense justice impartially, so that "pauperes et divites" may cool their passions. At II.19 there is a parallel to "keping lordes in hir degree" and "tyranny": if the king does not govern himself according to the good counsel "dominorum et procerum regni," he may be deposed. These and other statements in the chronicles (above, Chap. Four, p. 154) indicate the background for Gower's Epistle, Alceste's speech, and the balade. Professor Arthur Hogue has pointed out to me that "doing right to poor and rich" was a common legal formula: cf. a petition presented to the royal court by one John Fesrekyn (1292), "Cher sire joe vus cri merci issi cum vus estis mis en lu nostur seinur le Roy pur dreit fere *a poveris et a riches* . . ." Selden Society, XXVII (1912), pp. iv, xxiii.

72. F. S. Haydon, ed., *Continuatio Eulogii Historiarum*, Rolls Series (1863), II.367. Referred to by Tatlock, *Development and Chronology*, p. 121n.

73. See Robinson's notes, p. 862.

74. Ernst Curtius, *Literature of the Latin Middle Ages*, p. 95, traces this complaint to classical origins.

75. R. M. Garrett, JEGP, XXII (1923), 64, argued that when the two

were commanded to write their parallel series of love stories, Gower took his order seriously whereas Chaucer took his as a joke and wrote a series of burlesques.

76. The connection between the omission of F 496–497 in G and the death of Ann and destruction of Sheene by Richard is discussed by Lowes, PMLA, xix (1904), 671; xx (1905), 781. Kittredge suggested that Gower's reference in the *Confessio* is what made Chaucer resolve to revise and finish the *Legend*, PMLA, xxiv (1909), 359.

77. Frederick Tupper, PMLA, xxix (1914), 93; J. L. Lowes, PMLA, xxx (1915), 237; J. M. Manly, *Some New Light on Chaucer* (1926). J. R. Hulbert enters a plea for a more universal interpretation in PMLA, lxiv (1949), 823.

78. For comment on this Kantian perspective see W. Ferguson, *American Historical Review*, lix (1953), 4.

79. On the tradition of pilgrimages see Muriel Bowden, *Commentary on the General Prologue to the Canterbury Tales* (1948), Chap. ii. Passages illustrating the figurative application of the pilgrimage motif are to be found in Owst, *Preaching in Medieval England*, p. 103.

80. For parallels to the procession of the Seven Deadly Sins in iconographic tradition (tapestries, illuminations, and the like) see Bloomfield, *The Seven Deadly Sins*, p. 422.

81. See above, Chap. Four, p. 137.

82. The vices found in both Gower's *Mirour* and Chaucer's Parson's Tale are in italics:

Mirour	Parson's Tale
I *Orguil*	Superbia
1 *Ipocresie*	12 Inobedience
2 *Vaine gloire*	11 Avaunynge
3 *Du vesture*	1, 35 Ypocrisie
4 Fole emprise	13 Despit
5 *Flaterie* (in PT under Ira)	6 Arrogance
6 *Surquiderie*	
7 *Presumpcioun*	10 Inpudence
8 Vaine curiosité	6 Swellynge of Herte
9 Derisioun	14, 15 Insolence
10 *Malapert*	Elacioun
11 *Avantance*	Inpatience
12 *Inobedience*	18 Strif
13 *Despit*	19 Contumacie
14 *Desdaign*	7 Presumpcioun
15 *Danger*	22 Irreverence
16 *Groucer*	20, 21 Pertinacie
17 *Murmur*	2 Veyne Glorie
18 *Rebellion*	3 Pride of dress
19 *Contumacie*	Pride in horses
20 *Contrarious*	Pride of table
21 *Contradiccioun*	
22 *Blaspheme*	

II *Envye*
  23 *Detraccioun*
    24 Malabouche
    25 *Disfame*
      26 *Vituperie*
      27 *Reproef* (in PT
         under Ira)
    28 *Dolour d'autry Joye*
    29 *Dissencioun*
  30 *Joye d'autry mal*

  31 Supplanticioun
    32 Ambicioun
    33 Circumvencioun
    34 Confusioun
  35 *Fals semblant*
    36 *Bilingues* (in PT under Ira)
    37 Falspenser
    38 *Dissimulacioun*

Invidia
  28 sorwe of oother mannes prosperitee
  30 joye of oother mannes harm
  26 backbityng or (23) detracccion
    38 preising by wickked entente

  24 turning goodnesse up-so-doun
    amenusing neighbors bountee
  25 dispreisynge of hym that men preise
    herkning gladly to the harm of
    oother
  16 gruchchyng or (17, 29)
    murmuracioun

83. *Reports of the Historical Manuscript Commission, Beverly* (1900), p. 128, provides an interesting historical account of the combination of estates, a procession, and the Seven Sins. In a *ludo pater noster* we find *Mercatores pagendam Invidiae*, with the guilds grouped under Superbiam, Accidiam, etc.

84. Owst, *Preaching in Medieval England*, passim, offers a full selection of parallels in the sermons. E. Flügel, *Anglia*, xxiv (1901), 437, lists many of the parallels to be discussed below, but nearly half of his parallels are from Wyclif and other clerical literature. It should be stressed again that it is not the mere existence of parallels between the *Mirour* and *Vox* and the *Canterbury Tales* that is important, but their number, pervasiveness, and pattern.

85. Tatlock, *Development and Chronology*, p. 184, was sufficiently impressed by the parallels to observe that "Flügel has pointed out that in the best of all his works, the *General Prologue*, Chaucer was not above frequently drawing phraseology from Gower's *Mirour de l'Omme*."

86. We must turn back to Ten Brink for the fairest assessment of the relationship between the individual and the type in the *Canterbury Tales*: "Chaucer's thinking and writing had assumed a more decidedly national and popular tinge with his increasing age and larger experience of life. After having gone through the French, the Italian, and the Latin poetry, he was now more interested in the modest productions of the English muse (partly from ethical and patriotic motives, partly also on aesthetical grounds), viz., in the Satires, the romantic poems, and the popular songs. He watched political events with the deepest interest, and particularly the movements in social and ecclesiastical affairs, and the intellectual currents of his time. His sympathy with Wyclifism, and with the great reformer himself, had subsequently become more significant. He did not join the ranks of his disciples; he remained what he had been—a good Catholic, with occasional attacks of scepticism; a worldling, with deep and often dormant religious feelings. But the moral greatness of the reformer, and his pure zeal for the Christian life and doctrine which was still working in many of his followers, in-

spired Chaucer with the greatest respect, and quickened his perception of the abuses and the moral sores in the church and in society. The *Vision of Piers Plowman* must have had a similar effect upon him.

From influences and interests such as these was formed the great, cosmopolitan ideal which Chaucer was nourishing as an artistic fancy. . . . The revelation of the characters of these mediaeval pilgrims, however, is not the only object of these Tales. Their object is of far wider reach. While each is in itself a finished work of art, they are intended, taken altogether, to complete that universal picture which the poet had in mind, viz., a picture at once of the real life of mediaeval society, especially of English society, and a reproduction, in a higher and condensed form, of that ideal world which hovers over this reality as a spiritual reflection. Hence, on the one hand, the variety of the characters introduced, with their different situations and ways of life; and, on the other hand, the universality in selecting the subjects and the forms of expression, the diversity in tendency, character, and style of the separate stories," *History of English Literature* (trans. 1883–96, II.140). All true, save that for the unprovable relationship with Wyclif and *Piers Plowman* we would substitute a demonstrable relationship with John Gower.

87. Ruth Mohl, *The Three Estates in Medieval and Renaissance Literature* (1933), p. 102.

88. There is a somewhat similar list in Flügel, loc. cit., p. 438.

89. See references in Mohl, p. 20, and H. S. V. Jones, MP, XIII (1915), 45.

90. R. L. Kilgour, *The Decline of Chivalry* (1937), Chap. I, documents Gower's criticisms.

91. Flügel, *Anglia*, XXIV (1901), 440.

92. Lowes, RR, V (1914), 368.

93. "Amore vincit omnia," Virgil, *Eclogue* x.69, but proverbial (Walz, no. 105b). Gower quotes it at VC, VI.999; *Cronica*, Prol.7; *Ecce patet tensus*, line 3.

94. Pride in horses is a vice of the court of Rome (MO, 18515) and of bishops (MO, 19329); cf. The Parson's condemnation (CT, X.430) and Owst, *Preaching*, p. 283.

95. Curates are criticized for wearing furred cloaks at MO, 20473; bishops at MO, 19327.

96. These accusations and indeed many of Chaucer's very words are to be found in "The Song Against the Friars," Wright, *Political Songs*, 1.263.

97. See also MO, 21613.

98. F. D. Matthew, ed., *The English Works of Wyclif*, EETS (1880), p. 296. See Flügel, *Anglia*, XXIV (1901), 467, for other references to "Pseudo."

99. Matthew, op. cit., p. 187.

1. Skeat identifies the figure of curses returning home to roost as proverbial, *Oxford Chaucer*, v.465.

2. CA, v.1825: "Crist wroghte ferst and after tawhte . . ."

3. See VC, III.191.

4. For a summary of the documentary evidence see Bowden, *Commentary*, Chaps. XVII–XVIII. Some of the more important collections of data are by J. A. Work, PMLA, XLVII (1932), 419; L. A. Haselmayer, *Speculum*,

XII (1937), 43; A. L. Kellogg and L. A. Haselmayer, PMLA, LXVI (1951), 251.

5. Manly, *New Light*, p. 108, and above, Chap. Two, note 55.

6. Chaucer accuses the summoner in the Friar's Tale of trafficking in vice (CT, III.1340), and Morton Bloomfield argues that even the Summoner in the Prologue (CT, I.663) was a vice lord, PQ, XXVIII (1949), 503.

7. Mohl, p. 278.

8. On "chevisaunce" see T. A. Knott, PQ, I (1922), 1; Manly, *New Light*, p. 193; and above, Chap. Three, note 55.

9. On Chaucer's choice of the nonvictualing guilds which had been most aloof in the parliamentary struggle of 1386, see E. P. Kuhl, *Transactions of the Wisconsin Academy of Sciences, Arts, and Letters*, XVIII (1916), 653.

10. Joseph Horrell, *Speculum*, XIV (1939), 82; G. Stillwell, ELH, VI (1939), 285; and a summary of the scholarship in Bowden, *Commentary*, p. 240ff.

11. Galway, MLR, XXXVI (1941), 1.

12. P. F. Baum, *Chaucer: A Critical Appreciation* (1958), p. 66.

13. E. P. Hammond, *Chaucer: A Bibliographical Manual* (1908), p. 254.

14. L. Bech, *Anglia*, V (1882), 313. The notes in Robinson's edition provide a summary of subsequent scholarship. The death of Cleopatra by jumping into a pit of snakes (CA, VIII.2572; LGW, 696) has been cited as a borrowing by Gower from Chaucer, but if this is the sum total of their mutual indebtedness in this series of companion love stories it argues against rather than for their association while they were at work on them. Tatlock and Brown, MLN, XXIX (1914), 97 and 198.

15. Carleton Brown, SP, XXXIV (1937), 8.

16. Tatlock, *Development and Chronology*, p. 112.

17. On Tyrwhitt see above, Chap. One, p. 27. For a summary of scholarly opinion see also Hammond, p. 278, and notes in Robinson's edition, p. 690.

18. See references in Robinson's edition, p. 691 (line 81). Latin text: *Appolonius de Tyro*, ed. A. Riese (Leipzig, 1871), p. 2. "Pavement" occurs in the Latin: "Et cum sui pectoris uulnus ferre non posset, quodam die prima luce uigilans inrumpit cubiculum filiae suae, famulos longe excedere iussit quasi cum filia sua secretum conloquium habiturus, et stimulante furore libidinis diu repugnanti filiae suae nodum uirginitatis eripuit. Perfectoque scelere euasit cubiculum. Puella uero stans dum miratur scelesti patris impietatem, fluentem sanguinem cupit celare; sed guttae sanguinis in pauimentum ceciderunt." In another text: "Scelesti patris impietatem puella mirans cupit celare sed in pauimento certa uidentur. Cumque puella quid faceret cogitaret, nutrix subito introiit."

19. *Metamorphoses*, V.302.

20. Macaulay, 2.483 cites Skeat's opinion and remarks, "It seems probable that Chaucer's tale of Constance was written earlier than Gower's, and it is likely enough that Gower was acquainted with his friend's work and may have conveyed some expressions from it into his own." No evidence suggested.

21. E. A. Block, PMLA, LXVIII (1953), 601, 614.

22. Ibid., p. 612.

23. M. Schlauch, in *Sources and Analogues*, p. 157.

24. Owst, *Literature and the Pulpit*, p. 389.

25. Robinson, p. 663 (line 449), and Bloomfield, *Seven Deadly Sins*, pp. 136, 194, 421.

26. The "marriage group" is here taken to designate the Wife of Bath's prologue and tale, and the Clerk's, Merchant's, and Franklin's tales. For a recent inquiry into the evolution of the Wife's prologue and the conception of the group, see R. A. Pratt, *Studies in Medieval Literature in Honor of A. C. Baugh*, ed. MacEdward Leach (1961), p. 45. A fuller summary of various theories is to be found in W. W. Lawrence, *Chaucer and the Canterbury Tales* (1950).

27. F. L. Utley, *The Crooked Rib* (1944); S. K. Heninger, JEGP, LVI (1957), 382.

28. H. B. Hinckley, PMLA, XXXII (1917), 292; C. P. Lyons, ELH, II (1935), 252.

29. These two themes are well brought out in Kittredge's pioneer discussion of the group, MP, IX (1911), 435, and also by R. K. Root, *The Poetry of Chaucer*, (1922 ed.), p. 240n.

30. W. W. Lawrence, MP, XI (1912), 247, traces the marriage argument back to *Melibee*; so also J. S. Kenyon, JEGP, XV (1916), 282.

31. G. H. Maynadier, *The Wife of Bath's Tale, Its Sources and Analogues* (1901), concludes that Chaucer's and Gower's versions are nearer akin than any of the other versions but that they go back to a common source, ultimately Irish. S. Eisner, *A Tale of Wonder* (1957) has tried to reconstruct this common source from Irish materials. B. J. Whiting in *Sources and Analogues*, p. 224, leaves the door ajar for the interpretation here advanced: "Chaucer's version and Gower's agree in certain marked points as against the other two versions, but they differ too much in other respects to make it possible to speak of a common source."

32. A few more echoes of the marriage argument may be noted: the bitter tongue of Tençoun that, like a smoking chimney and leaking roof, drives a man from home (MO, 4118; CT, III.280; also in *Melibee*, CT, VII. 1085; *Piers Plowman* B. XVII.315; Hilton's *Scale of Perfection*, I.liii). "Prodegalité" will open her cask to no almoners "si noun de Venus et de Marte" (MO, 8412; CT, III.618 where Mars is likewise Marte). The fierce counterattack of the accused wife (MO, 8809ff; CT, III.226ff). The discussion of the functions of the organs of generation (MO, 20716; CT, III.115). At the wedding feast of Sin's first daughter are to be found the same guests as those who witness the conclusion of the Merchant's Tale: "Au table q'estoit principal,/ Pluto d'enfern Emperial/ Ove Proserpine s'asseoit" (MO, 961). The description of Vaingloire's "damoiselle" Flattery (MO, 1372) reminds us of the Merchant's fawning Placebo (CT, IV.1478). Under Lachesce we find the wretch who, like the old knight, defers repentance until he has his fill of sinning (MO, 5678; CT, VI.1248). "And clappe it out as doth a belle" for speaking (CA, V.4640; CT, VI.331; TC, II.1615). "And fyr, whan it to tow approcheth" for sexual attraction (CA, V.5623; CT, III. 89). "And in the lawe a man mai finde,/ Hou god to man be weie of kinde/

Hath set the world to multeplie" (CA, v.6421; CT, III.28). "For whan a man mai redy finde/ His oghne wif, what scholde he seche/ In strange places to beseche/ To borwe an other mannes plouh" against adultery (CA, VII. 4218; CT, v.1003). "May" a nickname for Ipotacie (CA, VI.518; CT, IV. 1693).

33. Lowes, MP, III (1905), 45.

Index

Alan de Lille, 219, 355
Alcuin, 186
Aldersgate, 62
Aldgate, 61
Aldington, 53, 334
Allen, R. J., 209
Allusions, 3; Gower to Chaucer, 6, 13, 119, 250; Chaucer to Gower, 6, 27, 287, 291
Anstis, John, 25, 33, 68
Apollonius of Tyre, 27, 289, 370
Apuldrefeld, Thomas, 314
Apuldrefeld, William, 47, 54, 314
Aquinas, St. Thomas, 160, 166, 168, 175, 178, 181, 225, 358
Archer, miniature of in VC, 145
Aristotle, 178, 181, 225, 300
Arnold, T., 29
Arnould, E. J. F., 354
Arundel, Thomas of, 100, 106, 111
Ashby, George, 3
Astrology, 169, 358
Athol, earls of, 41. *See also* Strabolgi.
Aterbury, Francis, 23
Audiau, Jean, 77
Augustine, St., 87, 143, 178, 262, 359

Bale, John, 17, 18, 91, 164, 321
Ball, John, 177
Barclay, Alexander, 7
Basil, St., 164
Baum, Paull F., 284
Baxter and Johnson, 341, 363
Beast symbols, 169, 171
Beaumont, family of Katherine Strabolgi, 46, 332
Bech, M., 285, 365, 370
Beichner, Father Paul, 150
Belletristic tradition, 147

Bennett, J. A. W., 191, 359, 362
Bemont, Charles, 345
Berry, William, 326
Berthelette, Thomas, 12, 16, 26, 29, 38, 40
Bethurum, Dorothy, 362
Bilderbeck, J. B., 365, 366
Biographia Britannica, 25, 324
Block, E. A., 290
Bloomfield, Morton, 357, 358, 367, 370
Boccaccio, 205, 222, 227, 230, 234, 252, 362
Boece, 62
Boethius, 225, 299
Bokenham, Osbern, 4
Book of the Duchess, 75, 172, 205, 207, 229
Born, Lester K., 359
Borradaile, Rosamund, 325
Bowden, Muriel, 367, 369
Brabourn manor, 39, 43, 328
Bracton, Henry of, 106, 111, 181
Bradley, H., 24
Brady, Haldeen, 361
Brockhull, Thomas de, 53, 334
Brokhull, John de, 314
Bromyard, John, 143, 146, 156, 206
Brown, Carleton, 286, 365
Browning, Elizabeth Barrett, 31, 34
Brunton, Thomas, 105
Brusendorff, A., 34, 361, 364
Bryan, W. F., and Germaine Dempster, 354
Buckley, Master, 18, 323
Burgh, Simon de, 54, 315, 335

Cambridge History of English Literature, 32, 352

Canterbury Tales, 13, 27, 33; clerical background, 252; composition of, 284; General Prologue, 251; pilgrims, 256; marriage group, 295, 371; Knight's T, 221, 237, 286, 293; Miller's T, 226, 271, 286, 293; Reeve's T, 286, 293; Cook's T, 286; Man of Law's, 27, 32, 242, 290; Wife of Bath's T, 195, 229, 293; Friar's T, 276; Summoner's T, 267; Clerk's T, 294; Merchant's T, 28, 294; Franklin's T, 295; Physician's T, 285; Shipman's T, 266, 271, 293, 296; Melibee, 290, 296; Monk's T, 226, 296; Nun's Priest's T, 226, 296; Manciple's T, 285; Parson's T, 140, 177, 255, 293, 367
Capitalism in Gower, 97, 348
Carlyle, R. W. and A. J., 358
Carmen super multiplici viciorum, 127, 151
Cassiodorus, 203, 360
Cato, 300
Caxton, 8, 12, 16, 40, 127, 329
Chancery, Court of, 55
Chaucer, Geoffrey, 1, 12, 33, 36, 57, 119, 125, 132, 344; Aldgate, 61; power of attorney, 61; literary development, 207; and Italy, 205; short poems, 74, 241; political commentary, 132, 243
Chaucer, John, 337
Chaucer, Philippa, 211
Chaucer, Robert, 337
Cheney, C. R., 354
Cheshunt, John, 80
Chesthunte, Thomas, 81
Chevisance, 98, 278, 348
Chirchehull, William de, 54, 314, 335
Cibber, Theophilus, 29
Cicero, 3, 143, 178, 217, 226
Cinkante Balades, 29, 67, 81, 126, 130, 135, 207, 220, 228, 233, 344; date, 72; MS, 71; forms, 75
Clay, C. T., 40, 326
Clifford, Lewis, 243
Cobham, John de, 51, 53, 314, 334
Cobham, Reginald de, 51, 327
Coffman, George, vi, 35, 128, 351, 353
Cohen, H. L., 81, 345
Colophons, Gower's, 88, 311, 352
Common good, 178, 191, 217
Complaint and satire, 3, 36, 153, 206
Confessio Amantis, 2, 5, 13, 21, 40, 59, 83, 108, 152, 207, 219, 226, 234, 252, 285, 295, 301; date, 116; MSS, 116; theme of, 185; revisions, 9, 68, 117, 136
Corner, G. R., 335
Corpus juris civilis, 155, 160, 193
Courtenay, William, 105
Cowden-Clark, Charles, 29
Coxe, H. O., 29
Cronica Tripertita, 21, 23, 33, 56, 68, 99, 105, 109, 152
Curtius, Ernst, 354, 366
Cusa, Nicholas de, 144

Dante, 3, 205, 210, 218, 228, 233, 252, 299, 361
Dart, John, 23, 324
Davis, G. E., 363
Dedwood, John, 127
De lucis scrutinio, 129
Deschamps, Eustace, 74, 240, 259, 294, 344
Dinaux, A., 361
Dodd, W. G., 365
Douglas, Gavin, 4
Dugdale, W., 345, 347
Dunbar, William, 5
Dwyer, Father J. B., 140, 144, 354

Ecce patet tensus, 130
Ecclesiastical courts, 159
Editions, Gower, 12, 29
Edward III, 1, 133, 175, 180, 221
Emden, A. B., 338
Epistle to the King, VC, 107, 183, 362
Equatorie of the Planetis, 61
Erasmus, 4
Erghum, Ralph, 105
Estrich, R. M., 365

Faceby, Yorks, 45
Fantasma Radulphi, 61
Farnham, Willard, 357
Favent, Thomas, 106
Feltwell manor, 50, 64, 67, 329, 339
Ferguson, A. B., 359
Ferguson, W., 367
Ferrers, family of Elizabeth Strabolgi, 332
Flower and leaf, 236
Flügel, E., 259, 368, 369
Forester, John, 346
Forester, Richard, 61, 338
Fortescue, John, 106
Fowler, R. Elfreda, 140, 144

Foxe, John, 7
Francis, W. Nelson, 354
Frebodi, John, 316, 335
French court poets, 74, 82
French prosody, Gower's, 344
Froissart, 74, 240, 344, 365
Frost, William, 362
Fuller, Thomas, 19, 323
Furnivall, F. J., 63, 140

Galway, Margaret, 34, 243, 351, 361, 366
Garrett, R. M., 366
Gaunt, John of, 24, 105, 124, 243
Gentilesse in marriage, 299
Gerson, Jean, 186
Gilbert, A. H., 359
Gloucester, Thomas of, 25, 30, 110, 124
Godfray, Thomas, 16
Godwin, William, 30
Goffin, R. C., 361
Gollancz, I, 61, 338
Gouer, John (steward of Earl of March), 343
Gower, Agnes, 58, 65, 341
Gower, John, tomb, 37; coat of arms, 18, 39, 326; collar of S's, 25, 38, 68, 342; real estate, 50, 58, 64, 67; marriage, 58, 65; grant of wine, 68, 342; in danger, 69; will, 65, 336
Gower, Margaret, 44, 328, 332
Gower, Robert, 41; daughters, 47, 332
Gower, Lord (George Granville Leveson-Gower), 29, 325
Gowers of Langbargh, Yorks, 45, 88, 330
Grandson, Oton de, 75, 344
Gravesende, John, 59, 81, 337
Green, R. H., 219, 362
Gregory, St., 169
Griffith, D. D., 241, 365
Grosseteste, Robert, 164, 169
Grossman, Ann, 357
Guillaume de Lorris, 77
Gunner, W. H., 336
Guyse, Anselm de, 44, 328

Hales, J. W., 32
Hamilton, G. L., 345, 359
Hammond, Eleanor P., 284, 322
H. aquile pullus, 99, 343
Hasted, Edward, 334
Hawes, Stephen, 5, 8
Hayselmayer, L. A., 275

Hearne, Thomas, 22, 26, 323
Hende, John, 63, 119, 339, 341
Heninger, S. K., 371
Henry IV, 9, 11, 26, 38, 68, 89, 111, 118, 121, 132, 221, 353
Héricault, C. D., 364
Hinckley, H. B., 371
Hoccleve, 3, 7, 62, 339
Hogue, Arthur, 366
Holdsworth, William, 199
Holzknecht, Karl, 123
Home, Gordon, 337, 353
Homer, 3
Homiletic tradition, 141
Horrell, Joseph, 370
House of Fame, 62, 208, 219, 233, 240, 250
Huntyngfeld, Henry, 336
Huntyngfeld, Walter de, 59, 336
Huppé, B. F., 347
Hyd, Absolon, 239

In Praise of Peace, 72, 127, 132, 203

Jean de Meun, 161, 228, 252
Jerome, St., 3, 294
Joan of Kent, 34, 113, 243
Johnson, Samuel, 5, 26, 322
Jones, P. E., 80
Jonson, Ben, 19, 252
Jusserand, J. J., 2, 177, 345

Kellogg, A. L., 275
Kentwell manor, 50, 53, 332
Kenyon, J. S., 371
Kilgour, R. L., 369
Kingis Quair, 3, 36
Kingship, theories of, 180, 198, 223, 362
Kittredge, G. L., 36, 72, 93, 240, 295, 357, 361, 364, 365, 371
Knighton, Henry, 350, 366
Knott, T. A., 370
Knowlton, E. C., 357
Koeppel, E., 360
Kuhl, E. P., 370

Lak of Stedfastnesse, 247
Lange, H., 365
Langland, 5, 105, 177, 206, 252, 349
Langlois, Ernest, 357, 362
Lateran Council, Fourth, 137, 140, 153
Latini, Brunetto, 198
Lawrence, W. W., 371
Legal associations and ideas, Gower's, 55,

57, 63, 111, 154, 160, 163, 167, 171, 199, 222, 287, 356
Legend of Good Women, 33, 75, 85, 113, 181, 235, 284
Leland, John, 1, 14, 24, 26, 34, 36, 38, 40, 57, 154, 207, 287, 321, 323
Lewis, C. S., 6, 36, 73, 187, 191, 359
Lewis, Ewart, 355
Literary circle, Gower's and Chaucer's, 61
Literary jealousy, tradition of Chaucer's, 31, 289
Livy, 285
Loomis, R. S., 215
Looten, Canon, 205
Lossing, Marian, 365
Lounsbury, T. R., 21, 323
Lovaigne, Nicholas, 52, 54, 315, 332, 335
Love, courtly, 229; sexual, 162, 229; vision, 237
Lovejoy, A. O., 161, 357
Lowell, James Russell, 2, 36
Lowes, J. L., 36, 205, 240, 243, 251, 260, 301, 361, 364, 366, 367, 372
Lucan, 3
Lück, E., 32
Lutterall, Elizabeth Dame, 67, 339
Lutterall, Hugh, 67, 341
Lydgate, John, 3, 4, 7, 364
Lyons, C. P., 371

Macaulay, G. C., v., 4, 12, 29, 31, 35, 37, 53, 57, 64, 72, 91, 96, 100, 116, 123, 135, 145, 156, 173, 198, 290, 321, 352
MacCallum, Mungo W., 205
MacCracken, H. N., 87, 321, 345
McDonald, Charles O., 362
McKisack, May, 131, 350
McNeil, John T., 354
Machaut, Guillaume de, 74, 241, 259, 344
Macrobius, 217
Magoun, F. P., 363
Maitland, F. W., 356
Manly, J. M., 251, 365, 367, 370
Mannyng, Robert, of Brunne, 138, 206
Manuscripts, Gower, 9, 88, 126, 303, 345, 352; *Cinkante Balades*, 71; *Mirour de l'omme*, 91; *Vox Clamantis*, 99; *Confessio Amantis*, 116
Marche, Lecoy de la, 355
Marriage of the daughters of the devil, 164

Marsh, G. L., 364
Martianus Capella, 164
Martin, Terence, 363
Map, Walter, 294
Matheolus, 293
Mauleverer, John de, 346
Mauleverer, Richard, 92
Maynadier, G. H., 371
Memento mori, 165, 166
Meyer, Karl, 26, 31
Milton, John, 129, 163, 206, 357
Miroir du monde, 140
Mirour de l'omme, 32, 62, 70, 106, 121, 135, 163, 174, 181, 194, 208, 212, 221, 227, 244, 251, 277, 300; discovery of, 91; date, 95; composition, 95
Mohl, Ruth, 256, 278, 348
Moland, L., 364
Moral philosophy, 225, 363
Morley, Henry, 29, 34, 64
Mosher, J. A., 355
Moubrays of Yorkshire, 43, 328
Multon manor, 64, 67, 329, 339
Muscatine, Charles, 224, 362

Naturalism of Chartres, 162, 219, 230
Nebuchadnezzar's dream, 186, 190, 354
Neve, William, 50
Neville, Thomas, 92
Nicolas, Harris, 1, 24, 26, 30, 39
Nicolson, William, 21, 26

Occam, William of, 178
O deus immense, 130
Ovid, 3, 147, 186, 229, 285, 355
Owst, G. R., 128, 142, 293, 358, 368

Pantin, W. A., 128, 348, 353, 354
Papworth, J. W., 326
Parent, J. M., 358
Parliament of Fowls, 75, 208, 210, 216, 229, 233
Passeles-Pashleys, 331
Patch, H. R., 214, 361
Pauli, Reinhold, 13, 29, 31, 34
Peasants' Revolt, 98, 106, 170, 349
Penitential tradition, 137, 354
Perrers, Alice, 96, 347
Peter, John, 36, 206, 354, 356, 360
Petrarch, 3, 4, 154, 205
Phillips, Edward, 19
Pintelon, P., 338
Pits, John, 19
Plato, 161, 186

Political opportunism, tradition of Gower's, 24, 29, 123, 133
Pourchace, 56, 287, 336
Pratt, R. A., 234, 361, 362, 364, 371
Praz, Mario, 205, 360
Price, D. J., 338
Pui, 78, 207
Pultney, John de, 47, 332
Pyncebeck, Thomas, 335

Quarrel, tradition of Gower's and Chaucer's, 27, 31, 289
Quixley, John, 86, 345

Raby, F. J. E., 356
Ravensere, Richard, 334
Rayed garments, 55, 336
Raymo, Robert, 356
Reason and law, 167
Rendle, W., 337
Rex celi deus, 72
Richard II, 1, 9, 13, 20, 23, 25, 31, 60, 72, 95, 105, 107, 111, 122, 131, 151, 180, 183, 200, 221, 236, 243
Richard of St. Victor, 186
Rickert, Edith, 323, 338
Riga, Peter, 147, 150
Riley, H. T., 79, 337, 345
Ritson, Joseph, 29
Robbins, Harry W., 357
Robertson, D. W., Jr., 354, 357, 360, 363
Robinson, F. N., 360, 362
Rolle, Richard, 228
Roman de la Rose, 77, 161, 164, 218, 285, 299
Romaunt of the Rose, 239
Root, R. K., 205, 360, 371
Roscelin, 252
Rouclif, Guy de, 62, 64, 339
Rouclifs of Yorkshire, 340
Rufinius, 160, 167

St. Mary Overys Priory, 13, 18, 58, 60, 93, 347
Salisbury, John of, 106, 175, 178, 350
Sarton, G., 338
Satire and complaint, 3, 36, 153, 206
Savage, Arnold, 341, 351
Say, Geoffrey le, 327, 337
Schism of 1378, 103
Schlauch, Margaret, 244, 350, 366, 371
Scott, Florence, 366
Scott, James Renat, 326

Scotus, Michael, 193
Scrope, Richard, 108
Secretum Secretorum, 184, 193, 198, 203, 245, 359
Seneca, 226, 300
Septvauns affair, 51, 276, 313, 334
Seven Deadly Sins, 141, 164, 251
Sexhow, Yorks, 45
Ship of state, 175
Sidney, Philip, 4
Siegmund-Schultze, Dorothea, 348
Sin and death, origin of, 163
Skeat, W. W., 24, 31, 62, 204, 242, 290
Snell, Frederick, 29
Social hierarchy, 170, 179
Speculum Meditantis, 91, 135
Speght, Thomas, 17, 21, 24
Spenser, Edmund, 252
Spenythorn, John, 50, 333
Spies, Heinrich, 32, 321
Spurgeon, Caroline, 7, 321
Staple court, 316, 335
Statius (Stace), 3
Steadman, J. M., 357
Steel, Anthony, 108, 111, 350
Steele, R., 359, 366
Stengel, E., 29
Stewart, George R., 215, 361
Stillwell, Gardiner, 96, 359
Stimulus diffusion, 204, 301
Stittenham, Yorks, 18, 38, 331
Stockton, Eric W., vi, 355
Stow, John, 19, 21, 37, 56, 91, 164, 326, 336
Strabolgi family, 42, 329
Strode, Ralph, 13, 20, 56, 61, 81, 225, 338
Structure and unity of Gower's poems, 94, 135, 162, 166, 174, 190
Sudbury, Simon, 105
Sypherd, W. O., 365
Syward, John, 50, 333
Syward, Thomas, 50, 333

Taine, H. A., 1, 36, 177
Tatlock, J. S. P., 31, 36, 214, 226, 234, 242, 288, 357, 361, 368
Temple, M. E., 359
Ten Brink, B., 36, 368
Tertullian, 359
Thirning, Chief Justice, 132
Thomas, Timothy, 24
Thomas, William, 24, 324
Thompson, Canon, 325, 337

Three Estates, 254
Thrupp, Sylvia, 332, 335, 337
Thwaites, John, 92
Thynne, Francis, 18, 38, 40, 323
Thynne, William, 13, 17, 21, 132
Todd, Henry, 17, 30, 34, 39, 322
Tout, T. F., 173, 338, 351
Traitié, 71, 83, 91, 94, 125, 130, 135, 161, 167, 203
Treatise on the Astrolabe, 61
Trivet, Nicholas, 290
Troilus and Criseyde, 3, 6, 13, 16, 20, 61, 75, 205, 207, 208, 218, 220, 225, 236, 237, 239, 250, 293, 295
Troubadour poetry, 77, 218
Tupper, Frederick, 251, 254, 367
Tupper, Martin, 32, 204
Tyrwhitt, Thomas, 13, 27, 30, 289, 291, 322, 364

Unwin, George, 345
Urry, John, 22, 26, 28, 30, 322, 324
Usk, Adam of, 113, 351
Usk, Thomas, 17, 21, 24, 62, 225, 339
Utley, F. L., 371

Valence, Aymar de, 329; Marie de St. Pol, wife of, 44, 329, 340
Virgil, 3, 4, 164, 172, 209
Viterbo, Godfrey of, 150, 152, 356
Vitry, Jacques de, 142

Vox Clamantis, 2, 21, 29, 38, 59, 72, 99, 145, 155, 170, 179, 200, 216, 243, 256; audience, 105; date, 106; MSS, 99; revisions, 102, 112, 136

Waddington, William of, 140
Waldeby, John, 144, 355
Waleys, Henry le, 79, 80
Walsingham, 105
Walz, G., 353
Ward, Adolphus, 29, 31
Warton, Thomas, 1, 72, 91, 343
Warwick, W., 28
Wedel, T. O., 358
Weese, W. E., 351, 366
Weever, John, 19, 38
Whiting, B. J., 371
Wickert, Maria, vi, 35, 103, 115, 144, 176
Wimbleton, Thomas, 177
Winstanley, William, 19
Wireker, Nigel, 147, 150
Work, J. A., 275
Workman, H. B., 338
Wright, Thomas, 34, 110, 351
Wyclif, John, 24, 61, 106, 128, 143, 177, 206, 270, 338, 369
Wykeham, William of, 105

Yonge, John, 200
Yunck, John A., 356